WHOSE NEWS?

To Sheila & Ray
Remembering the good times in Istanbul!
Warm regards,

Ammu

(June 1998)

WHOSE NEWS?

The Media and Women's Issues

Edited by
Ammu Joseph and **Kalpana Sharma**

Sage Publications
New Delhi ■ Thousand Oaks ■ London

To our parents

Copyright © Ammu Joseph and Kalpana Sharma, 1994

All rights reserved. No part of this book may be reproduced or utilized in any form or by any means, electronic or mechanical, including photocopying, recording or by any information storage or retrieval system, without permission in writing from the publisher.

First published in 1994 by

Sage Publications India Pvt Ltd
M-32 Greater Kailash Market I
New Delhi 110 048

Sage Publications Inc
2455 Teller Road
Thousand Oaks,
California 91320

Sage Publications Ltd
6 Bonhill Street
London EC2A 4PU

Published by Tejeshwar Singh for Sage Publications India Pvt Ltd, lasertypeset by Micron Computers & Allied Services, New Delhi and printed at Chaman Enterprises, Delhi.

Second Printing 1997

Library of Congress Cataloging-in-Publication Data

Whose news?: the media and women's issues/edited by Ammu Joseph and
  Kalpana Sharma
    p.   cm.
  Includes index.
  1. Women in the press—India. 2. Women in mass media—India.
 3. Mass media and women—India. I. Joseph, Ammu, 1953-
 II. Sharma, Kalpana, 1947-   III. Title: Media and women's issues.
 PN5377. W58W46 305. 4'0954—dc20   1994   94-8044

ISBN: 0-8039-91525 (US-hbk)   81-7036-380-2 (India-hbk)
          0-8039-91533 (US-pbk)   81-7036-381-2 (India-pbk)

Contents

Preface

PART I: THE ENGLISH LANGUAGE PRESS

1. Introduction   15
   Ammu Joseph and Kalpana Sharma

   Daily Newspapers

2. Dowry Deaths: Crime Without End   33
   Kalpana Sharma and Ammu Joseph
3. Rape: A Campaign is Born   43
   Ammu Joseph and Kalpana Sharma
4. The Shah Bano Controversy: A Question of Maintenance   51
   Kalpana Sharma and Ammu Joseph
5. Female Foeticide: The Abuse of Technology   64
   Kalpana Sharma and Ammu Joseph
6. The Roop Kanwar Tragedy: In the Name of Tradition   70
   Ammu Joseph and Kalpana Sharma
7. **General Interest Periodicals**   88
   Kalpana Sharma
8. **Women's Magazines**   113
   Ammu Joseph

PART II : THE INDIAN LANGUAGE PRESS

9. Introduction   135
   Kalpana Sharma and Ammu Joseph
10. The Hindi Press   139
    Shubhra Gupta
11. The Tamil Press   168
    Prasanna Ramaswamy and Vasantha Surya
12. The Bengali Press   190
    Maitreyi Chatterjee
13. The Gujarati Press   224
    Sonal Shukla

PART III : TELEVISION

    14.   A Critical Focus   245
               Deepa Dhanraj

Postscript   292

Notes on Contributors   301

Appendices   303

Index   327

Preface

Women's issues are usually not the stuff of which headlines are made. Nor are gender-related concerns considered good copy. When such questions do draw the attention of the media, they are often either sensationalised, trivialised or otherwise distorted. In a nutshell, their coverage can be summed up as a series of hits and misses.

Although women account for just a little less than half the population of India, they are not seen as an important constituency by most people in decision-making positions. This is true of those in the media, government, academia and traditional development agencies. Women, especially the poor majority of them, often bear the brunt of the chronic problems which beset the country and, in addition, carry the heavy burdens related to the gender-based division of labour and the general devaluation of women by society. Yet, they rarely make it to centre stage in the nation's affairs.

In the past ten years, however, women's issues have increasingly, though sporadically, begun to make news and be considered worthy of comment. This is largely due to the growth of the contemporary women's movement in India, with women's groups becoming steadily more active and vocal. The print and visual media, in turn, have responded to this greater volubility by giving women's issues more prominence. But enhanced visibility—whether in the press, on television, in advertising or in cinema—is not an unmitigated good as the few studies in this area point out.

The idea of a detailed and systematic study of the portrayal of women in, and the coverage of issues of special concern to women by, the media arose out of our involvement with women's groups active in this area.

Although several women, within and outside the media, have written and protested about the more blatant forms of sexism that appear in the media, we found a paucity of empirical and analytical studies which explore the more subtle distortions that tend to occur when the media focus attention on women. These distortions are partly the consequence of overt biases and partly due to the very structure of the different media. As journalists who have held decision-making positions in both mainstream and alternative publications, we decided to undertake a study seeking to enhance our understanding of the media's perception and presentation of women's issues.

We have focussed on two major media in this book—the press (English as well as four regional languages) and television—hoping to supplement and compliment the few existing studies on the subject. Television is the single most widespread and influential medium in India today. The only available study of the portrayal of women on TV, by Anita Dighe and Prabha Krishnan, is a pathbreaking, detailed analysis of one month's telecast in its entirety.[1]

The study on television and women in our book, by film-maker Deepa Dhanraj, is based primarily on the women-centred serials which were telecast virtually simultaneously in the mid-eighties, after Doordarshan went commercial and began national network programmes. These have been viewed in the context of the evolution of women's programming on Doordarshan. The analysis goes beyond surface content to include a feminist critique of the form and implicit ideology of the serials.

The landmark study of women and the press in India by Vimal Balasubrahmanyan provides an excellent overview of the subject.[2] In our documentation and analysis we have tried to deepen our understanding of press performance in relation to issues of special concern to women. The coverage given by a cross-section of newspapers and magazines to five women's issues which attracted media attention over a period of about ten years has been examined in detail. In the process we have gained some insights about press responses to the different campaigns launched by the women's movement.

The broad objective of this book is to enable media professionals and lay consumers of the media to critically view the messages conveyed by the mass media, especially with regard to women, and develop an understanding of the factors which govern and shape media content and emphasis.

---

[1] Prabha Krishnan and Anita Dighe, *Affirmation and Denial: Construction of Feminity on Indian Television*, New Delhi, 1990.

[2] Vimal Balasubrahmanyan, *Mirror Image*, Centre for Education and Documentation, Bombay, 1989.

Accessing Yesterday's History

We would like to place on record some of the difficulties encountered in data collection. This is important because it highlights the unfortunate devaluation of record-keeping and documentation even by well-endowed media organisations. We hope this will prompt institutions to examine and assess their archival facilities and, where these are found wanting, resolve to improve their efforts towards preserving material for future reference.

Most newspaper organisations have some kind of a records room where bound copies of past editions are stored (only three of the five newspapers covered in the study have gone in for microfilming—clearly a more durable, if expensive, option). But the location and physical qualities of these archives indicate how low they figure on the priorities list of these institutions.

In *The Statesman* (Calcutta), for example, old newspaper files have been banished to a distant attic, far from the air-conditioned comfort of the editorial offices. This can be accessed only after traversing vast workrooms where time has obviously stood still for a century; bemused staff, startled by the intrusion of the outside world, dust the files while wondering how to accommodate the determined visitor in their cramped and steaming surroundings.

The Hindustan Times (Delhi) charges a fee for access to its old files, but the small, airless room lined with dusty shelves assigned for the purpose boasts only one small table surrounded by a few broken chairs.

The Madras headquarters of *The Hindu* has a well-equipped library where newspaper files are preserved on microfilm. However, the Bangalore office, which produces a local edition of the paper and is housed in an independent building on spacious grounds, does not preserve files for more than a couple of months.

At the Bombay office of the *Indian Express*, the librarian sits in a makeshift alcove—originally a shaft where the lift was located—sending up material requested as if from a well. *The Times of India's* Bombay office has a usable library although it could do with more space and less clutter.

In an act of inexcusable vandalism, *Eve's Weekly*, India's oldest English language women's magazine (which temporarily ceased publication in 1990), has reportedly sold all its past editions as waste paper. This accounts for certain gaps in our study of this magazine. We were unable to scrutinise letters to the editor on the issues concerned as we were told that all the files had been disposed of. The least the proprietors could have done was to ask members of the editorial staff whether they had any use for old files; many, including journalists who had worked earlier with the magazine, would have been pleased to either buy them for their personal collection or help place them in a library.

Our deep appreciation goes out to the Nehru Memorial Museum and Library at Teen Murti House (Delhi) which preserves a range of publications on microfilm, as well as in neatly kept bound files, and provides a quiet and pleasant environment for research. Unfortunately, the annexe of the famous National Library in Calcutta, where magazines are stored, is in a sorry condition; there are many issues missing from the dust-laden 'files' loosely tied up with string.

Researchers working on the regional language press faced many more difficulties, including refusal of access to files by several newspaper organisations even after the nature and purpose of the study were explained. Some, admittedly, had reason to be unwelcoming, having earlier experienced vandalism at the hands of would-be researchers.

Hunting down copies of television serials was an even worse nightmare. The copyright rests with the producers, most of whom are elusive in the extreme. Despite dogged chasing, a clear explanation of the purpose for which the serials were required and the offer of blank videotapes for copies to be made, only six ultimately obliged. Several were not quite sure where their copies were; one did not even have a master version of his own serial.

Doordarshan was equally unhelpful, having neither the right to lend or copy the masters they retain (they do have further telecast rights) nor the facilities for researchers to view tapes within their premises.

As a result, it was impossible to adhere to our original selection of serials for analysis, which aimed at a representative cross-section of different genres (soap opera, situation comedy, fiction-based, information-oriented, and so on). There is clearly an urgent need for a proper television archives in India. At present the vast bulk of programmes telecast by Doordarshan are promptly erased and thus inaccessible to future media researchers. Storage facilities for the tapes that are kept—recordings of programmes on the arts and sports—are inadequate. According to newspaper reports, Doordarshan is likely to lose even the 10 per cent of the recorded material of the last twenty years, which has has been retained, because it is stored in a cramped, poorly air-conditioned room.

Even those interested in documenting and studying current media messages and willing to do their own taping are handicapped because Doordarshan does not provide detailed and reliable information about scheduled programmes. The daily programmes list given to newspapers is too skeletal to be of any practical use; further, Doordarshan is notorious for last-minute changes and lack of punctuality even in the case of newscasts.

This book would not have been possible without a generous grant from the Norwegian Agency for International Development (NORAD). We were also fortunate that The Concerned for Working Children, Bangalore, gave us access to their computers for both the quantitative data analysis and typing the bulk of the manuscript.

We wish to acknowledge the assistance and support given to us by: Meher Ghyara, who typed our project proposal; Pramoda Kantraj, who did our data analysis; Jeanne Prasad, who helped in data collection for the periodicals section; Harsha Rao, who loaned one of us a computer for six weeks; and Anna Joseph, who read the manuscript and gave us her valuable comments as an active consumer of the media.

Ammu Joseph and **Kalpana Sharma**

I

THE ENGLISH LANGUAGE PRESS

1

Introduction

Ammu Joseph and **Kalpana Sharma**

The press is not the most important means of communication in a country like India, with its large illiterate population. Yet, because of the prevailing power structure, which is dominated by those with access to education, the written word carries weight which is out of proportion to its outreach. Therefore, its ability to influence the attitudes of both ordinary readers and policy-makers cannot be underestimated.

The importance of the print media has been enhanced by the role of the press during India's struggle for independence. The press was the vehicle used by the more important leaders of the national movement —from Lokmanya Tilak, who founded the Marathi newspaper *Kesari*, to Mahatma Gandhi, with his *Hind Swaraj, Young India, Harijan* and other publications—to communicate their ideas to the then rulers as well as to fellow citizens. Repressive press laws during the British Raj gave the indigenous press what M. Chalapathi Rau, veteran journalist, terms its 'reforming and crusading zeal.'[1]

This historic role of the press and the journalistic efforts of those who led the struggle for freedom ordained an adversarial role for the fourth estate vis-a-vis the imperial government. But after Independence, the crusading, anti-British, nationalist press assumed, by and large, a supportive attitude towards the State.

---

[1] Chalapathi Rau, *Press in India*, Allied Publishers, New Delhi, 1986.

Many of the norms dictated by this early, congenial relationship between the press and the State continued to govern the nature of Indian journalism for several years after Independence. There was an implicit acceptance of what represented the 'national interest'—particularly, though not exclusively, with regard to foreign affairs.

A major break with the old tradition came in 1975 with the imposition of Internal Emergency restrictions, including press censorship. For the first time in free India, censorship laws, which had been considered repugnant during the Independence movement, were imposed. The benign face of the State suddenly took on a more menacing appearance for the mainstream press. Yet, the response to censorship was not resistance of the kind seen during British rule, but passive compliance, barring some initial protest and the brave resistance put up by a few small publications.

The Emergency experience, however, signalled the end of one kind of journalism and heralded a more vigorous, investigative style of newsgathering and writing. It also paved the way for greater coverage of human rights issues and the condition of marginalised social groups.

This period also coincided with increased awareness about women's oppression and the need for emancipation, both globally and nationally. The years following the Emergency witnessed the beginnings of nationwide campaigns by women's groups who coalesced to demand changes in laws, of special concern to women, beginning with those relating to dowry. A number of these campaigns received fairly prominent coverage in the press.

The Language of the Elite

While these changes could be perceived throughout the print media, they were particularly evident in the English language press. The latter occupies a position of special privilege and eminence in India although its audience is substantially smaller than that of the regional language press.

According to a readership survey by the Operations Research Group, just 5 per cent of the adults in India read English language newspapers. In most states the regional language readership is many times higher. For instance, in the highly literate state of Kerala, 57.8 per cent of the people read Malayalam newspapers and magazines while only 5.8 per cent read English publications. The highest readership for English publications is in the four metropolitan cities of Bombay, Delhi,

Calcutta and Madras. But even in these cities the readership of local language publications is at least twice as high.[2]

However, the English language press continues to enjoy a position of prominence that is quite disproportionate to the size of its readership. This is really a legacy of India's colonisation experience which made English the language of the ruling class and the elite. The situation remains much the same nearly five decades after Independence.

In recent times, there has been a decided shift away from English dominance in national politics. Caste groups uninfluenced by western education, and therefore not fully conversant with English, have succeeded in capturing political power, particularly in the 'Hindi belt'. Yet, even the non-English speaking politicians cannot, or at least do not, ignore the English language press—as is obvious from their frequent references in Parliament to stories from the English press.

The power of the English language press is further enhanced by its class composition. It is run by the same dominant group to which it primarily caters. This is an important consideration in assessing media coverage because the nature of the press, to a large extent, determines what constitutes 'news'. The traditional definitions of news, accepted by the mainstream English language press in India, conform to the generally liberal, yet elitist, values espoused by the relatively affluent, upwardly mobile, university educated, upper caste urban male.

For example, while these newspapers accept that the interests of minorities and other marginalised groups should not be entirely ignored, their principal preoccupation remains with the ruling class. And although there is increasing coverage of human rights violations and struggles for social justice, this perspective is not always integrated into news coverage or editorial comment.

Similarly, in relation to women's issues, most mainstream newspapers do not pursue an openly anti-women line. This is at least partly because the ideal of the equality of the sexes is enshrined in the Indian Constitution. Measures to ensure equal participation in national life as well as eliminate discrimination and oppression are among the accepted social goals of the country—reiterated ad nauseum by all the major political parties. However, it does not necessarily follow that the press does not neglect or trivialise women and many women's issues.

Further, commitment to vaguely liberal norms can be deceptive. It may prevent the appearance of overtly communal, openly casteist or

---

[2] Centre for Media Studies, *Media Scene in India: Highlights from ORG-NRS 1989-90*, New Delhi, 1990.

blatantly sexist writing in the mainstream English press. But it does not ensure the incorporation of the perspectives of women and other powerless groups into press coverage.

What is News?

Apart from history and class, a number of other factors influence the English language press and affect its outlook on issues of special concern to women.

Dominant perceptions of what constitutes news are among the most important determinants of coverage. According to generally accepted definitions, events rather than processes make news. A violent episode merits front-page coverage while a peaceful state of affairs is not considered nearly as important. The magnitude of the event, whether in terms of the area affected or the number of people involved, also determines its importance as news. An unusual, out of the ordinary event—of the man bites dog variety—is considered newsworthy, whereas normal, everyday life attracts less notice. By conventional standards people can also make news—but not all people. The activities of the wealthy and powerful rate more highly than those of the poor and marginalised, including women. The opinions of the dominant sections of society are also given more weightage and, therefore, more coverage.

The unquestioning acceptance of such definitions by the majority of journalists affects the coverage of women and their concerns directly and adversely. Most issues of special concern to women do not fit into the traditional concepts of what constitutes news. First, most women in India (and elsewhere) are neither affluent and influential nor in positions of authority and dominance. As American media analyst Harvey N. Molotch explains, 'Women are not in control of society's institutions. Traditional dependence by the media for spokesmen (literally) from the top of such institutions means that the sexism which blocks women's mobility in other realms accumulates to block women from even knowing that they exist as a public phenomenon.'[3] The absence of women from the news pages is what Gaye Tuchman terms 'symbolic annihilation'—a combination of condemnation, trivialisation and erasure.[4] The invisibility and inaudibility of women in society is thus further perpetuated and enhanced by the media.

[3] Harvey N. Molotch, 'The News of Women and the Work of Men' in Gaye Tuchman et al., eds., *Home and Hearth, Images* of *Women in the Mass Media*, Oxford University Press, 1978.
[4] Gaye Tuchman, 'The Symbolic Annihilation of Women by the Mass Media' in *ibid*.

Second, event as opposed to process orientation necessarily results in the neglect of issues concerning women because many of them are linked to processes rather than events. A number of serious women's issues are not overtly violent or dramatic and, although often involving large numbers, the affected persons are not necessarily part of a readily identifiable group or concentrated in a particular geographical area. Further, many aspects of women's oppression are so commonplace and widely accepted that they are not considered sufficiently extraordinary to merit coverage.

This is reflected in the kind of women's issues which receive attention from the media. Violent atrocities against women provoke far more coverage than less gruesome but no less debilitating forms of oppression.

This reality has, in fact, influenced the choice of women's issues covered in the present study. A review of over ten years of newspaper coverage clearly revealed that the events and issues of special concern to women which really caught media attention were dowry deaths, rape and sati. The Shah Bano controversy was deemed worthy of coverage mainly because it was viewed as a legal, religious and political question, which held out a threat of conflict, rather than as a women's issue. Sex determination tests and female foeticide received some coverage because of the concerted efforts of those involved in the campaign against these practices; however, they did not excite as much attention as the other, more dramatic issues in which violence was either inherent or implicit.

Issues related to women's work, health, position in society and experiences within the family—the everyday conditions of their lives and the deprivation and tyranny they are routinely subjected to— prompted far less coverage. When such issues infrequently made it to the media, it was because they were referred to by one or other of the traditional sources of news—the government, the police, Parliament, the courts, national or international organisations, well-known personalities (especially politicians), conferences and workshops, etc. Significantly, there is another reason for the media's focus on atrocity-related issues. Dowry deaths, rape and sati also happen to be the issues on which some of the most active, vocal and visible campaigns by women's groups were based. Press coverage of campaigns is predictable.

Even within the broad category of women's concerns, the dominant notions of what constitutes news privilege certain disciplines and groups. Events and issues involving politics, economics, law, religion—in that order—are invariably at the top of the ladder of newsworthiness.

This explains the wide coverage given to the question of Muslim Personal Law brought up by the Shah Bano case. Further, as seen in this instance among others, the opinions of the powerless, including women, and the impact of events and issues on them are, more often than not, overlooked. Again, in a riot situation, it is the views of 'the authorities' and the leaders of various groups that are sought; the impact on ordinary people, particularly women, does not usually enter the picture.

Women and News

Commenting on the implications for women of these traditional definitions, Molotch holds that the formal news business is not just the powerful talking to the less powerful but 'essentially men talking to men. The women's pages are a deliberate exception: here it is the case that women who work for men talk to women. But in terms of the important information, the news pages, women are not ordinarily present.... News is a man's world.'[5]

Although this is gradually changing in India, with many more women entering the daily press as reporters instead of being confined either to the news desk or the features and magazine sections of newspapers, the continuing predominance of men—across the board and especially in decision-making positions—cannot be disputed. This is particularly evident in the regional language press where the entry of women into the field has been much slower.

The advent of women reporters and the presence of some senior women journalists in positions of responsibility have made a significant, if limited, difference to the coverage of women's issues by the press. The most important factor contributing to this process of change is, perhaps, the opening up of communication channels between the press and women's groups. This has come about through the involvement of journalists (including a few male) in the women's movement as participants or sympathisers.

Although the relationship between the press and the women's movement in India has not always been entirely smooth, women's groups here have greater access to the media compared to their counterparts in the West. Also, English language newspapers in India do not resort to the overt sexism, racism and pornography evident in the tabloid or gutter press of countries like the United Kingdom.

---

[5] Molotch, 'The News of Women and the Work of Men in *Ibid*.

Further, women's groups in India have not experienced the kind of media silence or open hostility evident in sections of the British press. In her analysis of the coverage of the women demonstrating at Greenham Commons against the Cruise missiles, Carol Addington found the British press to be biased. Her survey confirmed the women's charge that the press was 'creating a climate of distrust and prejudice against women working for peace. Our voices are silenced and facts are distorted in ways which incite more violence and bigotry against us.'[6] Not only were the efforts of the Greenham Commons women ignored, but they were constantly referred to in derogatory terms as headlines screamed 'Pigs Jibe At Police After Gays Hit Nukes Demo' (*Sun*) or 'Who's Afraid Of Wimmin?' (*Observer*). With headlines like 'Reds Tune Into Cruise Signal,' the 'gutter' press particularly took every opportunity to suggest that the group was infiltrated by communists.

While the press in India does not entirely ignore women's events or processes concerning the less powerful, including women, such coverage tends, by and large, to be fairly superficial. Of course, even this limited gesture can be positively exploited as is evident from the press survey that follows. Women's groups in India have been able to project at least parts of their struggle fairly effectively through the press.

Nevertheless, the gender perspective has not yet been properly integrated into the process of newsgathering. Thus even when an incident touches the lives of women, their views are rarely sought; even when an issue concerns them directly, their voices are barely heard. For the decision-makers in the newsgathering establishment, they are still not important constituents except in very specific contexts: as consumers who form an important target audience for the advertisements on which the media's viability depends or as victims of atrocities. In that sense, women continue to be 'the other' as far as the press is concerned.

The Study

This study of the print media was designed to span roughly a decade, from 1979 to 1988. Rather than examine the coverage of all issues concerning women over this period, it was decided to focus on five landmark issues. The choice of four of these five issues—dowry deaths,

---

[6] Carol Addington, 'Greenham and the Media' in Kath Davies et al., eds., *Out of Focus, Writing on Women and the Media*, The Women's Press, London, 1987.

rape, sex determination tests and sati—was partly determined by the fact that the women's movement had drawn national and media attention to them. The fifth issue, the Shah Bano controversy, came into national focus essentially because of its religious and political dimensions. However, its importance as a gender issue stemmed from the fact that the woman in question had demanded maintenance after divorce.

The periods for monitoring the coverage of these issues in the selected newspapers and periodicals were decided on the basis of when these five issues were in focus nationally—either because of campaigns by women's groups or, as in the case of Shah Bano and sati, because political parties had also drawn attention to them by taking up some aspect of the issue. It was felt that a scrutiny of three to four months per issue, when media attention was at its height, would give a fair idea of the coverage and the comment that they invited. For example, an issue like dowry deaths first came to the media's attention in early 1979 and continued to remain sporadically in the news up to 1984 when amendments to the dowry law were passed by Parliament; the sati controversy was confined to the latter part of 1987, immediately after the death of Roop Kanwar in Deorala in September.

For the section dealing with the English language press, five daily newspapers, four periodicals and two women's magazines were selected. Each of the regional language sections looks at one daily newspaper, one general interest magazine and one women's magazine.

English Language Newspapers

The prime consideration in the selection of daily newspapers for the study was regional representation and prominence as reflected in circulation. The leading English language daily in each region was chosen—*The Hindustan Times* in the north, *The Hindu* in the south, *The Statesman* in the east and *The Times of India* in the west. In addition, the *Indian Express*, with the greatest spread (fourteen editions in different parts of the country except the east) qualified as the fifth paper for study.

The data collected from the survey of the press was quantified both in terms of the total number of items on each issue and their break-up across separate categories—that is, special story, editorial, edit page article, magazine article, etc. The qualitative analysis was done by looking at the placement of the item within the publication and analysing its content.

The placement and type of coverage given to an issue signify the relative importance granted to it by a newspaper. Between news and views, for example, the latter is considered more weighty within the press, if not among readers (it is well known that the readership of the editorial page is much lower than that of the news pages, but it is assumed that opinion-leaders read editorials and other commentative pieces).

Among the news pages, the front page obviously gets top billing because it clearly commands the largest readership. On page one, the top left-hand position is considered the most prominent and is referred to as the lead. Generally, the more important news items appear on the top half of the front page as this is the most visible part of a paper when kept folded in half on news-stands. The next most important position on the front page is the 'anchor' position—that is, the article spread across the bottom of the front page.

Special reports are based on exclusive material gathered by a paper's correspondents or on-the-spot reconnaissance in a developing story or special surveys by the staff (usually published along with their names, known as bylines in journalistic parlance). News features/analyses provide background information or interpretation or both. These two categories indicate some special interest in the subject on the part of those who head the newspaper hierarchy as usually such reports are specially commissioned. The use of photographs and boxes (items with rules around them, often printed in bold characters) also suggests an attempt to draw attention to an event or issue.

Routine reports are generated in the normal, workaday manner. They are based on news gathered either on regular beats, such as the police, the courts, Parliament, the ministries and political parties, or at press conferences, public meetings and conferences organised by various groups. Since they do not suggest any special effort on the part of a paper to extend coverage, they are clearly less significant.

In terms of quality of coverage, the number of editorials is particularly telling because it indicates how seriously the editorial hierarchy of a paper takes note of an issue. However, while evaluating the editorials for this survey, their focus was also scrutinised: Did they articulate the women's perspective or dwell on the political, legal and/or religious aspects of the issues concerned?

The number of editorial articles is of somewhat less consequence because it does not accurately reflect the editorial hierarchy's interest in the issue. Few newspaper editors today consciously plan the editorial page, commissioning articles on current issues they consider important. Most often, edit page articles are written by a senior person on the staff or an outsider (usually of some eminence) on their own initiative. Nevertheless, they are noteworthy because they contribute in one way or another to the visibility of and debate on a particular issue.

Feature articles carried in the Sunday magazine supplements of newspapers can afford to be more detailed and evocative since they have less inflexible deadlines and fewer space constraints than daily news reports. By including the necessary background material and giving a human face to the subject under discussion, they are generally quite successful in drawing attention to a problem. This is why coverage in the Sunday magazine supplement assumes importance.

However, the different Sunday magazine sections vary in character and do not necessarily reflect the general bent of the newspaper to which they belong (because they usually have separate editors who work under the editor-in-chief but are often allowed a fair degree of independence and autonomy). The outdated definition of 'hard' and 'soft' news—the former traditionally associated with narrowly political and economic issues (seen as serious and important) and the latter with social and cultural issues (not considered quite as major and significant)—plays a part in determining the content of the Sunday supplements. These and other features sections of a newspaper are considered the natural resting places of, say, women's issues while the news pages are supposed to be reserved for 'the real action.'

The Sunday sections of the five papers included in the survey are quite different from each other. Most magazine supplements publish articles on a wide range of topics, such as the arts, culture, cinema, health, science, sports, travel and leisure, in addition to comics, astrological forecasts and other trivia. However, during the periods surveyed, the Sunday magazines of *The Times of India*, the *Indian Express* and *The Hindustan Times* also typically carried topical, news-related features, whereas the Sunday supplements of *The Hindu* and *The Statesman* tended to be less responsive to current affairs.

The number of letters to the editor reflects reader interest in an issue; it is usually assumed that for every reader who actually writes in, there are ten who had every intention of doing so but never got around to it. Most newspapers welcome letters to the editor but set aside limited space for them—so the number ultimately published does not necessarily tally with the number received (see Appendix B).

This, then, was the context within which the coverage of the selected issues, in the five English-language newspapers included in the survey, was assessed. Of the five issues, sati received the maximum coverage, closely followed by the Shah Bano controversy. While dowry deaths and rape were given almost equal coverage, the debate on the misuse of sex determination tests evoked the least interest. (For the detailed quantitative analysis, see Appendix A).

The quantitative data, however, has limited significance. It includes everything from front page stories to tiny crime briefs, from editorials to letters to the editor, from photographs to regular columns. This can be deceptive because even if a newspaper has published the greatest number of items on an issue, it may not have commented on it, thus diminishing its editorial importance.

The sati and the Shah Bano issues received the most attention in the press, both quantitatively and qualitatively. While there are several explanations for this, it is significant that hardly any of the editorials or editorial page articles dealt with these two issues from the women's viewpoint. The political, religious, legal and (particularly in the case of sati) broadly sociological aspects of these issues virtually eclipsed the fact that at the epicentre of both stood two women, representative of countless others; that neither debate made any sense unless they were viewed from the gender perspective and analysed in terms of women's status in society.

During the Shah Bano controversy, for instance, the editorial comment centred on the Muslim Women (Protection of Rights on Divorce) Bill or the implications of the resignation of politician Arif Mohammed Khan from the Rajiv Gandhi government over this issue. The advocacy in the editorials largely revolved around the adoption of a uniform civil code. Not a single edit suggested that the Shah Bano issue should lead to greater introspection about the status of all women, irrespective of religion, outside the institution of marriage; or, at the very least, to an examination of the situation of all divorcees, no matter what their creed. A couple of newspapers, however, did allow this aspect of the issue to be addressed through edit page articles, mainly by women, written with a feminist perspective.

Similarly, on the news pages hardly ever were the voices of women heard recounting their experiences as divorcees (during the furore over the Shah Bano case) or widows (in the period after Roop Kanwar's death). Nor was much attention paid to the social and economic status of women in general, and divorcees and widows in particular, not only in the communities concerned but also in much of Indian society. Both approaches would have provided a context within which the problems raised by a particular legal case and an individual death could have been understood and, perhaps, tackled.

Emerging Trends

Several discernible factors and trends emerge from the survey of the coverage of the five women's issues in the selected dailies.

Quantum of Coverage: For one, there seems to have been an overall increase in quantitative coverage over the years surveyed, from a total of 150 items on dowry deaths in all five papers in 1979 and early 1984 to as many as 498 items on the Roop Kanwar tragedy in the last months of 1987. Although these numbers in themselves do not tell the full story, the increase in volume is nevertheless significant.

The Proximity Factor: It is also clear from the survey that proximity has a definite impact on the extent of coverage. The fact that the dowry death phenomenon and the campaign against it were, at least initially, centred in and around the capital accounts for the Delhi-based *The Hindustan Times* carrying seventy items on the subject while the Calcutta edition of *The Statesman* had just thirteen.

Similarly, the Bombay-based newspapers, the *Indian Express* and *The Times of India*, gave the greatest coverage to the amniocentesis and female foeticide issue, possibly because the campaign against the misuse of sex determination tests was launched in Bombay. By the same token, the poor coverage in *The Statesman* of practically all the issues is at least partly explained by the fact that women's groups in Calcutta were, perhaps, not as vociferous in their protests and other interventions.

Dominant Norms: By the time the sati issue hit the headlines with the death of Roop Kanwar in Deorala, proximity was no longer a major determinant of coverage. For, although *The Hindustan Times* once again gave the issue more coverage than any of the other papers, all of which have Delhi editions (including *The Hindu*, a late entrant into the Delhi market), the difference was not so marked. This may, of course, be partly because it had become such a politically controversial issue that no self-respecting newspaper, regardless of its home base, could afford to ignore it. However, even this is significant because it suggests that when a women's issue fits the dominant definitions of newsworthiness, it can move up in the hierarchy of news items and consequently get greater coverage.

It was the commonly accepted norms which ensured that both the Shah Bano controversy and the sati issue merited much wider coverage than any of the other five issues. Both issues involved the law, had communal overtones and were politically sensitive; in the case of sati there was an unusual, violent and gruesome episode to report in addition to an eventful aftermath. In contrast, an issue like the sex determination tests controversy, which involved a disturbing process rather than a dramatic event, was accorded a much lower priority in terms of both news coverage and editorial comment.

Male Perspective: At the same time, the treatment of the Shah Bano issue, which received relatively wide coverage in quantitative terms, conformed generally to what one can term the 'male view' of news. Thus, the main emphasis was on aspects which would presumably interest those considered the primary consumers of the print media— middle-class males. The views of the women directly affected by the controversy were rarely sought and the problem of maintenance after divorce, faced by women of all religions and classes, was scarcely addressed. This 'symbolic annihilation' of the female view on what was essentially a women's problem illustrates well how the media can compound the marginalisation of women in society.

Structured Ad-hocism: The dissonance between the editorial position taken by some newspapers and the bias in their news coverage or choice of headlines—apart from the advertisements they publish—reveals a central feature of the press in India: structured ad hocism. Themes which fall within the conventional definitions of 'hard' news, such as politics, economics and the law, are almost automatically commented upon. News relating to these as well as to events with a component of violence is routinely carried because this is seen as the real business of newspapers. Equally significant aspects of a nation's life—such as the social and cultural, traditionally viewed as 'soft' areas—are covered if and when journalists on the staff are able and willing to write on them.

Editorial writers in mainstream papers who have made such subjects their primary areas of concern, either out of conviction and choice or by default (because these are the only issues left, others having been cornered by their more senior colleagues), have found that there is practically no discussion on the position their newspaper should take. Thus, for instance, in those cases which are clearly 'women's issues,' such as dowry deaths or rape, the individual edit writer is generally left to more or less guess the ostensible policy of the paper on such issues (which, if it exists, is rarely articulated with any degree of clarity even to senior staff). As a result, contradictions invariably abound; apart from vague editorials lacking coherent positions, there are often differences in perception between one edit and another on a particular subject. This does not signify a change in the paper's stand but reveals that it never had one; consequently, senior staff members writing edits can express what amounts to their individual opinions.

Frustrating as it often is, especially for concerned women working within the press, this ad hocism does, strangely enough, have some advantages. In fact, the Indian women's movement has been able to capitalise on it effectively at times. Access to the news or edit pages in most western newspapers, which tend to be more tightly run than their Indian counterparts, is relatively difficult. Women's groups here have succeeded in getting their press releases printed; most of their events, such as demonstrations and conferences, covered; and their analyses of issues, often written by women activists themselves, published on the edit page or elsewhere (even if some of these were not displayed as prominently as they would have liked them to be).

However, this laissez-faire attitude can be a double-edged sword. It leads to certain contradictions in the editorial content of newspapers that the lay reader, who is not aware of the ad hoc manner in which newspapers function, would find confusing. For example, the *Indian Express* adopted a liberal stance on rape. However, on the day the daily highlighted the rape of women during the Narainpur atrocity (10 February 1980) the Sunday magazine section of the paper featured a supposedly humorous piece by someone using a nom de plume, which stated:

> I dislike masculine women. Today's wives are so conscious of their equality they're forgetting their personality requirements. Women are soft, gentle and feminine. They should not be ashamed of it. They should stay soft, gentle and feminine instead of turning into half-baked human concoctions, neither here nor there.

Another example can be found in *The Hindu*. Its daily column on aspects of Hinduism generally reflects an extremely conservative and narrow vision of the female sex and its role in society. Yet the paper adopted a progressive editorial line on rape and the campaign against it. However, during the same period, this religious column featured an exposition on 'The Heritage Of Indian Women' (24 March 1980) which, at a time when rape was being brought out of the closet, was particularly inappropriate:

> For a woman, the most worthy and priced (sic) possession is her chastity .... Irrespective of her husband's status, she will admire and revere him and also encourage him to succeed in his endeavours and lend all support. She will also refrain from bringing him any discredit. Should it require any sacrifice on her part to enable him to uphold his prestige, she will not mind it.

Similarly, the unusually prominent position given by the *Indian Express* to the advertisements of the Vishwa Hindu Parishad (VHP) illustrates the contrast between the editorial stance of a paper and its actual content. During the height of the Shah Bano controversy, this newspaper carried an advertisement released by the VHP (26 September 1987). It was placed in the top right hand corner of the page opposite the edit page—a position where advertisements normally never appear. Entitled 'Respect For Womanhood,' it commented:

> Hinduism has the greatest respect for womanhood. It was Hinduism which first declared that God resides where women are worshipped. Hence there was no difficulty for a woman to become the PM of India. Instances like (sic) Shah Bano case never arose in Hinduism. Women lost all their glory and liberty in the dark period of history when India was invaded by barbarians.

Similar was the tone and tenor of an advertisement issued by the VHP, which appeared in the same position, during the sati controversy. However, then the focus was not on the position of women in Hindu society but on the question: Are Hindus communal? Yet, the editorial columns of the paper did not contain any overtly communal statements. Of course, decisions about advertisements are generally taken by the management without prior consultation with the editors.

Women Journalists: The fact that some newspapers, particularly *The Statesman*, carried proportionately more editorials than news reports on these issues is explained by the presence of senior women journalists in the newspapers and their spheres of influence. Although progressive-minded male journalists have also made a notable contribution to the coverage of and debate on women's issues, the increase in the number of senior women journalists has had a noticeable impact on the number of editorials written on women-related subjects. In the past, most of these would probably have been overlooked, with only the most obvious meriting a mention.

Newspaper Style: Apart from this, several factors directly connected to the nature and structure of the press influence the coverage of women's issues. One of these is the particular style of a newspaper. Some of the divergence in the quantity and quality of coverage can, at least partly, be attributed to differences in the approach and character of the selected five newspapers.

For instance, true to its image, *The Hindu* rarely trivialised or sensationalised any of the issues surveyed. But, by the same token, it did not often stray beyond the bland, straightforward chronicling of events either. Nor did its reportage show much initiative, sticking close to traditional sources of news—such as the Parliament, the courts and the police—which tend to sanitise problematic issues and give legitimacy to their coverage on the pages of a traditionally conservative newspaper. (It must be noted, however, that the paper has of late been making efforts to be more dynamic without sacrificing its credibility and now pays far more attention to women's issues, among others.)

Similarly, it was typical of the muted idiom of *The Times of India* to underplay news about events, like rape, with potentially prurient and sensational overtones. (The paper has, however, undergone a noticeable change in more recent years; this was evident in its prominent coverage of the Pamella Bordes scandal involving an Indian call-girl in the UK, a subject that would have been treated very differently in the early eighties.) The same restrained tone is characteristic of *The Statesman*.

In contrast, papers like the *Indian Express* and *The Hindustan Times* pride themselves on being more forthright and display news about violent events much more explicitly than the other three. The difference in the kind of photographs used in these two newspapers and the others, even for routine crime stories or reports about a road accident or acts of terrorism, also illustrates this marked dissimilarity in styles.

Patriarchy Unquestioned: A close study of content reveals that few articles and none of the editorials on these issues really questioned the fundamentally patriarchal structure of Indian society or the family, which is the source of the problems women face. So, for instance, while the history or sociology of sati was traced and the communalisation and politicisation of the issue condemned, no editorial pointed out that the custom had arisen in the past and persists sporadically today essentially because a woman in Indian society had and has no value outside the institution of marriage. And that here, too, her worth was and is defined primarily by the males in the family.

Likewise, in the Shah Bano controversy, no editorial asked why the wrath of a community should be aroused merely because a woman demanded her right as a citizen, irrespective of religion. For doing so, she was denigrated in a humour column and largely ignored in the news columns; her brave stand was used as the hook on which several writers hung their pet theories on what was wrong with the Muslim Personal Law and how the community must reform itself. No concern for women, not even for the woman at the centre of the controversy, was reflected in such writing.

Communalisation of Issues: Indeed, the paucity of articles by women activists on the Shah Bano controversy can be attributed to the confusion created within the ranks of feminist organisations by the communalisation of the issue. Most women's groups are generally in favour of a uniform civil code that gives all women, irrespective of caste or creed, fair and equal rights in questions of marriage, divorce and inheritance. However, during this period, they hesitated to state their position because Hindu fundamentalist organizations, with whom progressive women do not identify, were arguing for such a code.

There was, therefore, a noticeable absence of statements from the women's movement on the issue except for a condemnation of the Muslim Women Bill. Secular women's groups by and large left it to radical Muslim women, like Shehnaaz Sheikh who had challenged the Muslim Personal Law in the Supreme Court, to raise the gender issues underlying the controversy. In other words, they were not able to function outside the communal parameters set by political forces.

Conclusion

This survey of newspapers over almost a decade has also indicated a noticeable decline in overtly sexist writing, even in 'third edits' —the slot used by some newspapers for humorous comment. Simultaneously, there has been a marked increase in coverage and analysis of a variety of other women's issues(other than the five surveyed), a trend not so discernible in the early eighties.

The historical legacy of the press in India, a generally liberal and reform-minded approach, has benefited the coverage of women's issues in the print media. The rise of the contemporary Indian women's movement, and the consequent increase in public consciousness about women's oppression and quest for emancipation, has led to the espousal of women's concerns by the main political parties in the country. While their commitment is clearly superficial, it has given women's issues a political legitimacy, thereby enabling them to fit into the mainstream notions of what constitutes news.

Although the press has played a significant role in publicising issues which readily conform to the traditional definitions of newsworthiness, other equally important women's issues that are less 'newsy' continue to be marginalised. In other words, what we would call the 'feminisation' of the news process has not yet taken place. This would involve paying as much attention to the process as to the event and making a deliberate attempt to seek the views of the inarticulate majority instead of routinely reporting on the prominent and the powerful.

This book is based on a detailed and extensive study, the complete report of which is available in limited numbers. In the interest of readability, much of the detail has been left out or placed in appendices. Nonetheless, the issue-wise documentation and analysis of newspaper coverage which follows does include fairly extensive quotations. These not only capture the mood of those times and the tenor of the discussions on these issues in the press, but also allow readers to judge for themselves the response of this cross-section of publications to issues of special significance to women.

2

DAILY NEWSPAPERS

Dowry Deaths: Crime Without End

Kalpana Sharma and *Ammu Joseph*

The institution of dowry, the price parents must pay to ensure a 'decent' marriage for their daughters, remains well entrenched in India even today. Despite the campaign against dowry launched by women's groups in the late seventies and early eighties, changes in the law and much writing in the press on the issue, the problem of dowry demands and the resultant harassment of young, newly-wed women continues.

There are many ways of looking at the dowry issue. As the eminent sociologist M. N. Srinivas, in his J. P. Naik Memorial lecture in 1983, stated:

> The first and the most obvious problem is the ambivalence which dowry rouses in the sociologist studying it. On the one hand, there is the feeling that the institution is an unmitigated evil and that it needs to be destroyed root and branch, and at the earliest opportunity, and on the other hand, the institution demands to be understood, its many ramifications traced, and its regional, caste and other variations recorded.

Yet fundamentally, the problems thrown up by the institution of dowry are essentially gender-specific. The crucial issue is the worth of a woman. Her parents pay for her to be taken off their hands by sending her laden with all manner of gifts for the marital home. And her worth, once she arrives there, is measured by the gifts she brings with her. In this exchange of goods between two households, the woman is almost incidental.

Dowry demands also reflect several societal factors linked to the institution of marriage and the status of women within it. The vulgarisation of the dowry phenomenon is closely related to the growth of the consumer culture and the availability of larger disposable incomes amongst the middle class. Although the desire for upward mobility has encouraged them to educate their women, a supposedly liberal education has not shaken deeply internalised beliefs about the status of the woman within the household.

While media reports on this issue concentrated on the villainy of the in-laws and their overriding greed for a larger dowry, the culpability of the parents, who failed to respond to the pleas for help from their beleaguered daughters until it was too late, was not fully acknowledged. The fact that women rarely receive a fair share of their parental property even when they have legal rights to inheritance was not adequately recognised as one of the factors contributing to this phenomenon.

Media attention was drawn to 'dowry deaths' in 1978-79 when there were reports of an increasing number of deaths of young brides in kitchen accidents. Although the first of the deaths recognised as a case of bride-burning occurred as early as 17 March 1979 (when Kanchan Sashi Bala, a twenty-four-year-old pregnant woman, died a hideous death from burns sustained in her marital home in Delhi), the first case to reach the media was the death of Tarvinder Kaur of Model Town, Delhi, on 17 May of the same year. It was the demonstration outside the house of Tarvinder's in-laws that, in fact, brought Kanchan Sashi Bala's death to light. Her mother, Satyarani, tracked down women's groups after reading about the demonstration in the press. These incidents marked the beginning of a change in media coverage of this issue which till then had consisted of small items routinely reporting these deaths on the city page.

The time frame for the study of this phenomenon was partly governed by the landmark events in the campaign organised on the issue. Following Tarvinder Kaur's death in May 1979, women's groups began investigating other such deaths and launched a campaign against dowry in Delhi. This, in turn, drew media attention to what came to be known as the 'bride-burning' syndrome.

By June and July of the same year, the campaign had become more vociferous and included demands for changes in the law and demonstrations outside Parliament House. While the campaign continued over the next three years, another landmark month was May 1983, when Justice S. M. Aggarwal, Additional Sessions judge in Delhi, awarded the death sentence to three people for the death of twenty-one-year-old Sudha Goel. (This judgment, however, was overturned by the Delhi High Court in November 1983.) In August that year demands for changes in the law were made during the monsoon session of Parliament. Amendments to the Dowry Prohibition Act of 1961 were finally tabled in Parliament in March 1984 and passed in the monsoon session of that year.

Keeping these high points of the campaign in view, months in 1979, 1983 and 1984 were selected for the study. While this piecemeal survey of the coverage of the dowry death syndrome and the campaign to change the law clearly does not give a full picture of the extent of discussion and reportage on an issue which persists till today, it indicates how the press responded when the campaign was at its height.

A North Indian Phenomenon

Of the five newspapers included in the study, *The Hindustan Times* gave the maximum coverage to dowry deaths. This is understandable as the issue was, initially, a Delhi and north-India phenomenon. Only later did the press in Bombay and Calcutta and, to a much lesser extent, Madras acknowledge that the crime was occurring in their cities, too.

Most of the coverage comprised news reports, there being very little editorial comment. Although *The Statesman* carried only thirteen items in all, it had three edits on the issue—the maximum number on the subject. Thus, scarce coverage on the news pages does not necessarily mean that the issue is not deemed important enough for comment.

In qualitative terms, the four-part survey by the *Indian Express*, which ran from 15 to 18 August 1983 on the news pages, under the general heading 'Why Women Burn', stands out as an exceptional piece of reportage and analysis. Two *Express* reporters, Sevanti Ninan and Sanjay Suri, methodically investigated thirty-three of the forty registered cases in which women had died of burns in Delhi in the first part of that year.

The reporters found that the majority of the deaths occurred amongst 'Delhi's upward thrusting lower middle class', that in two-thirds of these cases the husband did not have a steady source of income, that additional problems were caused by minimal physical living space, and that the parents of the girls were equally guilty because they were not willing to accept the social slur on the family caused by a broken marriage. They concluded:

> Implicit in such social complacence is a cultural acceptance of harassment of women. What emerges as crucial from this scrutiny of deaths by burning is a total lack of a woman's status in her husband's family or in her own, in the eyes of law or in the eyes of society.

This survey is significant for a number of reasons. First, it was the only instance of investigative and in-depth reportage on the dowry death syndrome by any of the five newspapers under study. The two reporters' conclusion, quoted above, was based on the investigation of specific cases of dowry deaths. Also, by commissioning its reporters to conduct such a survey, the *Indian Express* indicated its willingness to carry in its news columns a 'soft' social issue—one which would normally have been relegated to the magazine section. Indeed, it is significant that the same paper did not pay much heed to the subject just four years earlier, in 1979, when a Delhi newspaper like *The Hindustan Times* daily reported dowry deaths.

Regional disparities in the coverage on this issue were most evident in the early part of 1979. In Delhi people realised that the daily city briefs in local papers about women's deaths from burns represented more than just accidents. On 3 June, by which time the anti-dowry campaign had picked up considerable strength following Tarvinder Kaur's death, *The Hindustan Times* carried a round-up report under the headline 'Dowry Death Almost Every Day'. Quoting a number of Delhi-based women's groups, it went into the background of Tarvinder's death and reported on the protest demonstrations in the capital. Similarly, the 12 June protest march against dowry by women's organisations and women's wings of political parties outside Parliament House was covered with a three-column photograph on the front page and a report on the back page. Sashi Bala's death was reported in some detail in the paper on 27 June through an interview with her mother, accompanied by a photograph of the young woman. Other reports of similar deaths also appeared on the front page. On the whole, however, such news continued to be published on the city page in the form of crime or city briefs.

In contrast, the Bombay-based newspapers, the *Indian Express* and *The Times of India*, gave very little coverage to dowry deaths over this period. *The Times of India*, Bombay, was on strike from 12 June to 22 August and so there were no issues of the paper over that period. The *Indian Express*, which had a full-fledged Delhi edition, was surprisingly lax in its coverage of this issue in 1979 as compared to 1983, when it devoted space on its news and editorial pages to dowry and related issues.

Although it is based in the south, where dowry deaths were then not as prevalent as in the north, *The Hindu* did take note of the campaign against dowry in 1979 with a round-up piece on a news page headlined 'Brides Are Not For Burning' (8 July 1979). The article described the phenomenon and the protests against it, without going into individual case histories.

It is noteworthy that by 1983-84 bride-burning had been recognised as a social malaise afflicting many parts of the country. This was reflected in the increased coverage in Bombay-based papers, compared to 1979 when not much space or attention had been devoted to the issue.

Front Page News

As in most of the other issues covered by this survey, in the case of dowry deaths, too, the subject was featured on the front page primarily when it could be linked to the law or debates in Parliament. Thus the Supreme Court judgment laying down that dowry demand constitutes an offence appeared on the front page of the *Indian Express* on 24 March 1984. This was one of the two items on this issue which made it to the paper's front page over the period surveyed.

On the other hand, a major anti-dowry rally in front of Parliament House on 27 August 1983—in which hundreds of women, including some leading opposition politicians, participated and over a hundred were arrested—did not make it to the front page of either the *Indian Express* or *The Times of India*. The former carried a report on an inside page with a heavily biased headline indicating the personal prejudice of the sub-editor on the job. The item mentioned that some disagreement amongst the participating women led those from the Congress (I), the then ruling party, to leave rally; the headline, however, stated: 'Anti-Dowry Rally Ends In Fiasco'. Yet, the very next day, the paper carried a three-column photograph of the rally it had dismissed as a 'fiasco' the previous day!

The Times of India did not give it even this much importance, relegating it to a single column item on an inside page. *The Hindustan*

Times mentioned the rally on its city page but did not play up the fact that Congress (I) women had jeered. *The Hindu* took note of it on page one in a brief report. While *The Statesman* failed to report it altogether, in response to the growing outcry against dowry and the increasing demand for changes in the law, it did devote the second of its three edits to the subject, just three days before the rally.

Inconsistency in Coverage

The May 1983 judgment by Justice S. M. Aggarwal in the Sudha Goel case—sentencing her mother-in-law, brother-in-law and husband to death—aroused considerable debate amongst women's groups and the legal community, provoking most of the major newspapers to comment on the dowry issue.

For instance, the only editorial comment in *The Times of India* (9 August 1983) took off from the Aggarwal verdict and two other judgments and stated that the 'present cases are likely to go some way to deter what is an unspeakable and yet widespread combination of heinous crime and social evil.' The editorial argued for a law on dowry while admitting that this in itself would not be enough. It concluded: 'Admittedly, dowry deaths do not disgrace the entire country.... But for as long as even a single bride is killed on account of dowry anywhere, the matter is one of shame for the entire nation.'

Despite the extensive news coverage given by *The Hindustan Times* to the dowry death phenomenon, it only carried one editorial, which did not make any exceptional points, repeating much of what other newspapers like *The Statesman* had already written. Headlined 'The Evil Of Dowry' (26 July 1979), it also placed the blame at the door of an ineffective law and police inaction. 'Public apathy and legislative loopholes have been abetting in making marriage a death-trap for an increasing number of women whose dowry is not big enough to please the husband's family.'

The Statesman was the first to publish an edit on the issue. In the first of its three edits (during the period surveyed), headlined 'Brides Without Dowry' (26 March 1979), the paper commented on the government's reported decision to make changes in the law banning dowries. It was unequivocal in its strong condemnation of 'the practice of extorting money and gifts and of ill-treating a bride who is not well-dowered.' However, it was cynical about the efficacy of more legislation, extending only 'a qualified welcome' to the proposal for changes in the law and suggesting that change could be brought about through 'social enlightenment.' It concluded that 'there is ample scope to do so under the 1961 law', adding a strange and unexplained corollary: 'without penalising parents who may wish to provide their daughters with a trousseau.'

Interestingly, reports of dowry murders and the proposal to amend the law cited in the edit, did not appear in *The Statesman* itself—at least not in the ten days preceding the edit which were monitored. This suggests that an editorial writer was more sensitive to the growing dowry death phenomenon than those responsible for the news pages.

The inconsistency that often characterises the editorial position of newspapers, particularly on so-called 'soft' issues, is evident in the last of the three edits carried by *The Statesman* on this issue. The edit was sparked off by the 'avoidable facetiousness' over women judges in the Rajya Sabha (24 August 1983). While calling for more seriousness on the part of the government and law-makers, it concluded that 'there should be no further delay in amending the laws relating to punishment for such crimes, establishing family courts, make [sic] the Dowry Act more realistic and enforceable and widening the definition of cognizable sexual assault.' This was in striking contrast to its earlier, more cynical, position on the efficacy of the law in such matters. Such contradictions occur because individual edit writers more or less dictate the paper's 'line' on subjects not taken too seriously by the majority of the senior editorial staff.

Despite the exceptional quality of some of its special news features on the dowry death phenomenon and on harassment of women in the cities, the *Indian Express* did not comment on it during the period surveyed. However, from 1983 onwards, there was a marked increase in editorials on women's issues, including one to mark International Women's Day in March 1984.

The Hindu, which had acknowledged the 1979 campaign against dowry, did not accord the 1983 developments much significance except as Parliament news. It did not carry a single editorial or edit page article on the subject.

Anti-Dowry Law

By 1984 the attention of women's groups was focussed on changes in the law. The issue had been raised and debated in Parliament for two years after a Joint Committee of both Houses, appointed in early 1981, to review the working of the Dowry Prohibition Act, 1961, submitted its report the following year.

Its recommendations included: widening the definition of dowry, making the offence cognizable, prescribing a minimum punishment, imposing ceilings on all marriage expenditure as well as gifts, and ensuring rigorous enforcement. This debate culminated in the tabling of the Dowry Prohibition (Amendment) Act in March 1984 and its passage during the monsoon session in August of the same year. As the survey period does not cover the passage of the law, the study does not record editorials, if any, commenting on the new legislation.

Interestingly, during the period when the new law was under discussion, newspapers editorially acknowledged the International Women's Day (IWD), 8 March—an event which had received only sporadic media attention in the past. While some devoted editorials to the women's movement, others featured edit page articles on the issue. *The Times of India*, for example, editorialised: 'Amongst all the movements of this century, the one with the greatest potential for revolutionising human existence is the women's movement.'

This shift in perception of the major newspapers was not a chance occurrence. It can be directly traced to the presence of journalists, including sometimes an editor, who considered the growth of the women's movement in India too important a development to be ignored.

The Sunday sections of *The Times of India* and the *Indian Express* carried reports and some comment on the anti-dowry campaign by staff writers as well as women activists. Except for a little more detail, as magazine sections can accommodate longer features, these articles essentially covered the same ground as the news reports and the editorials elsewhere.

'Women's Libbers'

The Times of India's Sunday supplement displayed schizophrenic tendencies during this period, featuring some good, in-depth and well-written articles on dowry or other women-related issues along with some outright anti-women pieces. For instance, in its 25 March 1984 issue, the *Sunday Review* carried a number of women-related articles on subjects such as the differential rates paid to male and female film stars and women's double burden of work. But the same issue also featured a strange editorial comment under the heading 'Women On The March':

Like all ideologues, women libbers (sic) must look ridiculous to many of us who are in their (sic) fifties and sixties. They tend to be sharp-tongued; they appear too self-righteous, rhetorical and argumentative; they are often too well-heeled to look credible representatives of Indian women. But they represent a genuine and growing constituency (the constituency of educated working women) even if members of that constituency themselves find them too aggressive.

Thus, in one paragraph the edit both condemned so-called 'women libbers' for not being representative and conceded that they do perhaps represent a 'growing constituency.' Then again it contradicted that point by asserting that members of this constituency may find them 'too aggressive.'

And as if this display of wobbliness was not enough to confuse the reader, the *Sunday Review,* in its regular Anti-Column by R.G.K., carried the following assertions on women under the headline 'Cannot A Woman Be A Woman?':

Women's libbers in India are a pitiable lot. They are all the time trying so hard to liberate other women that they themselves remain in chains. At one time their prophetess was Germaine Greer. Now Ms Greer has shifted her ground in a manner most women are prone to shift their ground. The trouble with our women's libbers is that they are not sure what they want. They are not even sure whether they should remain women or be something else. Sometimes they despise sex, sometimes they glory in it. To speak of the joys of motherhood seems to them old-fashioned—or are they seeking the advice of foreign libbers?

Conclusion

The coverage of the dowry issue illustrates well the impact of the women's movement on the media. In both quantitative and qualitative terms, there was a noticeable improvement in coverage by at least three of the five papers—*The Hindustan Times*, the *Indian Express* and *The Times of India*—coinciding with the campaign organised by women's groups on this issue. Without this, it is entirely possible that dowry deaths would have continued to appear as two-line items under crime briefs on the city page of most newspapers. It is noteworthy that the more in-depth articles came towards the middle of the decade, in 1984, when women's groups had become vocal and visible in their demands for changes in the laws on dowry and rape.

However, proximity played an important part in determining the quantum of coverage. With the dowry death phenomenon first surfacing in the north, the campaign by women's groups was initially Delhi-based; consequently, the coverage in papers with a base in the capital was decidedly greater than in *The Hindu* and *The Statesman*, published from Madras and Calcutta respectively.

On the other hand, this issue also revealed the preoccupation of the press with events rather than processes. In the period surveyed, few of the analyses cared to look more closely at the processes and the institutions in Indian society which had given birth to such a phenomenon. Although the condemnation was universal and no attempt was made to justify the phenomenon, much of the analysis remained superficial.

At the same time, the campaign by women's groups, white it did draw media attention to the specific issue of dowry deaths, made little impact on openly sexist writing which continued to appear alongside several sensitively written articles on women. The third edit slot, for instance, continued to take the occasional swipe at women or 'women's lib'—that all-encompassing phrase used to define any group raising its voice on a women's issue. It is evident that editors saw no contradiction between the pro-women position taken in editorials and articulated in edit page articles and the anti-women bias of some of this so-called humorous writing.

The unquestioning acceptance of law as a tool of social reform was also evident in much of the editorial comment. Changes in the law were recommended and commended. There was little discussion on the limitations of the law or the additional supports outside the State structure which would be essential to ensure the efficacy of legislation dealing with social crimes. The unwritten, but generally accepted, social compact that governs many of the positions taken by the mainstream media on such issues is an acceptance of the State as the arbiter in dealing with crimes against the so-called weaker sections. Dissenting voices, which actually question the motives of the State and its agencies and highlight structures which perpetuate patriarchy and oppression, appear only in the alternative media—in magazines like *Manushi*.

3

DAILY NEWSPAPERS

Rape: A Campaign is Born

Ammu Joseph and Kalpana Sharma

The campaign against rape is generally regarded as the catalyst which sparked off the contemporary women's movement in India. Although the agitation against dowry and bride-burning did predate the anti-rape campaign by about two years, it was initially confined to Delhi where the first cases of dowry death came to light. On the other hand, the fight against rape, while spearheaded by women in Bombay, was soon taken up by women's organisations in different parts of the country; the agitation took on the dimensions of a national campaign almost from the beginning.

Rape became a major public issue in January 1980 after an open letter to the Supreme Court, written by four lawyers, was circulated to concerned women in different parts of the country. The letter criticised the Court's judgment in a case involving the rape of a minor girl, Mathura, by policemen within the precincts of a rural police station in Maharashtra. It particularly condemned the insensitivity of the judges to the powerlessness of a poor, teenaged girl trapped inside a police station by two drunken men in uniform, and the unquestioning acceptance by the highest court of traditional assumptions about women and rape—for example, that a woman's morals and previous sexual history are pertinent to a rape case.

A campaign initiated by a lawyer's critique of a court judgment for naturally focussed on legislation. A major demand of the women's groups involved in the agitation was that the law relating to rape be changed to prevent the recurrence of such sexist judgments. Legal reform was, thus, central to the campaign although issues such as the definition of rape, its root causes, its impact on victims and social attitudes were also discussed.

The latter aspects were, perhaps, not sufficiently elaborated upon in the media. As a result, while pressure from women's organisations did force the government of the day to amend the law relating to rape (leaving many loopholes, as usual), the attitudes of members of the judiciary—as of society—remain much the same even today.

In fact, the 1989 Supreme Court judgment in the Suman Rani case—delivered exactly ten years after its controversial decision in the Mathura case—echoed its infamous predecessor so faithfully that it seemed as if a time-warp was in operation. The fact that in 1990, a full decade after the launch of the anti-rape campaign, a national conference on rape was held in Bombay to review the continuing judicial injustice done to victims of the violent crime is revealing indeed.

The first period selected for review (15 February-15 April 1980) spans the build-up of the anti-rape campaign, its climax with demonstrations organised around the International Women's Day and its reverberations beyond 8 March. The second period (25 July-25 August 1983), coinciding with the monsoon parliamentary session when the proposed amendment to the law relating to rape was expected to be tabled, covers the considerable debate on the legal aspects of the issue. As it happened, the Bill was introduced and passed only in the winter session, so that the 18 November-3 December 1983 period has also been reviewed.

The fact that dowry deaths and rape were the earliest issues to be taken up as campaigns by the contemporary women's movement is at least partly responsible for the relatively muted and scanty coverage accorded to them by the press. The women's movement was then at a nascent stage and, despite the great enthusiasm and fervour, it was not really equipped to orchestrate, widen and deepen public debates on issues of special concern to women. The subsequent proliferation of women's organisations in different parts of the country, the rise of women's studies as an academic discipline and the increased networking among concerned groups as well as individuals (symbolised by periodic national conferences) have contributed to the growing ability of the contemporary women's movement in India to make its voice heard.

The involvement of several women journalists in the movement played a significant part in ensuring media coverage. But it is clear that their efforts might not have been so effective were it not for the fact that they encountered no major obstacles—either because many senior journalists (mostly male) supported the causes they espoused or, more often, because the issues were not considered important enough for the decision-makers to formulate a coherent policy.

Anti-Rape Campaign

Rape did make it to the front page in all the newspapers at least once. The *Indian Express* was virtually the only paper which considered the formation of the Bombay-based Forum Against Rape, which spearheaded the anti-rape campaign sparked off by the Mathura case, sufficiently important to give it front page coverage (in the anchor position on 6 February 1980). This is clearly indicative of a deliberate editorial decision; the *Express* obviously saw the initiative as a precursor to more significant developments. By contrast, *The Times of India* (22 February 1980) announced the constitution of the Forum and its public meeting against rape in a single-column report on a left hand page towards the end of the paper.

The amendment to the law relating to rape, which was passed nearly four years after the launch of the campaign, did not receive much attention from the press. *The Hindustan Times* was the only paper which ran an edit on the passage of the amendments to the laws relating to rape and dowry. The *Indian Express* did carry a report on its front page, but in a small, single-column item. It did not deem it necessary to comment on the event.

During periods of heightened interest in a particular issue, often related news—which might otherwise have been routinely handled—is also emphasised. For instance, *The Hindustan Times* highlighted the item that American rapists were given a choice of chemical and physical castration with the headline 'Castration For Rape.'

By faithfully reporting public meetings as well as parliamentary debates on the issue, newspapers often threw up interesting bits of information. For example, *The Times of India*, in its report on the Lok Sabha debate on a private member's resolution on the subject, recorded that attendance in the House was thin, with a total of only six (women) members present when the debate was resumed.

The Statesman's report (2 December 1983) on the passage of the rape Bill in Parliament recorded the fact that only fifteen members turned up for the vote. It also quoted lawyer and member Ram Jethmalani of the Bharatiya Janata Party on the anti-rape legislation. He apparently thought the penalty provided for was too severe since rapists needed treatment rather than punishment. And he felt that the provision to make rape by a man of his wife punishable was a 'devious means to prevent sex with minor wives.'

All the papers, except *The Times of India*, published an editorial prompted by the anti-rape campaign revolving around the Mathura case. *The Hindustan Times* carried an additional one after the amendment to the rape law was passed by Parliament.

The *Indian Express* was the most prompt in commenting on the rape issue. In an edit appearing as early as 4 March 1980, it heralded the anti-rape demonstrations planned by women's organisations in Bombay and Delhi on the International Women's Day.

The edit published by *The Statesman* (8 March) actually predated any news report on the rape campaign in the paper. This was typical of the coverage given by the paper to all the issues reviewed—its editorial page invariably paid prompt and serious attention to each issue while its news pages lagged considerably behind in both immediacy and scope. This marked discrepancy is at least partly explained by the presence of a woman assistant editor on the editorial staff during this period. She could write edits on such issues but, because of the division of responsibilities between news and views, had no influence over their coverage on the news pages.

Women Out of Focus

In terms of focus, the *Indian Express* editorial (4 March 1980) stood out as the only one which dealt with rape squarely as a tool of women's oppression. As its headline 'Crimes Against Women' suggests, this edit viewed rape as one of many such crimes, on par with bride-burning and eve-teasing, in that it stemmed 'from the basic attitude of treating women as commodities.' It also pointed out the role of the communications media in transforming society and creating 'a modern community where the rights of women are not trampled upon with impunity at every step.'

Although rape did not merit an edit in *The Times of India*, the paper did feature a 'Current Topic' on the subject as early as 23 February 1980. (In *The Times of India*, brief comments on issues judged not important enough for an edit are published in this section of the editorial page.) Apart from the *Indian Express* edit, this was the only editorial comment which dealt directly with the women's question inherent in the issue. Supporting the call by women's organisations for a revision of the rape law, it cited research studies conducted in other countries to assert that among the root causes of the crime is the male urge to dominate and exercise power over the weaker (sic) sex. It urged Indian law-makers to pay heed to research findings which have established that there is no significant difference between the psychology of rapists and that of ordinary men. This progressive viewpoint was obviously slipped in by a sympathetic journalist with access to the editorial page since the issue was not considered worthy of an edit by the editorial hierarchy.

One other edit, published in *The Hindustan Times* (3 December 1983) the day after the Criminal Law (Amendment) Bill was passed by Parliament, focussed on crimes against women and, thereby, touched upon the question of women's oppression. Dealing with both dowry-related violence and rape, it declared that there was 'nothing more heinous than the rape of a woman.' It then went on to hail the new legislation as a step in the right direction, specially commending its acceptance of the concept of custodial rape. However, it deplored the fact that only a handful of MPs had participated in the debate, and finally ended by stating that it was up to social groups and women's organisations to ensure that the law was implemented.

Crime and Punishment

All the other edits focussed primarily on the crime and punishment aspects of the issue. Of these, *The Hindu's* editorial (31 March) was, perhaps, the most comprehensive, commenting in detail on the Mathura case and the campaign around it. The uncommonly long edit raised three main points: it questioned the Supreme Court's failure to take into account not only the age, status and consequent vulnerability of the victim, but also the violation by the police of the Criminal Procedure Code (CrPC) in summoning the girl to the police station in the first place; it contrasted the Court's decision in this case with its condemnation in another of the practice of calling women to police stations when the CrPC clearly states that they are always to be questioned at their place of residence; and it stressed the need to go beyond changing the law to sensitising people in the judiciary and the executive to the intricacies of the issue. The last point, particularly, assumes significance in the light of what has transpired in many rape cases in the intervening decade.

Among editorial page articles, one piece in the *Indian Express* and another in *The Hindustan Times* were distinguished by their analysis of rape from the women's perspective. They were also timed to coincide with the climax of the anti-rape campaign on the International Women's Day in 1980.

The Hindustan Times' timely edit page article, which preceded the paper's edit on rape, appeared on 7 March—the day before the demonstrations planned for IWD. Written by activist Amrita Chhachhi and headlined 'Stop Rape', it discussed different aspects of the problem: demystification of rape as well as rapists, legal loopholes, the genesis of the anti-rape campaign and, finally, the mass demonstrations scheduled for the next day. Whether or not this article was commissioned by the paper, the fact that it was published to coincide with an important date in the campaign suggests some support for the struggle.

The timing of the women-oriented edit page article in the *Indian Express*—a sensitive and insightful one headlined 'Rape And The Indian Woman' by author Nayantara Sahgal—was also significant. It appeared on 6 March—two days after the paper's editorial on the subject and two days prior to the anti-rape demonstrations planned for IWD. This was followed by another edit page article on 8 March. Written by Rami Chabra in her regular column on women's issues, it was headlined 'The Mathura Case And Rape Law'. The piece commented on the case, the campaign and the law, concluding: 'The battle to eradicate rape will have to be long drawn out and fought on many fronts. This will require the cooperation and goodwill of all thinking men and women.'

The juxtapositioning of editorial attention with the activities of women's groups campaigning on the issue suggests a deliberate decision within the paper's hierarchy to lend support to the struggle. The implied seriousness with which such a large newspaper chain dealt with the issue was bound to have an impact on the government and Parliament.

However, the last edit page article carried by the *Express* (22 November 1983) was not as sensitive to the women's question as the others. Written by M.P. Nathanael, a senior officer of the Central Reserve Police Force, its tone and content were clearly at variance with the paper's own perspective. The article dealt with police rape from the point of view of policemen. The piece did make some valid points about the low social and educational status of the rank and file policeman, as well as the poor pay and facilities he enjoys—all of which understandably affect his psychological well-being and attitude to society and work. But the writer revealed his basic insensivity by explaining away custodial rape as the natural consequence of such neglect and deprivation, accepting that women are natural targets of sexually starved, frustrated and vengeful men with a grouse against society, and failing to address the issue from the victims' viewpoint.

The *Times of India*'s only editorial page article on rape (11 April 1980) echoed these views. Written by retired police officer N.S. Saksena and headlined 'Police And Women', it also sought to explain rather than condemn the factors which lead to custodial rape.

Legal Questions

The Sunday magazine supplements of all the papers except *The Statesman* and *The Hindu* had features on rape. While the two articles in *The Hindustan Times* and the one in the *Indian Express* concentrated on the legal aspects of the issue, *The Times of India*'s article analysed the socio-economic roots of the crime.

In his serious piece in *The Times' Sunday Review* (9 March 1980), Achin Vanaik, then an assistant editor of the paper, demolished some of the myths attached to rape. For instance, he stated unequivocally that it was not an act of sexual frustration but one 'of violence, of domination, of humiliation.' He also linked rape to 'the politics of sex and class' and described the crime as 'the most ancient and evil of all social acts.'

The Hindustan Times' Sunday magazine (23 March 1980) published a well-displayed lead article by Kusum, headlined 'Violence Against Women: The Mathura Case In Retrospect,' on its cover page. The piece reviewed the case, the judgment and the law, stressed the need for social change and called upon the judiciary 'to mitigate the suffering of victimised women and not add fuel to the fire.'

Another article on the subject appeared on the features page of *The Hindustan Times* (21 March 1980). Written by the paper's legal correspondent, Krishan Mahajan, it provided details of the case and recalled the controversial judgment delivered by the Supreme Court. It is noteworthy that Mahajan's legal column often highlighted issues of special relevance to women, as did reports by M.J. Anthony, the legal correspondent of *Indian Express*. Thus, legal columns need not be dry, esoteric exercises but can actively raise public awareness about social issues and the law.

A timely article in the Sunday magazine of the *Indian Express* (17 February 1980) appeared just as the campaign was getting under way. Headlined 'The Law Behind Rape,' the article by Githa Hariharan discussed the inadequacies of the existing laws relating to the crime.

Conclusion

The most remarkable feature of the coverage accorded to the anti-rape campaign sparked off by the Mathura case is the evident coordination between certain newspapers and the movement. For instance, the climax of the campaign around 8 March 1980 was not only announced by some papers but also actively supported by a concentration of edits, other comments, features and/or reports timed to coincide with IWD.

This is explained partly by the involvement of journalists in the campaign, as activists or sympathisers, and partly by the fact that some women activists and commentators contributed timely articles which were promptly used. This kind of serious media attention cannot but have had some impact on the government of the day.

However, only two editorials and one 'Current Topic' item focussed on the gender question, examining the relationship between violence and women's oppression. Most of the others typically dealt with the legal aspects of the issue. The two editorial page articles analysing rape from the women's perspective were contributed by women outside the newspaper. At the same time, the one feature which discussed the gender-related as well as socio-economic roots of the crime was by a sympathetic male on the editorial staff.

The editorial and features pages of most of the papers seem to have been more responsive to the issue than the news sections. None of the news reports reflected original work or contributed a great deal to an understanding of the subject.

Another noteworthy point is that the attention span of newspapers is not very long. Notwithstanding the extensive coverage at the height of the campaign, little notice was taken of the new rape law when it was finally passed nearly four years later—only one paper commented on it in an edit. With no one specially assigned to the equivalent of a women's beat to keep track of developments in this field, the absence of follow-up is only to be expected.

4

DAILY NEWSPAPERS

The Shah Bano Controversy: A Question of Maintenance

Kalpana Sharma and ***Ammu Joseph***

In April 1985, on the eve of his retirement as Chief Justice of the Supreme Court of India, Justice Y. V. Chandrachud delivered a judgment for which he will long be remembered. In the case of a seventy-year old Muslim woman from Indore, Shah Bano, he ruled that she was entitled to a maintenance amount of Rs 179.20 from her ex-husband who had divorced her some years earlier. Shah Bano had been granted this amount by a lower court after she filed for maintenance under Section 125 of the Criminal Procedure Code, but the judgment had been challenged by her former husband who claimed that under Muslim Personal Law a man was only obliged to pay maintenance for the period of *iddat*—that is, for three months after the divorce.

The Shah Bano case will go down in legal history because it brought to the fore many fundamental questions about personal law, secular statues and whether the latter can overrule the former. In the end the issue was decided politically with the passage of the Muslim Women (Protection of Rights on Divorce) Bill. This excluded Muslim women from the purview of Section 125 CrPC. It laid down that the Wakf boards or the community would have to support deserted or divorced destitute women, and that the former husband was under no obligation to pay maintenance beyond the *iddat* period stipulated by Muslim Personal Law.

The Shah Bano controversy was, essentially, a gender issue. Here was a seventy-year-old woman who held that her husband had deserted her and then, as an afterthought, divorced her without making any provisions for her maintenance. Thanks to the support of her sons, she was able to fight the case through several courts—an opportunity denied to the majority of women.

However, newspapers writing on the case failed to touch on this central point. Nor did they ask or explain why Shah Bano had to resort to a section of the Criminal Procedure Code under which the maximum maintenance she could get was a pitiful Rs 500. One of the few writers who did bring this out was Madhu Kishwar, editor of the feminist journal *Manushi* (No. 32, 1986).

Kishwar articulated an important perspective for evaluating media coverage of the Shah Bano issue by pointing out two aspects that were misreported. It was generally assumed that Justice Chandrachud was the first judge to grant maintenance to a Muslim woman under the CrPC. Kishwar enlightened readers on two previous precedents set by the Supreme Court: the Fuzlunbi vs K. Khader Vali case (1980) and the Bai Tahira vs Ali Husain Fissali case (1979). The crucial difference between these two judgments and the Shah Bano one was that the former did not emphasise the fact that the contestants belonged to the Muslim community; the issue was considered purely as the legal right to maintenance under secular law. In the Shah Bano case, however, Justice Chandrachud made a point of noting that the woman fighting for maintenance was Muslim, thereby inviting the wrath of Islamic fundamentalists. Wrote Kishwar: 'By singling out Muslim men and Islam in this way, Justice Chandrachud converts what is essentially a women's rights issue into an occasion for a gratuitous attack upon a community.' In other words, the contents of the Chandrachud judgment laid the ground for turning what was essentially a gender issue into a religio-political-legal one.

The other fallacy propounded by the media, according to Kishwar, was that by granting maintenance under Section 125 of the CrPC, the Supreme Court had overruled Muslim Personal Law. She recorded many instances of lower courts granting maintenance under this provision to Muslim women, pointing out that many women, including Muslim women, preferred to use Section 125 of the criminal law because cases under civil law, such as the Muslim Personal Law, could drag on for several years. Few journalists were aware of this.

Instead, wrote Kishwar:

> Ever since the Supreme Court judgment in the Shah Bano case, the newspapers have been gleefully reporting each case of a Muslim woman getting maintenance in the lower courts as yet another 'victory'—in seeming ignorance of the fact that many such awards were made prior to the Shah Bano judgment.

She also showed that the incidence of polygamy and desertion by Muslim and Hindu men is almost identical—in fact, at one point higher amongst Hindus than Muslims. But this was hardly ever brought out by the press, which chose to project the problem as specific to the Muslim community. She concluded:

> Unfortunately, the media has helped cloud the real issues. Instead of using this occasion to start a real debate on how to remove various disabilities imposed by the legal system on women of different communities, it has highlighted the issue of injustice to Muslim women, in order to whip up anti-Muslim hysteria.

The analysis of the coverage of the issue in the print media which follows, suggests that Kishwar was not far off the mark. In fact, the communal fallout of this issue put a brake on women's groups which would otherwise have responded in a more direct way. Many women's organisations had long been recommending the adoption of a uniform civil code. However, once the Shah Bano controversy erupted, several Hindu fundamentalist groups also began arguing for a uniform civil code and used the issue to point out alleged shortcomings not just in Muslim Personal Law but in Islam. Not wishing to be associated, even indirectly, with such a position, most women's groups chose to remain silent on the question of the law. Instead, they voiced concern for divorced and deserted women of all communities.

The months selected for the survey were: November-December 1985 when, following Shah Bano's repudiation of the Supreme Court judgment, the demand for a law excluding Muslim women from the purview of Section 125 CrPC gathered momentum; and February-March 1986, when the tabling of the Muslim Women Bill led to the resignation of Arif Mohammed Khan, the Minister for Civil Aviation in the Rajiv Gandhi cabinet.

The Human Interest Angle

The *Indian Express* and *The Times of India* highlighted the human interest angle of the story much more than the other three papers. The latter carried a 1500-word article by Saeed Naqvi, a freelance writer, on 4 December 1985, albeit on page twelve. Headlined 'Drama Behind The Shah Bano Case,' the article was the first account of the pressures on Shah Bano, the struggle for dominance between different Muslim factions and the former husband's determination to teach all a lesson through Shah Bano. The writer had spoken to the people concerned, including Shah Bano, and the reader got a vivid idea of the situation she was confronted with in the wake of the judgment.

The Times of India was also one of the few dailies which attempted to project the plight of other Muslim divorced women through a report, datelined Pune 10 March 1986, carried in the anchor position on page one. It put forth the views of divorcees and their parents, describing the hardships they encounter once they are abandoned by their husbands.

Yet the same paper carried a news agency report, on Shah Bano's determination to reclaim her *meher*, on 10 March 1986, headlined 'Shah Bano Wants Pound Of Flesh.' The tone of the headline seemed to suggest that the woman was demanding something that was not entirely her right. The report, on the other hand, described the pressures on Shah Bano. Asked if she was not creating a fresh controversy, she said:

> My religious leaders forced me not to accept maintenance because, according to them, it is against the Shariat. But now I have decided I will not leave this matter just like that. I am determined to secure all those rights which have been provided in the Shariat exclusively for women. And *meher* is one of them.

In contrast, the same item appeared in the *Indian Express* under the straightforward headline 'Shah Bano Moves Court, Claims Meher.'

The *Times of India* headline, at variance with the substance of the story, indicates the attitude of the sub-editor on duty rather than that of the reporter who wrote the story. Such headlines, however, do not necessarily reflect deliberate policy. A sensitive and alert editor can, and often does, reprimand the sub-editor if he/she feels that a headline is inappropriate or misleading.

The *Indian Express* was the other paper which made some attempts to report the views of Muslim women. For instance, an item on 31

January 1986, reporting a women's dharna to demand a common civil code, quoted some of the participants. One Naseem Begum, who had been married for twelve years and divorced for five, wanted to know: 'Why should men be so deceiving *(sic)* that they force women to go to court to claim alimony?' It also carried interviews with Muslim women who had something to say on the subject. Thus both Meherunissa Dalwai of the Muslim Satyashodhak Sangh, who had led the Talak Mukti Morcha in Maharashtra, and Supreme Court lawyer Sona Khan were interviewed on 12 March and 22 March, respectively, in some detail. Khan was quoted as saying: 'Ignorance of what is written in the Koran leaves the Muslim woman dependent on the interpretation of the maulvis and the mullahs. Many Muslim women were afraid to speak out against the proposed Bill for fear of being divorced by their husbands.'

The Statesman, in one of its eight edits on the issue ('A Flawed Leadership,' 2 March 1986), commented that 'what Muslim women think of this (the proposed law) may never be fully known for not many of them are articulate.' But it did not make much of an effort to seek their opinions. For instance, in an otherwise commendable story by Hasan Suroor ('Many Muslims Oppose The Bill,' 9 March) based on interviews in Bihar and Uttar Pradesh, only two women were interviewed. An elderly male school teacher quoted in the article pointed out that the mullahs' claim that the Bill enjoys majority support 'simply ignores the views of countless women whose voice is muffled by their fathers, husbands and the mullahs.' Yet this forced silence was not sought to be broken by the correspondent.

Several articles related to the issue of maintenance were highlighted by a number of newspapers. They bear out Kishwar's point that ignorance about the past prompted the press to emphasise every decision on maintenance under Section 125 CrPC as a special happening. For instance, the *Indian Express* boxed a news story by the United News of India (UNI) on 16 March 1986, headlined 'Shah Bano Verdict: A Judicial Forerunner In Madras.' The story quoted a 1984 Madras High Court judgment, delivered by Justice S. A. Kader, on a petition filed by Ameer Amanullah challenging a lower court's order granting monthly maintenance of Rs 100 to his ex-wife Mariam Beevi and Rs 50 to their child.

The only 'human interest' story that stood out in *The Hindustan Times* was negative in some ways. The paper chose to devote a full page, with a specially emphasised introduction, to an article by Saeed Naqvi whose stories on this issue had appeared in many other papers. While in *The Times of India* Naqvi wrote about the pressure by fundamentalists to make Shah Bano retract her statements and refuse the maintenance awarded by the court, in *The Hindustan Times* (29 March 1986) he wrote a rather sensational report on how the wife of Shah Bano's younger son was being beaten by him and her mother-in-law.

Without directly stating it, the report seemed to imply that Shah Bano's behaviour towards her daughter-in-law somehow detracted from her claim to maintenance. The author also used rather exaggerated terms to describe the illiterate old woman—'the champion of oppressed Muslim women' and 'the symbol of women's rights.' Shah Bano had merely sought a measly maintenance amount from her prosperous lawyer ex-husband. By deliberately using such phrases to describe her in a story about her alleged mistreatment of another woman, the author seemed to be undermining the validity of Shah Bano's claim. Such reports, by counterposing two unrelated situations, tend to discredit the struggle of ordinary women for justice and reinforce the common belief that women are their own worst enemies.

Political Overtones

When an issue acquires political overtones it automatically attains prominence; for then even if it remains essentially a 'women's' issue, it ranks high in the traditional hierarchy of newsworthiness. Thus, the resignation of Arif Mohammed Khan on 26 February 1986 gave the issue fresh visibility, with all newspapers frontpaging the event. In the days that followed, other developments, such as Congress MPs' opposition to the Bill and women's organisations' attempts to press for its withdrawal, also drew media attention.

While all the papers featured the announcement of his resignation on page one, *The Times of India* went further. It carried two long anchor articles, 'The Arif Mohammed Affair' (1 and 2 March 1986), by Arun Shourie who was shortly to join the paper as its executive editor. Shourie's pieces were neither on the law, nor on Shah Bano nor the status of divorced Muslim women. They focussed almost entirely on Arif Mohammed Khan and the politics in the Congress party that led to his exit. These two articles were followed up with an edit on the resignation. In contrast, the *Indian Express* treated the news routinely and did not comment on the resignation. *The Statesman* did carry an editorial comment on 2 March, two days after the resignation, but its focus was the Muslim Women Bill and Rajiv Gandhi's inconsistency rather than Khan.

The position taken by these newspapers in their editorial columns is, perhaps, most indicative of their approach to this issue. While some of the newspapers had a consistent approach, others tended to strike in all directions.

For instance, in its six editorials which followed in rapid succession, the *Indian Express* consistently argued for the acceptance of a common civil code. Interestingly, it changed the nomenclature after the first edit (18 November 1985), which appeared before the Muslim Women Bill had become an issue, to an 'optional civil code' (5 December) and then to a 'Family Laws Act' (23 December). The edit argued that such a law would not affect 'those who prefer to follow existing or reformed personal laws' but 'would allow any citizen who sees his or her personal law as inadequate to seek satisfaction in common family law.'

The Statesman, on the other hand, was less focussed in its eight editorials. All the edits were on specific events following the Shah Bano furore and none advocated any solutions to the problem.

The Hindustan Times, which gave substantial news coverage to the issue, with fifteen items on the front page, devoted only two edits to it. The paper, in its 23 November 1985 editorial, favoured a 'common civil code conforming to the basic tenets of Islam.' It condemned the violent attacks on supporters of the cause of divorced Muslim women in Maharashtra, stating that this was indicative of a 'concerted attempt by obscurantist sections of the community to thwart the reformist movement building up within.'

Like the *Indian Express*, *The Times of India* also indicated its preference for a uniform civil code in its editorials. However, unlike the former, it did not push the case for it consistently. Instead, *The Times* argued that 'essentially the battle for reforms within Indian Islam is to be fought and won within the community.' Yet the same editorial (18 November 1985, headlined 'Muslim Social Reform'), pointed out that the Supreme Court was not wrong in going beyond the Shah Bano case to recommend the implementation of a uniform civil code because 'there is a general consensus that there should be a uniform civil code for all Indians.' But it admitted that the vast majority of Muslims have not been part of this consensus.

This last point is significant. *The Times of India* seemed to suggest that a uniform civil code was acceptable as long as the majority opinion was in its favour and even if the minority community did not support it. Also, the editorials tended to emphasise the unwillingness of some elements within the Muslim community to respond to reform without balancing this with the fact that militant Hindu parties were demanding change within Muslim Personal Law and pushing for a uniform civil code not because they saw this as good but because they wanted to expose the alleged inadequacies of Islam.

The Muslim Women Bill

The introduction of the Muslim Women Bill, followed by the resignation of Arif Mohammed Khan, drew the greatest amount of comment and writing on the legal, religious and political aspects of the issue. All the four papers criticised the Bill in their edits, dubbing it regressive. *The Times of India*, which had been generally supportive of the government of the day on other issues, carried a sharp edit entitled 'Scrap The Bill' on 28 February 1986, the day after Arif Mohammed Khan's resignation. The paper commented:

> There can be no question that the Muslim Women (Protection of Rights on Divorce) Bill is a wholly retrograde piece of legislation and that its introduction in the Lok Sabha represents a violation of the assurance the Prime Minister had given: he has not held the wide consultations he had promised and he has blatantly disregarded the opinion of educated Muslims. But the fact of support for it in the Muslim community cannot be denied. Whatever the factors at work behind the closed doors of South Block, it is shocking beyond words that a Prime Minister, who had made 'march into the 21st century' his battlecry, should have endorsed a march into the 7th century for one-eighth of the Indian people. The measure must be scrapped.

The Hindustan Times was equally strong in its criticism of the Bill. Headlined 'A Retrograde Step' (22 February 1986), it condemned the 'electoral calculations behind the misleading Bill,' questioned its implementability and concluded: 'The government has pre-empted the rational debate on the issue favoured at one stage by caving in to the fundamentalists' chorus for restoring the status quo' and by aiding 'the efforts of orthodox sections in thwarting the reformist movements that have been building up within the community.'

The legal and religious angles were predominant in most of the commentative pieces which appeared on the edit pages of the newspapers surveyed. A majority of these articles did not examine the law specifically in terms of its effect on women but went into the minutiae of whether the new law was necessary and the motives of those promoting it.

The Times of India outdid all the others in the number of articles it carried on the question of law and religion. At least two of the writers who featured on its edit page, Zarina Bhatty and Vasudha Dhagamwar, did emphasise the women's viewpoint even as they looked at the issue from the legal angle. However, the paper carried a number of other articles which discussed the question of Muslim Personal Law and whether maintenance beyond the period of iddat could be construed as violative of the Shariat. Danial Latifi, Shah Bano's lawyer, who fought her case in the Supreme Court, wrote a two-part article on the edit page on 12 and 13 March 1986, arguing that the Muslim Women Bill violated 'Islamic civilisation.' Subsequently, the paper carried another two-part series, by W. M. Shaikh on 14 and 15 March 1986, which looked at personal laws in other Muslim countries. The author argued against polygamy and for court-controlled divorce.

In her two-part edit page article (10 February 1986), lawyer Vasudha Dhagamwar placed the issue squarely in a gender perspective when she wrote:

Let us face it: the whole outcry that has gone up against grant of maintenance to Muslim divorcees is aimed at keeping Muslim women down...it is a shame that many of us have been unable to see through these tactics (of Muslim fundamentalists), which is why women activists are not taking as bold a stand as they should on this issue.

The Hindustan Times carried mainly legalistic comment pieces. H. B. L. Nigam (2 November 1983) discussed reform in Islamic law in other countries, focussing particularly on the guidelines issued by the Supreme Judicial Council of the Islamic Republic of Iran. A month later (3 December), lawyer Salman Khurshid, in a two-part article headlined 'Moulvis, Maintenance and Ministers,' declared himself against the Supreme Court's judgment and any changes in the law. Like many others, he failed to consider the problems or the rights of Muslim women under the existing law. The balance was somewhat righted by an edit page article by Kusum on 25 February headlined 'Undoing Shah Bano Case'. It traced the legal history of Muslim women's fight for maintenance and asked, 'Is it proper to barter away the rights of Muslim women who constitute half the Muslim population in the country?'

The *Indian Express* responded to the question of the law only after the Muslim Women Bill came into focus. In fact, the first major edit page article on this issue was written by L. K. Advani of the Bharatiya Janata Party (7 January 1986). Titled 'Shah Bano Case: Government Must Not Capitulate,' the article dealt mainly with the law and urged the adoption of a uniform civil code, a measure which the paper had also been advocating through its editorials. The issue was presented as a struggle between fundamentalists and secularists, the assumption being that the former were Muslims while the latter belonged to the Hindu community. Lawyer A. G. Noorani's two-part article on 21 and 22 March 1986 in the same paper, however, did not project such a perspective and was essentially a legal critique of the Muslim Women Bill.

Strange Humour

The Hindustan Times added another dimension to the issue through the supposed humour of its regular columnist, Rajinder Puri. His articles reflected his anti-women bias. Commenting on Shah Bano's stand, Puri had the following to say in his column titled 'One Woman' (5 March 1986):

> There is a woman who has given a headache to many people.... Only the woman herself did not get a headache. She continued to exercise a woman's prerogative of changing her mind with painful regularity. And by creating havoc in the minds of many, and in the careers of a few, she spectacularly demonstrated the power of women. Just one woman. Shah Bano.

A later column (26 March), titled 'Bill For Maintenance Of Women,' quoted the following imaginary conversation with a friend: 'Women expect maintenance for all sorts of frills and luxuries which can drive the poor male insane...(they are) only interested in buying sarees, perfumes and lipstick.' The writer called for a Bill for the maintenance of wives all over the country as, even though he was not divorced, 'I have this problem of maintaining my lawful happily married wife!'

Blatant Communalisation

Newspapers rarely carry advertisements commenting on controversial political or communal issues—these appear mainly in the run-up to elections. The *Indian Express*, however, chose to run a series of three-column advertisements, released by the Hindu revivalist organisation, the Vishwa Hindu Parishad, during this period. They were placed unusually in the top right hand corner on the page opposite the edit page. (Advertisements rarely appear in this position, the edit page being second only to the front page in importance for news stories. They are usually carried on the bottom half of the page.) The one entitled 'Respect For Womanhood' (5 February 1986), at the height of the controversy, stated:

> Hinduism has the greatest respect for womanhood. It was Hinduism which first declared that God resides where women are worshipped. Hence there was no difficulty for a woman to become the PM of India. Instances like Shah Bano case never arose in Hinduism. Women lost all their glory and liberty in the dark period of history when India was invaded by barbarians.

Such a blatantly communal piece of writing was shocking in itself. What was worse was that a major national paper gave it an important editorial position, thereby silently endorsing it.

The Gender Perspective

The Sunday magazine section of the *Indian Express* stood out amongst the five Sunday supplements surveyed for the consistency with which its articles on the Shah Bano issue emphasised the gender perspective. It published a total of five articles on the issue, two of which were featured on page one. *The Times of India* also gave the issue some importance; it carried three articles, of which one was a lead story. *The Statesman* did not have a single article on this subject in its magazine section, conforming to its set style of running only 'light' pieces on and for women. Both *The Hindustan Times* and *The Hindu* carried one article each.

All the five articles in the *Express Magazine* looked at the issue in terms of the impact of the existing and new laws on women. Anjali Mathur (16 March 1986) pointed out that the question of maintenance for divorced Muslim women had become communalised. She stressed that both Muslim fundamentalists and Hindu chauvinists claimed to be protecting the rights of women, yet neither had asked whether the Muslim Women's Bill benefits women 'in their search for equality, or increases their dependence on society.'

A page one story in the *Express Magazine* by Shahida Lateef (30 March 1986) traced the historical process 'by which a decimated and insecure Muslim community embraced the status quo for important political gains, sacrificing in the bargain the position of its own women.' She argued:

> In modern Indian conditions, divorced women require financial support, not as a charity but a rightful return for the years during which the woman's labour and support helped the husband to acquire economic and social assets of which she should get her just dues.

In contrast, the *Sunday Review* of *The Times of India* (15 March 1986) featured a long and detailed page one story by Arun Shourie entitled 'In The Name Of Muslim Personal Law.' The article went into details about personal law and criticised the Muslim Women Bill and those pushing it. However, it did not dwell on the specific impact of the law on women; Shah Bano was used as a hook on which the author could hang his personal views on the Muslim Personal Law.

The Hindu, which had otherwise given little prominence to this issue as a whole, carried a long article by a former Supreme Court judge, Justice V. R. Krishna Iyer, headlined 'Shah Bano Showdown' (2 February 1986) in its Sunday magazine section. The piece gave a detailed description and analysis of the case as well as its legal and constitutional ramifications. But even this renowned advocate of human rights, including women's rights, touched upon its implications for women only in passing.

Conclusion

None of the papers surveyed adequately dealt with the potential impact on women of the Supreme Court judgment in the Shah Bano case and the Muslim Women Bill which followed. *Express Magazine* stood out as an exception in this regard, as also two of the edit page articles in *The Times of India*. Otherwise, the preponderance of articles, edits and news stories tended to dwell on the political, legal or religious aspects, overlooking the women's question.

While the overall coverage of the issue was not overtly communal, there was an underlying bias in some of the editorial comment. For instance, the insistence that a uniform civil code was the best solution, a line pushed by all the five newspapers, reflected an unquestioning belief that what was acceptable to the majority community, that is Hindus, should also be accepted by all minorities, especially Muslims. A more blatantly communal view was evident in the text of the VHP advertisement run by the *Indian Express* at the height of the controversy.

Press responses to the Shah Bano controversy also underlined the fact that a women's issue merits front page treatment mainly when it turns 'political' in the narrowest sense of the term. For instance when the Congress (I), in an obvious effort to woo Muslim fundamentalists for electoral gains, floated the idea of the Muslim Women Bill, all the newspapers recognised its importance. There were numerous editorial comments on the legal aspects of the issue and its political fallout—brought into sharper focus by the resignation of a Union cabinet minister. Yet, most of the comment failed to recognise the basic issue: the position of divorced or abandoned women in Indian society, irrespective of their creed.

The central point about the impact of such laws on women emerged only in articles by women, many written on their own initiative. Their well-argued pieces were probably accepted because they did not contradict the papers' editorial positions but, instead, brought in a different dimension.

Coverage of the Shah Bano controversy illustrates how women's voices are rarely heard in the press—the 'symbolic annhilation' Tuchman writes about. Women's issues are taken seriously only when they enter the male spheres of politics and law. Under normal circumstances, reports about divorced or abandoned women fighting for maintenance are given cursory attention on the news pages, if that, and rarely commented upon.

Finally, unlike dowry deaths and rape, where campaigns by women's groups were primarily responsible for media attention, this issue did not benefit from the clear articulation of the gender question by the women's movement. As a result, the issue was politicised and communalised and the centrality of the question of maintenance after divorce was almost completely overlooked.

5

DAILY NEWSPAPERS

Female Foeticide: The Abuse of Technology

Kalpana Sharma and Ammu Joseph

The use or misuse of new developments in science and medicine have only recently been viewed critically by feminists in India. They have raised questions about the family planning programme and the kind of contraceptives it advocates since these have failed to demonstrate that the health of the woman is a central concern. Medical prescription, especially for pregnant women, has been another subject of investigation.

In the early eighties, some women's groups in Bombay found that the medical technique of amniocentesis, which involves the removal of amniotic fluid from the placenta to detect genetic abnormalities, was being misused to discover the sex of the foetus. Furthermore, women not wanting another girl child were being persuaded to have abortions even after the twentieth week, although this is considered dangerous. Some clinics provided both sex determination tests and abortion facilities.

This led to the formation in 1986 of the Bombay-based Forum Against Sex Determination and Pre-Selection, comprising men and women, including some doctors. They launched a campaign not just to raise awareness about the misuse of these technologies but to also show its link to the status of women in India, denied even the chance to be born.

The periods selected for this study were mid-June to mid-August 1986 when the campaign against female foeticide was launched, and December 1986, when a private member's Bill to curb this practice was under discussion. Also surveyed was January 1988, following the Maharashtra government's announcement of its intention to introduce a law restricting the use of sex determination and pre-selection techniques.

Although the debate on the issue continued through 1988, especially on the edit page of *The Times of India*, the selected months mark the periods when the issue was most in focus. The coverage over these months, therefore, gives a fairly good idea of the extent of interest in the subject. The discussion in the 'Letters to the Editor' columns of the *Indian Express* and *The Times of India* is particularly revealing as it provides an insight into the perceptions of readers (see Appendix B).

Minimum Coverage

Compared to the other issues surveyed in this study, this subject received the minimum coverage altogether and in individual newspapers. Although the Bombay-based papers, the *Indian Express* and *The Times of India*, did carry more than the other three, mainly because the campaign against amniocentesis was launched in Bombay, their coverage was extremely scanty.

In quantitative terms, the *Indian Express* gave the most coverage, including one edit, while *The Hindu* carried only four items, of which not a single one was an edit.

Like other issues, once the subject acquired legal dimensions, it merited the front page. Therefore, in January 1988, when the Maharashtra government announced its decision to ban sex determination tests except under strict supervision, the news was displayed on the front pages of both *The Times of India* and the *Indian Express*. *The Hindustan Times* and *The Hindu* also carried this news, but on the inside pages.

Earlier, the subject had figured either as small news items somewhere on the inside pages or as features in the magazine section. The one exception to the rule was *The Times of India,* which carried an edit page main article by Achin Vanaik on 20 June 1986, around the time the issue was raised by the Forum. The writer placed the subject in the wider social context without underplaying the centrality of the women's question.

Most of the editorials generally disapproved of female foeticide and either recommended a strict law to control the misuse of the technology or commended the Maharashtra government for taking the initiative. The *Indian Express*, for instance, welcomed the new law in Maharashtra in its edit (4 January 1988) headlined 'Well Done': '...for female foeticide at one end and sati at the other illustrate only too starkly "the womb to tomb" oppression of women in Indian society.'

A Different Note

The Statesman, however, struck a different note in one of its three edits. In a comment (18 December 1986) which was basically in favour of the Maharashtra government's plan to amend the Medical Termination of Pregnancy Act in order to prevent female foeticide, it raised a problematic point which had anti-abortion overtones: 'An amendment might help, but only if the fine print is carefully noted and abortion is not so readily available on demand.' Its edit of 17 January 1988, following the Maharashtra ban, however, struck a more decidedly pro-women note when it stated that 'other states would do well to follow the example of Maharashtra.' The paper argued:

> The demand that such tests should not be allowed is prompted as much by consideration of the mother's health and the safety of the unborn child as by objections to the grim practice of systematically destroying one gender, a form of discrimination that has sombre implications not only for the status of women but, ultimately, for the social fabric as a whole.

The editorial in *The Hindustan Times* following the Maharashtra ban (4 January 1988) pointed out the crucial role of media intervention in the issue when it wrote: 'In fact, the private clinics offering this test gained notoriety when the media began spotlighting the abuse and rank commercialisation of this important scientific discovery.'

Apart from such editorial comment, which was fairly general in nature, there was no detailed discussion on the law and its efficacy or on the question of conflict with other laws, such as the Medical Termination of Pregnancy Act.

Difficult Dilemma

Coverage of this subject posed a difficult dilemma for editors who disapproved of female foeticide and did not want to give free publicity to the methods available for sex determination and pre-selection. They found that even routine reports, or articles written by people critical of these methods, unwittingly publicised hitherto unknown techniques, inviting queries from readers.

For instance, the 29 June 1986 edition of *Express Magazine* carried an article about a new technique for sex pre-selection, devised by a Dr Ericsson, which was being introduced in India. Written by Manisha Gupte and Ravi Duggal, who were active in the campaign against female foeticide, it had a discernibly critical perspective. The very headline of the article ('A New Way To Eliminate Women?') indicated their position. The writers deliberately avoided giving specific details about the doctor who was introducing the technique and instead used this development to comment on what the issue reveals about the situation of women. They wrote: 'The status of Indian women is pitiful enough when they are born as "unavoidable evils" but it will be much worse when they are born despite a planned conspiracy to eliminate them.'

Despite all efforts to discourage and discredit this trend, the editor of *Express Magazine* received queries about the doctor from as far away as Jullunder in Punjab. Obviously, even negative publicity on such an issue can prove useful to those wishing to propagate these techniques; thus, even those critical of such practices can inadvertently contribute to their publicisation.

A few articles managed to go beyond reporting on the misuse of these technologies to discussing the more fundamental questions raised by the issue. Vanaik's piece in *The Times of India* (20 June 1986) was one such write-up: 'This problem of sex determination tests and selective abortion, or female foeticide, as it is aptly called, has at least three dimensions—misuse of science and technology, social oppression of women and abuse of human rights.'

Conclusion

This issue received uniformly minimal coverage, although newspapers published from Bombay, where the campaign was launched, gave it marginally more attention. This could be due to a combination of several factors. First, female foeticide was essentially seen as a middle-class, urban problem, involving a relatively small section of society.

Secondly, the first evidence of misuse was collected by groups which had already taken a position on the issue. It is possible that some newspapers, chary of any kind of flag-waving, were cautious about accepting such data. Nevertheless, none of them took the trouble to verify the facts. For instance, one of the most startling statistics put out by the Forum Against Sex Determination and Pre-selection in 1986 was that out of 8,000 foetuses aborted following amniocentesis in one Bombay hospital, 7,999 were female. Newspapers either published these statistics unquestioningly or avoided them altogether—not entirely surprising as most newspapers tend to reproduce figures without double-checking them as long as they come from what are perceived as 'reliable' sources.

Another possible reason for the cautious approach of newspapers towards this issue could be their reluctance to question the credibility of the medical profession. Journalists investigating medical ethics and malpractice have encountered considerable resistance from editors. This is partly because professional medical bodies have successfully lobbied newspaper owners and editors to promote a positive image and to prevent articles which raise uncomfortable questions. It is not unknown, for instance, for reporters of particular newspapers, whose proprietors have close connections either with a hospital or some leading doctors, to be told specifically that they are not to include any critical references to these institutions or individuals in their stories. As a result of this nexus, health activists have found it extremely difficult to encourage newspapers to conduct investigations into medical malpractices involving over-prescription or wrong medication leading to ill health and sometimes even death.

Also, unlike dowry deaths, or rape, or sati, or even the Shah Bano controversy, female foeticide is not obviously linked to the question of violence against women, although it could be argued that it constitutes violence against the female gender. The risk of projecting it as violence against the unborn foetus, however, is that it can be seen as support for the 'pro-life' lobby. Most of those campaigning against female foeticide would not wish to be identified with an anti-abortion position which curtails a woman's right to reproductive choice.

Furthermore, although some of the statistics gathered by activists were dramatic, it was difficult to prove conclusively the nexus between sex determination tests and female foeticide. The women who opted for abortion on discovering the gender of the foetus were not always willing to admit, on record, that this was the reason. The law permits abortion in a number of situations, the most common being 'failure of contraceptive.' In fact, it is this very difficulty, of proving deliberate female foeticide, which has detracted from the efficacy of the Maharashtra law restricting sex determination tests.

Finally, the coverage of this issue illustrated how the dominant orientation of news coverage towards events can lead to the neglect of a process like female foeticide. If activist groups had not made the connection between the increasing number of clinics offering sex determination tests and the rise in abortions, and conducted independent investigations that established that these tests were indeed being used for female foeticide, it is more than likely that the press would have missed out on this issue altogether.

6

DAILY NEWSPAPERS

The Roop Kanwar Tragedy: In the Name of Tradition

Ammu Joseph and *Kalpana Sharma*

The fiery death of 18-year-old Roop Kanwar on the funeral pyre of her deceased husband on 4 September 1987, a bare seven months after her wedding, sparked off a heated controversy over the macabre ritual of widow-burning which had been banned by law over a century earlier.

News about the tragedy first appeared in national dailies around 12 September in the form of a captioned news agency photograph showing *trishul*-wielding Rajput youths guarding the site of the so-called 'sati.' By 16 September, when the *chunri mahotsav*—a ceremony meant to honour the woman who had 'become a sati'—was scheduled, most major papers had journalists on the spot to cover it.

This prompt, active and almost universal response can be traced to a number of factors. For one, the press in India had undergone quantitative as well as qualitative changes during the period under review. The magazine boom of the late seventies was followed by a proliferation and diversification of newspapers. The resulting plurality of publications meant readers could no longer be taken for granted and this tended to inject new vigour into many aspects of the journalistic endeavour.

Also, the experience of the Emergency years had made the press more alert and assertive in its news-gathering activities; it had inaugurated the era of investigative journalism. In addition, the Emergency left a legacy of heightened public interest in current affairs, which acted as an additional spur to the press.

The women's movement had also developed and strengthened during the eighties, in terms of both activism and scholarship. For instance, by the time 'sati' once again reared its ugly head in the shape of Roop Kanwar, at least two major research studies by Indian feminists were available which could provide background information and analysis about different aspects of the practice. Women's groups and their protests were no longer confined to Bombay and Delhi. In this instance, women in Jaipur played a major role in anti-sati activities, ranging from legal action through marches and demonstrations to articulation of their views in the media. Women also kept a close watch on media performance, even going so far as to gherao the editor of a leading Delhi-based Hindi daily for what they considered an offensive, pro-sati editorial.

The positive contribution of women media professionals was also more organised by this time—for instance, the Women and Media Committee of the Bombay Union of Journalists sent a fact-finding team to Deorala, where the macabre death had occurred, and produced a detailed report, *Trial By Fire*, which was released to the press. Mediastorm, a group of women film-makers from the Jamia Milia University in Delhi, made a timely documentary which was shown nationally on television. Doordarshan itself featured an early television discussion on the subject in which concerned women were able to voice their views.

Further down the line, when the anti-sati legislation was being contemplated by the government, women lawyers drafted a bill for dealing more effectively with the problem of sati and other crimes against women and girls committed in the name of religion or custom, as well as with the perpetuation or glorification of such religious practices and customs. The multi-pronged response by concerned women and the increased visibility and volubility of the movement was bound to have an impact on press coverage of the issue.

Two other possible reasons for the extensive coverage given to the 'sati' controversy have to do with the nature of the press and the way it determines news values. The fact that the issue quickly acquired communal overtones and political significance certainly augmented media interest. And given the media's propensity for dramatic and outrageous events, the brutality inherent in the gruesome practice and the violence threatened by its protagonists, it is not surprising that the issue attracted considerable news coverage.

Roop Kanwar's controversial death was used by opinion leaders among the Rajputs of Rajasthan to heighten the community's sense of identity and fuel its quest for political power. Coinciding as it did with the rise of Hindu revivalism in the country, the young girl's demise was hailed as a supreme sacrifice—one which upheld a glorious tradition sanctified by religion; any opposition was described by religious fundamentalists as an attack on faith and accepted custom.

The extensive debate on the question of religious sanction which preceded the enactment of the 1829 legislation abolishing sati did not inform the contemporary discussion to any appreciable degree. Further, the question why women must invariably be sacrificed at the altar of religion and tradition was hardly addressed except by progressive women and a few concerned men.

In fact, the pro-sati lobby managed to enlist public support for the practice from Rajput women by projecting the issue as one of protection of the interests of the community. It also erected an effective barrier around Deorala village, making it difficult for concerned women and the press to elicit the real views of Rajput women. Despite this, there were indications that the information and views propagated by the lobby were not universally accepted.

The fact that at the time Rajasthan was ruled by the Congress (I) party, then also in power at the centre, and that politicians belonging to opposition parties were active on the pro-sati side added fuel to the fire. This is particularly significant in the light of the condemnation of the state government by both sides—one accusing it of inaction and complicity and the other alleging state interference in religious tradition.

Another point worth noting is that a number of prominent public figures, including members of the erstwhile royal family of Jaipur, the then speaker of the Lok Sabha and various other politicians (apart from the ones openly supporting sati), were accused of participating in sati-related ceremonies before as well as after Roop Kanwar's death.

An interesting aspect of media coverage highlighted by the 'sati' controversy concerns the use of language. Despite the confusion over whether Roop Kanwar went willingly to her death, consciously chosing to 'commit sati,' and despite the debate about the existence of such a thing as 'voluntary sati,' most newspapers routinely used words like 'sati' and 'self-immolation' without quotation marks, (one paper even resorted to capitalisation), giving currency to the disputed assumption that Roop Kanwar's death was indeed a case of 'sati'. Further, several reports on the *chunri mahotsav* described it in glowing terms; the writers were obviously awe-struck by the picturesque, emotion-charged and widely attended ceremony even while clearly disapproving of the unnecessary and cruel death of the young widow.

The period selected for study comprised the three and a half months immediately following the news about Roop Kanwar's death—mid-September to end-December 1987—during which the *chunri mahotsav* took place, anti-sati legislation was passed by the state and central governments, and public concern and media attention were at their peak.

Maximum Coverage

In terms of prominence and space, the 'sati' issue received more coverage than any of the other issues studied. It made its way to the front pages of all the newspapers, prompted several special reports and analyses, invited a large number of editorials commenting on various aspects of the issue, spawned magazine features providing details and historical background, and brought forth a spate of letters to the editor. While proximity did play a part in determining the total amount of coverage, the lack of it does not seem to have seriously inhibited *The Hindu* or *The Statesman*, published from Madras and Calcutta respectively (with Delhi editions), which made respectable showings in terms of coverage of this particular subject.

All the papers carried news about Roop Kanwar's death and subsequent developments on their front pages and sent reporters out to give more detailed coverage. Apart from this, some of these mainstream dailies used articles by a number of outsiders—social activists and lawyers—not just in their opinion columns, but in prominent positions in their news columns. For instance, the *Indian Express* carried an eye-witness account of the *chunri mahotsav* ceremony, by Gandhian social worker Vishal Mangalwadi, on its front page dated 19 September.

Mangalwadi's special report was exceptional because, in addition to witnessing the *chunri mahotsav*, he took the trouble to speak to women present on the scene. His article highlighted the terrible fate of widows and the pathetically low status of women, especially outside the institution of marriage, in Rajasthan. He also quoted people present at

Roop Kanwar's death, vividly documenting the horror of a young girl being buried alive under firewood, screaming for help, receiving none and the fire being relit to ensure her end, with crowds of people watching all the while.

The most controversial of the many special reports published by *The Hindustan Times* was one by staffer Sandhya Jain. It appeared on 28 September and sparked off demonstrations by pro-sati Rajputs as well as a legal suit by Roop Kanwar's brother against the paper. What incensed sati supporters and the family concerned were the disclosures in the report that Maal Singh, Roop Kanwar's husband, had been undergoing treatment for impotency, shock and depression; that the couple had spent only twenty days together; and that Roop Kanwar had been involved with another man and had, in fact, eloped with him prior to her husband's death.

Although 'pro-sati youth' burned copies of the paper outside its Jaipur office for the alleged 'character assassination of the "sati",' *The Hindustan Times* went ahead and published a second report by Jain (29 September) which dealt with the political significance of the event but also reasserted that Roop Kanwar was murdered in cold blood.

Not many papers sought out Roop Kanwar's natal family. The most noteworthy of the special stories which appeared in *The Statesman* were those which focussed on this aspect. Written by correspondent V.P. Sharan (8 and 14 October), one reported on the likelihood of a sati temple coming up in Ranchi, where Roop Kanwar's family is supposed to have originated, and the other was based on an interview with her brother, who claimed that Roop was a devotee of Rani Sati.

The alternative legislation proposed by women based in the capital—the draft Crimes Against Women and Girls in the Name of Religion or Custom (Prevention and Abolition) Act, 1987—did not receive much press coverage. It was designed to deal with the many manifestations of the sati syndrome and more effectively combat its perpetuation and glorification, as well as practices such as witch hunting and child sacrifice. Even the Delhi-based *The Hindustan Times* did not refer to it directly. However, some of the points covered by the proposed law were raised in a letter to the editor by Kusum, who later wrote an article on sati published on the editorial page.

The ideas underlying the draft legislation were featured quite prominently in *The Times of India*. The paper, in fact, broke tradition by carrying an article by two outside writers— Lotika Sarkar and Radha Kumar—on an important news page (opposite the editorial page). The article (5 December) was actually a commentative piece which analysed the government's proposed legislation and suggested deletions and amendments which would make it more effective in preventing unnatural widow-death. *The Times of India's* decision to run this openly commentative and advocative piece by persons associated with the women's movement and to accord it such a prominent position, normally reserved for news reports by staff and news agencies, is fairly significant, especially since the paper's edit on the subject echoed the arguments in this article.

In terms of an implicit editorial stance, it is significant that while the *Indian Express* reported the pro-sati views of the Shankaracharya of Puri in the anchor position on the front page (3 October), *The Times of India* placed its single column item on his statement at the bottom of a left hand page in the latter half of the paper. *The Hindu*, *The Hindustan Times* and *The Statesman* also reported the Puri Shankaracharya's views on their inside pages.

The contrast assumes further meaning in view of the unusual decision of the *Express* to carry an advertisement on the page opposite the editorial page, in the prominent top right hand corner—if ever this important page in any major paper features an advertisement, it is confined to the bottom of the page. Sponsored by the Vishwa Hindu Parishad, one of the chief promoters of contemporary Hindu revivalism, the advertisement (26 September) was headlined 'Are Hindus Communal?' Although it did not specifically discuss sati, it is significant that the only other time an advertisement was spotted in this position during the entire survey period coincided with the Shah Bano controversy; that advertisement, also placed by the VHP, sought to establish that 'instances like the Shah Bano case never arose in Hinduism.' Considering the context—the controversy over Roop Kanwar's death—it is clear that the purpose in this instance was to diffuse the furore over 'sati'.

Use of Language

The absence of clear directives from senior editors to the news desk often leads to discrepancies between a paper's editorial position on an issue and its news coverage of it. In the case of 'sati', this was particularly noticeable in the use of language.

For instance, while practically every mainstream daily condemned 'sati' and clearly viewed Roop Kanwar's death as socially-sanctioned murder or society-induced suicide, several newspapers carried a Press Trust of India (PTI) report (17 September 1987) on the *chunri mahotsav*, in which the event was described as a 'moving ceremony' held to commemorate 'the young bride (who) had burnt herself alive on the pyre of her husband.' The use of such descriptions suggests an unquestioning acceptance of the event and the version propagated by supporters of the concept and practice of sati, but few papers saw it fit to edit them out.

The common use of terms such as 'self-immolation' gave currency to the questionable assumption that Roop Kanwar had freely chosen to die on the funeral pyre of her husband. Similarly, only *The Times of India* consistently used inverted commas around the word sati to implicitly question the idea that Roop Kanwar's death was a case of sati. But in one report even in this paper, a page one box item (17 September) on the *chunri mahotsav*, the very purpose of using quotation marks around the word 'sati' was negated by the inclusion of phrases such as 'committed "sati"' and 'immolated herself.'

The Hindu capitalised the first letter of the word 'sati' even in editorials roundly condemning the whole affair. The only exception was an editorial page article, by an unnamed Delhi staff reporter, in which the word was put within quotation marks. Even after a reader objected to descriptions of Roop Kanwar's death as 'sati,' the paper did not change its way of referring to the incident.

The Women's Question

In their editorials all the papers unequivocally deplored the re-emergence of 'sati' in modern India. In fact, virtually all of them used exceptionally strong words in their edits, vividly expressing their revulsion at and condemnation of the revival of the practice and the failure of the Rajasthan government to stop the *chunri mahotsav*.

The Statesman, in its first edit (15 September) headlined 'Up In Flames,' connected the crime with other horrific anti-women practices: 'With dowry deaths and female foeticide, the latter half of the 20th Century has enough horrors of its own without dredging up a barbaric practice which remains repugnant to every civilised feeling in spite of the religious sanction it once enjoyed.'

Contrasting widow and bride-burning, it pointed out that the latter crime was at least carried out in private and considered shameful enough for its perpetrators to deny that they had any part in the woman's ordeal, whereas the former was done in public 'to the hysterical applause of the gathered community.' It was the only paper to make this relevant point. The edit concluded with the warning:

> If the denigration of women is now allowed to acquire the halo of deification, it is going to make even more daunting the task of rooting out deep-seated prejudice and all the brutality that it gives vent to. In such an event, the cause of women will not be the only victim.

While *The Statesman* edits did connect sati to other forms of women's oppression, this point was more directly articulated by two other edits—one in the *Indian Express* and the other in *The Hindu*. The latter, in fact, dwelt on this aspect of the issue in its very first edit (17 September) headlined 'A Horrifying Episode'. In what was a comprehensive analysis, the editorial placed the practice in the context of women's low social status and linked it with different oppressive customs and assaults against women as well as other vulnerable sections of the population. Calling widow-burning an obnoxious practice, it strongly disapproved of 'the theory that a woman can have no life apart from and beyond that of her husband.' It called upon the administration 'to show a much greater seriousness in putting an end to such barbaric practices.'

The *Indian Express* raised the women's question in its last edit on the subject (22 December), through a strongly worded reaction to the attempt by the Rajasthan government to stop Swami Agnivesh and other anti-sati *padyatris* from entering Jaipur. Taking off from this episode, it went on to connect sati to the wider issue of the oppression of women, describing 'the murder of Roop Kanwar' as 'a blot on our society' and the callous behaviour of politicians, pro-sati marchers and the Dharam Raksha Samiti as 'a ghastly stain on our society and country.' It did not fight shy of describing Roop Kanwar's death as murder—the only paper to do so in two separate edits (10 October and 22 December). The latter stated: 'Here we are debating esoteric points of constitutional law and here are thousands upon thousands revelling in the murder of a young girl, a murder for greed.'

The *Indian Express* was also the only paper to discuss strategy and advocate activism on this issue. For instance, even in an edit basically focussing on legislation, such as its 3 October comment on the Rajasthan Sati (Prevention) Ordinance, it stated: 'The evil has to be fought on the social and educational plane. Every social worker or reformer has to be a soldier in the war against sati'. In response to the National Convention Against Communalism and Separatism, it devoted an edit (16 October), headlined 'But Will They Act?', to the question of strategy. Stating that it would not do to merely denounce the inhuman practice in speeches or criticise the government for its inaction, it said: 'The participants in the Convention should take the lead in launching a massive counter agitation in the district where Roop Kanwar... is sought to be deified.' Admitting that such attempts could alienate a large number of voters, it asked whether the non-communal parties were 'prepared to launch such a campaign in that district and isolate those who are trying to resurrect a gruesome custom?' or 'those... concerned about the threats posed to national unity by communalism' were willing 'to pay the price?' This, it concluded, was 'the real test of their commitment to secularism.'

On the face of it, this *Express* edit seemed to support a secular movement to combat practices such as sati, raising a valid point about how far the so-called anti-communal forces would be willing to go in this process in view of the possible political repercussions. And yet it was this same paper that published the pro-sati views of the Shankaracharya of Puri prominently on its front page and carried the Vishwa Hindu Parishad advertisement.

The Law and 'Sati'

As many as ten of the total edits on 'sati' in all the dailies related to legislative and judicial matters. For instance, all the newspapers, except *The Times of India*, had edits on 3 October 1987 on the Rajasthan Sati (Prevention) Ordinance. While *The Statesman* expressed its customary cynicism about legislation, *The Hindustan Times* welcomed what it called 'fool-proof measures to save the lives of widows and thereby end a sinister practice.'

All the papers except *The Statesman* commented, between 16 and 18 December, on the central government's Commission of Sati (Prevention) Act, 1987. While *The Hindustan Times* (16 December) welcomed the new law and recorded the fact that it was 'partially a response to the country-wide agitations, particularly by women's organisations,' *The Hindu's* editorial (16 December) was critical of both the delay in 'legislative response at the national level' and the provision for the death penalty (citing the worldwide trend away from capital punishment). It was also sceptical about the move to bar entry into Parliament and the state assemblies of any person convicted under the law. *The Times of India* edit (17 December) reiterated the points made in the analysis of the law by Lotika Sarkar and Radha Kumar, pointing out some of the modifications required to make it really effective. In its comment (18 December), the *Indian Express* recommended that women's organisations be consulted before the rules under the new law were framed.

Role of Politicians

All the papers, except *The Statesman*, roundly criticised the role of the Rajasthan government as well as politicians, with a total of five edits focussing on this aspect of the controversy. In a typically forthright edit headlined 'Remove Him,' the *Indian Express* (10 October), for example, declared that Harideo Joshi, then Chief Minister of Rajasthan, 'must be removed from office for the things that he has failed to do in regard to Roop Kanwar's murder.' Despite its traditional support for the main opposition parties, the paper called on them 'to expel those of their leaders who attended the rally' (in Jaipur, against the Rajasthan ordinance). It went as far as to name the Janata Party and its state president at the time, Kalyan Singh Kalvi, who 'featured prominently in the proceedings and who was earlier present at the *chunri* celebration at Deorala.'

Only the *Indian Express*, in its 16 October and 22 December edits, commented on the communalisation of this issue. In the latter edit, it questioned the credibility of those who claimed to speak for the entire community of Rajputs and the right of the Dharma Raksha Samiti to speak for 'Hinduism itself.'

Clear Condemnation

The focus of the edit page articles in the five newspapers ranged from historical and sociological analyses to discussions on the gender question, the role of religion in society, the part played by the government and politicians and, finally, the legislative response. Clear categorisation is difficult because most of the articles touched upon several of these issues. But all except two were clear in their condemnation of the practice which had led to Roop Kanwar's untimely and ghastly death.

The Times of India's single but relatively timely editorial page article, which predated its first editorial on the subject by more than a month, was headlined 'Disgraceful Sati Episode: High Social Price Of State Inaction.' Written by Praful Bidwai, then senior assistant editor, it argued against the concept of voluntary sati, citing historical evidence regarding coercion. He also gave a political perspective to the controversy, especially in terms of Rajput identity and the role of the State. He made no bones about his stand on the issue, stating at the very outset that Roop Kanwar was 'burnt alive on her husband's funeral pyre,' and suggested that the practice originated in 'men's deepest insecurities about women and their obsession with proving to themselves that their women can have nothing worthwhile, literally not even life, beyond them—the goal of a woman's life is death, with man.'

L.S. Rangarajan referred to more recent history in his exploration of Mahatma Gandhi's stand on sati in the *Indian Express* (27 October). Quoting Gandhi himself, the article described how he tackled fundamentalists and refused to lend respectability to sati even to the extent of appreciating the courage of the young women who died on their husbands' funeral pyres. 'Why should I take upon myself the sin of even unconsciously leading astray some ignorant sister by my injudicious praise of suicide?' Gandhi was quoted as saying. According to the author, neither sati nor compulsory, lifelong widowhood had scriptural sanction—a point already expressed forcefully by Vishal Mangalwadi in the *Indian Express* (23 September).

Activist Brinda Karat, writing in *The Hindustan Times* (9 October), dealt with the issue in the context of the political and economic history of the country and women's role and status within it. She argued that the major issue the women's movement needed to contend with was 'the increasing power of religious fundamentalists to inflict the most barbaric crimes and atrocities on women, with a widening base of social consent which, in turn, strengthens the negative perceptions women may have of themselves.'

The role of religion in society was the focus of three editorial page articles in *The Statesman*, including a two-part piece by its editor, Sunanda K. Datta-Ray, headlined 'Hinduism On The March: Still Fighting Yesterday's Battle' (27 September). While the article did not exclusively focus on sati, it was clearly prompted by the controversy over the hoary practice and took a clear stand against both sati and its promoters. It began by contrasting the views of the Shankaracharyas of Puri and Kancheepuram—the former defending sati and the latter disavowing it. The writer went on to discuss the interaction between temporal and spiritual authorities, seen particularly in the spectacle of 'functionaries of the state paying obeisance to gurus and godmen who stand for an altogether different order.' He pointed out that medievalism would naturally trample over modernism, especially at the folk level, if political leaders continued to favour the former.

Justifying 'Sati'

Two editorial page articles—one in the *Indian Express* and the other in *The Statesman*—stood out for their seeming justification of sati in the guise of sociological explanations for the custom. Both writers chose to present the issue as a tussle between tradition and modernity, suggesting that those involved in the anti-sati campaign were too alienated from traditional India to understand the practice and its roots.

The article by sociologist Ashis Nandy in the *Indian Express* (5 October) represented a departure from the tone and substance of the coverage given by the paper to this issue. While ostensibly not in favour of sati, the writer nevertheless criticised the uproar over the practice, suggesting that it was based on poor understanding and a devaluation of traditions held dear by Indians unsullied by modern, western ideas. The argument presented in his piece, headlined 'The Sociology Of Sati,' is aptly summarised in the following sentence: 'However satanic it (sati) may look to us, the urban, westernised Indians, sati reaffirms, even if in a bizarre, violent and perverted fashion, respect for self-sacrifice, in which even the idea of self-sacrifice sounds hypocritical.' It is possible that the *Indian Express* published this piece by a well-known academic in the interest of a debate on the issue since it did succeed in drawing several letters to the editor in response.

An article strangely reminiscent of Ashis Nandy's piece appeared on *The Statesman's* edit page exactly a month later (5 November). Written by Patrick D. Harrigan, a foreign scholar at the American Institute of Indian Studies in Madurai, it was headlined 'Tyranny Of The Elite? Bringing Bharat Mata Up To Date.' The author was clearly critical of the attempts by 'a handful of English-educated exponents of social progress' to reform the 'ignorant masses' by imposing 'foreign' values on them. 'Bharat Mata,' he wrote, 'is great precisely because her children are free to live and die according to principles' but he feared that this freedom was facing danger from the intolerance of the elite.

From his description of Roop Kanwar's death it is obvious that

Harrigan was quite awe-struck by the event (as were many of the British observers who wrote accounts of sati during the Raj). According to him, there was nothing astonishing about a Rajput widow performing the rite of sati because, in doing so, she was simply demonstrating her assent to the set of principles and beliefs that makes her a Rajput in the traditional sense. He did not hide his disapproval of city-based feminists and the English-language press who, in his view, had orchestrated a 'unanimous barrage of rabidly anti-sati sentiment.' He claimed that the complete absence of dialogue or discussion between pro- and anti-sati groups was shocking, not only to 'the foreign scholar but also, presumably, anyone else sharing an interest in the survival of democratic as well as traditional institutions in 20th Century India.'

Thus, while the general tenor of the editorials and edit page articles was unequivocally against the practice of 'sati' and sceptical about the government's seriousness in dealing with the underlying reasons for the revival of the practice, articles such as those by Nandy and Harrigan expressed a school of thought among intellectuals outside the press which sought to explain rather than condemn the event. Readers' responses to these articles, in the form of letters to the editor, also suggest that many of them were open to such ideas and did not always agree with the stand of the mainstream newspapers (see Appendix C).

Myth or Faith?

The only edit page piece to focus directly and specifically on Roop Kanwar's death and its aftermath, headlined 'The Making Of A Dangerous Myth,' appeared in the *Indian Express* (23 September 1987). Based on the report of the fact-finding team of the Women and Media Committee of the Bombay Union of Journalists (BUJ) which went to Deorala to conduct an independent inquiry into the incident, it was written by staffer Geeta Seshu, a member of the team. The article highlighted sections of the BUJ report which provided hitherto unknown information about the incident, particularly the terror experienced by Roop Kanwar prior to her death. It also quoted the report on the Rajput community's response to the incident, asking whether it was a spontaneous expression of faith or a myth deliberately promoted by vested interests to gain economic and political mileage. The report's unique analysis of the press coverage of the incident—which found that some newspapers, particularly sections of the Hindi press, had glorified the act and Roop Kanwar—was also mentioned.

The Sunday sections of the newspapers carried long articles on the issue, some of which touched on the debate between tradition and modernity raised earlier by Ashis Nandy. Others questioned whether 'sati' could ever be deemed as voluntary, discussed the efficacy of laws to curb such social evils, and described the status of widows and other women outside the institution of marriage.

'Miracle-studded Crimes'

The most important of these articles, which appeared in *The Times of India's Sunday Review* (25 October), was written by Kumkum Sangari, who has done considerable research into the phenomenon of sati in post-Independence India. Headlined 'There Is No Such Thing As Voluntary Sati,' it placed Roop Kanwar's death in perspective by pointing out that it was basically 'a metropolitan event staged in an obliging village.' Sangari refuted Ashis Nandy's tradition vs. modernity position, suggesting that the event did not place the two in opposition but, rather, served to iron out the contradictions within the two. The point made by society through Roop Kanwar's 'sati' was, she said, that 'our daughters may study till class ten but they can still become devis. Education actually enables us to perform such miracle-studded crimes with greater dexterity.' Asserting categorically that 'there is no such thing as voluntary sati,' she cited evidence from history, art as well as modern-day interviews to buttress her stand:

> We were told by the family of a Rajput sati that armed guards were and are used to ward off evil tantrics and to cut off the head of the woman if she changes her mind and dishonours the family. Add the haste, family pressure, opiates, the photographs of women imprisoned by wood and coconuts in a neck-high pyre, and the very notion of 'voluntary' sati becomes a mystification.

This authoritative statement that coercion was the norm rather than the exception, by a person who had herself done the research to substantiate it, represents a significant contribution to the available information base about sati.

Another article notable for its authenticity was that written by Nalini Singh in her regular column in the *Express Magazine* (13 December) which generally focussed on the experiences of people in rural India. In this instance, she dealt with the women of Rajasthan and the impact of the Women's Development Programme on their status. She spoke to widows and, by describing their lives in their own words, managed to paint an uncommonly vivid picture of their plight:

> At the very moment a dead man's body is removed from the house for cremation, a black sheet is drawn around the widow. For a year she is not to be seen by males or married women. She sits on the floor within this black cubicle, knees pulled to the chest and head touching the knees. For ablutions and bath she leaves the cubicle at night. Saltless food is brought to her. Before a meal she must cry.... Since a widow sits in one posture for several hours and months, her knees get stiff, she has to be assisted to walk and she dies from illness before her time. Of course, as long as she lives, she performs heavy household tasks in seclusion, like grinding grain on the *chakki*.

Two articles—one in *The Hindustan Times* and the other in the *Indian Express*—analysed the issue in the context of gender relations. In the former (18 October), Rajasthan-based activist Srilatha Swaminadhan examined the part played by childhood socialisation, the romanticisation of sex roles, as well as the victimisation of widows in the promotion of practices such as sati, voluntary or otherwise. Headlined 'Satisfying The Male Ego,' the article stressed the need for long-term and continuous efforts to ensure that women had economic security and dignity as equal human beings, warning that the commercialisation of Roop Kanwar's death could lead to pressures on the next young widow to follow her example. She also drew attention to the lobby of intellectuals who were against the fundamentalism of minorities such as Muslims and Sikhs but justified sati on pseudo-religious, spiritual and philosophical grounds.

The Express Magazine's monthly column on women's issues (4 October), by the then editor Kalpana Sharma, discussed the link between the importance accorded to the institution of marriage, the status of women within marriage and the justification put forward for practices like sati.

Historical Aspects

Two features focussed on the historical aspects of the issue. In a two-part article in *The Times of India's Sunday Review* (20 and 27 December), Iqbal Kaul traced the history of the practice and the beliefs attached to it, taking care not to suggest that there was any justification for the custom. *The Statesman's Miscellany* (8 November) published a historical account of the phenomenon under the headline 'When Sati Was The Rule'. The piece (author unknown) quoted old records to highlight details of the 'ghoulish practice' and establish that it did not die out with Lord Bentinck's ban.

The Hindu's Sunday supplement did not carry any features on the 'sati' controversy. But an interesting article on the subject appeared in the 'Open Page' features section of the daily (27 October 1987). Written by Swami Harshananda of the Ramakrishna Math in Allahabad, it was headlined 'A Formidable Challenge That Can Be Met' and, indeed, posed quite a challenge to anyone trying to figure out the writer's position on the issue.

In the final analysis, it seems as if the Swami was against forcible sati, which he described as 'first degree murder' and which he believed had to be roundly condemned and squarely dealt with by 'the long and strong arm of the law of the land.' But judging by his romanticised description of Roop Kanwar's death—'the self-immolation of a youthful bride on the funeral pyre of her deceased husband'—and his criticism of the protests against it, he did not seem to consider it a case of forced sati.

Among the points he made in his article were the fact that the practice of widow-burning was not restricted to the Hindus of India; that over time it had become a mere ritual, with the widow free to leave the pyre before it was lit; that only the Vishnu Dharma Sutras sanctioned the practice and even then it was left to the widow to decide whether she wished to die; and that a custom once observed mainly by the royalty and nobility was adopted by others because of 'superstitions among the ignorant masses and their clever exploitation by economic vested interests.'

Declaring that not all satis were forced, he said the courage and sense of honour of the women who voluntarily died with their husbands had to be admired because they remained true to the 'highest ideal of Indian womanhood'—which was, according to him, chastity and personal purity. While he then went on to question the need for women to die just because their husbands were no more, he obviously endorsed the idea that widows had to lead a life of austerity and deprivation. 'Really speaking, a widow has much greater opportunity for spiritual progress... the stringent rules imposed on a widow in her personal life (were) approximate to the code of conduct of a sannyasin or a monk....'

Admitting that Hindu society had meted out cruel treatment to women 'during the middle ages,' he suggested that it was necessary to now propagate the idea that 'women can do better things in life than dying on the funeral pyres of their dead husbands' so that the sati problem would 'die a natural death.' His final advice to widows was:

> There is a popular saying that marriages are made in heaven. If this is so, then let our widowed sisters and mothers wait for their marriages to be continued or dissolved in heaven by the Power that made them, but live HERE happily till they go to that heaven!

Conclusion

By 1987, when the 'sati' controversy shocked the nation, the press was able to respond with a fair amount of professionalism and sophistication. Not only did all the major national dailies cover the issue extensively on their news pages, taking the trouble to carry on-the-spot and special reports, but they also devoted considerable attention to it on the editorial page. The Sunday magazine sections of most papers also discussed the issue through a number of features.

The multi-pronged strategy of the women's movement and the willingness of women activists and researchers to write in the 'mainstream' press certainly helped in widening and deepening media coverage of the issue, especially in terms of keeping the women's perspective in view.

However, the unprecedented coverage given to the issue was primarily because it conformed to established news values: it concerned a brutal incident which held potential for further violence through social conflict; in addition, it promised religio-communal and political repercussions. That these aspects of the issue were of the utmost importance is clear from the fact that only a minority of the editorials and edit page articles focussed directly and specifically on the gender aspect; most of them dealt with matters of religion and politics, in addition to legislation.

The structured ad-hocism which governs the functioning of the press was evident in press coverage of the 'sati' controversy. It was most obvious in the dissonance between editorial condemnation of the incident, on the one hand, and glowing accounts of the *chunri mahotsav* as well as the unquestioning use of words like 'sati' (minus quotation marks) and 'self-immolation,' on the other.

It is also remarkable that only the *Indian Express* (which carried a Vishwa Hindu Parishad advertisement and prominently displayed the pro-sati views of the Shankaracharya of Puri) questioned the communalisation of the issue. To their credit, however, all five papers were unequivocally against the revival of the practice of 'sati' and this stand was reflected in their edits in no uncertain terms.

7

General Interest Periodicals

Kalpana Sharma

Magazines often make a more lasting impact than daily newspapers on the views and perceptions of readers because they have a longer shelf-life. While people tend to glance through newspapers, reading a few items that catch their eye, most people buy magazines specifically to read the articles featured in them. Thus, a study of the print media would be incomplete if it did not also analyse magazines.

For the purpose of this study, three general interest magazines and one Sunday newspaper were selected. The choice was dictated partly by their location and partly by the extent of their reach. They were *Sunday*, a weekly published by the Ananda Bazar Patrika group of Calcutta; *India Today*, a fortnightly published by Living Media Pvt. Ltd., New Delhi; *The Illustrated Weekly of India*, a Bombay-based weekly published by Bennett Coleman & Co. Ltd., and *The Sunday Observer*, a Sunday broadsheet newspaper with Bombay and Delhi editions which was launched by Jaico Press in 1981 and bought over in 1989 by Observer Publications.

Originally, the study also planned to look at *The Week*, published by the Malayala Manorama group based in Kerala, in the interest of regional representation. But since it did not exist during most of the study period, it could not be included. The same was the case with *Frontline*, a fortnightly publication of the Madras-based publishers of *The Hindu*.

In terms of actual location, therefore, the four publications cover only Bombay, Delhi and Calcutta. However, all four aim at a national audience. Even *The Sunday Observer*, originally more or less confined to a Bombay readership, had launched its Delhi edition and was circulating in several other major Indian cities in the latter part of the survey period.

While *Sunday*, *India Today* and *The Sunday Observer* are clearly geared towards topicality, particularly in political developments, the profile of *The Illustrated Weekly* has been more diffuse and variable. In the late seventies and early eighties, it was a general interest magazine in the broadest sense of the term, hardly responding to current developments. In the latter part of the eighties it became more topical but continued to publish a mixture of news-related and issue-based articles.

The Sunday Observer is, of course, different from *India Today* and *Sunday* in that it is a broadsheet Sunday newspaper while the others are magazines. Since it can accommodate features on the latest news events right up to Saturday night, it enjoys some of the advantages of a daily newspaper in terms of topicality. At the same time, being a weekly, it has time to prepare in-depth analytical and investigative features.

Although some of the criteria for judging coverage in these four periodicals necessarily vary because of differences in format and periodicity, their coverage of the five selected issues, when compared, reveals how the same issue can be handled in different ways.

The Sunday Observer could not be studied over the early period surveyed for the dowry deaths issue (1979-80) as it had not begun publication by then. But for the other four issues, the selected periodicals were surveyed throughout the periods under study.

The importance given to an issue by magazine editors is indicated by its placement within the periodical. Cover stories or special reports generally appear in the first half of a magazine while lighter features are generally relegated to the latter half of the publication. Another criterion used to judge the importance of a magazine feature is the use of photographs. The three magazines studied make effective use of black and white and colour photographs to give their lead stories additional emphasis. A one-page feature without a photograph attracts less attention than, say, an article of the same length, spread over two or three pages, with several attention-drawing photographs.

The time frame for the study of each of the five issues in the selected periodicals was four to six weeks longer than that used for the dailies, taking into account the slower response time of periodicals.

The Illustrated Weekly had the maximum number of items (44) on the five issues, followed by *The Sunday Observer* with 38, *Sunday* with 24 and *India Today* with 23. But the number of individual items does not necessarily indicate the amount of space devoted to the subject. For instance, while *The Illustrated Weekly* had only one piece on amniocentesis, it was spread over four pages; whereas the two articles in *India Today* were much shorter reports, with neither the depth nor the analysis found in the former.

Qualitatively, the coverage varied greatly from issue to issue. For instance, the Calcutta-based *Sunday* gave far more comprehensive coverage to the amniocentesis controversy than *The Illustrated Weekly* and *The Sunday Observer*, which are based in Bombay where the campaign was initiated. The last-mentioned publication, however, surpassed the other three in its comprehensive coverage of the Shah Bano issue. In contrast, *The Illustrated Weekly* completely overlooked the gender angle in the Shah Bano controversy, concentrating instead on interpreting the Koran and Muslim Personal Law. *India Today*, while maintaining a more or less consistent standard in its coverage of all five issues, was far ahead of the others in the sensitivity with which the sati issue was handled—it was the only publication to focus on the plight of widows.

Dowry Deaths

The major anti-dowry campaign began in Delhi in May 1979 after the death of Tarvinder Kaur, culminating in the demonstration on 12 June in front of Parliament House by a combined front of women's groups. Only *India Today* and *Sunday* carried stories in this early period. *The Sunday Observer*, as has been mentioned, began publication only in late 1981. *The Illustrated Weekly* was not as news-oriented then as it is now; therefore, while it may have featured the issue at some point, it did not do so over the period surveyed.

While *India Today* carried a cover story on dowry and a total of four items over the period surveyed, including one letter to the editor, *Sunday* had only three items, neither of which was a cover story.

India Today carried a two-page special report headlined 'The Dowry System: Brides Are Not For Burning' in its issue of 1-15 July 1979. Using Tarvinder Kaur's death in May—'one link in a long chain of deaths'—as a starting point, it described the campaign launched by women's organisations against the evil practice. The article was accompanied by photographs of Kaur at her engagement, her charred body and demonstrators outside the residence of her in-laws.

Although the report was quite comprehensive and included a representative number of interviews with women activists, correspondent Sunil Sethi's tone was not quite in keeping with the seriousness and tragic implications of the subject. Taking a jibe at women's groups, he wrote:

> Other women's organisations, seeing a good thing going, have jumped onto the bandwagon, in what is dangerously becoming a join-the-club affair. Says Amiya Rao, a social worker and member of Delhi's municipal corporation, 'I think many of these women's organisations are a lot of hot air.'

Further, his conclusion was quite incomprehensible: 'Each year,' he wrote, quoting Sarla Mudgal, another woman activist, 'there are about 25 cases of death by burning brought to her notice. How fatal has 1979 proved? She has handled 13 cases so far, she says, keeping a straight face. The turnover in the bride-burning business is obviously quite high.'

The use of a glib phrase like 'bride-burning business' suggests a lack of sensitivity. There was little analysis in the report, and selective quotes from different women merely projected the author's own perception that women's groups were capitalising on the tragedy. Such deliberate slants nurture a generally negative attitude towards women's groups fighting on these issues.

In contrast, the report in *Sunday*, which appeared more than a month later (19 August 1979), was more straightforward. The two-page special article, headlined 'Bitter Dowry,' was reported from Delhi by Mandira Purie and led with the case history of Kanchan Chopra—one of the 'long list of innocent young girls who have been victims of the characteristic Indian greed for more dowry.' It quoted Chopra's father, a woman police officer, a woman lawyer and a woman activist. In addition, it referred to the law and to studies on the incidence of the phenomenon.

The contrast between the two stories is important. It reveals how almost the same set of facts can be used to project different attitudes towards women's issues and groups. It also highlights the virtue of allowing the people involved in such struggles to speak for themselves so as to enable readers to come to their own conclusions.

The earlier smug tone of the *India Today* writer, Sunil Sethi, was modified somewhat in his next story (16-31 August 1979) which appeared as a large box item headlined 'Dowry: Tales Of Horror.' It told the harrowing tale of two Delhi-based mothers of dowry victims and their search for justice. Photographs of the dead women and their mothers accompanied the piece.

India Today ignored the next peak period of the anti-dowry campaign —July-August 1983. But *Sunday's* columnist Khushwant Singh took note of the demand for legislation to curb the evil in his column 'Gossip Sweet And Sour' (17 August 1983). Writing authoritatively and clearly disapproving of dowry, he was, unfortunately, short on substance and faulty in his analysis. For instance, he stated categorically: 'The pressure for larger dowries is due to the general rise in prices and the current obsession with gadgetry.' As if to substantiate his belief that the dowry phenomenon was linked with economics and not women's status, Singh went on: 'If the bride happens to be an earner, she is better treated because her earnings are regarded as an interest on the amount spent on the son's education.'

Finally he traced the origins of the problem to the conferment of equal property rights on Hindu and Sikh women and the liberalisation of divorce laws. As a result of these two developments, the author concluded, 'the traditional concept of marriage as a (life-long) sacrament crumbled and it assumed the worst aspects of a contractual relationship. There was a throwback and primitive instincts resurfaced.' Elsewhere in the article, Singh had observed that bride-burning is almost unknown among Muslims (although this is no longer so) and that 'a Muslim marriage was always a contract.' This contradiction was not addressed or resolved.

Magazines generally do not control what their columnists write; so Khushwant Singh's views are his own and not those of the magazine. Nonetheless, *Sunday* did not take a consistent interest in the dowry issue. Apart from the special report in 1979 and Singh's column, the only other mention of dowry over the period surveyed was a small box item in 1984, by Vimal Balasubrahmanyan, on a dowry death case in Hyderabad/ Secunderabad. There was no discussion of the anti-dowry law and the legal changes being demanded by women's groups.

India Today, however, did respond to the growing clamour for changes in the law. Headlined 'Dowry Law: Debating The Delay,' the article by Sumit Mitra (April 1984) gave details of the suggestions made by the joint committee of both Houses of Parliament, as well as of studies conducted by the women's organisation, Saheli. This was a straightforward, factual report, quite unlike the 1979 story by Sunil Sethi.

Rape

The coverage of rape in the periodicals studied, although not extensive was, nonetheless, fairly comprehensive. Articles on this crime continue to appear in such magazines even today, usually when an incident involving rape hits the headlines. For instance in 1990, the rape of two nuns in a convent in the town of Gajraula in UP prompted spot reports. Sometimes such stories are accompanied by more analytical and commentative pieces about the inadequacy of the law or the inability of the authorities to punish rapists. Over the period surveyed, however, the focus was primarily on the rape law and the changes demanded by women's groups campaigning on the issue.

The Illustrated Weekly accorded the subject the maximum coverage, with a total of three features spread over eight pages. While *Sunday* carried a three-page feature, *India Today* had two one-page stories and *The Sunday Observer* (which did not exist when the anti-rape campaign was launched in 1980) had two items on its news pages—neither of which appeared on page one. None of the publications considered the issue serious enough to run as a cover or special story. Thus, both in quantitative and qualitative terms, only *The Illustrated Weekly* gave the issue considerable prominence.

Both the reports in *India Today* focussed on the law. The first, a well-rounded report by Chitra Subramaniam (16-31 March 1980), described the anti-rape campaign by women's organisations which reached a high point on 8 March 1980, International Women's Day. The other article was more specifically on the rape law. Titled 'Rape: Controversial Code,' the well-researched report by Sunil Sethi (31 December 1983) presented a detailed analysis of different aspects of the proposed legislation against the background of the Mathura rape case and the genesis of the anti-rape movement.

The Illustrated Weekly was the only magazine that actually looked at the other dimensions of rape. For instance, a one and a half page report by Gita Narayan (15 June 1980), titled 'Rape: The Shame Of A Nation,' discussed the repercussions of rape on the victim, especially the concept of 'tainting,' and exposed the inadequacies of the law. The author emphasised that although the crime was perpetrated against women by men, it was men who had defined it and drafted the law. Narayan also touched upon the social factors behind rape, which the articles in *India Today* had not mentioned, suggesting that it was an expression of domination and of the male view of women as property. As a result, she wrote, the act of rape was often used to punish not the victim but, through her, the male kinsmen. The author also brought out the double oppression of poor women in this system.

Serious, analytical and in-depth articles published in *The Illustrated Weekly* in the early eighties contrasted greatly with its later style. For instance, a feature on rape just two years after the above article (outside the survey period) was a superficial piece, verging on the sensational. Written by Payal Singh (23 March 1986), the article featured a child victim of rape who had been forced into prostitution. No effort was made to hide the child's identity. Instead, spread over four pages were two large photographs of the child, with the text occupying only four columns, which emphasised her youth and her vulnerability. The introduction stated: 'Fourteen-year-old Naseema's story is different. She isn't just another rape victim. But a child who was raped by her father and then sold by him.'

Such treatment of a serious subject suggests voyeurism rather than concern for the welfare of the individual concerned or the issue of rape. If Naseema's story was intended to be an illustration of the horror of child rape or of one of the reasons why women enter prostitution, the identity of the victim should have been hidden. By spreading her photographs over two pages, giving her story in lurid detail and projecting her like some minor celebrity, the magazine displayed scant regard for the possible consequences of such unasked for publicity.

The different types of features on the rape issue in the same magazine illustrate well how the subject of crimes against women can be used to serve entirely different ends. In the Gita Narayan piece, the object was clearly to inform and to present the various dimensions of the issue. The report by Payal Singh, however, capitalised on an individual's tragedy to attract readers. While it may be true that people like to read about other people, such commercial exploitation of rape victims is unjustifiable.

The Illustrated Weekly carried two more articles on the subject, including a commentative piece by sociologist and feminist Gail Omvedt (8 April 1984) which placed the issues of dowry deaths and rape in the larger context of the status of women.

Both *Sunday* and the *The Sunday Observer*, on the other hand, dealt with the subject only as news reports. The former had a feature on rape (30 March 1980), comprising reports from Bombay and Delhi, which focussed mainly on the vulnerability of women in city suburbs and included some details about the Mathura case, the Supreme Court verdict and the anti-rape campaign in the capital. The latter carried two short reports on its news pages, neither of which had accompanying photographs.

On the whole, all four periodicals dealt with the subject fairly seriously during the period surveyed. None of them succumbed to the temptation of using an issue involving violence against women for purely voyeuristic purposes. In recent years, unfortunately, such stories have featured in several periodicals, including *Savvy,* a new women's magazine.

What was missing in the coverage of this issue in all four periodicals was a comprehensive discussion on the loopholes and possible improvements in the law. As this was the central focus of the anti-rape campaign and the crux of the parliamentary discussions on the subject, it is unclear why these periodicals did not pay more attention to this aspect. A possible explanation could be that law is a fairly dry subject whereas the question of violence against women is more evocative and likely to hold reader interest. Since 'selling' publications and 'grabbing' reader interest are strong motivations in all commercial publications, it is perhaps only to be expected that descriptions of rape cases took precedence over serious discussions on the law.

The Shah Bano Controversy

The Sunday Observer's coverage of the Shah Bano controversy was comprehensive both quantitatively—eleven items, of which five were carried on the front page—and qualitatively. The paper ran a full-page, detailed interview with Shah Bano, which most magazines and newspapers had not bothered to do. It also carried articles on the case, its political fall-out, the views of Chief Justice Y. V. Chandrachud, whose judgment in April 1985 triggered the controversy, and the impact of the Muslim Women (Protection of Rights on Divorce) Bill on women.

While *The Sunday Observer, India Today* and *Sunday* did focus on Shah Bano herself (actually taking the trouble to seek her views) and also highlighted the gender angle, *The Sunday Observer* more effectively than the others, *The Illustrated Weekly* ignored this aspect of the issue altogether. Instead, the magazine concentrated on the religious and legal aspects of the controversy, looking at the politics of the issue in passing. The women's perspective was absent from its six articles on the subject, which occupied a total of thirty pages and included one cover story.

The most outstanding feature on this issue was a full page report by Jyoti Punwani in *The Sunday Observer* (24 November 1985) titled 'The Strange Case Of Shah Bano'. The writer's interview with Shah Bano recounted why she had rejected the Supreme Court judgment on maintenance. Punwani was able to present a clear picture of the pressures put on this frail old woman by the community; for instance, the publicity given by the Urdu press to the views of the maulvis Shah Bano had initially refused to meet. Apparently, none of this had an impact on her until the Muslims of Indore, her home town, took out a silent procession against the judgment and deliberately marched past her house. That is when she gave up. The article also described the enormous influence that Shah Bano's former husband, a noted lawyer in Indore, wielded in the community. A box item accompanying the article presented the legal issues, including the possibility of a review of the Supreme Court's decision.

This article stood out because it was one of the few which presented the problems faced by the woman at the centre of the controversy in her own words. *India Today* for instance, which often carries several interviews in one edition, did not publish one with Shah Bano although its correspondent, Tavleen Singh, spoke to her and included her comments in a two-page report (15 December 1985).

Sunday also incorporated the views of Shah Bano in its three-page special report by Ritu Sarin (1-7 December 1985) headlined 'Shah Bano: The Struggle And The Surrender'. Apart from interviewing Shah Bano, the reporter spoke to her ex-husband, her daughter-in-law, the Qazi of Indore and a Muslim lawyer. She also provided background information on the case and dealt with the subject as a women's issue—not just a communal or legal one.

The Illustrated Weekly treated the entire controversy as a religious issue—five out of its six articles dealt with the Shariat. Its coverage vividly illustrates how the politico-religious aspects of such an issue can completely eclipse the gender question. First, Arun Shourie wrote a three-part series on the Koran and Muslim Personal Law headlined 'The Shariat' (5, 12 and 19 January 1986). Although serious and analytical, the articles essentially presented Shourie's interpretation of the Koran and his view that there are several anti-women edicts in

Muslim religious texts. Such a view was bound to be disputed, as indeed it was through a two-part rejoinder by Rafiq Zakaria.

In the first of his three articles, Shourie contended that Muslim Personal Law was based not on a correct interpretation of the Koran but on how the clerics had chosen to interpret it. Re-examination of the Muslim Personal Law in the light of modern, secular principles, he argued, should not be seen as offensive. He suggested that the good provisions of the existing law should be retained while the iniquitous ones ought to be discarded.

His second article argued that the Hadis, the account of the traditions of the Prophet, were probably unreliable as they were often manufactured by dynasties to establish their rights and virtues. In his opinion, only about seventy verses could be relied upon to build the edifice of personal law. The author held that much of Islamic religious texts reflected folklore, superstition and beliefs that existed at a particular time rather than eternal truths. Thus, among other things, they sanctioned the principle of an eye for an eye and the continuance of slavery and justified the most heinous crimes under the label of Jihad.

Only the third article in the series tackled the question of women. Here the author looked at the provisions of Muslim Personal Law on questions of polygamy, divorce and alimony, maintaining that all these discriminated heavily against women. While polygamy was sanctioned by the Koran and sanctified by the example of the Prophet, who had nine wives, in matters of divorce the husband had absolute, unfettered and exclusive power to cast aside his wife, who had no corresponding right. Apart from the *iddat* period, equivalent to three menstrual cycles, when the husband was obliged to pay maintenance to the ex-wife, his only other obligation was to return her dower. To support this thesis, Shourie picked what he considered significant quotes from the Koran. Some of those which appeared in the article are:

> Your wives are your field. Go in, therefore, to your field when or how you will, but do first some act for your soul's good.

> Men are the managers of the affairs of women. For that God has preferred in bounty one of them over another and for that they (men) have expended of their property (dower, maintenance), etc.

> The whole world is to be enjoyed, but the best thing in the world is a good woman.

> The woman is like a rib; if you try to straighten her she will break.

So if you want to get benefit from her, do so while she still has some crookedness.

The author concluded that a new draft civil code should be framed according to modern secular principles after re-examining all personal laws, not just the Muslim one.

Shourie's three-part series was problematic for a number of reasons. He could be accused of giving a subtle anti-Muslim twist to the issue by quoting the Koran selectively to support his views. For readers not familiar with Muslim religious texts, the wealth of material presented by the author imbued the article with credibility. A lay person would not have been in a position to detect any deliberate design behind the choice of quotations. It is possible that Shourie's pieces served to colour the views of non-Muslim readers on the position of women under Islam.

Rafiq Zakaria's 'In Defence Of The Shariat' (2 and 9 March 1986) attempted to right the balance by pointing out that Shourie's views were based on selective documentation and, hence, were untenable. He argued that in reality Koranic verses are extremely complex and their subtleties are lost in translation. However, like Shourie, Zakaria too failed to provide a clear picture of the situation of Muslim women in India; instead he concentrated on disproving some of Shourie's assertions.

The Sunday Observer also discussed Muslim Personal Law but from a different angle. Writing in the 8 December 1985 issue, Javed Gaya, a Bombay-based lawyer, opposed the imposition of a uniform civil code. He suggested that the Muslim community perceived itself under siege because of the response of the liberals who dominated the English-language media and the judiciary. The plight of Muslim women, he argued, was only a part of the larger tragedy facing the community; by picking on only this aspect and overlooking the larger problem, the liberal media invited the charge of fostering anti-Islamic feelings. At the same time, the author held, the debate sparked off by the Supreme Court judgment on the Shah Bano case could only be beneficial; he hoped that as a result the appalling consequences of excessive use of oral talaq (divorce) would be addressed squarely.

While such an article is difficult to classify, it represents an important point of view which, unfortunately, did not find a place in many other papers. It was part of an attempt by liberal, educated Muslims to bridge the gap between progressive non-Muslims and Islamic fundamentalists. The main thrust of this argument was that the strong reaction in the Muslim community against the Supreme Court judgment arose out of a history of alienation and that the issue had to be viewed within this context.

It is significant that, barring *The Sunday Observer*, which carried a special feature on 4 May 1986 presenting the views of Muslim women on the Muslim Women's Bill, none of the other publications bothered to take into account the views of the concerned community.

For instance, *India Today* carried a four-page report under 'Current Events' headlined 'The Muslims: Anger And Hurt' (15 March 1986), but most of it focussed on the political fall-out of the Shah Bano controversy. Shah Bano herself featured only in a small gossip item in the Eye-catchers column (15 March 1986). 'Not content with being the Muslims' cause celebre,' the item stated, 'the Begum' was being 'egged on by her ambitious son' to try for a Rajya Sabha ticket, 'if you please.'

The political fall-out of the Congress (I)'s plan to push through the Muslim Women Bill also drew the attention of the periodicals surveyed. For instance, the only cover story on the subject in *Sunday*, by Sumit Mitra (9-15 March 1986), dwelt on Arif Mohammed Khan's resignation and its political implications. The women's question came up in passing because members of Khan's 'close circle' enumerated their objections to the Bill, giving details of how the proposed law would go against the interests of women. A divorced Muslim woman, who had called on Khan, was also quoted in the article.

Similarly, *The Illustrated Weekly* carried a two-page interview with Khan, entitled 'The Dissenter' (16 March 1986), accompanied by a box item in which his wife Syeeda Reshma, a Supreme Court lawyer, was also interviewed. While Khan defended the Supreme Court judgment, his wife argued that the new law would encourage oral divorce. She feared that as the majority of Muslim women were illiterate and poor, and therefore not in a position to approach the courts for redress after divorce, their problems would be multiplied. Asserting that the Supreme Court judgment was not un-Islamic, she was surprised that the Muslim Women Bill was formulated without consulting those who would be directly affected. This was the only mention of the impact of the new law on Muslim women—in the thirty pages devoted to this subject over six editions of the magazine.

Khan featured a second time in *Sunday* in a two-page feature (18-24 May 1986) headlined 'I Refuse To Follow The Shariat Of The Muslim League.' The article consisted of abstracts from a number of Khan's speeches in different parts of the country and established that he saw the issue and the Bill as a question of women's rights. He argued that Islam, by its very nature, cannot be against assistance to indigent divorcees. He questioned politicians who had not done or said anything about the failure of many men to even follow the Shariat in terms of payment of *meher*, return of the divorced women's property, and so on.

This article is interesting because it makes it clear that Arif Mohammed Khan viewed the Muslim Women Bill in the context of women's rights. Yet few questions, in the plethora of interviews with him in newspapers and periodicals, related to this. Instead, they focussed almost entirely on the political compulsions of his decision to resign from Rajiv Gandhi's cabinet. This is another illustration of the overwhelming and exclusive interest of the press in party politics. The importance accorded to this in the hierarchy of news often obscures other issues.

Only *The Sunday Observer* spoke to the person who triggered the controversy—Justice Y. V. Chandrachud of the Supreme Court. In an interview by Ajoy Bose on 8 December 1985, the former chief justice held that the unfavourable reaction to his judgment was sentimental rather than rational, political rather than sociological.

The Shah Bano issue posed a difficult dilemma because of the communal overtones of the campaign for and against the Muslim Women Bill. In such an atmosphere, articles by non-Muslims pointing out the fallacies and inadequacies in Islam and in Muslim Personal Law, however well-intentioned or well-researched, could easily be construed as covert bigotry. At the same time, even liberal Muslims who at other times would not identify with fundamentalists in their own community, seem to have hesitated to write critically about their religion or law, in case their views were exploited by Hindu communal forces. Women's groups were faced with a similar problem.

Articles on this subject must, therefore, be assessed against this background. Javed Gaya's article in *The Sunday Observer* is particularly significant as he attempted to move the discussion away from Muslim Personal Law vis-a-vis women—a point belaboured by Arun Shourie in his three-part article in *The Illustrated Weekly*; instead he tried to place the issue in the context of the condition of the Muslim community as a whole.

In fact, feelings were so highly charged during this period that a Muslim woman scholar, who had studied personal law, was deeply offended that her article favouring the Muslim Women Bill was placed on the same page that carried one by Shehnaaz Sheikh, a woman activist from Bombay who had challenged Muslim Personal Law in the Supreme Court. The former feared that this could be seen as support for the latter's position. Both articles appeared in the *Express Magazine* in 1986, outside the survey period.

Overall, most of the publications surveyed paid more attention to the legal and political ramifications of the Shah Bano controversy than the gender question.

Female Foeticide

The misuse of medical technologies for sex determination and pre-selection, leading to female foeticide, was covered minimally in the four periodicals under study. Although the campaign was concentrated in Bombay, the Calcutta-based *Sunday* accorded the issue maximum attention. It also devoted more space to this subject than to either dowry or rape.

Sunday carried four reports, of which three were specials, while *The Sunday Observer* had three items—a special report, a diary item and a letter to the editor. *India Today* and *The Illustrated Weekly* published two items each. Both carried a letter to the editor. In addition, the former featured an item in the current events section while the latter published a comprehensive special report which looked at all aspects of the issue.

Sunday was the only publication to have taken the trouble to conduct its own multi-pronged investigation into the extent of the problem. The special feature (24-30 January 1988) was obviously prompted by the proposed Maharashtra legislation. The timely seven-page article, accompanied by photographs and boxes, was headlined 'Boy Or Girl?' Incorporating reports from correspondents in Delhi, Bombay, Amritsar and Calcutta, the story went into the history of sex-testing, presented case studies and featured interviews with activists, doctors, concerned government servants, as well as clinic operators. Boxes accompanying the story dealt with clinics, the new threat of sex pre-selection and the various methods of sex detection and selection.

In an earlier issue, too, the magazine had demonstrated its interest in the subject. The first report published in *Sunday* during the period under review was a two-page special (8-14 June 1986). Headlined 'The Unwanted Girl Child,' correspondent Olga Tellis' report was accompanied by a box on the various techniques of sex determination and pre-selection. It also featured the famous UNICEF photograph which poignantly illustrates the neglect of female children—a mother with male-female twins, the former a healthy toddler, the latter a starving spectre of a child. This well-researched piece contained a wealth of information and presented both sides of the controversy. However, the fact that the writer was against the practice was apparent in the overall tone of the article.

The Illustrated Weekly carried a four-page spread on the subject, accompanied by photographs (14 September 1986). Written by Bharati Sadasivam, the detailed and analytical article reflected a clear pro-woman perspective. It described the growth of clinics which advertised amniocentesis as 'humane and beneficial,' a test having '98 per cent accuracy.' Given the socio-cultural bias against women, the author stated, it was inevitable that the original purpose of amniocentesis, detecting genetic abnormalities in the foetus, would be obscured and that doctors would exploit its potential as a method to prevent the birth of unwanted daughters.

Sadasivam touched upon a point which others writing on amniocentesis had failed to raise: namely, its disturbing implications for the country's population programme. Family planning theorists believe that by reducing the birth of girls, who grow up to become the 'breeders,' the test provides an ideal and rational solution to the population problem. The article also highlighted the campaigns launched against female foeticide in cities like Delhi and Bombay and the demands for a law to check the misuse of such technology. It concluded that amniocentesis must be viewed as the latest manifestation of society's continuing devaluation of women and as part of the emerging trend of patriarchal control over women's reproductive functions.

The detailed articles in *Sunday* and *The Illustrated Weekly* were not matched by those in *The Sunday Observer* or *India Today*. This is particularly surprising in the case of the former as the campaign against female foeticide was Bombay-based. Thus, the Bombay dailies had shown greater interest in the subject than their counterparts in other cities. Yet *The Sunday Observer*, whose main edition originated in Bombay, carried just one special report headlined 'Fresh Bid To Ban Sex Tests'. Written by Jyoti Punwani (10 August 1986), it recounted the campaign launched by the Forum Against Sex Determination and Pre-Selection and the group's suggestions on a law to curb the misuse of technology for such purposes. In addition, it published a short diary item on the Maharashtra government's announcement in January 1988 regarding the introduction of a Regulation of Use of Pre-natal Diagnostic Techniques Bill.

The coverage of this issue in the four publications suggests that periodicals too respond more to events than to processes. However, unlike the coverage in daily newspapers, some of the articles in these publications did present the issue in the context of the status of women.

The Roop Kanwar Tragedy

Periodicals were able to cover the death of Roop Kanwar in Deorala from several angles. First, the news itself: although daily newspapers covered the events that followed her death in considerable detail, periodicals were able to incorporate background information about the area and the tradition of sati in their reports. Secondly, the law: the revival of 'sati' in this century, despite a nineteenth century law banning the practice, raised serious issues about the efficacy of social reform legislation. Thirdly, the sociological perspective: the Deorala incident and the Rajput community's assertion of its right to customary practices raised the question of 'tradition' versus 'modernity'. It also reactivated the debate about voluntary versus forced sati, given the historical evidence of considerable social, psychological and sometimes even physical pressures on the woman to kill herself or be killed. And finally, the women's question: the status of widows in Indian society.

Neither *The Illustrated Weekly* nor *India Today* featured the issue as a major cover story although both had two special reports on the subject. All four publications made generous use of photographs, including the now-famous picture of Roop Kanwar on her wedding day—up for sale in Deorala after her death. On-the-spot reports from Deorala and its environs were carried by all the periodicals except *Sunday*. However, the latter did carry a cover story on Hindu revivalism, a fall-out of the Deorala incident, in addition to a special report focussing on the media response to the issue. *The Sunday Observer* published two special reports, apart from featuring news connected with the issue on its front page three times. Both *India Today* and *The Sunday Observer* have editorials but only the former commented on the issue. The other publications featured opinions by columnists or special writers.

The Illustrated Weekly was surprisingly prompt in its response to the Deorala incident. It carried a report headlined 'Shame', by freelancer Rajni Bakshi, in its issue of 4 October 1987—exactly a month after Roop Kanwar's death. The article focussed on the arrangements made by Roop Kanwar's family for the *chunri mahotsav*. It also reported the protests by women's groups in Jaipur, their moves to stop the ceremony and the reaction of local men who felt there was nothing wrong in what they saw as women's belief in sati.

The writer pointed out that neither education nor fifteen years of exposure to modern media like television seemed to have changed people's attitudes. A senior local journalist from a leading Hindi daily was quoted as saying: 'So what if there is one sati after every 30 or 40 years? No force has been used and, anyway, blind faith is there all over India.' His contention was supported by Ghanshyam Tiwari, a Bharatiya Janata Party politician, who asserted: 'In Sikar district there is no village without a sati temple. Every married woman first goes there and the woman prays to remain a *suhagan*.' Roop Kanwar's brother, interviewed by the writer, conceded that the practice of sati should not continue. 'But this does not alter his family's pride over a girl who was neither brainwashed, doped or forced into committing an act they believe has wiped away the sins of seven generations,' she commented.

Bakshi's second report from Rajasthan in *The Illustrated Weekly* (1 November 1987), headlined 'The Rajput Revival,' focussed more specifically on the Rajput revival which had manifested itself through rallies in support of sati. She linked the emergence of groups like the Dharma Raksha Samiti to the new religious militancy in the state. She also highlighted the contention of women's groups that 'sati' needed to be viewed within the broader context of atrocities against women. These groups had condemned the use of religion and caste as instruments for the exploitation and subordination of women. By incorporating the views of these women's groups in the report, the author reminded readers of the centrality of the women's question which would otherwise have been lost in the mire of religion and politics.

Similarly, the report in *India Today* by Inderjit Badhwar, headlined 'Sati: A Pagan Sacrifice' (15 October 1987), sought the views of women's groups. Spread over four pages, with colour as well as black and white photographs, the story presented a comprehensive account of the events connected with Roop Kanwar's death as well as its fallouts, such as the economic windfall to the village. The author highlighted the fact that, far from being a socially backward village, Deorala boasted seven schools, a dispensary, and so on. The report also touched upon the debate over voluntary versus forced sati and quoted women activists on the reasons for the prevalence of 'sati.'

The Sunday Observer produced a full-page special report by Shiraz Sidhwa under 'In Focus' as early as 20 September 1987—just a week after the *chunri mahotsav*. The introduction to the report, headlined 'Sati: Who's Guilty?', read:

> What can you say about an 18-year-old woman, married barely seven months ago, who flings herself onto her husband's funeral pyre? That it was the insanity of the moment, an act of adolescent despair, which drove her to suicide Romeo and Juliet style? That it was an act of coercion, a heinous murder by scheming in-laws? Was it that the hapless Rajput girl could not face the bleak years of widowhood that loomed hopelessly ahead? Or was it misplaced spiritual belief, reinforced by years of indoctrination and frequent visits to sati temples that led to this barbaric last rite?

The writer did not express any view on whether Roop Kanwar's death was suicide or murder; nor did she attempt to fully answer some of the questions posed in the introduction. The report was basically a reconstruction of events, containing neither comment nor analysis. In a box item, the author cited instances where the government had been able to prevent the sati ritual using existing laws and suggested that the Deorala incident could only have taken place with the tacit agreement of the authorities.

The Sunday Observer continued to closely follow developments in Deorala and Rajasthan till January 1988, running three reports on its front page. The news stories exposed the lackadaisical attitude of the Rajasthan government—despite the promulgation of the 1 October ordinance, it did not prevent the construction of a platform for the sati *sthal* in Deorala. The story by Ruchira Gupta, headlined 'Roop Kanwar Was Not Very Religious' (18 October 1987), quoted Roop Kanwar's elder brother Mool Singh. He flatly denied that his sister was excessively religious as had been suggested by some people; neither could he recall Roop ever talking about the legendary Rani Sati. Although she routinely visited the temple, it was, he pointed out, not out of any special sense of devotion.

The Sunday Observer also ran a front page report (13 December 1987) exposing the presence of sati temples in Bombay, accompanied by a photograph of local women's groups demonstrating against the glorification of sati in a locality where such a temple exists.

The Deorala incident made the press more alert about similar occurrences elsewhere. For example, a report by Minu Jain on the op-ed (opposite-editorial) page of *The Sunday Observer* (17 January 1988), headlined 'Sati Or Murder?', dealt with the death of a woman called Shakuntala in Lalitpur in UP on her husband's funeral pyre. *Sunday* also carried a four-page report on the same incident by Nirmal Mitra (24-30 January 1988), which concluded:

> Either way, the only definite fact to emerge from this mysterious but sordid saga is that women in India continue to lead miserable existences as second class citizens. If Shakuntala was murdered for the sake of property, this of course is an outrage and a scandal. But if she did choose to kill herself out of love for the rogue and womaniser who ruined her life, then that is even sadder.

The only cover story on this issue in *Sunday* (25-31 October 1987), headlined 'The Angry Hindu', did not go into the Deorala incident. Instead, it focussed on the rise of Hindu revivalism following the incident and condemned the government for its paralysis and complicity in the gruesome affair. The article also analysed the new anti-sati ordinance.

It is significant that both *Sunday* and *The Sunday Observer* took early note of media response to this issue. The former's first report on the subject headlined 'A Burning Issue,' by Kuldeep Kumar (11-17 October 1987), appeared in its media column. Accompanied by photographs of the *chunri mahotsav* and the anti-sati protests, the report focussed on the controversial editorial in the Hindi daily *Jansatta* (an accompanying box provided the full text of the edit in English), pointing out its contradictions and factual errors. It also referred to the coverage of the incident in another Hindi newspaper, *Rashtradoot*, as well as the 'malaise of obscurantism' among politicians of all hues. It asked: 'Has the situation come to such a pass that even in the last years of the 20th century, opinion makers in our society cannot distinguish between the decadent, inhuman aspects of our cultural and religious tradition and its universal essence?' Apart from criticising the Hindi press, the report took note of the more progressive views of the editor of the *Navbharat Times* and the statement by prominent Hindi writers and journalists condemning the *Jansatta* edit.

Shiraz Sidhwa's report on media coverage in *The Sunday Observer* (27 September 1987) preceded the *Sunday* report. It focussed more specifically on the local press in Jaipur which had played up and romanticised Roop Kanwar's story by carrying details about what it termed 'the supreme sacrifice.' This article was significant as it was the first to draw attention to the mythologising power of the print media on such an issue.

The law became the focus of much of the discussion with the passage of the Rajasthan ordinance banning sati in November, followed by demands for a Central law and the tabling of the new Bill in Parliament in December. While *The Sunday Observer* carried a critique of the Central law by Radha Kumar (13 December 1987) before it was tabled in Parliament, both *Sunday* and *India Today* dealt with the law only in passing. Kumar pointed out that although the Bill was an improvement on the Rajasthan ordinance, it had several objectionable clauses and loopholes: punishments for the woman attempting 'to commit sati'; inadequate differentiation between different kinds of abetment, direct and indirect; severe penalties which would deter potential witnesses; and grave omissions in the definition of what constituted glorification of sati.

Only *India Today* cared to look at a fairly obvious human interest angle—the condition of widows—in its eight-page special report (15 November 1987) headlined 'Widows: Wrecks Of Humanity' by Inderjit Badhwar. Backed by reports from other centres, it provided precisely what was needed in the aftermath of the Roop Kanwar tragedy—a context for analysing and understanding the event. The report described the status and experiences of widows in different parts of the country, investigated government programmes for them and recorded the efforts of voluntary organisations as well as individual women in fighting the oppression and exploitation of widows.

The introduction to the article spelt out why this timely project was undertaken:

> There is a convenient penchant to sweep under the rug some of the most grotesque evils that plague society until some apocalyptic incident jolts people from their escapist reveries. Roop Kanwar's sati provided such a catalyst. It awakened people not only to the sheer horror of the act itself but also forced a re-examination of the larger subject of crimes against women.... To understand why a widow might try and take her life, *India Today* talked extensively to women who had lost their husbands and to activists who have worked for the betterment of their plight.... Widowhood is still an instant certificate of penury, privation and mental torture from which there is no escape.

> Rural or urban ... the common thread that unites these widows in a chain of misery is the forcible deprivation of property and economic independence. Even though the law—the Hindu Succession Act—confers equal property and inheritance rights on women, widows are rarely given their fair share.

This feature stands out because it illustrates how the press can move beyond event-oriented, time-bound, reactive reportage to writing that can enhance public understanding of not just events but the issues which they bring into focus.

It is significant that *India Today* (3 October 1987) chose to use the one page it reserves for editorial comment to state the magazine's position on sati. This gave weightage to its coverage, as it signalled the importance accorded to the subject by the editors. Headlined 'Moral Bankruptcy,' the strongly-worded edit affirmed the positive role of the press and women's organisations who 'rightly refused to ignore a pagan practice.' The edit emphasised that social reform legislation during the pre-Independence days stood a chance of being effective because the reformists devoted their lives and souls to the causes they held dear and refused to pander to superstition. However, today the 'moral bankruptcy of the Indian State and its rulers' was evident. The absence of moral and political will in effect implied social sanction to 'the forces of exploitation and obscurantism,' the edit stated.

In contrast, both *Sunday* and *The Illustrated Weekly* carried articles which attempted to explain sati. For instance, in the first issue of the former which touched on this subject (11-17 October 1987), columnist Khushwant Singh referred to what he termed the 'self-immolation' of Roop Kanwar. Headlined 'Sati And Hindu-Sikh Psyche', the column divided Indians into two categories: the vast majority, which still harbours respect for a widow who ceremoniously mounts her husband's pyre, and the minority of modern, westernised Indians who decry the act as barbarous. Suggesting that the latter 'get more publicity because of a like-minded media,' Singh continued: 'But if they think that sati-supporters are a lunatic fringe who will soon be wiped out, they are in for many unpleasant surprises....' The writer went on to state: 'Even I who condemn sati as a remnant of medieval barbarity feel a glow of pride when I read of Rajput women committing *jauhar*.... Sati is only a singular manifestation of the mass *jauhar* mentality.'

In her three-page article in *The Illustrated Weekly* (28 February 1988), sociologist Veena Das took a somewhat contradictory and obscure stand. The introduction to her article read:

> Recurring instances of sati in modern India lead to two kinds of reactions: first, passionate condemnation; second, angry defence of the custom. For the former, sati is a sign of the savagery of Hinduism; for the latter it is a sign of heroism such as that displayed by a soldier who dies in war for his country.

The author suggested that the British used the prevalence of sati as objective evidence of the barbarity of Hindus, thus legitimising the civilising mission of British rule. Das then dwelt on the savagery versus heroism debate. She held that the defenders of modernity refuse to discuss why death in war should be valorised but not voluntary death in sati. In her view, the same collective pressure that was responsible for a person's decision to die was at work in the case of soldiers going voluntarily towards death in war. Das held that for a society that offered such few channels for heroism, Roop Kanwar's 'sati' provided a few moments of transcendence for many people.

In this survey of periodicals, Das was the only writer who tried to give a sociological gloss or 'explanation' for sati. All others, barring Khushwant Singh, condemned it. Her article was representative of an argument heard elsewhere over that period—sociologist Ashis Nandy wrote in a similar vein in the *Indian Express* (and later, outside the survey period, in *The Illustrated Weekly*), as did an American scholar, Patrick D. Harrigan, in *The Statesman*. This viewpoint took as given the concept of voluntary sati while consistently ignoring historical evidence about the coercion usually associated with the practice. Such articles diverted the debate from the basic issues of the status of women in modern Indian society, particularly outside marriage, to obscure questions of heroism and cultural identity.

In contrast to Veena Das's article, Justice V. R. Krishna Iyer's two-page comment in *The Illustrated Weekly* (8 November 1987) was uncompromising in its condemnation of the sati tradition. He stated that wherever issues of the 'weaker gender' were at stake, the law was often dead or still-born. Despite the guarantee of equality between the sexes in the Constitution, the author argued, terrible discrimination was practised against Indian women in the form of female foeticide, discrimination in education and employment, bride-burning, rape, murder, discrimination in marriage and inheritance, and the *devadasi* system.

The author pointed out that the existing laws and constitutional guarantees could be used to prevent such crimes in the future. He cited precedents where existing provisions in the Indian Penal Code had been used in the past to punish those abetting sati. He attributed the unwillingness of the government to act to its reluctance to alienate Rajput fundamentalists. He also made an important statement when he asserted that the right to life, guaranteed under Article 21 of the Constitution, outweighed the right to practise religion where there was a conflict between the two.

In his weekly column 'Byline' in *Sunday* (18-24 October 1987), M. J. Akbar restricted his comment to the political aspects of the issue. The former editor of the magazine used the occasion to attack the opposition, specifically V. P. Singh, for its silence on the sati issue. He could not, however, contrast the opposition's position with exemplary behaviour by the party then in power at the Centre—the Congress (I), of which Akbar was by then an open supporter. He resorted instead to quoting from Jawaharlal Nehru and speculating on how Nehru would have responded in such circumstances. The writer made no comment on the issue of sati specifically.

India Today sullied its otherwise commendable coverage of this issue by carrying an article written by one of its regular columnists, Rajinder Puri. In his 'Last Word' column, headlined 'The Male Opinion' (15 December), Puri made light of the issue by conducting a mock survey among men, named Dowry Chand, Kanjoos Lal, Swami Phoka Shloka Mal, Prof. Nasbandhi Singh, Sifarish Kumar, etc., which revealed that they were all against sati. The so-called humour in the column was in bad taste, trivialising as it did so tragic an event as Roop Kanwar's death. As recorded elsewhere in this survey (see section on newspapers), this particular columnist clearly has a penchant for making fun of women and issues that are of particular concern to them.

Although some individual writers in the periodicals covered in the survey rationalised the existence of 'sati', it is significant that none of the publications indicated any editorial support for the practice or for the people attempting to revive it. Almost all of them acknowledged the centrality of the status of women to this issue and highlighted the efforts of women's groups to bring this into focus.

Conclusion

The coverage of the selected five women's issues by the four periodicals surveyed indicates a trend similar to that in the newspapers included in the study. In all of them the Shah Bano and 'sati' controversies received the maximum coverage. The sex-determination question received uniformly poor coverage in most of the periodicals as well as in newspapers. *Sunday* was an exception in that it had four pieces on the subject—more than the number carried on either dowry deaths or rape.

As in the case of newspapers, issues with legal, political or religious ramifications in varying combinations are accorded more importance than purely 'social' issues. Therefore both the Shah Bano and 'sati' controversies, which had all these dimensions, took up maximum space, while dowry deaths and rape, despite having legal implications, lagged far behind.

The improvement in the quality of coverage given to women's issues in some publications is another noticeable trend. This was particularly the case with *India Today*. By the time the 'sati' issue hit the headlines, it had a well-developed features section and made good use of photographs and layouts to bring out different aspects of this issue—particularly the social dimensions, which others had ignored. At least on the 'sati' issue, it was the one publication which did not let the political angle eclipse the human and social implications of the problem.

Sunday, on the other hand, seems to have gradually become more politics-centred. Its coverage of both the dowry deaths issue and amniocentesis consisted of factual and fairly original reporting. However, its handling of the Shah Bano and 'sati' controversies showed an interest in the political ramifications rather than the women's question or the sociological context. For a magazine which had distinguished itself by excellent investigative and human interest stories in the early years of its existence, this signalled a noticeable shift in focus.

Throughout the period under review, none of the periodicals exploited the subject of crimes against women for prurient purposes. However, the example from *The Illustrated Weekly* (outside the survey period)—the insensitive manner in which the story of a child rape victim was played up—shows how easily this can be done.

Finally, the study reveals the dilemma faced by periodicals which do not wish to inflame communal sentiments when dealing with issues like the Shah Bano case or the Roop Kanwar tragedy. With both issues having taken a communal turn, presenting the different points of view in the controversy was akin to walking a tight-rope. Only the accomplished were able to maintain a balance. As the press often, wittingly or unwittingly, confirms unspoken prejudices, its role in ensuring that negative and regressive attitudes are not reinforced at such times is all the more crucial.

8

Women's Magazines

Ammu Joseph

Women's magazines occupy a peculiar position in the media world. Precursors of the trend towards special interest publications, they existed long before the recent boom in specialised magazines. Although they cater to a much wider audience than many others in this genre, they are considered less than equal even among specialised publications. They are, in many ways, the pariahs of the press—ignored by the majority of media professionals, belittled by the rest and taken less seriously than even a men's magazine which depends for its audience on nude photographs of women and prurient humour.

The publishers of these magazines view them chiefly as money-spinners which deliver a valuable captive audience to eager advertisers. Their editorial staff is divided between those who treat their work as any other job and those who, propelled by missionary zeal, are determined to open the eyes and widen the horizons of the women they address, thereby helping them improve their lives and social status. Their readers are, for the most part, unaware of the grand designs of publishers, advertisers and committed journalists but continue to patronise these magazines mainly because of their combination of utilitarian and entertainment values.

Women's magazine bashing is a favourite pastime among those who deign to notice (if not read) them, both within the press and the women's movement. Serious journalists who work on the staff of these magazines find themselves in the same position as bright students who choose to major in an 'arts' subject, with concerned seniors suggesting that they are wasting their time on the side-lines when they are good enough to be in the 'mainstream.'

A particularly telling example in this context is the experience of one woman journalist who left the staff of a women's magazine to freelance. Praising her first major piece in a men's magazine, a senior colleague generally considered sympathetic to the women's cause wondered what she had been doing holed up in her former publication for so long. Only when she listed the serious stories she had written for that magazine over the years did he realise that he had erroneously assumed the contents of all women's magazines to be uniformly vapid and inconsequential. Both also recognised the irony implicit in the view that an article in a men's magazine represents entry into the mainstream.

While people in the press tend to ignore or trivialise women's magazines, many in the women's movement demonise them. Critiques of 'commercial women's magazines' in alternative women's publications and other fora invariably attribute questionable, if not diabolical, motives to both their publishers and their editorial staff. They suggest that these magazines play an integral part in a grand conspiracy hatched by the promoters of capitalism and patriarchy—represented by the press barons, advertisers and renegade women journalists—to keep women in their lowly place.

There is, admittedly, much that is open to criticism in women's magazines as they exist today and many critiques have made valid points about the weaknesses and inherent contradictions of these publications. However, the critiques themselves are not without problems, based as they commonly are on a faulty understanding of the basic realities of the press in general and women's magazines in particular. Concerned women working within these magazines are often disappointed that they are unable to use such feminist critiques to bolster their own on-going internal battles for change—the factual errors, misrepresentations and conspiracy theories in these treatises make them vulnerable to easy dismissal by editors and publishers.

Commercial women's magazines have, in their own way, been catering to a section of the population normally neglected by the so-called mainstream press. Even the most traditional of them have been slowly and silently changing the outlook and lifestyles of a couple of generations of women. And at least some of the changes have been for the better as far as women's self-confidence, awareness of the world, expression of their thoughts and feelings, and other such intangibles are concerned.

Some of the communication gaps between women on either side of the women's magazine divide were narrowed by their common involvement in the women's movement. The resulting interaction and dialogue on the subject led to the publication of articles by women activists on a variety of serious topics in some women's magazines. This gave a new dimension to these publications and radicalised them to a certain, however limited, extent. The process was most evident during the campaign against rape at the beginning of the eighties—the symbiotic relationship allowed for prompt and detailed coverage of the issues involved in at least some of the 'traditional' women's magazines.

The late seventies and early eighties were relatively heady days in this respect. The women's movement in India, impelled by the United Nations-declared International Women's Decade and by Indian women's own observations and experiences within their particular contexts, gathered momentum with the demonstrations against dowry deaths in 1979 and the anti-rape campaign in 1980. These efforts generated public interest and helped create an environment in which at least some women's issues—notably atrocities against women—were deemed worthy of media attention. The involvement of women journalists in the movement (as activists or sympathisers) contributed to the visibility of these issues in newspapers and magazines. Coverage in the mainstream press not only increased public awareness of both the issues and the movement, but also made it easier for interested editorial staff within women's magazines to orient their publications towards issues of serious concern to women.

However, in the latter half of the eighties, commercial pressures began to impinge on the efforts of the staff to keep up the serious focus. The advent of television advertising sent ripples across the gamut of the print media. With a large chunk of the advertising lucre diverted to the electronic media, newspapers and magazines had to compete for a much smaller share of the publicity pie. In the process, the marketing and advertising departments of publications began to increasingly interfere in editorial matters, in what was ostensibly an attempt to make their profiles more appealing to advertisers.

In women's magazines, these developments led to pressures on the editorial staff to 'lighten' their contents. In many ways, this meant retracing some of the steps taken a few years earlier. Of course, since the commercial world has now jumped onto 'the new woman' bandwagon, a veneer of liberation is 'in' and, therefore, permissible. To this extent, women's magazines continue to publish occasional articles on current women's issues.

But the consumerist tendencies which have characterised Indian society since the late eighties have rubbed off on women's magazines in a fairly significant way. With their very raison d'etre intimately tied up with their ability to attract consumer advertising (mostly targeted at women), these magazines always paid attention to women's role as consumers. However, the focus has since shifted. The emphasis is now on the woman in a consumerist culture.

In earlier times, for example, women's magazines were among the first to promote consumer rights, with popular columns analysing products or providing a forum for the airing of consumer grievances. But now this aspect has been diluted and, to an extent, replaced with features focussing on currently fashionable activities such as private enterprise and personal investments.

It is difficult and dangerous to generalise, but it seems as if the concept of women's emancipation has lately undergone some change in women's magazines, influenced both by the general consumerist trends in society and the pressures from powerful commercial interests. The idea that liberation lies in yuppiedom and in women gaining access, quickly and efficiently, to that world, seems to have gained currency.

There appears to be less room for serious attempts to understand the poor status of women irrespective of class, caste, creed and other divisions; to look at gender as a major factor in determining social, cultural, economic and political power; to keep in view the ground realities faced by the majority of Indian women, and so on. The focus now seems to be on helping middle and upper-class readers become superwomen-cum-little women—the entrepreneur or professional par excellence who is also the hostess with the mostest, the super-efficient housekeeper, the smart and decorative wife, as well as the loving and attentive mother.

It is against this background that the coverage of select women's issues in *Eve's Weekly* and *Femina*, the two leading English language women's magazines, must be viewed.

Eve's Weekly and Femina

Eve's Weekly is the oldest English-language, nationally-circulated women's magazine in India. Published by Eve's Weekly Pvt. Ltd., then owned by the J.K. Somani business house, it was launched under a male editor. The magazine's first woman editor was Gulshan Ewing, who had earlier worked as assistant editor of the other major, national, English language women's magazine—*Femina*. She continued to edit the weekly until 1989—that is, throughout the ten-year period covered by this study. *Eve's Weekly* was closed down by the management in 1990, despite efforts by the staff to save it, on the grounds that it was no longer a financially viable publication. It was re-launched by its new owner, Vineet Jain, in 1992 as a monthly.

Eve's Weekly began as a socialites' magazine, covering fashionable people and events in addition to providing tips on clothes, grooming, cooking, needle-craft and other matters assumed to be of particular interest to women. Although it moved beyond that profile in the late seventies and eighties, vestiges of its former avatar could be found in the regular 'People and Events' and colour pages till the end.

Femina is a fortnightly women's magazine owned by Bennett Coleman Pvt. Ltd. Although younger than *Eve's Weekly*, it soon overtook the latter in circulation, thanks chiefly to the strength of the newspaper group behind it. But, like *Eve's Weekly*, it was initially edited by a male. The editor of *Femina* during the period under review was Vimla Patil.

Like its older counterpart, *Femina* has gone through periods of seriousness and superficiality. While it has always had the usual ingredients of a traditional women's magazine, such as fashion spreads, grooming guides, recipes and homecraft instructions, it has also carried some noteworthy regular features at various times. For example, *Femina's* consumer complaints column was a pathbreaker, as was its excellent if short-lived literary section which featured samples of women's writing in different regional languages.

On the whole, however, during the period under review, *Femina* emerged as the less serious of the two in terms of coverage of controversial current issues concerning women, such as the five selected for this study. This is particularly surprising because although *Femina*, like *Eve's Weekly*, has a small staff, the fact that it is a fortnightly allows for a little breathing space between production-related duties. Secondly, as a member of *The Times of India* stable, it has access to writers from other publications of the group as well as to better financial resources. Despite these advantages, *Femina's* coverage of all five issues was both quantitatively and qualitatively poorer than that of *Eve's Weekly*.

Over the total period of thirty months spread over the ten years covered by this study, *Eve's Weekly* published twenty-one features (plus one short story) on the five selected issues while *Femina* published only eleven. All except one of *Eve's Weekly*'s features were full-fledged articles, a page or more in length. On the other hand, three of *Femina's* eleven items were less than half a page long.

Selecting limited periods for monitoring coverage of issues poses a problem in respect of magazines as not all reports on the subject show up in the precise months included. This method is particularly restrictive for features magazines (like *The Illustrated Weekly of India*, *Eve's Weekly* and *Femina*) since they have a much longer lead time than newspapers and newsmagazines. Some allowance for this factor has been made in the study by extending the survey period in the case of periodicals to thirty months, compared to twenty for daily newspapers.

The women's magazines present an additional problem in this regard. Unlike the news-oriented publications (dailies as well as periodicals), which tend to react to particular events and issues and have concentrated coverage of these while they are 'news,' women's issues are more or less integral to women's magazines (in their new avatars); and as part of their ongoing agenda, tend to turn up in one form or another (not only articles but short stories, letters to the editor, book and film reviews, etc.) over much longer periods.

One example is the dowry issue—a stock-in-trade of women's magazines read in the main by middle-class women affected by the practice. In the case of *Eve's Weekly*, the issue would crop up time and again in fiction, readers' letters, and as a part of larger features. For instance, the magazine devoted a whole edition in the late seventies to exploring and exposing the sexist nature of many marriage customs, including dowry, in different parts of India.

Similarly, articles on maintenance for divorced Muslim women (inspired by the Shah Bano case) were noticed in *Femina* during the survey period but also outside the specified months. *Femina* also published one of the first thoroughly researched articles on the amniocentesis question as early as in 1983, long before it became a media issue and outside the period allocated for this subject by the study.

Such continuous attempts to stimulate readers' opinions against exploitative practices are not registered in this survey because the periods for study were determined by the way the 'mainstream' press, with its definition of news, tends to cover women's issues.

Dowry Deaths

While *Eve's Weekly* promptly responded to the dowry death syndrome, which caught media attention in May-June 1979, *Femina* did not carry a single article on the phenomenon over this early period.

Though the *Eve's Weekly* article was timely, appearing within weeks of the launch of the campaign, in the edition dated 7-13 July 1979, its opening paragraphs tended to trivialise the issue. Headlined 'Burning The Bahu,' the article by Ila Kapoor opened with a case history of 'beautiful, smartly turned-out, well-spoken' Mona, with an MA from Delhi's fashionable Lady Shri Ram College,' which did not immunise her against complaints of inadequate dowry by her mother-in-law. While this lead paragraph was perhaps intended to invoke human interest, it seemed to suggest that dowry harassment was particularly reprehensible when it was directed against a woman with so many virtues—as if the victimisation of someone with fewer endowments would be somehow more acceptable.

The article then went on to discuss other cases of dowry death handled by the Delhi-based women's group, Mahila Dakshata Samiti. It also quoted women's organisations such as Nari Raksha Samiti and the All-India Women's Conference on the issue. Among the suggestions made by Mahila Dakshata Samiti on combating the problem were: setting up family courts and enacting legislative measures to make requests for dowry and wife-battering cognizable offences. But by restricting itself to human interest details and neglecting to provide an analytical context for the case studies, the article basically skimmed the surface of the issue.

By 1983, when Justice S.M. Aggarwal's sessions court judgment in the Sudha Goel case—awarding the death sentence to her husband, mother-in-law and brother-in-law—had become a talking-point in the media, both the magazines carried features on the subject. But in each case, the articles tended to be descriptive rather than analytical.

However, *Femina* did publish a commentative piece the very next month (23 September-7 October 1983). Written by Vimla Patil, editor of the magazine, this equivalent of an editorial was a confused piece of writing which almost suggested that the writer was looking for some justification for dowry. For instance, the introduction to the article stated:

Ritika, a student of law, was married at age 25 and gave up further education to look after the home. No dowry was paid at her marriage. At the age of 45, her husband wants her to leave because he is having an affair with a colleague. She has no means of supporting herself or any income since she did not receive a dowry or fight for her share of the inheritance from her parents.

The article argued that inheritance rights are crucial to the well-being of women; it pointed out that most women either have no rights to property or are brought up in such ignorance about money matters that they blithely sign away whatever they do get without a thought about the future. Even those who are given dowry, she wrote, seldom have any access to it, let alone control. Ostensibly presenting a case for women's economic independence, and ignoring the point made earlier about women's lack of awareness about and access to money (whether in the form of inheritance or dowry), she stated:

Since Indian women are still largely uneducated and not earning, some manner of giving them economic relief will have to be found. If dowry is completely done away with, and succession is not implemented, women are going to be sufferers of a worse fate in the future, unless we naively presume that all husbands are generous and gentle.

She also argued that the concept of dowry and succession go hand in hand. Before the Succession Act, she wrote, a Hindu woman could not inherit property but was given dowry for economic security: '... no one would find anything wrong with dowry if it is a gift given in goodwill and love to a daughter and is treated strictly as her security and her personal property.'

In sum, the author seemed to be suggesting that if dowry were treated as something given to the woman for her security in the event of desertion, divorce or widowhood, it would be acceptable, especially since the laws relating to inheritance are inadequate and those concerned with alimony and maintenance not strictly implemented. In attempting to bring out the complexity of the issue, which she felt ought to be considered before amendments to the anti-dowry law were finalised, Patil came across as less than forthright in her condemnation of dowry as a practice.

She made no reference whatsoever to the phenomenon of dowry harassment and the related deaths of young brides. Further, by dealing with the subject solely in terms of inheritance rights, she totally neglected to address the problem from the viewpoint of those who have no property worth the name but are nevertheless miserably and inextricably caught in the dowry trap.

The article was accompanied by a box item, headlined 'Compare And Contrast,' by Gita Piramal. It merely described two weddings—one an instance of child marriage and the other of arranged marriage—which were similar only in that they took place in the same year (1982), that the participants belonged to the same caste and that dowry was handed over in both cases. This piece, too, referred to questions to be taken into account before framing a new dowry law but failed to make any concrete points.

The coverage of this issue by both magazines was inadequate in all respects—quantity, quality, as well as timeliness. It was confined to reportage and narrow, superficial and confused analysis. The views of ordinary women—the magazines' target audience—went unheard, as did the voices emerging from the women's movement, which had been galvanised by the dowry death phenomenon and fought long and hard against it.

Rape

By the time the campaign against rape was launched, *Eve's Weekly* was somewhat better prepared to meet the challenge. It featured a total of eleven articles and one short story on the subject during the seven months surveyed. Eight of the articles, as well as the short story, appeared in a special supplement on rape, in the edition dated 8-14 March 1980, to coincide with International Women's Day and the high point of the campaign which had developed around the Mathura case.

On the other hand, *Femina* carried just two delayed articles on the subject, the coverage being even scantier than that given to dowry. Once again, it took no note of the vociferous anti-rape campaign which originated in Bombay (where the magazine is based) and made no mention of the raging controversy throughout the period surveyed in 1980. It was only in the 1983 period under review that two articles turned up. The first article dealt with a women's fight for justice on behalf of an eight-year-old rape victim. The second was an interview-based piece on various people's reactions to the Supreme Court judgement in this case. But they failed to acknowledge the anti-rape campaign which, by then, had led to a Law Commission report on the law relating to rape and a draft Bill which was expected to be tabled in the August session of Parliament. Neither article really dealt with the question of legislation, let alone any of the other issues raised by women's groups.

Eve's Weekly's special supplement on rape indicates a concerted effort by its editorial staff to focus readers' attention on the issue. It was tackled in a variety of ways. Apart from the four main feature articles, the edition carried a one-act play on rape, a short story which had police rape as its theme, an interview with the director of Women Organised Against Rape (an American group), a piece focussing on young people's views on the crime and a brief report on the anti-rape campaign taking shape in Ahmedabad.

This kind of onslaught, representing a major departure from the magazine's usual style of dealing with many different subjects in a single edition, was perhaps the result of the involvement of some staff journalists in the anti-rape campaign in Bombay. The fact that several women activists involved in the movement contributed to the supplement also points in this direction.

Unfortunately, this otherwise strong edition was marred by its inappropriate cover—it featured a serene young woman peacefully strumming a *tanpura*. Although the special supplement was announced with a band across the cover stating 'It's Time We Looked Rape In The Face,' as well as highlights of some of the main features, the passivity of the woman in the photograph cannot but have obscured the activism reflected inside the magazine. Also incongruous in this setting were some of the other inevitable and typical features in the edition, such as one on electrolysis for men, another on fashions for tiny tots, and so on.

Of the four major articles on the subject, two took off from the Mathura rape case and the campaign building up around it to focus on different aspects of the crime and attitudes towards it. The one by activist Subhadra Butalia, headlined 'The Rape Of Mathura,' went into the details of the case, its passage through the various courts and the open letter to the Chief Justice of the Supreme Court by four law professors criticising the court's verdict; she also pointed out the connection with other rape cases, calling attention to the responsibility of the state, specifically the judiciary, to curb and punish such atrocities against women.

The second of these articles, by (then) assistant editor Ammu Joseph, dealt with commonly accepted myths about rape—which invariably blame the victim—in a discussion on the perspective sought to be promoted by the newly formed Forum Against Rape, Bombay. It emphasised the fact that all women are vulnerable to rape, irrespective of 'character,' age, looks and economic status; showing how even those relatively protected because of their class are nonetheless trapped because the fear of rape effectively restricts their participation in many aspects of life. The article also outlined the long and short-term objectives of the Forum's anti-rape campaign and, significantly (because this was again an unusual move for any commercial publication), invited interested persons to contact the organisation through the magazine.

The other two of the four major features broke new ground as far as the debate on rape in the media was concerned. The one authored by activist Vibhuti Patel, headlined 'Rape As A Means Of Social Oppression,' recalled the myriad instances of custodial and mass rapes clearly intended to terrorise and subjugate powerless individuals, as well as groups and communities struggling for their rights (such as workers, dalits, minorities, etc.). Patel described in detail the findings of a group called Atyachar Virodhi Samiti, which had visited affected areas during the Marathwada riots to investigate the condition of dalits in general and the atrocities reportedly perpetrated on dalit women.

It is significant, in the context of this study, that the team apparently decided to focus particularly on the latter aspect because 'it was the one least highlighted by the press.' Patel also noted that 'the press had not considered it necessary to convey to the public even a fraction of the atrocities that confronted us there.' Thus a lowly women's magazine made up for the sins of omission of the more prestigious 'mainstream' press.

The final major feature headlined 'Can A Man Rape His Wife?,' was also virtually a first, appearing at a time when even anti-rape groups had not adequately or satisfactorily dealt with the question of marital rape. The article, by freelancer Milika Hariani, included interviews with Indian women from various social strata on this taboo topic; quoted the well-known book, *Against Our Will*, by Susan Brownmiller on the subject; and presented the legal position on rape within marriage in India as well as in some other countries.

The question of law was tackled in *Eve's Weekly* through an article by Nandita Haksar in its 26 November-2 December 1983 edition (also referred to but not counted in the dowry deaths section). This dealt with legislative and judicial responses to both rape and dowry and concluded that they often do little more than recognise the existence of these problems. In the case of the proposed amendment to the rape law, for instance, the writer commented that it 'appears to protect the police rather than women,' since the recommendations of the Law Commission had not been incorporated.

Eve's Weekly's coverage of the rape issue more or less kept pace with the women's movement's response to it, articulating new perspectives on an old crime, highlighting its socio-economic aspects and openly discussing previously taboo topics like marital rape. The imaginative use of different forms to drive home the point in the special supplement no doubt ensured that all its readers were exposed to new ideas through one feature or another.

However, the failure to convey on the cover the new radicalism evident inside must have obscured even a major effort such as the special supplement. The cover was one of the several features of the traditional women's magazine format that proved impervious to the efforts of staff attempting to change the orientation of the magazine. Another weakness of *Eve's Weekly's* coverage was that it did not directly highlight the human angle; it could have conveyed the trauma faced by rape victims through authentic case histories.

In its scarce coverage of the rape issue, *Femina* revealed its distance from the emerging women's movement in India, as well as its unresponsiveness to a crime so central to women given the debilitating impact that fear of rape has on practically every aspect of their lives. The magazine made no reference at all to the use of rape as a tool of class and caste oppression; nor did it pay serious attention to the question of law which was hotly debated during the survey period. Not only did *Femina* fail to analyse the issue and present it in the context of women's oppression, it also neglected the human dimension by not publishing anything on the trauma experienced by rape victims and the absence of facilities to help them cope with it—a fault was shared by both magazines.

The Shah Bano Controversy

Compared to its coverage of the rape issue, *Eve's Weekly's* response to the Shah Bano controversy was muted and limited. During the five months surveyed, it published only two articles on the subject. The first appeared in December 1985 following Shah Bano's repudiation of the Supreme Court judgment in her favour. The second one was carried in April 1986—during the controversy over the legislation excluding

Muslim women from the purview of Section 125 of the Criminal Procedure Code, which deals with maintenance for indigent divorcees, irrespective of creed.

Femina's coverage, with only one delayed article during the period under review, was even more insubstantial. The fact that it did not pay prompt or sufficient attention to such a raging controversy related to women's rights tells its own story.

Neither *Eve's Weekly* nor *Femina* interviewed Shah Bano or other poor Muslim women, the ones most likely to be adversely affected by being placed outside the purview of Section 125 of the CrPC. This was a major failure on the part of these women's magazines—when, surely, one of their primary duties is to give voice to the silent majority of women normally ignored by the 'mainstream' media.

However, *Eve's Weekly's* article in the edition dated 14-20 December 1985—after the furore over the case had forced Shah Bano to retract, and moves were afoot to ensure that Muslim women did not have access to redress under Section 125—did provide a context in which the arguments for and against the Supreme Court judgment could be viewed and understood.

Headlined 'The Muzzling Of Minority Women,' the article, by Ammu Joseph (then no longer on the staff), took off from Shah Bano's forced capitulation to the dictates of religious fundamentalists to tackle several myths about the implications of the Supreme Court judgment and its aftermath. The article placed the issue in the context of the poor economic, social and educational status of the majority of Muslim women and concluded: 'The Shah Bano case does not involve Muslim Personal Law alone. It is a question of social justice in general and women's rights in particular.'

Femina's only article on the subject, headlined 'A Burning Issue,' projected the views of women activists of various organisations on the controversy. While some interviewees were for and some against a common civil code, others said it was not a question of personal law alone but of the rights of Indian women as citizens of India. However, the views of the writer, Neerja Pahwa, were not entirely clear.

The only article pertaining to the Muslim Women Bill which appeared in *Eve's Weekly* was an interview with activist and film actress Shabana Azmi (who happens to be a Muslim). But the interview, by freelancer Jyoti Lajmi, merely presented Azmi's views on why she was opposed to the Muslim Women Bill. Given that the Bill had become so controversial politically and would potentially affect the lives of millions of Muslim women, it is surprising that neither magazine thought of discussing the legislation in greater detail.

In fact a whole range of issues raised by the Shah Bano controversy—such as anomalies in divorce and maintenance laws (both secular and religion-based), the implications for women of a Uniform Civil Code, the plight of the majority of divorcees irrespective of creed, the situation of poor Muslim women, the oppression of women by religious fundamentalism across the board, and so on—were inadequately covered by both *Eve's Weekly* and *Femina*.

Even if circumstances prevented an interview with Shah Bano herself, there was nothing to stop these Bombay-based women's magazines from listening to the voices of ordinary Muslim women in the city. Their failure to talk to even Shehnaaz Sheikh, a woman activist and Muslim divorcee also engaged in challenging the Muslim Personal Law in the courts, speaks poorly of their interest in the issue. *Eve's Weekly's* interview with a film star, however concerned and progressive, was surely not enough.

The absence of more detailed coverage is particularly incomprehensible in women's magazines. They are not constrained by the pressure of daily deadlines and are, therefore, better placed to run stories based on serious analysis as well as authentic interviews which can give a human face to current affairs.

The only possible explanation for this lapse is the pressure on these magazines to remain light and frothy, to refrain from becoming too political or serious. Although there have been periods, as during the anti-rape campaign, when at least *Eve's Weekly* was able to overcome these pressures, it is evident that such occasions were exceptions and not the rule. However, it must be noted that—by default or otherwise—neither magazine succumbed to the communal overtones which had overtaken the debate on the issue in many other publications. Further, they did not lose sight of the centrality of the women's question, as did much of the 'mainstream' press, which focussed almost entirely on the legal and political aspects of the case.

Female Foeticide

Compared to their coverage of the Shah Bano controversy, both *Eve's Weekly* and *Femina* gave slightly greater coverage to the sex determination tests and female foeticide issue, with a total of three articles each during the survey period of seven months.

Femina's pieces were all short, superficial reports in the current events sections of the magazine ('Jottings' and 'Keeping Track'). Considering that the campaign against the practice originated and was most vocal in Bombay, where both the magazines are based, *Femina's* cursory coverage of the issue is puzzling. Its three items consisted of a brief review of a short film on the issue called *Samadhaan* (23 July-7 August 1986), another short item on a survey conducted by the pharmacy college of the SNDT Women's University and a report on a workshop focussing on the social and legal aspects of sex determination.

Eve's Weekly's coverage, featuring three full-fledged articles, was relatively comprehensive. However, it continued to concentrate on reportage rather than analysis. Sandhya Srinivasan, in an article headlined 'The Blatant Misuse Of Amniocentesis Tests' (7-13 June 1986), focussed primarily on the physical ill-effects of the widely-available 'service.' Significantly, she also noted two other unfortunate aspects of the practice: it led to women's psychological devaluation of themselves and it would result in a further skewing of the sex ratio, already unfavourable to women.

Srinivasan wrote on the subject again in the edition dated 13-19 February 1988. Obviously prompted by the Maharashtra government's announcement in January regarding the introduction of legislation to ban the controversial tests, the article was headlined 'Banning Sex Determination Tests: How Much Will The Law Help?' It presented the various arguments advanced by those ranged on either side of the controversy and reviewed the campaign that had led to action by the state.

The author attributed the success of the campaign to the wide media coverage of the issue (not substantiated by this survey, which has found that the press gave it minimal coverage compared to the other issues) and the fact that no vote banks were involved. The article concluded by pointing out that a major change in social attitudes would be required to stamp out such practices.

In both these otherwise pro-women articles, Srinivasan cavilled against the labelling of this problem as a women's issue. In her first piece, she stated that sex determination had to be viewed as a social rather than a women's issue (which seemed to suggest that women's issues are either not social issues or are less serious than 'wider social issues'). There was no elaboration on this point but in her second article, too, she privileged social issues by stating that the campaign was greatly helped by the fact that the problem was not presented as a women's issue. Once again, she did not explain her obvious preoccupation with this point.

A box item accompanying Srinivasan's second article provided details of the proposed legislation and the recommendations of the Forum Against Sex Determination and Pre-Selection—giving readers the benefit of precise information.

Eve's Weekly's third article, by activist Vibhuti Patel in the edition dated 20-26 December 1986, reported on a procession in Bombay of proud parents with daughters. This demonstration was organised by the Forum Against Sex Determination and Pre-Selection to create public awareness about the link between the devaluation of girls and the misuse of medical techniques such as amniocentesis and the development of sex pre-selection methods. The article, appropriately headlined 'So That Our Daughters Can Live With Dignity,' quoted speakers at the rally, including children who declared: 'I am proud to be a girl.'

Although *Eve's Weekly* did give considerable coverage to the issue, specially in comparison to *Femina*, it failed to articulate the feelings of ordinary women on the subject. This was unfortunate because so much of the debate on the controversy centred around a woman's right to choose the sex of her babies; her own preference for such tests; her having the option of aborting a female foetus, given that in our society giving birth to a girl does not carry social prestige, and so on. An authentic assessment of what a cross-section of women actually thought and why would have been a useful contribution, well within the capability and brief of a women's magazine. Also, while *Eve's Weekly* did include some discussion on the proposed law, it did no better than the rest of the press in terms of verifying the statistics and other data bandied about by proponents as well as opponents of the practice.

The Roop Kanwar Tragedy

The Roop Kanwar tragedy and the controversy over the re-emergence of 'sati' in modern India, which caught the attention of the mainstream press, also drew prompt response from both the women's magazines. Although *Eve's Weekly* did not carry an on-the-spot report, it responded promptly with a timely article on the subject (3-9 October 1987). Written by the (then) assistant editor, Pamela Philipose, it was forcefully headlined 'Murder In The Guise Of Glorifying Sati Mata'. The strong headline was matched by an evocative introduction:

What is the force that makes four thousand people watch impassively as a young woman burns to death before their eyes? What is the force that convinces an 18-year-old girl that her life is without value once her husband of eight months has died? What is the force that causes a practice that has been condemned and outlawed 158 years ago to splutter alive every once in a while?

The tone of the article was also passionate: 'To those who hesitate to condemn sati because of its religious significance one asks: human sacrifice was once an accepted religious practice and still has votaries. But does that mean you won't condemn it?' The writer pointed out that the practice of sati only underlined the fact that a woman's life has no value in itself, no meaning apart from that of her husband. The article unequivocally equated sati with murder. An accompanying box item traced the history of the practice and undercut arguments in its favour which relied on the assumption that sati enjoyed religious sanction.

Femina also responded promptly to Roop Kanwar's death with a timely piece, headlined 'Sati In 1987,' in the edition dated 8-22 October 1987. The author, *The Times of India* staffer Saroj Natarajan, put the tragedy in the context of women's status and the prevalent attitudes to widowhood. Even the reactions of the dead woman's parents, the article pointed out, revealed the continuing prejudices against women in modern India.

Both magazines carried articles about the legal aspects of the issue. The one in *Eve's Weekly*, headlined 'Can This Law Prevent Sati?' (9-15 January 1988) placed the burning of widows in the context of witch-hunting, ritualistic child murders, the dedication of girls as *devadasis*, the rise of religious fundamentalism and communalism, etc. The author, freelancer Jean D'Cunha, went on to critique in fair detail the Commission of Sati (Prevention) Act, 1987. She concluded that the Act would be effective only if it incorporated the recommendations of women activists.

Femina analysed the law in a piece, headlined 'The Burning Problem,' by staffer Satya Saran (23 January-7 February 1988). It was basically a curtain-raiser on the one-day workshop organised by the magazine in February 1988 'to reiterate the protest felt by women all over the country.' Detailing the provisions of the Commission of Sati (Prevention) Bill, it recorded both the division in public opinion on the issue and the viewpoint of religious fundamentalists who saw opposition to the practice as an attempt to obstruct religious freedom. (This was followed by a one-page report on the workshop, which fell outside the survey period.)

Although both *Eve's Weekly* and *Femina* highlighted the centrality of the women's question and critiqued the law relating to sati, they neglected to give voice to the women concerned. Neither published articles incorporating interviews with women—whether in Deorala or in cities like Delhi and Bombay where sati temples and Rani Sati worshippers are known to exist.

Nor were any of the other issues thrown up by Roop Kanwar's death—such as the plight of widows, the failure of education to change attitudes to women, the oppression of women by religious fundamentalism, the exploitation of women in the name of communal identity, and so on—tackled by the magazines, at least during the survey period.

Conclusion

In sum, the two leading English language women's magazines left much to be desired in their coverage of the selected issues, in both quantitative and qualitative terms. The only notable exception was *Eve's Weekly's* treatment of the rape issue—it was accorded the seriousness it deserved.

However, it must be noted that, unlike general interest publications which focus on women's issues primarily when they reach a dramatic flash-point, these magazines do pay fairly consistent attention to a wide range of issues of concern to women—their target audience. In this respect, they are more in tune with process-related subjects than with event-centred ones.

Also, the uneven quality of their coverage of serious issues, evident from this study, is closely related to circumstances beyond the control of the editorial staff, such as poor payments for articles and the low standing of women's magazines among good writers.

These factors do not, however, excuse their conspicuous failure to provide ordinary women with a forum for airing their views on these subjects—the one area in which they could have perhaps surmounted their difficulties and used their special focus to advantage. Further, despite their customary dependence on and preference for human interest stories, these magazines by and large failed to present the human dimension of many of these issues.

Still, a comparative evaluation of their coverage of the selected issues reveals that *Eve's Weekly* was the more serious of the two during the survey period. Both the magazines are bound by similar commercial compulsions and have been under pressure, especially since the latter half of the eighties, to 'lighten' their contents in order to stay ahead in the race for advertisements. So the difference in their approaches must be attributed, at least in part, to their staff. For example, the involvement of staff journalists in the women's movement throughout the period under review made a significant difference to *Eve's Weekly's* handling of issues taken up by women's groups.

The findings of this survey suggest that the very nature and traditional format of commercial women's magazines inhibit the serious presentation of issues. The underlying assumption that governs the overall editorial policy—formulated in the vaguest of terms by the publishers—is that women are not interested in serious issues. The natural corollary is that if the magazines' staff wish to expose their readers to grave matters of particular relevance to women, they must make such subjects palatable through light treatment.

The publishers and, often, the editors of women's magazines also tend to be wary of the 'feminist' label. They, therefore, try and steer clear of open advocacy, whatever the merits of an issue. This is partly because of the media's obsession with the holy cow of 'objectivity' —regarded as an essential ingredient of profession-alism—despite the proven fact that the concept of media objectivity is highly suspect. But it is also out of the fear that a campaigning tone might put off the (predominantly male) decision-makers in the advertising world and make them look for more appropriate vehicles to get their messages across to 'normal' women.

These inherent characteristics of commercial women's magazines make it difficult for their staff, however senior and serious, to make fundamental changes in the basic structure and thrust of these publications. They can, at best, make a difference for a while on certain issues—as in the case of *Eve's Weekly* during part of the survey period, when it managed to break through commercial and other barriers to provide serious coverage to some issues.

But as long as society continues to regard women primarily as homemakers—whatever else they may do with their lives—women's magazines will continue to present and cater to them as such. It is to the credit of these magazines that, despite their obvious limitations, they have periodically tried to reflect the changing profile and aspirations of at least the urban, educated woman, their typical reader, as well as to question—albeit in a schizophrenic manner—the status quo in gender relations.

II

THE INDIAN LANGUAGE PRESS

9

Introduction

Kalpana Sharma and **Ammu Joseph**

The coverage of women's issues in the English print media and in the Indian language press differs in a number of ways. This variation can be attributed to several reasons. For one, even today English continues to be the language of the ruling class, while the indigenous languages are read and spoken by a much wider spectrum of classes. Therefore, although the English language publications have a smaller readership than several regional language publications, the former are deemed more influential because they cater to the economically and politically powerful elites.

Secondly, English has the advantage of being spoken in pockets throughout India. As a result, only English language publications can claim a 'national' status. Each regional language is naturally rooted in the history, culture and social structure of a specific part of the country. These languages boast literary traditions that match those of several major world languages. Indeed, each one of the four languages included in this study—Hindi, Bengali, Tamil and Gujarati—is spoken by more people than many international languages. But the influence of publications in these languages remains restricted to the regions where they are spoken.

However, barring those in the four metropolitan cities of Delhi, Bombay, Madras and Calcutta, where English language publications are well-established, most literate people in India read at least one local language newspaper regardless of their knowledge of English. In fact, even in the four metropolises many families read both an English and an Indian language paper. Thus the influence of regional language publications, taken together, is considerable notwithstanding the continued domination by English of the national scene.

The regional language press claims, perhaps with some justification, that it is closer to its constituency than the English language press. According to some journalists, Hindi newspapers reflect more accurately the feelings and aspirations of people living in the Hindi belt than any English language newspaper, even when the latter is published from the Hindi heartland. Says Mrinal Pande, editor of the Hindi weekly newsmagazine, *Saptahik Hindustan*, 'The English writer does not live in the same universe he is reporting about; he just pays an occasional visit.' She asserts that reportage in the English language press entails processing events through a linguistic and social filter that necessarily differentiates them from what she considers the more authentic and rooted approach of the language press.

Pande's point is borne out to some extent by the survey. A common feature of the publications in all the four regional languages, which sets them apart from the English language press, is their use of language. Indian languages are more expressive and are generally used more emotively than English. Regional language publications also have the advantage of being able to report what people have stated in their own tongue, unlike the English language press which has to rely on poor and often inadequate translations.

However, for this very reason the regional language press runs the risk of being more inflammatory than the English press. For instance, the latter has rarely been accused of arousing communal passions. On the other hand, there have been several instances where regional language publications have been indicted for directly contributing to communal tensions.

Their proximity to a more conservative and traditional readership also makes regional language publications prone to reactionary views. For example, a retrogressive edit such as the one on sati in *Jansatta* would never have appeared in a mainstream English language newspaper. Likewise, the role of the Hindi press in Rajasthan during the sati controversy, when it openly glorified the custom, was far from laudatory. At the same time, some of the most sensitively written reports on the Roop Kanwar tragedy and its implications appeared in the Hindi daily, *Navbharat Times*; its coverage was extensive and it carried several strong editorials, including one that directly challenged the position taken in the *Jansatta* edit.

Representing as they do four disparate regions, differentiated not just by language but distinct social and cultural histories, the press in the four languages selected for this study display special characteristics. For example, Gujarati women actively participated in the national movement; this ethos is reflected in the coverage of women's issues in some Gujarati newspapers. *Janmabhoomi/Pravasi*, a leading Gujarati newspaper, has carried regular columns and fiction by known feminist writers and activists for over a decade. Its publications division has also brought out books written by these women.

Despite differences in readership profiles and other characteristics, there is a common turning-point in the coverage of women's issues by the regional language and the English press. Around the mid-eighties, there was a marked upswing both in the number of items and in the quality of reporting and comment on these issues even in Indian language publications. This suggests that the women's movement, which has sometimes been criticised for being urban, middle-class, elitist (and by inference dominated by English-speaking women), did make an impact even on the regional press.

However, women's magazines in regional languages differed greatly from their English language counterparts in their coverage of the five issues surveyed. While the latter did address them in their own fashion, the former appeared to be more preoccupied with the perceived traditional interests of women, such as the home, cooking, marriage, clothes, etc., than with larger social issues.

The contents of the regional language press were analysed using the same criteria as those used for the English language press. However, in each of the four regional languages, only one newspaper, one general interest magazine and one women's magazine were studied. The individual researchers have explained the reasons for their choice of publications. Only in some instances was it possible to select and study the largest circulating publication in each category. In fact, some of the regional language researchers faced more acute problems than their English language counterparts in terms of the non-availability of back issues or the reluctance of managements to allow access. As a result, in the Gujarati section, for example, some of the data is incomplete.

A study restricted to just three publications in each of the four languages clearly does not allow credible generalisations on the nature of the press in these languages. Further, as the study is largely confined to the most widely circulated publications, representing the mainstream in the regional language press, it does not cover the plethora of smaller publications which are not necessarily governed by the same values.

The four studies that follow, therefore, touch just the tip of the iceberg. However, even this limited survey has thrown up valuable insights about the treatment of women's issues in a cross-section of the regional press. It is evident that the press, in each of these as well as other languages, requires to be studied in greater detail.

10

The Hindi Press

Shubhra Gupta

The importance of the Hindi press lies in one immutable fact: Hindi daily newspapers top the list in terms of both number of publications and circulation. According to the twenty-ninth annual report of the Registrar of Newspapers of India (RNI), Hindi claimed the highest number of newspapers (6,370) during 1984, followed by English (3,961) and other languages (Bengali, Urdu and Marathi). In circulation, too, Hindi scored over English by 1.18 crore copies.

The sheer number of Hindi dailies indicates that the news and views contained in their pages have a higher readership than those that appear in dailies published in any other language. In addition, the National Readership Survey (NRS) for 1989, conducted by the Operations Research Group (ORG), came up with some interesting figures for the Hindi-speaking belt. The share of English newspapers and magazines in the total readership of this area is 3.8 per cent, while that of Hindi publications is 15 per cent.

For the purpose of this study, the *Navbharat Times* (*NBT*) was chosen instead of the *Punjab Kesari* in the daily newspaper category. Although the former falls short of *Kesari's* circulation, its readership base in the Hindi belt is wider; *Punjab Kesari*—as its name suggests—sells mostly in Punjab. The NRS puts the *Kesari's* total readership at 2.3 per cent, compared to *NBT's* total of 1.9, but in the state-wise break-up of readership *NBT* clearly scores higher everywhere except in Punjab.

Of the Hindi newsmagazines, *Maya* was chosen in place of the Hindi edition of *India Today* because the latter only entered the market in 1987. Over the decade under study, two other leading general interest Hindi magazines, *Dharmyug* and *Saptahik Hindustan*, moved hesitantly towards coverage of political trends and 'hard' news—both as cover stories and in the rest of their contents, although their forte in the earlier years used to be non-topical feature stories and first-rate fiction. Circulation-wise, however, both these magazines are behind *Maya* and *India Today* (Hindi). The newsmagazine, *Ravivar,* managed to achieve high circulation figures when it first began in 1977 (reaching over a lakh). But its readership slipped over the years till it finally closed down just before the Lok Sabha elections in 1989.

In the third category, comprising women's magazines, *Grihshobha* is the undisputed leader both in terms of circulation and readership; its nearest rival is *Manorama*. Other women's magazines, like *Vama* and *Meri Saheli* (its masthead carries actress Hema Malini's name as editor) were never able to break the stranglehold of these two. Subsequently, in any case, *Vama* ceased publication.

NAVBHARAT TIMES

The *Navbharat Times*, published by Bennett Coleman & Co. Ltd., was the only one of the three chosen publications which provided fairly comprehensive coverage of the selected issues over a decade. The frequency of reports on women's issues and the increasing space given to women's problems in the paper reflect the growing awareness of these problems in society and the media. Also, the paper rescued women-related issues from the 'mahila pristh' (women's pages) and brought them instead into the main editorial pages.

The process of granting editorial respectability to women's issues—reflected in the allocation of more space, prominence and seriousness—received a major boost through the efforts of the then editor-in-chief Rajendra Mathur (who passed away in April 1991). Executive editor S.P. Singh (who subsequently left the paper) dates it approximately to 1983 onwards:

> Around 1983-84, some important amendments to the laws governing rape and dowry were made; these developments were naturally reflected in our pages in the form of edits and editorial page articles. It had nothing to do with my ascendancy but my being there helped

because I do think such issues should be dealt with much more seriousness.

Dowry Deaths

In the late seventies and through the eighties, reports about burning brides were treated routinely in newspapers; they were generally placed inconspicuously on inside pages, usually under city briefs. Headlines like 'Yet Another Woman Burns To Death' ('Ek aur jal kar mari') were symptomatic of the callousness of both society, which was killing its brides, and the media, which was content to act as a recording device. It is significant that, in the five months chosen for study, of the twenty-four stories related to dowry deaths, only three were special stories (features), two were letters, while the rest were all routine reports.

Interestingly, several other small news items which reported deaths by burning did not mention dowry at all. For instance, a brief report on 17 March 1979, headlined 'Aag laga li' ('Sets Herself Alight'), read like this: 'A 16-year-old Seva Nagar resident was admitted to hospital with severe burns. She had poured kerosene on her body and set fire to herself. The girl is in no condition to give a statement.' End of item. In another brief (14 August 1983), headlined 'Pati aur nanad ne jalane ki koshish kari' ('Husband And Sister-in-law Try To Burn'), the burnt girl reportedly complained of harassment. Again, there was no mention of dowry.

The first item which actually mentions dowry is a 19 March 1979 story on page four: 'Kingsway Camp resident Sita Devi filed a report accusing her son-in-law and his family members of having burnt her daughter for dowry. Enquiry is underway.' The item appeared clubbed with other city briefs.

The issue made it to the front page twice. In the first instance, a box item (22 August 1983) featured a gazetted officer in Lucknow who became a rickshaw puller to gather enough money to dower his two sisters. The second report (31 August 1983) informed readers about a Supreme Court judgment which laid down that any demand made by the bridegroom's family during the wedding ceremony would be termed a dowry demand and be deemed a culpable offence.

Other than these few examples, most dowry-related stories were tucked away inconspicuously. In one instance, a small item, 'Dahej ke karan bahu ki hatya' ('Bride Murdered For Dowry'), was placed among the classified advertisements on page two (8 August 1983)!

Except for three features, there were no editorials or serious, analytical pieces on the subject in the specified period. The first of these, 'Dahej ko mitane ka upaay: prem vivah' ('Love Marriage: A Way To Eradicate Dowry') by Akhileshwar, appeared in the Sunday magazine section, *Ravivarta*, on 8 August 1983.

The article reported the outcry against the evils of dowry in recent years but said that it had by and large been ineffective. It went on to suggest that there was a gap between the vocal critics of the dowry system, who came from affluent, English-educated backgrounds, and the average Indian. If the decision to marry were left to the girl and the boy, it pointed out, there would be no dowry problem. Questioning whether society was ready for this solution, it concluded: 'Dahej pratha hamaari dharmik aasthaaon se judi hai' ('The practice of dowry is inextricably linked to our religious beliefs').

The other article, a two-part feature, was also carried in *Ravivarta*. It appeared on 7 March 1984, the eve of the International Women's Day. Written by Gurcharan and Bharat Dogra, with the first part headlined 'Chote gaon ka bada karishma: Dahej ko sada ke liye vidaa' ('Small Village's Big Miracle: Farewell To Dowry'), it described the unique effort of a small Haryana village to abolish dowry. The second part discussed the failure of a similar effort in another village, Bahadurgarh in Rohtak district, also in Haryana.

Going by the stories which appeared in the *Navbharat Times*, it would seem that no editorial effort was made to place the practice of dowry and dowry-related deaths in the larger social context or to extend the coverage of this issue to the main news pages of the newspaper. Reports did appear after the event (on a dowry death, a demonstration, a statement by the authorities); but the fact that there were no serious, well-researched articles exploring the reasons for the pernicious practice and no editorials (at least in the period when this issue was in the limelight) indicates the low priority given to this issue. This is particularly surprising for a newspaper read in North India where the dowry death syndrome first came to light.

Rape

Of the eighteen stories published by *NBT* on this issue, sixteen were routine reports. Most of them documented the fact of a rape, sometimes giving a few details about how, where and when it happened. These stories were usually placed on the city page. Occasional reports—dealing with a demonstration against the rising rape graph, a memorandum to the Prime Minister, the government's assurance on steps to be taken for tackling violence against women or amendments to the rape law—did appear on more prominent pages. Typical of the city page reports was a one-paragraph brief headlined: 'One Arrested On Charge Of Raping A British Woman' (15 February 1980) or a report on the rape of a Harijan girl in the village of Lehranpur (21 February 1980).

However, a month later, on 9 March 1980, the demonstration against rape by various women's groups, students' organisations and trade unions of Delhi, on the International Women's Day (8 March) made it to page one.

On the same day, 9 March, the Sunday magazine section, *Ravivarta,* carried the first serious, hard-hitting story against rape. Written by Ashok Ojha and headlined 'Har baar purush apradhi hota hai aur nari shikar' ('The Man Is Guilty Every Time And The Woman A Victim'), it made a strong case against the weakness of rape laws in the country. The woman in the dock during the trial, it said, becomes the target of abuse, with barbed comments about her 'character,' which is doubly unjust after the crime of rape. The article lamented the fact that the 'willingness' of the woman is linked directly to the presence or absence of injury marks on her person; the horrible fact of rape is side-lined in the process. The writer condemned the prevailing male-centric, opinionated approach, affirming that in cases of rape the man is always guilty.

A week later, on 18 March 1980, a memorandum submitted to the Prime Minister by several women's organisations was reported on page one. The government's request to the Law Commission to devise a plan for the protection of women all over the country was carried as the third lead of the front page on 24 March 1980. The report stated the government's intentions of amending the penal code in accordance with the Commission's suggestions.

The only article on the subject to appear on the edit page during this period (29 March 1980) discussed the inadequacies of the law against rape and demanded effective steps to check such crimes. It also suggested the institution of in-camera trials for rape.

With only two serious articles on rape appearing in the *Navbharat Times* during this period, it would seem that the human dimension was not taken serious note of by the paper. The routine reports read like any other local event; and, like the stories on dowry deaths, were frequently placed among other items of city news, often fashioned from police handouts which include reports on suicides, burglaries and other crimes as well as accidents.

The Shah Bano Controversy

The Supreme Court judgment in favour of Shah Bano's plea for maintenance created a stir all over the country but the clamour from Muslim fundamentalists dragged it into a controversy which ultimately negated its effect—it forced a weak government to pass the Muslim Women (Protection of Rights on Divorce) Bill. Introduced in Parliament amidst severe disapproval from women's groups, intellectual and public opinion, as well as a section of the Muslim leadership, the Bill was an attempt to reverse what the Supreme Court had sought to categorically establish: that under Section 125 of the Criminal Procedure Code, all women were equal and that husbands—Muslim or otherwise—of indigent divorced women had to pay towards their maintenance.

Commenting on Shah Bano's apparent retraction of her original stand and her call for a reversal of the Supreme Court judgment in her favour, a lead edit (19 November 1985) in *NBT* said:

> The historic Supreme Court judgment has created ripples of consternation among conservative Muslim elements. Shehnaaz Sheikh's case is still undecided. Meanwhile, in Kerala, Zuleikha Bibi has been threatened with a horsewhip by the Muslim Jammat. Here we were thinking that such retrogressive elements would be shown up for what they are. Now comes an astonishing reversal: Shah Bano's thumbprint has appeared on a statement which demands that the judgment be taken back, calling it interference in Muslim Personal Law. Under what conditions did a woman, who is 65 and illiterate, affix a thumbprint to such a blueprint can well be imagined.
>
> But we cannot ... laugh at the people who drafted the statement—these are the people who are talking of Shariat courts, to be run by the All India Muslim Personal Law Board, which alone would judge the personal problems of Muslims. These can at best be called out of court settlements. Otherwise what would be the veracity of our courts? That this situation has come to pass is the direct result of equivocation on the government's part (dulmul sarkar ki neeti). It calls for a struggle against all those who want to cash in under the guise of religion and sectarianism.

A superb cartoon in *NBT* (22 November 1985) showed Rajiv Gandhi in a burqa looking coyly at the Muslim vote; the caption at the bottom read: 'No interference with Muslim Personal Law.'

Two small stories (28 November and 25 December 1985) placed the whole issue in a human context. The first reported that a woman had been awarded Rs 150 a month as compensation from her husband who had remarried. The possibility of the Shah Bano case having influenced the favourable judgment was highlighted. The second story had a similar focus: Asahrbi, who had been thrown out of her house by her husband without a divorce, had been awarded Rs 150 a month as compensation. Another woman, Shahnaz Bi, had been awarded Rs 100 a month from her former husband Yusuf. The meagre amounts for which these women had to move the courts speaks volumes about their profound deprivation and miserable living conditions.

The plethora of letters on the subject published by the *NBT* reflected the conflict of opinion among people at large. While a few called it anti-Islam, most were in favour of the judgment and its implications. Among them, one from Sayid Bashir Ahmad of Sonepat (15 March 1986) was immensely moving: 'I was in my mother's womb when my father said "Talaq, talaq, talaq," and sent my mother out on the streets to beg. Where were these protectors of Islam then?' It was the cause of such women that the Supreme Court championed and the Bill demolished.

NBT was vociferous in its disapproval of the Bill. In a lead edit (24 February 1986), it castigated the government for bowing to obscurantism and fundamentalism; calling the Bill an ill-judged, hurried move, the edit warned against its devastating impact on women for whom the Supreme Court judgment had come as a beacon of hope. By this action, said the edit, the Prime Minister had gone back on his word and betrayed the cause of women for political reasons.

Another edit commended the 26 February resignation of union minister Arif Mohammed Khan on this issue. Appropriately headlined 'Arif ka mantrimandal ko talaq' (Arif Divorces Cabinet), the 28 February edit called it a 'historic resignation and a principled gesture,' a shot in the arm for the rights of Muslim women.

Yet another edit (9 March) raised doubts about those whose advice had been sought for formulating the draft bill. It asked whether the Shariat Board and fundamentalist opinion mattered more to Rajiv Gandhi than the divorced women themselves who had gone to him to petition their case. Nowhere in Islam, claimed the edit, are the wife's family and the Wakf Boards held responsible for her after a divorce.

The Bill, it concluded, was an insult to Islam and sanctioned excesses in the name of religion.

Also powerful was an edit page main article (13 March 1986) by Suryakant Bali. Headlined 'Muslim Women's Bill: Congressi and Computeri Uttaron Ke Pare,' it stated that the Muslim women's question was beyond the Congress and its computers. The article analysed Rajiv Gandhi's attitude towards secularism and found him wanting. Without a deep sense of history, it stated, no party or leader can deal with *sampradayikta* (communalism).

Female Foeticide

The problems raised by the misuse of the amniocentesis test, such as female foeticide, did not find much space in the columns of *NBT*. Some ascribe the paucity of articles on this subject in the paper to the fact that it was seen as an urban, higher income group phenomenon. But this could well be too simplistic a reading, especially in view of the growing evidence that the tests are not confined to major cities.

According to writer and editor Mrinal Pande, another reason why relatively little space was devoted to the issue in *NBT* could be the fact that it is a medical subject; since most writers are not conversant with these matters, they hesitate to write much about them. But this argument is only applicable to reports on the technicalities of the test; it does not hold for discussions on its social implications, its philosophical assumptions and its impact on the personal choices of women.

It could be argued that for a majority of *NBT* readers, amniocentesis is not as endemic a problem as matters relating to the working mother and her children, birth control and family planning, expectant mothers' health and baby care. It must be admitted that on such questions *NBT* has scored over many of its rivals. However, the five articles which did appear were uncomprisingly against the practice of sex determination.

The damages caused by the test were taken note of in a lead edit on 7 January 1988, shortly after the Maharashtra government's decision to ban sex determination tests. While holding out a word of praise for the state government, the edit argued that the ban was not enough. The prejudice against women, in a society which claims to worship them, is so deep-rooted that it would take time for people to understand that the birth of a girl is not an act of divine misfortune. It pointed out that the misuse of the medical technique of amniocentesis had led to horrific results. From 1977 onwards, several clinics in Bombay and elsewhere had committed female foeticide in the garb of amniocentesis. The edit suggested that doctors should be made to pledge that they would not reveal the sex of the foetus and would recommend abortion only in cases where an incurable disease had been detected. Foeticide, it concluded, is not just an evil—it is a crime.

The Roop Kanwar Tragedy

Unlike the sporadic reportage on dowry deaths and rape, the coverage of Roop Kanwar's death in Deorala in the *Navbharat Times* was both comprehensive and sensitive. It carried 177 news items on this subject. While the stories kept the readers apprised of events as they unfolded, the strong editorials as well as the well-written analytical articles provoked them to think during the months when the tragedy was the focus of media attention.

NBT made its stand clear in several editorials, denouncing the incident in unequivocal terms. The first of these (19 September 1987) took exception to the editorial in *Jansatta*, another prominent Hindi daily (published by the *Indian Express* group), which came out in support of sati *pratha* (the practice of sati).

(The *Jansatta* editorial, a page one double-column piece which raised hackles all over the country, suggested that Roop Kanwar's act, her 'sati,' was neither a question of women's rights nor of discrimination between men and women. The issue, instead, was one of religious and social beliefs. To condemn sati *pratha*, it said, was to completely misunderstand Indian *parampara* and *dharm* (tradition and religion). Such criticism was confined to those influenced by Christianity (*Isai dharm*) and Western education. According to the edit, the practice of sati could make sense only to those who believed that death did not come as the end: that it was just a transitionary phase in the soul's journey from this life to another. Coming when it did, the editorial was seen as both retrogressive and provocative; the edit writer clearly did not see anything wrong in Roop Kanwar's death.)

The *NBT's* lead edit declared that those who were glorifying sati by citing religious texts and tradition were no less than fascists. It pointed out that to support the practice of sati was tantamount to regarding the woman as a man's personal property, with no right to live after the man's death. 'Yeh ek gahri purush asuraksha se paida hua rog hai' (This is born out of men's deep sense of insecurity), it said.

Several articles written by *Navbharat Times* correspondents Manimala and Vishnu Khare, as well as a number of other writers, exposed the hollowness of the so-called religious and social beliefs which justified such a heinous act by portraying it as not merely excusable but desirable. The anomaly presented by a nation heading for the twenty-first century while consigning its women to their husbands' funeral pyres was highlighted in these articles.

Manimala's impassioned writing on the issue was impressive. In a series of well-researched stories, she established that there was no eye-witness to support the claims of Roop Kanwar's parents-in-laws that she voluntarily committed sati. The writer also pointed out that the tragedy was being used to extract political mileage and the media response in general was questionable.

In a half-page story (4 October 1987), headlined 'Gunahgaar poora Deorala gaon hai' (The Whole Village Of Deorala Is Guilty), Manimala put together several first-person accounts of those who were present at the time of the 'sati'. Questioning the 'voluntary' nature of the act, which Roop Kanwar's parents-in-law were at pains to emphasise, the author stated:

> The truth is that all of Deorala, including her in-laws, wanted Roop Kanwar's death (Maut chahiye thi, zindagi nahin). The question of whether she did it voluntarily or not is pointless: she died because 300 people willed it and these people are answerable for her death.

In an edit page article on 12 October 1987, the same author discussed the politicisation of Roop Kanwar's death in 'Roop Kanwar aur Rajnaitik dal' (`Roop Kanwar And Political Parties'). She concluded that all parties were equally guilty of letting political considerations prevail over humanitarian concerns.

In 'Deorala ki Roop Kanwar aur akhbaron ki bhumika' (Roop Kanwar Of Deorala And The Role Of Newspapers), which appeared the next day (13 October 1987), Manimala pointed out that virtually all mediapersons automatically used the word 'sati' instead of suicide or murder. She said, 'For us to launch discussions on sati in this day and age is in itself shameful. Today we must discuss why it wasn't stopped.'

In the 13 November 1987 issue of *Ravivarta*, the Sunday magazine of the paper, her article, headlined 'Kisne suna hai stree ka sahi swar?' ('Who Has Heard The Real Voice of Woman'?), took a look at injustices against women. Roop Kanwar's 'sati,' she wrote, negated the nation's claims of what it had so far accomplished in terms of education, administration, progressive thinking, etc. (To translate loosely in the above manner what was originally written as 'Shiksha, prashasan aur naitik tatha baudhik vichar' unfortunately takes away from the punch and tone of the original article).

The hands which lit the pyre are now turning the pages of the Hindu dharmashastras to support their action. Have the shastracharyas (masters of the shastras) ever listened to the voice of women? Men have been speaking for centuries and they have lost the capacity to listen; it is they who determine the lives and dreams of women. A bride's father gives away his daughter to another man ('*kanyadaan*') who takes her to use as he wishes and then proceeds to justify her life and death.

This and the other articles by Manimala reveal a deep consciousness about the roots of the issue. They put into ironic perspective the nation's claims of marching towards a progressive future even as it insists on observing and justifying the hidebound traditions governing the lives of its women.

In an op-ed (opposite editorial page) article on 25 September 1987, Vishnu Khare quoted from the Vedas to disprove the myth that 'sati' was in any way sanctioned by them. The gist of his argument was: 'Vidhwa ko sati banana avaidik hai' (To cause a widow to commit sati is against the Vedas).

In the 27 September 1987 edition of *Ravivarta* (Sunday magazine section), an analytical feature by Lata Karandikar raised several disturbing questions about a society which condones sati. She asked:

Isn't sati another form of dowry death? Wasn't Roop Kanwar's 'sati' regarded as a question of social prestige for her parents, in-laws and for Deorala? Roop Kanwar's father wasn't illiterate. Yet he claimed that after the 'sati,' Roop Kanwar had become a devi (goddess) and had increased his social prestige (samaajik pratishtha badhaayi hai).

When the people themselves are deifying 'sati' and holding *chunri mahotsavs*, the author pointed out, it is not entirely fair to blame the government, the courts and the police. According to Karandikar, sati is clearly connected to our social beliefs:

None of our shastras talk of sati as an imperative for a widow. But in our society widows are being forced to die daily deaths because there is no place for them; and then there is Roop Kanwar who is actually consigned to the flames. What is the difference? Nothing will change unless society's attitudes do.

Two op-ed articles, in the 29 September 1987 edition, looked at Roop Kanwar's 'sati' from another angle. In the first piece, headlined 'Dasvin tak padhi sati roop kanwar ki siksha,' educationist Krishna Kumar examined the failure of the education system which produced a Roop Kanwar. 'Even after ten years of association with such a system, she couldn't protest, she couldn't take a stand. Of what use is such an education?' he asked. The article by Kiran Arora, headlined 'Aarthik Daastan Banati hai Vidhva ko Sati,' attributed the degradation of women in many forms, in this case 'sati', to their economic dependence. The article made a case for monetary selfhood, which would go a long way towards curbing exploitation, according to the author.

In a brilliantly satirical piece (6 October 1987), the paper's ace columnist Sharad Joshi (who died recently) took a look at the tamasha (carnival) created out of the tragedy. Headlined 'Deorala ka arthik rang chokha ho gaya'('Deorala's Economic Prospects Brighten'), the article pointed out that the 'sati,' by attracting crowds and the curious hordes, had brought undreamt of prosperity to Deorala. Other villages, it noted with biting sarcasm, were busy praying for their own sati to invite similar bounty. In a similar view, Joshi's earlier column of 29 September, unequivocal in its assertion that full-fledged murder had been committed in the name of sati, observed that the 'sati-*sthal*' had been deified to boost 'dharmik tourism.'

On the whole, the *Navbharat Times* showed a distinct increase in serious, research-based stories on women in the post-1984-85 period. This quantitative as well as qualitative improvement after the mid-decade mark reflects the concerted efforts of women's organisations and rising public and media consciousness about the miserable condition of women.

The quality of coverage given to the Roop Kanwar tragedy best exemplifies this heartening trend. It demonstrates the contribution a committed woman journalist, like Manimala, and a sensitive editor can make to the debate on a delicate issue—one which touches religion, that too practised by the majority of its readers. *NBT's* stand on the 'sati' issue was notable especially in comparison to other Hindi newspapers, like *Jansatta* or the *Rajasthan Patrika*, which tried to justify the practice in the name of tradition.

The progressive change in *NBT's* position on such issues can best be seen by comparing its coverage of the dowry deaths issue with that of 'sati'. In the former case, it had carried an article suggesting that much of the fuss about dowry was being made by urban, English-speaking women; in the Roop Kanwar instance, not once did the paper suggest, as had several other Hindi newspapers (and some writers in the English press), that only westernised urban women were objecting to the practice.

NBT continued to devote much greater space to women's issues in the latter part of the eighties. Well-known women columnists wrote about a whole range of problems faced by women: the price of independence, the impact of development, occupational hazards at the workplace, and the double burden borne by the majority of them. Editorials commented on laws affecting women or their image in the media.

MAYA

Maya, published by Mitra Prakashan of Allahabad, began as a high quality literary journal in 1929; after completing nearly fifty years in this form, it was converted into a newsmagazine in 1978. Shortly thereafter, it became the highest selling Hindi newsmagazine. Its monopoly of the market was unaffected by the arrival of *Ravivar* and continued till the Hindi edition of *India Today* hit the stands. Since then its readership has dipped.

The reasons are not difficult to gauge. Since its launch as a newsmagazine in 1979, *Maya* has concentrated on news from the states where it has maximum sales. Even now, its highest circulation is in Bihar. So, in an average *Maya* issue, there are always three or four hardcore political stories on Bihar, Rajasthan and U.P., apart from a couple of articles based on events in the capital. There was not much change in its editorial content over the decade under study. It struck a winning formula by publishing, in addition to reports on current events, the misdeeds of political figures (especially their sexual misdemeanours) and salacious stories about film stars as well as other public figures.

India Today in Hindi, on the other hand, relies upon its English edition to provide the reader with a much wider spectrum of news and views. It is also much better produced than *Maya,* whose bad printing and non-glossy paper are thus shown up to its disadvantage. This has spurred the latter to improve its layout and paper quality.

When women and women's issues make an appearance in *Maya,* they tend to be treated lightly and with damaging frivolity. The style and content of the women-related stories border on the tawdry and vulgar. In the four or five years prior to this survey, however, this overt misuse of women had decreased. In fact, a few years ago, *Maya* began its first column by a woman writer, Mamta Kalia, who discusses serious women-related issues, among other subjects, in this slot. But there has been no corresponding effort to publish full-length articles on the issues under consideration in this study. *Maya* still does not give any weightage to stories which are not political or connected with political persons.

The 15 November 1985 edition was fairly typical of the *Maya* editorial mix—a lead story on Bihar; a report on how the brother of the then chief minister of Madhya Pradesh, Motilal Vora, acquired land; another article on the threat of nuclear attack from Pakistan; and, finally, a feature headlined 'The Kiss And Our Actors And Actresses' (focussing on the question: will they or won't they get AIDS?). The last story went into the details of Rock Hudson's death due to the HIV virus and claimed that film stars in Bombay are, consequently, petrified of kissing on screen.

Since the mid-1980s, other Hindi general interest magazines, such as *Dharmyug* and *Saptahik Hindustan,* seem to have taken the cue from the changes in newspapers, both in terms of the growing volume of coverage given to women's issues as well as the seriousness with which they are handled. Such issues now have a different tone and content and find increasing space in these two features magazines. In fact, Mrinal Pande, after taking over the editorship of *Saptahik Hindustan*, has been using her past experience of writing on women's issues and editing *Vama* to good effect; the magazine now carries topical stories on women as opposed to the earlier predilection for just using beautiful female faces to adorn the cover.

A newsmagazine which stood out for its progressive stand on women's issues was *Ravivar*. Right from its inception in 1977, it made consistent efforts to deal with women and feminist concerns with due seriousness. A detailed look at some of the stories done by the magazine supports this observation. Unfortunately, this magazine was closed down in late 1989, just before the Lok Sabha polls.

In the periods chosen for study, there were only three stories in *Maya* on the selected topics: two on Shah Bano, one on sati and none on the other three issues.

The Shah Bano Controversy

The 15 March 1986 edition featured an interview with Shah Bano which did not find mention in the strapline (the band on the top-right corner) of the cover. The correspondent's question to the old woman, asking what she expected from her visit to Delhi ('Dilli aaker kis tarah ki keemat vasoolna chahati hain?'), indicated slight hostility.

The next edition highlighted the Muslim Women (Protection of Rights on Divorce) Bill on the cover. The vexed question of Personal Law was dealt with at length in interviews with Muslim leaders and leading political figures. The accent was on the political implications of the government's proposed Bill; Shah Bano was mentioned only in passing.

An exception was a story on the Wakf Board which appeared on 3 June 1986 (out of the study period). It looked sympathetically at the problems faced by divorced Muslim women and questioned whether the Wakf Boards were in a position to deal competently with compensation. It condemned the Rajiv Gandhi government for passing a retrograde, regressive Bill, describing it as 'giving in to the Shahabuddins and Banatwalas.'

The Roop Kanwar Tragedy

The only feature on the sati issue during the period surveyed appeared, belatedly, in January 1988. It comprised a one and a half-page interview with Swami Agnivesh (a social reform-oriented man of religion), accompanied by a factual report on the government's steps against Agnivesh's *padayatra*, which contrasted the progressive viewpoint of the Arya Samaj with that of Rajput fundamentalists.

Going by the absence of serious, well-researched articles on women, it is clear that no editorial thought was given to issues of concern to them. *Maya's* failure in this particular respect parallels the tendency of most Hindi magazines and journals to give women's issues the go-by unless they can be used as fodder for gossipy titbits or sexual titillation.

For instance, an article on modelling in the January 1979 edition interspersed pictures of half-clothed women, looking provocatively at the reader, with the text which addressed that all-important question: Is it necessary for models to reveal all? The cover story in the same edition was on women and politics. There was no attempt at serious analysis; the article was full of unpleasant speculation and innuendo—who favours whom, which powerful male politicians play godfathers to whom and who, presumably, goes to bed with whom.

RAVIVAR

The coverage of women's issues in *Ravivar*, also a general interest magazine, was markedly different from that in *Maya*. *Ravivar* began the first serious, issue-based column by a woman, on women, in a Hindi newsmagazine. In fact, when Alka Saxena, encouraged by editor Udayan Sharma, began the column, entitled 'Saheli,' in 1984, she was still a post-graduate student. It was an investigative column, another first, in the sense that it was based on spot reports and interviews instead of armchair analyses. Saxena later joined the magazine as a trainee reporter and did some extremely interesting, path-breaking stories on women.

In the edition dated 27 April-3 May 1986, 'Saheli' focussed on the story of a woman telephone operator in Gujarat who was refused maternity leave on the grounds that her marital status was not stated clearly on any of her certificates at the time she took the job. The woman's explanation was that she had simply retained her maiden name after marriage; she had, in fact, been married for five years. In the ensuing exchanges, the then minister for women and youth affairs, Margaret Alva, wrote to the then home minister, P. Chidambaram, for a just hearing of the case. The telephone department had claimed that the operator had been living with a married man and so was not eligible for maternity leave under central secretariat rules. The column discussed the implications of the tussle between the operator and the administration.

Ravivar's triumph was a story published after the landmark judgment in the Maya Tyagi rape case, accompanied by an interview with the victim herself (14-20 February 1988). The policemen who killed her husband and gang-raped her in Baghpat (50 km from Delhi) were indicted, eight years after the incident occurred in June 1980, in what was one of the strongest judgments in legal history—six were awarded the death sentence and four got life sentences. The interview, supplemented by Saxena's account of how she reached a reluctant Maya Tyagi, of the fiercely protective attitude of her family and the animus against all presspersons in the village, constituted a moving document— the story of a woman who was publicly widowed, humiliated and raped.

Another unusual story by Alka Saxena took her to a thirteen-year-old Adivasi girl, who had given birth to a baby daughter, in a remote village in Vidisha district of Madhya Pradesh. Ramvati, herself a child, did not know how she had become pregnant; she did not know what it was to become a mother. She told *Ravivar* that the Thakur, sixty-five-year-old Vir Singh Dang who owned the small outhouse she and her mother lived in, took her inside forcibly and 'did all this.' 'Ham jante nahi the ki kya baat hai, ki baccha ayega' ('I did not know what it was, I did not know there would be a baby'). She said she had kept quiet because the Thakur had warned her not to tell her mother. According to her mother, Tunda Bai, it was only when Ramvati's belly began to show that she suspected something. But by then it was too late. Tunda Bai accused Vir Singh of raping her daughter. The Thakur denied the charge, claiming that it was a conspiracy.

The report, appropriately headlined 'Bacchima' ('Child Mother'), brought out the slow response of the district administration, the milieu of the village and the conditions in which Ramvati lived. That such an incident could occur at the end of the International Women's Decade reveals the continuing oppression of Indian women.

In an editorial in the same edition, Udayan Sharma commented on Ramvati's world:

> This issue has nothing to do with Neena Gupta (the actress who became an unwed mother with great pride) nor with those scores of teenage girls in the U.S. who have children because of early knowledge of sex. This has to do with a 13-year-old girl who was forced into motherhood. But because such issues have nothing to do with a political system which runs on notes and votes, there is no one to hear Ramvati's case or to ensure that justice is done.

Sharma made the pertinent point that if Ramvati had lived in Lucknow or Delhi or Bombay, the media would have taken more interest instead of just dismissing her in five cursory lines:

> Women's organisations would have demonstrated at the Boat Club. But Ramvati lives in a remote village in Madhya Pradesh and she is unaware of her rights. Women's organisations have confined their

attention to Delhi and other big cities: will they ever get out of the city lights and go to far-flung villages where those Ramvatis live?

Another story, by Milapchand Dandiya in the edition dated 27 November-2 December 1988, followed up *Ravivar's* August 1988 expose of the family of a member of the Rajasthan Legislative Assembly which had been killing its newborn baby girls for three generations. The original report had resulted in a case against the MLA, Brajendra Singh, his grandmother and other members of his family. This follow-up piece showed how the government had dragged its feet, refusing to accept the facts even after an inquiry had established strong evidence of the crimes.

There are several other examples of *Ravivar's* investigative reports focussing on women, their plight and problems, as well as their development and advancement.

GRIHSHOBHA

Published by Delhi Press, publishers of the English women's magazine *Women's Era*, *Grihshobha* (launched in 1979) is the highest selling women's magazine in Hindi. An average edition of *Grihshobha*, like its popular competitor *Manorama*, contains regular columns on 'personal' problems (concerning sartorial, social and sexual matters), fashion, knitting or sewing patterns (depending on the season), film and gossip columns, agony and advice columns, several pages of recipes, as well as three or four short stories.

The predominant concerns of the market leaders in the Hindi women's magazine segment are the 'good woman' and 'marriage'. Most features, repeated in one form or another in each edition, revolve around one intrinsic and immutable fact: that the Indian woman today faces challenges which would have been unimaginable even a decade ago. The pressures have changed; she may now have to go out and supplement the husband's earnings or even opt to pursue a chosen career. However, according to these magazines, such pressures have to co-exist with the values cherished by generations of women, epitomised in the belief that the only lasting and fulfilling happiness a woman can achieve is to get married and stay married.

Of course, every other fortnight, stories are woven around certain uncomfortable social realities—that not all marriages are happy or successful, that the divorce rate is going up, that there are such things as adulterous relationships. But all through these articles there runs a strong moralistic vein which expresses regret that such things actually come to pass. Their message, perhaps not spelt out in black and white but implicit nevertheless, is: get your act together and fall in line because otherwise not only you but your children will also suffer, as will your parents and unmarried sisters.

Both *Grihshobha* and *Manorama* often come out with special editions focussing on subjects like 'Ten Ways To Keep Your Marriage Happy,' 'The Importance Of Love In Marriage,' 'How To Deal With An Errant Husband,' etc. (Needless to say, neither has anything to say about the possibility of a woman desiring change in her marital circumstances.) Although the magazines are clearly targeted at the woman reader, they address her vis-a-vis the man around whom her life revolves. Not surprisingly, both *Grihshobha* and *Manorama* have a large number of male readers who follow with salacious interest readers' queries on sexual problems or, say, features on such topics as 'Different Kinds Of Kisses' ('Tarah Tarah ke Chumban'), and so on.

During the period surveyed, there were in abundance special editions on Holi and Diwali, cosmetics and beauty care, as well as sex (the problems and joys of). Immensely popular columns, with contributions by readers, which continued during these periods were: 'Meri Suhaagraat' ('My Wedding Night') and 'Hai, Main Sharam se Laal Hui' ('Oh, I Went Red With Embarrassment'). Articles in the former column contained coy references to the sexual act, much of the space taken up by the preliminaries which lead up to consummation. Most of the incidents described in the latter column had to do with something 'naughty' said to or done with a fiance or husband or in the home of the parents-in-law.

The treatment of sexual mores in these magazines is a fascinating mix of the frank and the coy. Words like 'masturbation' or *'hast maithun,'* seen as *aprakritik kriya* or an unnatural act, as well as 'virginity', 'semen', etc., are decidedly out of the closet. But normally every article begins with several initial paragraphs devoted to fudging before it comes to the point. Some particularly bad pieces read like soft-core pornography, negating any educational intent that the magazine may have had.

There is no doubt that magazines like *Grihshobha* and *Manorama* are often the only convenient source of this sort of information for their readers. The contents mix is evidently monitored to keep both ends of the middle class happily engrossed. Columns on 'Meri Suhaagraat' ('My

First Night') and other first person experiences which involve romance, love and passion are read by all women. In the useful information bracket there are features on subjects like 'How To Set A Table' and 'Table Manners' (providing instructions on such niceties as what to do with a napkin ring once the napkin is out and whether ice-cream should be eaten with a fork or a spoon).

The accent of these magazines is primarily on women maintaining beautiful homes, making interesting things, keeping themselves pretty for their men and keeping their beds warm for them. In at least ten issues of *Grihshobha* over the past four years, the theme of the cover feature has been: It is a sin to say 'no' to an amorous husband. The argument is that since men are endowed with carnal desires, it is their right to claim fulfilment of these and, therefore, that to refuse them does not become the *adarsh patni* (ideal wife). The authors of these articles hint darkly that to spurn a husband is to send him straight into another woman's arms. Clearly, the message is: If the reader does not want such disasters to befall her, she would do well to always be welcoming and acquiescent towards her husband. Nowhere is it acknowledged that the woman may also have her own rhythms of desire and passion. In short, according to these magazines, a woman's sexuality depends upon the husband's advances.

According to observers of the Hindi press, this reflects the sort of sexual half-life led by the majority of women. Most of them have been conditioned to view sexuality in itself as negative—something that is confined to prostitutes and the 'other woman'. Sexual union with a man other than the husband or before marriage is a sin; with the husband, sex serves a worthy end: procreation. This is probably why the slightly hectoring tone of the articles and short stories goes down well with the readers.

An adulterous relationship always comes to a sorry end in the fiction published by these magazines, serving the dual purpose of allowing forbidden pathways to be explored even while warning against them. In other words, reading about such issues (seldom tolerated even in conversations in most homes) satisfies the readers' curiosity and, in most cases, sublimates their half-felt longing for such adventures.

Columns dealing with 'personal problems' provide an interesting index of the kind of confusion and anxiety caused by the prevalent sexual code comprising guilt and repression. In answer to one question, for example, one advice column tried to persuade the reader that kissing was not a dirty activity.

A letter from a twenty-two-year-old woman stated that she was in the habit of *aprakritik* (unnatural) sex and also that by mistake she had established *samlingi* relations (the references were obviously to masturbation and lesbianism in that order). She wanted to know whether she should still get married and whether she would contract AIDS as a result of her activities. The editorial confidante praised the woman for giving up these 'unnatural' acts and warned her not to revert to them in the future. The agony aunt also reassured her with the assertion that AIDS does not spread very quickly among women.

Another letter-writer was assured that her attraction for her male domestic help was merely sexual and that a marriage between a *naukar* (servant) and a *maalik* (master) could never work.

A wife who complained that her husband was habituated to *hast maithun* (masturbation) and spurned sex every day because of his habit was told: 'After marriage, most men give up masturbation on their own; you must arouse him by your efforts.' The matter-of-fact manner in which these columns discuss masturbation as the norm among unmarried males is quite startling. In fact, it is doubtful whether any English language periodical, except perhaps the 'men's magazine,' *Debonair*, would discuss this practice so openly and clearly.

This schizophrenia is characteristic of almost all the fiction, articles and columns in *Grihshobha* which deal with sex. On the one hand, there is an amazing frankness about the usage of specific terms and explicit examples; on the other, there is a constant attempt to counter this with the moralistic tone adopted in the editorial perspective.

Tender romance took up a great deal of space in *Grihshobha* during this period; the innocent, wistful approach to love, leading inevitably to marriage, is virtually propagated as the sanctioned manner of wooing. It seems as if the readers of *Grihshobha* are encouraged to go in for 'love' and 'romance' before marriage if this leads to the altar; they are also furnished with tips on how to keep these ingredients alive after the knot is tied because they are essential for a happy married life.

So there are countless articles on such topics as: how to keep husbands happy, whether newly-wed women should keep going off to their parents' homes (they shouldn't), whether they should work if their husbands feel threatened (they shouldn't), the importance of candle-lit, intimate evenings with the husband, the question of sex appeal and how to acquire it, the advisability of not telling the husband of her own past indiscretions but bearing up nobly if he had had other relationships, and so on.

Jobs or careers and the 'new' challenges and problems that follow in their wake were the focus of attention in several editions of *Grihshobha* during the survey period but these issues were clearly not perceived as the most important aspects of a woman's life. Their overall perspective seems to be that a woman stepping outside her house can expect to be as constrained as she is within the home; that, in fact, she has to be constantly on the watch in her behaviour with male colleagues and superiors and careful about what she does with her salary. *Grihshobha* does not approve of too much independence: small rebellions are acceptable in the name of progress but any action which militates against male suzerainty or the rights of in-laws are definitely frowned upon.

Middle-class Indian mores are assiduously encouraged by *Grihshobha*. In a September 1986 feature headlined 'Jism nari ka, libaas purush ka' ('Body Of A Female, Clothes Of A Male'), the trend of wearing 'male' clothes and going against *Bhartiya sanskriti* (Indian tradition) was deplored. A woman who followed this fashion, claimed the article, lost her husband to another—so beware of wearing 'pant-shirt'. Another edition (July 1985) highlighted the evils of watching blue films: 'Cracks appeared in their married life.' The moral of the story, clearly, was: nice, middle class people would be destroyed by indulgence in *paschim adhunikaran* (western modernisation). Patronage of blue films, in *Grihshobha's* book, is obviously a modern, western evil.

Maintaining the status quo while affording frequent peeks into other lifestyles seems to be the predominant theme of *Grihshobha* and other similar magazines. What is really disturbing about this determined attempt to keep things fundamentally as they are is that serious and vital issues get ignored or are dealt with in an extremely reactionary manner.

Not surprisingly, therefore, topical issues which claim top priority in newspapers and newsmagazines take a decisive backseat in *Grihshobha*, *Manorama* and other Hindi women's magazines. In fact, in the period selected for study, *Grihshobha* published only two articles on the chosen issues: one on sati and the other on rape. Not a single piece appeared on the dowry death phenomenon, the Shah Bano case or the amniocentesis controversy in the specified periods, when public interest in these issues was at its height.

Dowry Deaths

The bride-burning issue was touched upon in an edition outside the period marked for survey (June 1986). Written by Uttamprakash Bansal and headlined 'Samasya ka doosra paksh,' the article discussed in a horrifyingly callous manner whether brides are actually burnt by husbands/in-laws or commit suicide, completely ignoring other salient points.

In support of his contention that the majority of such cases are either accidents or suicides, the writer pointed out that the restrained lives led by newly-wed women in unknown households often became unbearable, leading to suicide. He then went on to argue that murder could be committed using a variety of methods, such as strangulation, poisoning or electrocution; death by any of these methods could be made to look like an accident. Therefore, he concluded, there was no reason why husbands or in-laws would always choose to burn the young women.

He further justified this conclusion by pointing out that it would not do the husband any good to dispose of his first wife in this fashion since no one would marry him again. The girls' parents, he claimed, would naturally say their daughters were murdered; otherwise they would not be able to claim whatever they had gifted to their daughters: 'Majboor ho kar, var paksh walon ko kahan kahan se paisa laakar, samjhauta karna padta hai' (In desperation, the boy's parents have to collect money and come to a settlement).

To the question why such 'accidents' happen only to daughters-in-law, never mothers-in-law, the author said that once there is a daughter-in-law in the house, the mother-in-law does not have anything to do with the kitchen. Besides, even if she does enter the kitchen, she would be wearing a cotton sari, not a nylon or rayon one—presumably only daughters-in-law wear synthetic fabrics! According to the writer, these are the reasons why there is little chance of a mother-in-law burning to death. In any case, concluded the story, committing suicide in this fashion is nothing new—it is part of our *sanskriti* (culture)!

Rape

The one feature published by *Grihshobha* on rape was not a full-fledged article at all. It was, instead, a brief report accompanied by a photograph in one of its regular columns, 'Samachar Darshan' ('News Round-up'). The item, which appeared in the May 1980 edition, was on a procession against rape taken out by several women's organisations in the capital on International Women's Day two months earlier.

Female Foeticide

Although *Grihshobha* did not publish anything on sex determination tests leading to female foeticide during the period under review, an interesting editorial on amniocentesis, based on a survey of readers conducted by the magazine, appeared in the October 1987 edition.

Quoting the results of a nation-wide survey on amniocentesis, carried out through coupons in an earlier issue of *Grihshobha*, the magazine's editorial claimed that 65 per cent of the readers were in favour of amniocentesis while only 35 per cent considered it immoral. It also said that 36 per cent of those who opposed amniocentesis were unmarried and 'therefore (would) not know the difference between a son and daughter.' The editorial concluded by saying: 'In this age of small families, when abortion has been legalised and made morally acceptable, amniocentesis should also be. A majority of readers also favours it.' The first twenty coupons received by the magazine had been awarded cotton saris!

The Roop Kanwar Tragedy

The macabre death of Roop Kanwar was accorded two and a half pages and four photographs, in the December 1987 edition of *Grihshobha* (three months after the Deorala incident), which featured on its cover 'Bunaai ke Aadhunik Barah Namoone' ('Twelve Novel Knitting Patterns'). Also given prominent display and space was a feature on adultery which attempted to answer the question: Are married women attracted to other men? The Roop Kanwar story, titled 'Ek Yuva Stree ko Jinda Jala Diya Gaya' ('A Young Woman Is Burnt Alive'), consisted primarily of a recapitulation of events. However, some sense of outrage at the injustice against women was evident, with the article strongly condemning the anti-women bias of outmoded religious and social rites.

But author Brij Mohan was not very kind to Roop Kanwar herself. He took note of the fact that she was an educated girl ('tenth pass') from an affluent family who was in the habit of frequenting beauty parlours to get her eyebrows plucked and her nails painted. He also reported, without substantiation, that at the time of her marriage Roop Kanwar was having an affair; her husband, who was aware of her activities, was unable to take any steps because he was weighed down by her 'strong' personality. The article stated with conviction that the husband, who was undergoing treatment for impotency, did not touch his beautiful wife on their 'first night.' The story went on to relate how Roop Kanwar went back to her parents' house and once again became involved with her old lover; she returned subsequently when her husband fell ill. Finally, the author went into the details leading up to the horrific tragedy.

The observation on Roop Kanwar's penchant for plucked eyebrows and varnished nails and the reference to an unidentified lover completely detracted from the seriousness of the crime of which she was a victim. The author did not quote any sources while making these allegations; he obviously relied on hearsay and other news reports. The moral of the story, as told in *Grihshobha*, seemed to be that girls who frequent beauty parlours, have an eye for men and cannot abide impotent husbands will, as a natural corollary, be burnt at the stake.

In an article published in the English language journal, *Mainstream* (20 August 1988), entitled 'Toiling Women In Hindi Journals,' writer and editor Mrinal Pande commented on the tone and content of *Grihshobha* and *Manorama*:

There is a definite bias against Western ideas and a leaning towards revivalist Hindu ideas, especially vis-a-vis the observance of social mores. But, even here, everything reflects a clear patriarchal ethos which is selective in its approach to Western ideas. So divorce is criticised as anti-tradition and anti-Indian culture, whereas the definitely Western technique of amniocentesis being used for sex-determination and female foeticide is praised and supported. Westernised social behaviour is criticised but Western fashions, food and table manners are highlighted and presented as worthy of emulation.

There is an overall emphasis on the values of an upwardly mobile middle-class, of good housekeeping, cooking, fashion and keeping up with the Joneses. These journals, thus, not only encourage male-female, middle-class and lower income group segregation, they justify and idealise it.

CONCLUSION

It became evident during the course of the study that the issues selected for monitoring were handled with due seriousness and depth in the *Navbharat Times*, less so in *Maya* and not at all in *Grihshobha*.

This trend broadly conforms to the differences in the coverage of these issues in daily newspapers, newsmagazines and women's magazines in general. On the whole, daily newspapers published from New Delhi or other state capitals in the Hindi belt, which enjoy a fairly large readership, reserve a reasonable quantum of space for such issues, but not all of them view these sympathetically or progressively. *Jansatta's* editorial on and the Jaipur-based *Rajasthan Patrika's* coverage of the sati controversy were, by and large, reactionary, according to Hindi media persons.

Few newspapers, even at the national level, can resist using exploitative photographs to illustrate the text of a story. The first, dummy issue of the Hindi edition of *The Sunday Observer*, for instance, featured a provocative photograph of a girl, revealing her cleavage and holding an apple between her pouting lips, to accompany a column on health. In the same edition, an article on women's property rights took the progressive stand that a woman had as much right to ancestral property as a man. This kind of contradiction seems part and parcel of the current concept of glossy journalism—newspapers sell primarily on the basis of how they are packaged.

In most regional Hindi newspapers—that is, papers published from small towns all over the Hindi belt—women's issues are dealt with superficially and, often, with a dangerous tilt towards titillation. For example, a report in *Awaz*, a Dhanbad-based paper, on the admission into hospital of a seriously injured nine-year-old girl read:

> According to a preliminary report, deep injury marks were found on the girl's private parts, which had been bleeding. Her face also had marks and it was swollen. The girl, in a comatose condition, kept repeating, 'Put my panties on, put my panties on.' She was only able to state that a man had taken her away the previous night.

Yet here, too, there are contradictions. The women's section, 'Mahila Jagat,' of the same edition, had an article against wife-battering. Quoting an unsourced survey, the feature claimed that wife-beating was rampant or common among all classes and communities except tribals. It deplored the fact that despite all the measures taken to better the lot of women, such atrocities continue. The article was obviously a hurriedly put together, indifferently written, patch-up job, but it signified an attempt to present a women's issue in a positive framework.

Maya, which calls itself a complete, topical newsmagazine, is in reality a hard-core political magazine; women's issues generally feature on its pages only when they acquire political significance or overtones or can be used to provide voyeuristic delight to readers. In the last five years or so, however, *Maya* has toned down the overt exploitation of women's issues. The explicit photographs of semi-nude women and the provocative stories it once used liberally had been phased out by the second half of the eighties. But that did not make the magazine more open to women's issues. There was no visible effort in the latter-day *Maya* to catch up with developments on this front; there was no attempt to focus on what most newspapers have begun to acknowledge as part of routine editorial content.

Still, in the mid-eighties, *Maya* began its first column by a woman, Mamta Kalia (a recognised figure in the Hindi literary world), which deals with women's issues, among other subjects. This marked a beginning, a departure from the rigid conventions of political reporting which had thus far been *Maya's* forte.

An exception in the newsmagazine category was *Ravivar*. From its inception in 1977, first under the editorship of S.P. Singh and later under Udayan Sharma, *Ravivar* did significant service to the women's cause. Unfortunately, it slipped from an impressive circulation of more than one lakh in the early eighties to less than half that number before finally closing down. The reasons for its demise can be attributed to the hike in cover price (from Re.1 to Rs.5) and lapses in marketing. Like *Maya*, it was also affected by the appearance of the Hindi edition of *India Today*.

The profiles of the leading Hindi women's magazines, like *Grihshobha* and *Manorama*, conformed to the established norms of the genre which view all serious issues as largely irrelevant to its predominantly female readership. A test case—which, unfortunately, failed—was the *Vama* experiment under Mrinal Pande's editorship. The magazine, launched in 1984, represented a startling departure from the tried and tested contents mix of crochet and knitting, recipes and interior decoration. Pande blames an unresponsive marketing department and some hostile reader opinion—so taken by the concept offered by women's magazines like *Manorama* or *Grihshobha* that they could not appreciate the worth and distinctiveness of *Vama*—for the demise of this innovative magazine. According to Pande, 'If *Manorama* gave them 120 sweater patterns, they thought we ought to give them 240.'

However, the mere fact that even traditional women's magazines are taking notice of some serious women's issues is a step forward. The features which deal with careers, the problems of working women, and so on, may be couched in conventional terms but, at least, they are being aired among women who cannot normally voice their feelings about such matters. This exposure may trigger off the beginning of an awareness which can only increase. Besides, the very fact that these magazines have to deal with issues of this type, albeit amidst all their recipes and knitting patterns, amounts to a tacit recognition that these questions have become central to the lives of a large number of women in this country. And that is a positive development, even if issues such as dowry death, rape and the Shah Bano case are still left to newspapers and newsmagazines.

The importance of the Hindi print media to some of the issues which form the focal points of this study lies in the fact that atrocities such as bride-burning and sati first came to light in or, in the latter instance, were even confined to communities based in the Hindi belt.

Therefore, coverage of such issues or the lack of it in the Hindi press provides accurate pointers to several factors—editorial attitudes (which fashion stories and determine editorial stance), the attitudes of the victim and her family, and public opinion, especially in the area where the victim lives. According to the majority of Hindi presspersons, Hindi journalists have an edge over their English counterparts in presenting a complete and accurate picture of the situation because they tend to use the same idiom that the victim, her family and, indeed, the majority of readers employ in their everyday lives. Mrinal Pande puts it thus:

> When a writer reporting in English on a dowry death describes a relative as 'remembering her great sorrow,' whereas the Hindi original is 'kaleja phat jaata hai' (the heart is broken), it is obvious that the English version is light years away from what comes through in the vernacular.
>
> We as a people are given to hyperbole—it gets bottled up or distanced in English. People who write in English are not involved with the kind of families in which dowry deaths occur—such things take place among the vernacular-speaking majority. The Hindi writer is closer to that oppressed class; the closeness comes through in the writing and is immediately absorbed by the reader. English writing becomes rarified through the linguistic filter as well as through a social filter. Writers in English do not live in the same universe they are reporting about, they just pay it an occasional visit. And readers of English, who have not even paid this universe a visit,

are very pleased with the ethnic touches in these sort of distress stories, so far removed from their universe.

Hindi writers feel that their stories are not confined to the event and what is being done or not done, as the case may be, in legal and administrative circles—the general preoccupation of the English press, according to them. While these aspects of the stories are important, they point out, it is also imperative to look at the social and economic matrix of the victim's life and examine the links with societal conventions and compulsions which lead to such atrocities. In their perception, Hindi writers understand the victim's world because that is where their own origins lie and, therefore, they do more justice to these stories than those who write in English. Because of this involvement, they feel, the tragedy is given the kind of urgency and immediacy and, what is more important, the context that is required for true understanding.

According to them, there are innumerable instances where stories dealing with the exploitation of women in the interior areas of the Hindi-speaking belt have made a splash in a local daily, been picked up by some of the Hindi papers at the national level and still remained non-issues for the English press. They say the English press sits up and takes notice only when an incident acquires major political ramifications, is situated in a major metropolitan centre or its impact is felt beyond its immediate vicinity, as happened in Roop Kanwar's case.

This opinion was voiced by all the three editors of Hindi publications interviewed during the course of this study. This was also the considered opinion of several lower and middle level journalists of Delhi-based Hindi newspapers and magazines, as well as of all the readers whose opinions were sought. These readers were familiar with the English press because they subscribed to at least one English daily or newsmagazine in addition to their intake of Hindi publications.

The new and growing trend of translating the work of Hindi writers for use in the regular columns of English newspapers indicates a dilution of the earlier strict demarcation between the Hindi and English streams in the print media. For example, the late Sharad Joshi, the *Navbharat Times* columnist and recipient of the Padma Shree award, appeared in translation in *The Times of India* till his death last year. Observers think this trend will go a long way towards bringing a new perspective to media debates on various current issues.

11

The Tamil Press

Prasanna Ramaswamy and **Vasantha Surya**

Among the 235 Tamil publications registered in 1987, there were twenty established newspapers and fifty magazines. Of these, *Kumudam*, a magazine consisting almost entirely of short stories, had the largest circulation of five and a half lakhs, followed by the daily newspaper *Dina Thanthi*, with over three lakhs. The latter is one of three broadsheet newspapers in Tamil which have a wide circulation, the other two being *Dina Mani* and *Dina Malar*. Of these, *Dina Mani*, which has a two lakh readership, is better suited for the purposes of this study for reasons explained later.

Tamil periodicals fall into four categories: magazines meant for a general readership, those specially targeted at women, literary or 'story' magazines and film magazines. For instance, *Ananda Vikatan*, *Thuglak* and *Kalki* aim at a general readership while *Kanaiyazhi*, *Kalaimagal* and *Kumudum* are literary and 'story' magazines. Film journals abound, many of them published by film personalities—for example, Bhagyaraj's *Bhagyam* and Bharatiraja's *Devi*, *Kumkumam* and *Vannathirai*. Many of the film-based periodicals count on women readers but some magazines like *Mangai* and *Mangayar Malar*, are aimed directly at women.

For the purpose of this study, *Ananda Vikatan* would have been the most appropriate choice in the general interest periodical category; it is perhaps the best known weekly magazine in Tamil for a general audience although *Kumudam* has enjoyed a larger circulation for some years. Launched by the film magnate, S.S. Vasan, in the thirties, *Ananda Vikatan* was intended as a counterpoise to the earnest *Kalki*. Unfortunately, however, the magazine's management would not allow the researchers access to their past issues. Consequently, *Kalki* was selected for review.

DINA MANI

Unlike *Dina Thanthi* and *Dina Malar*, which are tabloid in their approach and content and aim at a burgeoning neo-literate population, *Dina Mani* is a fully-developed newspaper with clearly demarcated editorial, news and feature sections. Its Tamil may not have the punch and gusto for which *Dina Thanthi* has become famous but it is clear and precise. The struggle between conventional literary forms and the rapidly-developing spoken language has produced a supple, modern prose style within the pages of *Dina Mani*.

The paper was established in 1933 and is part of the *Indian Express* group of newspapers. Its readership consists of the educated middle-class which is largely bilingual, especially in Madras. According to the associate editor Kasturi Rangan (who later became the editor in 1990 but was unceremoniously removed from that position in 1992), the bulk of its readers are teachers and small business people, as well as 'everyone in public life....Karunanidhi will ignore what is written in the English papers but he will not ignore *Dina Mani*.' Rangan said that while the paper's readership used to be predominantly Brahmin sometime ago, it now encompasses all the educated castes. He claimed that up to twenty people read each copy of the paper.

Sometimes, special articles from its sister publication, the *Indian Express*, are translated and reproduced in *Dina Mani*. In political and economic affairs the editorial stance is right of centre. Its news reports and comment on issues concerning social change, however, are marked by a certain earnestness. Explains Rangan:

> We have traditionally followed the forward-thinking ideals of Subramania Bharati. We fully endorse what he has said about women's place in society, especially how they have to go forward fearlessly. The old view of women is not our view. They don't just belong in the home; they have an equally responsible position in society as men do, if not more....

Elaborating why he thought women were more responsible, he went on:

> Women are responsible for the family and child rearing. The Illatharasi (queen of the home) ideal is very true and men's character is very much influenced by women. For instance, a corrupt officer can be deterred by his wife if she says they don't need that kind of money! So we condemn any kind of neglect or indignity done to women. The Kannagi concept—rigid moral rules for women alone—is not the way we look at women. Women are by nature upholders of moral values and so they should come out of rigid roles.... Right now what is needed is an all-round entry of women in all fields, though I personally feel that certain professions are more suited to women—teaching, electronics, and so on, which require patience and precision....

Dina Mani displays a cautious interest in pursuing progressive goals. Notwithstanding Rangan's 'We want broad-mindedness, not petty or narrow views!', such goals are watered down perceptibly when they come into conflict with religious, specifically Hindu, sensibilities. For instance, the Shankaracharyas come in for uniformly favourable coverage—though this was hardly Bharati's attitude. When it comes to the crunch, *Dina Mani* is a conservative newspaper, albeit one with a conscience.

Three types of women appear on the pages of *Dina Mani* regularly: those who are in the news because of their association with the performing arts, such as classical dance; those who are featured because of their brilliant performance in academics, especially in terms of examination results; and those who happen to inaugurate functions covered by the press. Female victims of murder or rape, as well as women who challenge the existing order, like Shah Bano, also find a mention in the paper's news columns. However, the tone adopted in such reports is markedly different from that used for the first category of women news-makers.

Dina Mani's layout differs from that of English language broadsheet newspapers. Not only are the pages thickly packed with print, but there are very few photographs, illustrations or even advertisements. Further, the paper does not conform to the spatial rules generally adopted by English dailies, whereby the importance of a report can more or less be judged by its position on the page, particularly in the case of the front page. Here, the size, type and prominence of the headline is more meaningful; a news item or article may be placed almost anywhere on the page, but its significance is indicated by the style of its headline and its spread across the page. For instance, reports with small, light headlines at the top of the paper's ten-column page are clearly not as important as centre-page pieces with larger, bolder headlines.

The paper, however, underwent a marked change after Iravadham Mahadevan took over as editor in 1987. Since then its design has visibly improved and its classification of different sections has become clearer. But more important, Mahadevan introduced a more coherent policy which was reflected in every aspect of the daily—not just the layout but the tone of the stories, the language and so on. There was a discernible shift in perspective from the right to the centre; this was particularly evident in the paper's coverage of the sati issue.

It is significant that between 1979 to 1987, the months monitored, *Dina Mani* did not carry a single editorial on a women's issue; but in 1988 alone there were seven editorials on a variety of women's issues.

Of the five issues studied, sati received the maximum coverage. Out of a total of thirty items, one was an editorial (the only one on any of the issues covered by the survey over the entire period of the study) and three were edit page articles. Thus, sati did not just receive a greater quantum of coverage than the other issues; it was accorded some importance editorially as well.

Although both the Shah Bano controversy and rape were covered in ten items each, the former was granted more prominence, both in terms of space and positioning. While three of the ten reports on the Shah Bano issue were placed on the front page, the majority of the rape items were routine news reports featured inside. Only six items related directly to the issue of dowry deaths although an additional ten routine crime briefs did suggest that the women's deaths reported in them could have been connected to dowry demands. The furore over sex determination tests appears to have escaped the attention of *Dina Mani* altogether.

Dowry Deaths

Despite the many dowry deaths recorded in New Delhi and other parts of northern India during the period surveyed, they were hardly covered in the south. It could, of course, be argued that the phenomenon was not, at the time, as prevalent in southern states as in the north. However, there are reasons to think that the issue was not pursued closely enough by the press based in the south. It is possible, for instance, that at least some of the deaths of young women reported with depressing regularity in a paper like *Dina Mani* could have been linked to dowry demands. However, as they were not investigated, there is no way of ascertaining whether this was the case.

The possibility is not too remote, considering the similarity in the causes of death of these women in the south and those in the north. For instance, *Dina Mani* carried several short, single-column reports from 2 July 1979 till 10 August 1983, reporting the deaths of women in kitchen accidents, while cooking, in 'domestic fire accidents,' as a result of gas cylinder explosions, 'while lighting a stove,' and so on. While these could have been genuinely accidental deaths, it is also possible that they were the consequence of harassment in the marital home, not too different from the circumstances that led to dowry deaths in the north.

The first item over the period surveyed, which actually mentioned the term 'dowry death,' appeared as late as 27 August 1983 and reported the death of a woman doctor. Only one other item which could be construed as a dowry death had appeared earlier (10 August); here the term used to describe the woman's death was *theekkuliththal* (immolation) as against the usual *theeppidithu irandhu ponal* (caught fire). Among the sixteen items which could be connected to the issue, only six mentioned dowry deaths specifically. Of these, one was the brief report on a suspected dowry death (mentioned above) while the other five were routine reports of discussions in Parliament on the subject. The remaining ten items were short reports on unnatural deaths which did not mention the possible link to dowry demands.

There were no analytical articles or editorials on the subject during the period surveyed. Even in later years, when there was a noticeable increase in the number of items on dowry deaths, the issue was not deemed important enough to warrant a lengthy feature article or an editorial comment.

Rape

Dina Mani's coverage of the rape issue followed the same pattern evident in its handling of dowry deaths. It consisted, in the main, of news reports on ministerial speeches or the pronouncements of other public figures who happened to comment on the issue. There was not a single editorial or analytical article on the subject.

Of the eleven items on rape that appeared over the period surveyed, eight were routine reports on the violation of women in different parts of the state and elsewhere. For instance, two of them concerned the commission of the crime by a politician, belonging to the Telugu Desam party in Andhra Pradesh who was subsequently suspended from his party (16 and 17 August 1983).

One particularly gruesome case of the gang rape of fourteen women working in a stone quarry in Hyderabad was reported in a casual manner (10 March 1980). The incident did not occasion any follow-up or comment; even the initial reports were tucked away in an obscure corner of one of the news pages, well-hidden from public attention.

The remaining three items consisted of a report on the central government's order laying down that women could not be summoned to a police station for questioning after sundown (15 March 1980); one on a statement in Parliament, by a woman member, which mentioned the Mathura rape case (14 March 1980); and a two-column spread on the amended rape law and its provisions (12 December 1983). The last was the most substantial of the news reports on the issue.

The language used to describe women of different classes becomes especially interesting in the coverage of rape. Working class women are referred to as *'penn'* while *'pennmani,'* *'maadhu'* or *'stree'* are some of the terms reserved for upper class, affluent women. Thus, women are defined according to their class even if they have experienced the common trauma of rape.

In contrast to its cursory coverage of the rape issue, *Dina Mani* devoted a great deal of space to news about beauty contests. While it often went out of its way to interview the contestants, the voices of poor, working class rape victims, such as those in the above incident, were never heard through its pages.

The Shah Bano Controversy

The Shah Bano controversy received as much coverage in *Dina Mani* as rape—a total of ten stories. The longest of these was a three-column discussion on the Muslim Women (Protection of Rights on Divorce) Bill while the shortest was a report on a judgment in a U.P. court granting maintenance to a Muslim woman. Not a single editorial on the subject appeared during the five months when the country debated the historic Supreme Court judgment and the law that followed.

News connected with the issue appeared on the front page three times. Predictably, these reports were preoccupied with the political dimensions of the issue. For example, a fairly long front page report (21 December 1985) began with a detailed account of the parliamentary speech of the Congress (I) MP, Z.A. Ansari, condemning the Supreme Court judgment and Chief Justice Y.V. Chandrachud. It is significant that while Ansari's speech was quoted in full, remarks critical of his views—made by another member of Parliament, Saifuddin Choudhury of the CPI(M)—were dealt with in brief at the tail end of the story.

When the Muslim Women Bill came up for discussion in Parliament in February, the issue once again made it to the front page (22 February 1986) in a fairly detailed story on the proposed legislation. On the same day, the front page boxed an item on Arif Mohammed Khan's resignation from the council of ministers.

Dina Mani did not publish a single item directly quoting Shah Bano, the woman at the centre of the controversy. Her name figured in a news item (10 December 1985) on the views of the then Muslim chief minister of Pondicherry, H.M. Farouk. When asked by a reporter about his opinion on the Shah Bano judgment and whether it was in conflict with the Shariat, he was reported as saying, 'Absolutely not. Why should it? Should you not pose the question to some of the Muslim judges as well?'

The only items in which Muslim women were mentioned were about cases in which they had claimed maintenance; the debate provoked by the Shah Bano case obviously augmented media interest in such cases. For instance, a news item on 3 February 1986 described the protest of a Muslim woman in Nagpur against her husband's illegal retention of her house and children after divorce. The tone of this brief report was noticeably sarcastic.

The choice of headlines for this item and another related report which appeared on the same day is significant for its definite bias. The item on the Nagpur woman was headlined 'Muslim Penn Uunnaviradha Mirattal' ('Muslim Woman's Threat'). The use of the word 'mirattal' ('threat') for a woman's legitimate fight for her rights contrasted sharply with the far milder term used in the headline for the other report. The second item (3 February 1986) was on the warning issued by a Kerala Muslim League MP that the government 'may have to face the consequences' if Rajiv Gandhi did not take measures to put the Supreme Court in its place, and if the Shariat was not respected. Here, the term used to describe the MP's strongly worded threat was 'korikkai' which means 'request.'

Despite the national debate sparked off by the controversy, *Dina Mani* did not publish any editorials or analytical articles on this issue. The majority of the news items focussed on official statements on the law or the discussion in Parliament on the Bill.

Female Foeticide

There was practically no coverage of this issue in *Dina Mani* over the months chosen for the study. The edition dated 15 October 1987 (outside the period under review) carried an edit page article by a staff reporter headlined 'Male Or Female? A Choice'. The article put together foreign and other news reports which suggested that sex choice technologies could be useful in aborting boys likely to be haemophiliacs.

One edit page article, appearing during the survey period, which made some mention of the subject was a book review by Dr M.S. Venkatraman of *Sexual Medicine* by K. Natarajan, MD. Though generally favourable, it criticised the author's implied acceptance of amniocentesis as a means of choosing the sex of infants. The review evoked a response from the author in the form of a letter to the editor which was carried on 30 January 1988. Dr Natarajan clarified that he did not support female foeticide but believed that parents have the right to choose the sex of their children.

The Roop Kanwar Tragedy

Compared to the other four issues, the events and debates following the death of young Roop Kanwar in Deorala received considerable coverage. There were a total of thirty items—three times more than those on rape or the Shah Bano controversy.

This issue also prompted the only editorial on any of the selected five subjects throughout the study period. In addition, *Dina Mani* published three edit page articles on the subject. Apart from routine stories, there were as many as six special articles on the news pages, four of which featured on the front page; the Friday magazine also carried one major article on sati.

Although Roop Kanwar died on 4 September and news about the incident began to trickle in a few days later, the first mention of the subject in *Dina Mani* appeared only on 16 September—the day of the *chunri mahotsav*. Significantly, it was an editorial that brought the

Deorala incident to the readers' notice. Headlined 'The Retreat Of Women,' the edit condemned the whole sordid episode and urged the government to take more responsibility in the matter. It noted that 'many parts of the country are still immersed in the 18th century' and expressed support to women's organisations which had demanded the arrest of the persons responsible for the crime.

News coverage of the issue revealed the clearly anti-sati editorial stance of the paper. Special stories (translated from English), such as the one written by Brinda Karat of the Janwadi Mahila Samiti and headlined 'The Sati Episode And The Women's Movement,' were accorded prominent positions and considerable spread (27 October 1987). By way of contrast, the statement of the Shankaracharya of Puri justifying the practice of sati was tucked away as a single column item on an inside page (5 October 1987). This is significant because the English language sister publication of *Dina Mani*, the *Indian Express*, displayed the Shankaracharya's statement in the anchor position on the front page.

The issue gained maximum prominence on the front page of *Dina Mani* when the then prime minister, Rajiv Gandhi, directed the Rajasthan chief minister to take steps to prevent glorification of sati (28 September 1987). The story was carried as the second lead and went beyond the Prime Minister's instructions to quote him: 'This event is humiliating to the whole nation and not only to all right-thinking and progressive people who will resist the practice of sati. Those who praise the murder of young girls in this way must be condemned.'

Another page one item was a special news report on the Rajasthan Ordinance which laid down the death sentence for sati abettors (1 October 1987). Apart from emphasising the criminality of the act and the culpability of those who abetted and glorified it, the article also provided background information. For instance, it reported the existence of 140 sati temples in the country, 40 of them in Rajasthan alone.

The rest of the coverage dealt with the central government's position on the issue, including statements by various ministers, the Rajasthan government's response, the Rajasthan High Court's verdict and other major events. However, while the paper carried an item on pro-sati demonstrations in Rajasthan, U.P., Gujarat and Haryana (9 October 1987), there was no item on the silent march against sati taken out by women's groups in Jaipur around the same time.

On the other hand, the paper seemed to give even-handed treatment to statements both for and against *sati*. The Vishwa Hindu Parishad and the Rashtriya Swayamsevak Sangh were given routine coverage. However, a special story, headlined 'Burn The Sati-Supporting Shastras!' (28 October 1987), highlighted the stand of the well-known Kannada writer, Dr Nirupama Niranjana, condemning the Puri Shankaracharya's views and urging his arrest. Inserted in the body of the report was a parenthetical explanation and analysis of the Shankaracharya's statement, indicating the editor's anti-sati stance.

Although the statement of the then president of the VHP, Vishnu Hari Dalmia, claiming 'Sati is divine' was reproduced (1 November 1987), it is noteworthy that his views were not reported uncritically. Instead, the reporter attempted to show up the contradictions in the VHP's position on the issue.

Despite its southern base, this regional language paper did not miss out on many major stories arising from the Deorala incident. For instance, a news report on 4 October 1987 went into the desire of Roop Kanwar's relatives to build a memorial for her in Ranchi, Bihar, said to be her birthplace. According to the report, 'Although the Centre expects all states to take action to prevent sati, no specific or complete guidelines have been given. Yet the Bihar government has announced its determination to stop the building of the memorial.'

All the three edit page articles in *Dina Mani* were translations of pieces that had appeared in the *Indian Express*. On 24 September 1987, a day after an article by Gandhian social worker Vishal Mangalwadi had appeared in its sister paper, a translation headlined 'How Sati Can Be Prevented' was published by *Dina Mani*. The article traced the historical background of the issue and Raja Ram Mohan Roy's crusade against sati. The author stated that Ram Mohan Roy was unable to shake off his feelings of shame and disgust at a practice which seemed to be 'clearly based on the greed of the male survivors of the deceased man.'

The other two edit page articles were similarly unambiguous in their anti-sati sentiments. The 11 October 1987 edition of the paper carried a translation of an article by Padam Rosha headlined 'Legal Ban Not Adequate To Banish Sati'. A special edit page article entitled 'What Gandhiji Said About Sati' by L.S. Rangarajan, the assistant director of the Mahatma Gandhi Publications Trust, was featured on 3 November 1987.

This was probably one of the most significant articles to appear in the paper over the period because it made clear the ideological basis of the paper's treatment of women's issues and social change. For the middle class, largely upper-caste, educated adult readers of *Dina Mani*, the Gandhian approach to social reform would be less threatening to family, caste and religious institutions than either Bharati's impassioned and idealistic views or feminism—radical or socialist. The ahimsa ideal, 'friendly persuasion,' and the lofty view of man-woman relations typical of Gandhism tend to be more universally acceptable than the dense rhetoric of militant feminism. Although the editor of *Dina Mani*, in an attempt to be 'fair,' accommodated all these approaches in the various articles carried on the issue, his own preference for the Gandhian perspective was articulated in this edit page article.

The readers of the paper responded in greater measure to this issue than to any of the others. Not a single one of the seven letters to the editor that appeared over this period was pro-sati or even attempted to explain or justify it in any way. Expressing disappointment and regret at the Puri Shankaracharya's support of sati, one reader wrote, 'If spiritual leaders like the Shankaracharyas encourage the evil forces behind sati, the ignorance of the people will grow' (13 October 1987). It is significant that this letter was given a fairly prominent position. The Shankaracharya mystique is powerful in Tamil Nadu but, by and large, it is the two southern Shankaracharyas (Kanchi and Sringeri) who are venerated in the state. To give credit where it is due, neither of them made statements endorsing sati. In fact, Shankaracharya Jayendra Saraswati of Kanchi has not only launched a programme of 'social awakening,' but is also well-known for his anti-dowry views. He also made a clear statement against sati.

The only magazine feature on the issue appeared as late as 20 November 1987. Headlined 'The Torture That Is Sati,' it featured interviews with three women on the subject—Kala Balasubramanian, a journalist; Mythily Sivaraman, general secretary of the Democratic Women's Association; and Mala, a domestic servant. The feature revealed a definitely pro-women approach although the writer, reportedly, had considerable difficulty persuading the editor of the magazine section to publish the article.

Overall, *Dina Mani's* coverage of the sati issue was consistent—its news pages faithfully reflected the anti-sati position taken in its timely editorial and editorial page pieces. This rare harmony between news coverage and comment indicates that the editor played a fairly major role in the placement and emphasis of stories on the news pages so as to ensure their concordance with the paper's editorial stance.

KALKI

Kalki is a weekly magazine belonging to the Kalki group of publications established by R. Krishnamurthi (Kalki), the well-known writer of historical and 'social' novels. The publishing group and the magazine itself are identified with the C. Rajagopalachari variant of Congress nationalism—a mixture of social idealism and cultural revivalism which greatly appealed to the upper caste, especially the Brahmin intelligentsia. This brand of journalism, however, is not at all highbrow. In linguistic and literary terms, it has shunned both the Dravidian and the Sanskritised pedantries, as well as the coarseness of new periodicals whose content often borders on 'soft pornography.'

Over the last ten years, *Kalki's* appearance has improved to some extent; there are also more features and cover stories on current events. Its format is slightly larger than that of other Tamil magazines. It uses both colour and black and white photographs, the latter generally for news stories.

Although it has a separate section on women, women's issues are viewed in a fairly conservative light. This is particularly evident in the short stories, serialised stories, cinema reviews and question and answer features—the mainstay of the magazine. Because *Kalki* does not respond directly to news developments, it tends to deal with women's issues at random, often not directly but illustratively—through short stories.

Dowry Deaths

On the dowry issue, for instance, although there were a total of six items over the period surveyed—more than for any of the other four issues—four of these were short stories pegged on the dowry issue. The phenomenon of dowry deaths, per se, was not discussed. In June and July 1979, when the anti-dowry campaign had reached a crescendo in New Delhi, *Kalki* dealt with the issue through two short stories by a male writer, Rajesh Kumar.

The first, headlined 'Sugirtha Will Not Put Up With Any More' (3 June 1979), narrated the anger felt by a young girl against dowry. However, according to the story, as soon as the *thali* (mangalsutra or special gold necklace worn by married women) was tied around her neck, she suddenly became a different person and urged her father to fulfil her in-laws' demand for a gold chain. The writer's explanation for this dramatic change in the girl was that before her marriage she had been concerned about dowry because she did not want to burden her father, but after the wedding she had become part of her husband's household and shifted allegiance to her in-laws. Obviously the author viewed the status quo as immutable and, therefore, acceptable.

The second story, in the issue dated 12 August 1979, used the dowry theme to highlight the qualities of an 'ideal' woman. It was about a mother-in-law and her two daughters-in-law. The one who did not bring a dowry was treated cruelly while the one who had been generously dowered was showered with affection. Finally, the former nursed the wicked mother-in-law during her illness while the favoured one preferred to go off to her parents' home for a holiday. Although the long-suffering, dutiful—and pregnant—daughter-in-law was urged by her parents to return to her natal home for the delivery of her child, her virtuous response was: 'My duty is to be here; all the gifts you have to give to me, you can come and give them to me here.'

Thus this story, too, stressed the duties of the woman rather than her rights. There was not even a hint of censure at the custom of dowry. The hideous outcome of the social pressure on young women for dowry—the dowry death phenomenon in the north—was never even touched upon. Even *Kalki's* review of the film *Dowry Kalyanam* (Dowry Marriage), focussing on the evil of dowry, merely commented on the acting, direction and music, totally ignoring the central theme of the film (24 June 1983).

At a time when women's organisations in the north were demanding tougher laws to curb the practice of dowry, *Kalki* ran a short story which put forward the most popular, traditional solution to dowry in Tamil Nadu. The story was about a girl who was shocked and upset by her lover's demand for dowry. She was finally saved by a millionaire college friend (snubbed by her several years earlier) who was prepared to marry her without a dowry! This is a familiar formula repeated fairly frequently in the Tamil press. The idea is that if one man is bad enough to demand a dowry, a saviour will appear to rescue the woman. Similarly, in the instance of rape, the preferred solution is for the rapist to marry the victim.

The totally uncritical endorsement of the dowry custom represented by these stories was somewhat balanced by a detailed feature which appeared in the edition dated 14 August 1983. Headlined 'Women Who Become Corpses In In-laws' Houses,' and spread over three pages, the story provided details of a number of bride-burning incidents in Delhi;

the formation of the Dahej Virodhi Chetna Manch, an anti-dowry coalition of women's groups, and the efforts made by women's groups in Delhi to spread public awareness on the dowry issue. The story was both positive and informative. It failed, however, to report on the Tamil Nadu situation.

There were other instances of *Kalki's* lack of consistency in its approach to the dowry phenomenon. For example, a few months after the informative feature mentioned above, *Kalki* ran what could be considered a positive short story—about a girl who refused to marry a man who demanded dowry (4 March 1983). Yet in its special issue on interior decoration (15 April 1984), the magazine proceeded to suggest alternatives to traditional dowry items—'Why don't you give sewing machines and washing machines to your daughter instead of silver vessels?' or 'You can use the old brass vessel given by your mother as a plant pot.'

To conclude, barring the one feature on the anti-dowry campaign in the north, the rest of the material touching on the custom of dowry in *Kalki* endorsed it in one way or another and emphasised the traditional duties of a wife in her marital home.

Rape

Although *Kalki* ran an editorial comment on rape, taking off from the Mathura rape case, it did not specifically address the issue through reports or articles over the period surveyed. In fact, a special issue on violence in society (25 March 1983—outside the survey period) failed to mention either dowry deaths or rape. Perhaps the editors felt that rape was an unsuitable subject given its image as a family magazine and the Tamil context where the press in general does not shy away from reporting rape cases in fairly lurid detail.

The edit (13 April 1980) was packed with information on the Mathura rape case and commented on the protest staged by women's groups in front of the Supreme Court. It concluded thus: 'While it is fair on the part of women to fight for better laws regarding this, it is highly improper to stage a protest in front of an office of justice such as the Supreme Court.'

Apart from the 'saviour' theme, another popular theme favoured by the Tamil press in the context of dowry and rape is one of divine retribution. This was echoed in one of the short stories that appeared in *Kalki* outside the period surveyed (27 May 1979). It revolved around a young girl whose rape, by her superior in the office where she worked, was accidentally avenged. The daughter of the rapist, living with her husband in another city, was raped by some local thugs and, unable to bear the shame, committed suicide. This genre of stories tends to look upon the rapist with sympathy.

The importance of the preservation of a woman's dignity and chastity at all costs was a recurring theme in several stories and features published by *Kalki* over this period. Perhaps the most vivid example of this was a report, in the edition dated 12 August 1979, on a tragic and shocking incident in Coimbatore. It involved the death of a teenaged school girl caused by repeated scorpion bites. The magazine applauded the modesty of the girl—not taking off her skirt in public even though she was bitten to death as a result of her modesty—and extolled the virtues of *Bharathappanpadu* (Indian culture).

Readers' responses to this story were even more revealing. In the very next issue, several letters from male and female readers praised the girl's decision not to reveal her body even when she was bitten by the scorpion many times.... The one letter which was critical of this was printed in a highly edited form. It stated:

> The whole of society ought to feel ashamed about putting a girl to death through conditioning based on false values. A woman is nothing but a body here: she is good if she doesn't reveal it and bad if she reveals it. As if the death, which was the result of society's wrong priorities, was not enough, the media's attitude that this is a matter of *panpadu* (culture) is disgusting. If an adolescent boy had done the same thing—that is not taken off his clothes despite a scorpion bite—what would *Kalki* have written?

The Shah Bano Controversy

Kalki did not run any feature articles or short stories even tangentially related to the issues raised by Shah Bano's fight for maintenance or the Supreme Court's judgment in her favour. It did publish two editorials, both of which focussed on the Muslim Women (Rights on Divorce) Bill rather than the issue of divorced women's rights to maintenance.

The edit that appeared on 23 March 1986, headlined 'The Midnight Bill,' congratulated Arif Mohammed Khan for a 'historic resignation, a decision made with deep morals and high principle.' It strongly criticised Rajiv Gandhi for bowing to obscurantism and fundamentalism for political reasons. Besides, it argued, the Personal Law can be followed by those who consider it important; but Muslims wishing to follow a uniform civil code should have the freedom to do so.

The 18 May 1986 edit, headlined 'The Adamancy Exhibited By The PM,' once again castigated Rajiv Gandhi for what it called the Black Act executed at midnight. It stated, 'It is indeed surprising that Rajiv Gandhi, who talks so much about the 21st Century, prefers Indian Muslim women to remain in the 18th Century.' This constituted the only mention of Muslim women in the magazine's scanty coverage of this issue. Otherwise, both edits were restricted to the political fall-out of the Muslim Women Bill.

Female Foeticide and The Roop Kanwar Tragedy

Kalki did not publish any articles on the controversies arising out of sex determination tests and female foeticide or the sati issue throughout the periods surveyed. Overall, the magazine's coverage of the issues selected for survey revealed its deep conservatism with regard to women and women's issues.

MANGAIYAR MALAR

With an estimated circulation of one lakh, *Mangaiyar Malar* is the leading women's magazine in Tamil. Its closest rival is *Mangai* which sells 45,000 copies. Established in 1982, the magazine belongs to the Kalki group. It is a decorous publication which eschews the pouting, busty cover girls, racy question-and-answer columns and reams of gossip on film personalities favoured by other women's magazines. Further, it does not concentrate on clothes and cooking as do some women's magazines in different languages, including English.

Mangayar Malar's preoccupation is with the concept of a 'lady.' It considers neither cooking nor clothes, politics nor atrocities on women as important as the making of a lady through education. It offers a mix of general information on culture, careers, child-rearing and 'husband-management,' health and nutrition, as well as recipes, household hints and, of course, short stories.

Women's issues are often dealt with indirectly through fiction which enables its upper class and upper caste readers to identify themselves with the heroines and their lives and problems. The short stories published in *Mangaiyar Malar* adopt a didactic tone, quite obviously exhorting women to run their lives better. It is certainly not as sensational or sentimental as fiction in other Tamil magazines.

Mangaiyar Malar is a direct descendant of such turn-of-the-century women's periodicals as *Madar Manoranjani* insofar as its purpose is concerned. It aims to bridge the information gap between men and women—a need felt keenly by old-time editors such as G. Subramania Iyer and Subramania Bharati but by and large neglected by contemporary editors. Education and social reform, then, and education and social change, now, are considered greater priorities than mere newsiness or topicality in the context of serious women's journalism in Tamil. However, there is a difference—the earlier women's magazines were more political than the present-day ones, perhaps because their editors were influenced by the freedom movement. What the old and new versions of women's magazines share is their definition of what constitutes good reading for women—and this has generally tended to be conservative.

According to Manjula Ramesh, current editor of *Mangaiyar Malar*:

As far as a women's magazine is concerned, I find South Indian women are not very receptive to very modern ideas. We want them to change, but the roots of change are important. Culture, values, traditions—these are basic for peace of mind and a balanced attitude. And women need these today more than anyone else...

The magazine's articles, features and stories are, therefore, replete with positive cultural reinforcements.

Why is there so little information and comment on political matters in *Mangaiyar Malar*? Says the editor:

We tried publishing political news for six months. But judging from the letters and from our discussion sessions with readers, there was no response at all. Women aren't very enthusiastic about politics because of what happened to Indira Gandhi and Jayalalitha. Any woman who goes into politics has her name dirtied. Look at our women MLAs! Even actresses don't get such a bad name as they do.

What about women's issues? According to Manjula Ramesh:

Well, we have always covered the more important ones. For

instance, Shah Bano, sati.... In general, we don't favour militant struggles, going on fasts, etc., to solve women's issues. Human problems are not solved dramatically, by political methods. They get solved as times change. And some don't seem to change at all. For instance, ill-treatment by in-laws. Even the most advanced women have very traditional views on certain things. And even women tend to give credit to men who get ahead but not to other women.

Sita had to prove her chastity only once, but today every woman trying to make her way in the world has to prove her chastity again and again! Today's struggles are terrible! The double standard continues.... A woman may be working, doing everything that men are doing, even better than they are, but when she comes home, she must be a willing slave! Indian men haven't changed. So it's up to women to educate their children for a new future....

Mangaiyar Malar takes its educational role quite seriously. Almost every issue has articles and snippets on health, exercise, yoga and nutrition. Gynaecological and other health problems, consumer problems and career opportunities are all dealt with in considerable detail, with a view to making them understandable to women with limited education. One whole edition was devoted to different aspects of banking, focussing particularly on the part played by women in banking operations.

Dowry Deaths

There was only one article on dowry deaths over the period surveyed although there were references to dowry in other articles and stories. Carried as a cover story (August 1983), spread over three and a half pages and accompanied by two photographs, it was a personalised piece by the editor, Manjula Ramesh, headlined 'For Days, A Turmoil In The Mind!' The article began:

> Every day, as I read the newspaper, my eyes fall on that sort of article. Reading it, the heart boils and turns to steam! Womanhood... how highly it was esteemed in the land of Bharat! Rivers and colours, deities and Nature herself were given female names, cherished and celebrated....

Moving on to the death of dowry victim Sudha Goel in Delhi and those responsible, she concluded, 'Are these human beings? Or are they fiends in human shape?'

This was a strong, persuasive piece, bound to appeal to traditionalists and modernists alike. It was reminiscent of old-time journalism which used the same approach to denounce child marriages and the ill-treatment of widows—appealing to the readers' conscience. And it is certainly a fact that child marriage is no longer practised among the middle classes in Tamil Nadu, and that widows are seldom shaven, confined and ill-treated as they used to be among the Brahmins of the state.

The tone of the article suggested that the editor felt compelled to deal with the issue although she would have preferred to deal with 'pleasanter' subjects which do not reveal the worst aspects of human nature. But once aroused, the fury—of the patient and the compassionate—was obviously uncontrollable. Her reaction seemed akin to that of Kannagi in the ancient Tamil epic, *Silappadikaaram*, where the heroine is gentle and tolerant by nature but driven to terrible fury when faced with royal tyranny and injustice.

Rape

There were no articles on rape during the survey period. In fact, there was not a single reference to rape in any of the issues studied over the entire period spanning nearly ten years. Sensationalised rape stories are commonplace in Tamil newspapers and magazines, fiction and films. *Mangaiyar Malar*, which sees itself as a family magazine, may not have wished to tarnish its image or expose children to such a subject.

The Shah Bano Controversy

The furore over the Supreme Court judgment in the Shah Bano case and the subsequent Muslim Women Bill was not covered by *Mangaiyar Malar* over the months selected for study. However, in June and July 1986, just outside the survey period, there was a two-part article on the subject by the writer Vasanthi which is worth noting. Together the two parts examined the Shah Bano case, its repercussions and its implications in a serious and thorough manner.

The first part (June 1986), a cover story which ran over three pages, was critical of the government. The article, headlined 'The Future Of Muslim Women,' candidly discussed the issues raised by the case and described the protests of women's groups. Advocating a uniform civil code, the writer made a sincere attempt to clarify all the legal aspects of the issue, putting on record the legal position of divorced women under Muslim law.

The second part (July 1986) was a livelier piece. Headlined 'This Is A Question Of Human Values,' it consisted of four interviews conducted by Vasanthi. One of the interviewees, Zoya Hasan of the Jawaharlal Nehru University, was quoted as saying:

> I never thought Muslim women would be so determined, forceful and motivated in their attitude towards this question. I feel that with such women in our society, there is room for optimism, if not today, then one day.... This is a law which directly attacks the rights of Muslim women.

On the communal dimension of the issue, Zoya Hasan was emphatic: 'It's an election stunt! Islam is being used to deprive Muslim women of their rights. The Bill takes us back to the 12th Century. And as far as I am concerned, this is an attack on all women.'

Reshma Arif Khan (lawyer wife of politician Mohammed Arif Khan) was no less forthright when she said the Bill was opposed to tenets of Muslim law. She also spoke out against oral divorce. On the role and stance of Muslim fundamentalists, she retorted, 'They have no vision of the future. They are male chauvinists in their very nature. Those who made this law have no respect for Islam and women should resist its enforcement. If women are serious, this can be resisted.'

The third interview included in the article was with an uneducated Bengali Muslim woman whom Vasanthi met on the street. Poor, divorced and tubercular, Noori had no hope that a second husband would treat her better than the first one did. 'It isn't customary,' she explained. Another woman from Kerala said:

> I never dreamt I would be divorced by my husband. We came back from the Gulf and when I went to my family for my confinement, he divorced me. The *meher* is only enough for a ring or a chain. How is that enough for maintenance? And now the new law has stopped me from appealing to the court.

Remarking that all the Muslim women she had spoken to had opposed the Muslim Women Bill, the writer concluded that this was 'a sign of hope.' Their opposition, she stated, also indicated that 'this is not a religious but a human issue.'

Female Foeticide

There was little coverage of this issue in 1986—when the extent to which sex determination tests were misused for female foeticide was first highlighted by the press, particularly in Bombay. This was also the time when a campaign demanding a ban on the misuse of such technology was launched. The subject first found mention in *Mangaiyar Malar* in the edition dated January 1987. The magazine reproduced a poster, by Praveen Karat and Anand Mazumdar to arouse public opinion against amniocentesis, featuring a photograph of Indira Gandhi with the caption: 'She would have died before she was born.'

The same edition carried a short feature headlined 'Women On Womanhood,' based on interviews with a cross-section of women, on the theme whether being born a woman was a misfortune and whether women by nature were inferior to men. Only one of the many women quoted in the article, a domestic servant, blamed her ills on her birth as a woman. Others had different things to say. For instance, a 60-year old glorified womanhood and referred to traditional practices which showed that girls were cherished. She said that to abort a female child was a *mahaapaavam* (major sin).

The magazine's almost total silence on this issue, which according to *Dina Mani* had become widespread in the southern districts of Tamil Nadu, can be partly explained by its apparent wariness against raising women's consciousness about their insecurity and vulnerability. The magazine tended to emphasise women's strengths. There were some articles aimed at educating women about abortion, sex, sterility and family planning. There was also a curious mention of the efficacy of rituals promoting fertility. However, as in the case of rape, there was a disinclination to deal with violence or the negative aspects of women's status.

The Roop Kanwar Tragedy

In November 1987, a full two months after Roop Kanwar's death in Deorala, *Mangaiyar Malar* came out with an article of some substance but not much originality on the subject. Entitled 'The Torture That Is Sati' (punning on the word sati, which means torture in Tamil), the article was written by G. Ramalakshmi and Khiyambur Sankarasubramanian.

> It is a lie that sati is a way of gaining *moksha* or establishing wifely loyalty and sacrifice. The truth is that a brother is unwilling to share paternal property with his brother's widow, as Raja Ram Mohan Roy believed. Is woman a living being or is she a piece of wood, a thing to be burnt on her husband's pyre? In what century are we living? Woman, too, must raise her voice against this, and both the central and the state governments must condemn it.

A box item in the same edition described the pitiable condition of widows in Rajasthan, including the fact that they may not remarry or cross the threshold of their houses or wear fine clothes or even eat good food. They are set aside, believed to be unlucky and forbidden from attending auspicious functions. The Rajasthan Ordinance against sati and its glorification were also dealt with.

The article and the box item together provided considerable information about the issue, placing it clearly in the context of women's status in society. However, the emphasis on sati as a Rajasthani phenomenon distanced it somewhat from readers of *Mangaiyar Malar*, based in Tamil Nadu.

The only other reference to sati over the period surveyed came in a letter to the editor in the edition dated December 1987. The reader referred to the November 1987 article and said it 'made my heart ache. To murder, and then to celebrate the murder with a festival—it makes us wonder if all human values have been entirely forgotten. How can there be such a defect in a nation which was ruled so long by a woman?'

While *Mangaiyar Malar* cannot be called a feminist magazine, it displayed some awareness of the major campaigns conducted by women's groups in the country. On the whole, its coverage did reflect the women's perspective. However, it essentially tried to tackle issues without upsetting the status quo or raising too many radical questions. In that respect, it remained firmly within the mould of mainstream women's magazines, even though in appearance and some of its contents it stood out as different.

12

The Bengali Press

Maitreyi Chatterjee

The Bengali language does not command the large readership of Hindi. It is spoken by an even smaller number of people than Tamil, Telugu, Malayalam, Marathi and Gujarati. Yet, thanks to the high level of politicisation and the considerable spread of education in the state, the average Bengali is an avid reader of newspapers and periodicals—seen as conduits of essential information on important national and international issues. The Bengali press, therefore, boasts a range of publications of high quality.

From among the several major Bengali dailies currently being published, the *Ananda Bazaar Patrika* (*ABP*) was the daily newspaper selected for this study. In terms of both circulation and readership base, it is well ahead of its closest rivals—*Aajkaal*, *Bartaman* and *Jugantar*. Besides, *Aajkaal* (launched in 1981) and *Bartaman* (launched in 1986) are new entrants in the field of dailies and were not around during the entire period covered by the study. *Jugantar*, which till the mid-1960s was the largest selling Bengali daily, was later overtaken by *Ananda Bazaar* and now lags behind even *Aajkaal* and *Bartaman*. The relatively low circulation of the other Bengali dailies—*Ganasakti* (a publication of the ruling Communist Party [Marxist]) and *Dainik Basumati*—left them out of the reckoning, even though *Ganasakti's* current circulation is 1,25,000.

The combined circulation of the three new entrants (4,07,000) —*Aajkaal* (1,75,000), *Ganasakti* (1,25,000) and *Bartaman* (1,07,000)—is not much higher than *ABP's* latest figure (4,00,032). While it is true that in recent years *ABP's* circulation has stayed at the four lakhs mark and that newer readers (especially in the younger age group) are opting for either *Aajkaal* or *Bartaman*, *Ananda Bazaar's* dominant position among Bengali newspapers still remains unchallenged. *Ananda Bazaar* also enjoys the rare distinction of being the largest circulated single edition daily among all Indian newspapers in English as well as regional languages.

Commenting on *Ananda Bazaar's* pre-eminence, one senior editor said it was quite unique. It is an integral part of the middle class Bengali home where its editorial approach is deemed to be correct. No other newspaper in Bengal enjoys this kind of cultural hold, particularly over the older age group, both urban and rural. To its readership, the *Ananda Bazaar Patrika* is **the** Bengali newspaper.

An editor who has worked as a stringer for both *Ananda Bazaar* and *Jugantar* suggested that the former owes its special position to its recruitment policy. Popular Bengali writers work as journalists for the paper. Promising writers are employed at handsome salaries. Their creative work is serialised and later published as books. The *ABP* publishing house also has a prestigious literary award. These factors, coupled with a professional approach, have made *Ananda Bazaar's* position among Bengali readers quite unassailable.

Desh, a weekly magazine of general interest published by the *ABP* group and selected in the general magazine category for this study, has been a pace-setting journal for more than fifty years. Originally conceptualised as a literary magazine, it has undergone several metamorphoses over the years to emerge in its present form as a general interest features magazine. Its contents comprise cover stories on current topics, serialised fiction (usually two novels at a time), a short story, poetry, comment on the literary scene, serialised essays on art, serialised features on the national movement and a big review section—incorporating art, books, music, theatre, dance and television.

Thus, *Desh* is not a newsmagazine in the same way as *India Today*. Neither does it have any real rivals although, off and on, other weeklies (*Paribartan*, for instance) and news fortnightlies (*Pratikshan*) have nudged it out of its complacency. Both these have since closed down. While it existed, the *Pratikshan*, a fortnightly, provided excellent coverage of issues like the Muslim Women (Protection of Rights on Divorce) Bill, the Roop Kanwar tragedy, the Pararia gang rape case, and so on. It had a balanced, non-paternalistic approach to women's issues. *Nabo*, a monthly with a plebian touch, and *Alokpat* (also a monthly), with its sensationalised, almost soft-porn slant, never posed any threat to the supremacy of *Desh* among Bengali periodicals.

The women's magazine scene has been rather bleak in West Bengal. In the late 1940s and early 1950s, *Mahila*, a monthly magazine, did quite well. It was a very traditional magazine, giving advice to women on how to be good wives and mothers. Virtue was its key word. Another monthly, *Basumati*, also carried a few women's pages that included fiction by women, recipes and embroidery.

Ananda Lok was never a full-fledged women's magazine. Basically a film magazine from the *Ananda Bazaar Patrika* stable, it carried some fashion and beauty tips as well as recipes, trying to double as a film-cum-women's magazine. Another magazine, *Naba Kallol*, catered to a semi-urban, middle and lower middle class readership, carrying pulp fiction (in the main), as well as beauty, health, fashion and cooking tips, with an eye on the female reader.

That was the range of Bengali journalistic endeavour targeted at women until *Sukanya* came along. Launched at the beginning of 1983 as a fortnightly by Ityadi Prakashani (floated by one of the directors of the Peerless group of companies), *Sukanya* was well received because it was the first Bengali women's magazine which dealt exclusively with women and subjects of special interest to them. So *Sukanya* fulfilled a genuine need. Later, *Sananda*, closely followed by *Manorama*, also filled a definite vacuum in the field of women's periodicals in Bengali.

ANANDA BAZAAR PATRIKA

Ananda Bazaar has taken the lead in covering women's issues. Although it publishes a 'typical' women's page once a week, featuring fashion and beauty care tips, recipes and superficial articles, it has also consistently focussed on women's issues in its Sunday magazine section. Usually serious, analytical articles on such subjects are given a berth under the review section.

One editor is of the opinion that the phenomenal increase in female literacy in Bengal and the growth in the Bengali female readership have compelled newspapers to include women's issues in their coverage in order to remain relevant. Thus the coverage given to women's issues is due partly to the need to discharge social responsibilities and partly to boost circulation.

By frequently publishing articles on women's issues by locally known women activists, the paper has built up a progressive image. Finally, it must be acknowledged that whatever the reasons for its coverage of women's issues, *ABP* has played an important role in promoting public awareness of such issues in Bengal, if only because of the paper's tremendous reach and influence.

The language advantage enjoyed by *ABP* is obvious. The dramatic manner in which news is presented in Bengali papers caters to their readers' penchant for the dramatic. English is impersonal by comparison. According to a senior editor and newspaper administrator, because of this a Bengali paper is regarded as the family newspaper, enjoying a bond with its readers; reading an English newspaper is more akin to listening to news over the radio.

Dowry Deaths

During 1979, when the media elsewhere had taken note of it, no news report, feature or editorial on the dowry death phenomenon appeared in the *Ananda Bazaar*. Considering the shared class background of the publishers, advertisers and readers of the paper, it is possible that the dowry issue and allied problems were seen as rather distant and more relevant to other sections of society. The 'upper' class tends to take for granted the fact that parents give daughters jewellery and other gifts at the time of marriage, the monetary worth of which would be commensurate with their social and economic status; in this milieu, the vulgar act of 'demanding' dowry does not generally arise. So the editors of the *ABP* perhaps decided not to allocate space to an issue of little direct relevance to their readership and from which, in their perception, no political or commercial mileage could be gained.

However, *ABP* published sixteen items on dowry in 1983 and 1984. The introduction of the dowry legislation in Parliament was reported with due prominence and details of all the important clauses and amendments. When the Bill was presented in the Lok Sabha, the news made it to the edit page; when it was presented in the Rajya Sabha, the report was put on the front page.

Also featured on the front page was the protest demonstration by women's organisations in Delhi in August 1983 accompanied with a photograph and the names of prominent protestors arrested for violating traffic rules. The event fit into the traditional definition of news because one of those arrested was Kanak Mukherjee, the Rajya Sabha MP from West Bengal.

'News sense' rather than concern for women's welfare put another dowry-related item of news on the front page on 31 August 1983. Headlined 'Demanding Dowry Is A Crime—Supreme Court,' the report centred around a bridegroom's demand for dowry to pay for the bride's passage to the United States of America. The prominence suddenly given to dowry-related news was clearly related to the currency given to the issue by the anti-dowry campaign. Similarly, on 8 March 1984 (International Women's Day), an agency report detailed statistics of the unnatural deaths of women in Delhi between August 1983 and January 1984. These cold statistics were very well used on the front page to drive home the enormity of the problem.

Ananda Bazaar's editorial on the subject, published on 23 August 1983, criticised the dowry system as a matter of 'shame in a relationship that should be a harbinger of love and understanding. This mercenary attitude to a long-term relationship like marriage is condemnable.' It is interesting that while it condemned dowry, the edit adopted a romanticised view of marriage, ignoring the harsh reality of marital oppression—the lot of a large number of women. Further, the paper made no attempt to analyse the socio-economic factors underlying dowry.

In its second edit on 12 March, the paper took a broad swipe at both the central and the state governments. While agreeing with Prime Minister Indira Gandhi's comment at an IWD meeting that women in India were *devis* (goddesses) only in name because in reality they were not given any respect, the edit was critical of her comment that neither patriarchy nor men were responsible for the dowry system. 'Coming from a woman PM this was regrettable,' the edit commented. The paper also challenged her claim that in post-Independence India the condition of women had improved. It then took on the government of West Bengal for claiming that the 165 dowry deaths in the state during 1981-84 represented an insignificant number. It warned that such complacency would encourage crimes against women. The edit was also critical of the women's movement for its failure to reach millions of victims.

Once again, there was no attempt to formulate a convincing rationale for the increase in dowry and related violence. There was no attack on consumerism. In fact, the paper carried advertisements by banks advising parents to save for their daughter's wedding, as well as companies which presented consumer durables as ideal wedding gifts.

Rape

Ananda Bazaar's coverage of the rape issue, which included reports on custodial rape as well as the rape of minors, was not sensational; the paper omitted the names of the victims and used sober language. There was a gratifying absence of expressions like *ijjat* (honour) and 'outraging the modesty of a woman.'

The paper wrote three edits on the issue. Commenting on the Mathura rape case (31 March 1980), the paper criticised the acquittal of the accused policemen as well as the legal definition of rape. It advocated that the law placing the onus of proof (that she did not provoke the rape) on the woman, be changed. Calling attention to the prevalence of rape of minors, the edit stressed that a sense of shame prevented nine out of ten women from reporting rape. It included an extensive quote from Chief Justice Chandrachud's speech at a conference of the Indian Federation of Lawyers which urged the judges not to limit themselves to a literal interpretation of the law but to go ahead and deliver a fair judgment, thus making the law effective and its interpretation dynamic. The tone of the edit was direct and non-paternalistic and it voiced the demands made by women's organisations regarding changes in the rape law.

Another edit (23 August 1983), headlined 'A Social Crime,' commented on the Rajya Sabha debate on the issue. It mentioned the dissatisfaction of women members who felt that the Home Minister's assurance on amendments in the rape law was inadequate. The edit supported the demand that the onus should be on the man to prove his innocence and suggested special courts for speedy justice. It said, 'There should be a change in the legal system to enable a rape victim to identify the rapist and depose without shame and fear.' The edit reflected sympathy for the victim and understanding of her predicament. The description of rape as 'a physical and mental torture' was a welcome depature from the usual platitudes about rape dishonouring women.

An edit headlined 'Law And Society' (6 December 1983), commented on the Bill and described rape as a serious social crime with implications for women's dignity and rights. It advocated the inclusion of child marriage under rape to discourage the practice. The edit rightly criticised politicians' attitude towards women's issues, revealed in their minimal presence (only fifteen MPs) during the passage of the Bill.

Incidentally, all the serious women's issues—such as rape and dowry—were dealt with on the edit page or general news pages of the *Ananda Bazaar*. The paper's women's page, 'Stree,' carried only light-hearted articles.

The presentation of the Rape Bill in the Lok Sabha on 2 December 1983 was not reported on the front page but the headline and space given to the item on an inside page gave it prominence. It discussed in detail the proposed amendments and mentioned the minimum sentence of seven years. The report pointed out that the Bill was first introduced in the Lok Sabha on 12 August 1980, highlighting the inordinate delay in passing it and the small number of MPs present to finally vote on it.

The Shah Bano Controversy

The in-depth and comprehensive coverage given to the Shah Bano case in *Ananda Bazaar* highlights the glaring difference in the paper's attitude towards purely 'women's issues' and issues that can be politically exploited. In its coverage of the Shah Bano controversy, the women's angle was relegated to the background. The real focus was on religious fundamentalism and fanaticism. *Ananda Bazaar* spared no pains to publicise the issue, even sending a senior editorial staff member to Indore to interview Shah Bano and her family.

The paper carried fifty-two news items on the subject, including contributions by political commentators like Kuldip Nayar and the paper's own columnist Sunit Ghosh. An entire pullout was devoted to the issue (12 March 1986) with contributions from Suman Chatterjee (a Delhi-based special correspondent) and Syed Mustafa Siraj, a well-known Bengali novelist as well as a senior member of the *ABP* editorial department. Five edits focussed on the issue which figured on the front page twenty-six times.

Of the news items, twenty-five were despatches by special correspondents, senior reporters and staff reporters. In addition, there were two special write-ups—one each by M. J. Akbar (editor of the sister publication, *The Telegraph*) and Ashish Ghosh, a political columnist. A page one photograph showed Muslim women demonstrating against the Bill in front of Parliament. Twice the issue was positioned as the main news of the day.

Demonstrations for and against the judgment, seminars, meetings, debates on the Bill—all the main events were covered by *Ananda Bazaar*. Its handling of the Shah Bano issue is an accurate indicator of the priorities of a large-selling language daily catering mainly to the educated middle class, both rural and urban. The political overtones of the award of maintenance to a divorced Muslim woman by the highest court of the country were fully exploited.

ABP's treatment of the Shah Bano affair was a triumph because, despite its covertly communal approach to religious issues, there was an attempt at maintaining a balance by equating Muslim fundamentalism with Hindu fundamentalism. This was especially true of its first edit on the issue. However, subsequently, an undertone of communalism did creep in.

In the first edit, the paper outlined the pressures that were forcing Shah Bano to forego her victory. It pointed out that progressive elements in the Muslim community had welcomed the judgment because they felt the need for changes in the Muslim Personal Law in keeping with the times. A parallel was drawn between reaction to the judgment by orthodox Muslims and the response of the majority of Hindus to the nineteenth century Hindu social reform movement for the abolition of practices such as sati and child marriage and the promotion of widow remarriage and women's education. It recorded that the British government had nonetheless passed the necessary laws.

The edit went on to say that it was unrealistic to expect fundamentalists to support change. The demand for social reform always emanated from a few liberal idealists and not from the majority in a community. This equation of Hindu and Muslim funadmentalism was certainly a big change because *ABP* is known to support the line that Muslims are more rigid than Hindus in their attitudes and that it is difficult to find liberals in that community.

The second edit on the subject (29 November 1985) reflected the expected *ABP* approach. It commented on the miserable conditions of Pakistani women and wondered whether Indian Muslims would like their women to share the same fate. (This sanctimonious remark obviously implied that the condition of non-Muslim women in India is better than that of Muslim women). Another comment—'support for the judgment has come from rational social reformers of both communities, indicating that not all Muslims are fundamentalists'—echoed the familiar communal line that most Muslims are orthodox. The edit pointed out that the Muslim community accepts the Indian Penal Code in matters of criminal law and asked why it was raising the bogey of the Shariat when it came to civil laws.

The interviews with Shah Bano, her husband, Mohammed Khan, and her son, Hamid Khan, published on 7 December 1985, were sensational and melodramatic, neglecting to touch upon the basic lack of rights suffered by women of all communities in India.

A third edit (23 December) was openly critical of the Prime Minister and suggested a meeting with Opposition parties as a prelude to the amendment of Section 125 to exclude Muslim women from its purview. Though it described the Supreme Court judgment as an attempt not at reforming Muslim Personal Law but at giving maintenance rights to a deserted woman irrespective of religion, the edit's clever reference to Shehnaaz Sheikh's petition against the Muslim Personal Law—'Even in the Supreme Court, a Muslim woman has challenged the Muslim Personal Law as discriminatory against women'—exposed a sophisticated and subtle communal approach. Criticising the fundamentalists' unwillingness to accept the Supreme Court's judgment, which amounted to questioning the jurisdiction of India's secular courts and laws, the paper stayed glued to the theme of 'a few liberal Muslims.'

Only the edit on 24 February 1986 took a sympathetic stand on the problems of women. It was critical of the emphasis on the Shariat Law in civil cases exclusively and stated that mercenary considerations were responsible for making women second-class citizens even within the family. Asking why the community did not demand punishment according to the Shariat for thefts and other crimes, it warned against the rise of fundamentalism in other communities, too, which would blur the humanitarian view on the issue. The focus on the discriminatory aspect of the new Bill gave the edit a human and pro-women perspective. Further, the reference to counter-fundamentalism at least shifted some of the focus from 'the few liberated Muslims' syndrome.

The last edit to appear on this issue during the survey period (28 February) commented on the Muslim Women Bill. The edit described it as a ghost of the two-nation theory, saying it harked back to the Middle Ages. But its insinuation, that fundamentalists would now feel encouraged to demand the amendment of Article 44 of the Constitution and thus bring about the death of the proposed Uniform Civil Code, had communal overtones masked by sophisticated secular rhetoric.

The news coverage of the issue ranged from the sensational and melodramatic—like the interviews with Shah Bano and her family (7 December 1985)—to the routine, such as the regular reports on the Muslim Women Bill and the parliamentary debate on it.

Predictably, news related to the Bill featured on page one. But the entire focus was on the communalisation of the issue, rather than on the deprivation of Muslim women under the new Bill. The issue of maintenance after desertion and divorce was pushed to the background. The emphasis rather was on how the government had surrendered to the fanaticism of the Muslim Personal Law Board and other fundamentalist Muslim organisations.

On 21 February, the Muslim Women Bill received page one coverage, complete with all the details of the provisions of the new legislation. The next day, the news of the deferment of the Bill was prominently published on the front page. Tagged on to this report was a small news item on the demand for a Uniform Civil Code submitted to the Prime Minister by the Muslim Satyashodak Mandal.

The presentation of the Bill in Parliament on 26 February was again the main news on page one, published along with a photograph. A Communist Party of India (Marxist) MP was quoted on the Bill: 'A black Bill that insults Muslims and is both anti-Muslim and anti-woman.'

Several reports thereafter reflected a cross-section of opinions against the Bill. According to Mansur Habibullah, law minister in the West Bengal cabinet, it was 'against Article 14 of the Indian Constitution.' Actually, no other newspaper in the region (including the English-language papers, *The Statesman* and *The Telegraph*) gave such comprehensive coverage to the issue.

The news of the resignation of Arif Mohammed Khan was again placed on the front page despite the announcement of the Railway Budget on the same day (27 February). Khan's statement—'Injustice has been done to divorced Muslim women'—was given prominence.

The women's angle was highlighted in a news item on 2 March which reported that Zoya Hasan, on behalf of the Committee for the Protection of Muslim Women's Rights, had presented to the Prime Minister a memorandum signed by 800 prominent Muslims. The memorandum supported Muslim women's right to start legal proceedings under Section 125 and condemned any attempt to deprive them of this legal remedy.

Another important piece of news which appeared in *Ananda Bazaar* on 5 March was not carried by any other paper of the region. It quoted Professor Ahra Rahnabad, wife of the Iranian Prime Minister Hussain Mussavir, on the financial entitlements of a divorced Iranian wife. The new Islamic law, based on the Shariat and drafted by eminent lawyers after consulting Koranic principles from archival texts, gave women in Iran the right to half the husband's assets and bank deposits in addition to maintenance during *iddat*. Since the implementation of the new law, she said, there had been a drastic decline in the divorce rate in Iran. By publishing this news with a big headline, *ABP* at least went beyond the 'oppressed Muslim women' theme.

The *ABP* supplement of the same day contained an interview with Arif Mohammed Khan. In keeping with his secular outlook, he pointed out that his opposition to the Muslim Women Bill was based on his knowledge of the Koran which he quoted to explain his stand. 'My protest is against the torture of helpless Muslim women in the name of Islam by those who have no proper understanding of its tenets,' he said in the interview.

The other article on the subject in the same edition, by the well-known novelist Syed Mustafa Siraj, was one of the best-written pieces on the subject in any language, surpassing even Madhu Kishwar's article in *Manushi*, reproduced by *The Telegraph*, Calcutta. It was well-reasoned, analytical and sympathetic to women without being paternalistic and presented a view of the problem from a wide-angle perspective without entering into sterile polemics. His description of the kind of women who are usually divorced (elderly, impecunious, ugly or sickly wives) and the deprivation of women under the new Bill (for example, deserted but not divorced Muslim women who could earlier get maintenance under Sections 125 and 127 were now ineligible for financial support) provided ammunition for a concerted movement against the Bill.

He demolished the argument about maintaining the traditions of minorities, saying that if such traditions are not in consonance with the country's ideals and human rights values, their abolition could not be said to be depriving the community of its rightful practices. 'Customs must conform to the humanitarian and liberal values of the modern times,' he wrote; citing the examples of cannibalism, human sacrifice, slavery and hideous physical punishments, he asked whether these could be justified as defence of minority rights: 'The Hindu Code Bill was not based on Manu's code but modern, secular values.' In conclusion he added an important point that many had missed: 'The new Bill has not put any restriction on casual talaq.'

This article is a brilliant example of how women's issues can be placed in the larger context of a newspaper's concerns by combining the political as well as the human ramifications of a subject. That the topic was given this kind of importance mainly because of its political fall-out reveals the devaluation of what are considered purely 'women's' issues—domestic violence, discrimination at work, women's health, and so on—in the planning of a big newspaper. The handling of the Shah Bano issue showed that news about it gained in importance only after it spilled over the local boundary of Indore and transcended the question of maintenance for a divorced woman.

Female Foeticide

Although people in West Bengal, as elsewhere in India, also have a strong preference for male offspring, the problem of the misuse of sex determination techniques leading to female foeticide has so far not been given much prominence in the Bengali press. Except for a few sporadic news items and some letters to the editor, there was very little on the subject in *Ananda Bazaar* during the period surveyed. This is surprising because West Bengal is a rich repository of proverbs and rhymes on the desirability of a male child; the inferior status of women is also propagated through the oral tradition.

The issue was possibly neglected editorially because the practice is relatively rare in the state. Not too many clinics offer these techniques in Calcutta, let alone in the rural areas. The two or three clinics in Calcutta which have the facilities do not indulge in brash advertising of the 'Spend Rs. 500 now and save Rs. 50,000 later' variety seen in Maharashtra and northern India. Instead, they rely on small advertisements in the personal columns of newspapers and are, in fact, extremely cagey about giving information or interviews. However, a survey carried out by the Child in Need Institute, of villages on the southern outskirts of Calcutta (Joka and Pailan), showed a positive response to the concept, with 18 per cent of women favouring female foeticide if the test were made available to them.

During the period under review there were only eight items on amniocentesis in *Ananda Bazaar*, five of them letters to the editor written by men. Besides two agency reports, there was one editorial on the subject. There was a total absence of well-researched or serious articles probing the obvious prejudice against the girl child, linking it to the dowry system and the prevailing value system that views girls as a liability. This is an accurate indicator of the priority accorded to what is seen as a purely women's issue by a major newspaper.

Incidentally, the news of female infanticide by a Rajput family in Rajasthan was given prominence because the father was a member of Parliament (belonging to the then ruling party) and the cause was taken up by a woman politician belonging to the then Opposition. Much political heat was generated by the media publicity. Although this incident occurred out of the period under review, it is mentioned here to demonstrate how women's issues without political repercussions are generally overlooked in the mainstream press.

The only editorial on the issue (29 December 1986), headlined 'Murder Of The Girl Child,' contained the familiar argument against the ban—that it would prevent the detection of foetal malformations. It shed no light on how many women really went in for the test to check the health and not the gender of the foetus. The edit's questioning of what the government was doing to effect a change in social values was fatuous. However, the edit did acknowledge the discrimination against the girl child which made a medical test a tool for female foeticide. Still, its outright dismissal of the ban on the plea that it would achieve nothing unless problems like dowry were tackled first was unnecessarily pessimistic and not very convincing.

The Roop Kanwar Tragedy

The first mention of Roop Kanwar's death appeared on 6 September 1987 in the form of an agency report placed on page six but printed in bold type under the headline 'Sati Daho.' The paper carried four editorials and a total of seventy-seven items on the subject. Its coverage of this issue was as comprehensive as that on the Shah Bano controversy.

Initially presented as an example of women's oppression, the issue assumed political dimensions in the latter part of September. It got front page coverage eighteen times and appeared on the edit page thirteen times. Gouri Chatterjee, a senior assistant editor of the paper, was sent to Deorala for on-the-spot coverage. Apart from the editorials themselves, there were two edit page articles, one by a senior political columnist and the other by a professor of history. In addition, the prestigious Sunday review page was devoted to the issue with two big articles.

Though *ABP* used agency reports in September, by the end of the month special despatches by staff reporters and special correspondents were more common. Considerable space was given to news about protests by women's organisations, not only in Rajasthan and the big cities but in distant places like Pune as well. News about the widely attended *chunri mahotsav* was pepped up with spicy details describing the pomp, the hordes of people rushing towards Deorala, the religious fervour, etc. At the same time, the conspicuous absence of the police and the total violation of government orders were highlighted.

The politicisation of the issue began on 22 September with the story about the on-the-spot report given to the then Prime Minister by the then minister of state for home, P. Chidambaram, blaming the state government, the Opposition and other social service organisations for the situation. Protest actions by women's groups got second priority to the pronouncements of political luminaries.

Increasingly, news items began to appear in which the focus gradually moved away from the question of human rights violations and women's oppression to the usual mutual mud-slinging by political parties. Typically, the first public condemnation of the incident by Rajiv Gandhi was published on the front page (28 September), as was the comment by Janata Party leader Kalyan Singh Kalvi that the construction of a memorial to Roop Kanwar was a personal matter concerning the family and that the government had no right to interfere.

While reactions by well-known figures received the expected prominence, the paper also reported, often on the front page, protests connected with the 'sati' incident such as the procession in Calcutta by the city branch of the Marwari Youth Forum demanding condemnation and punishment of the guilty (11 October 1987).

The brouhaha over the Deorala incident had an interesting fall-out in Calcutta. It trained the spotlight on the existence of old sati temples which, at the time of the Rani Sati Mela at Jhunjhunu in Rajasthan, held celebrations on a grand scale. These included annual processions, puja (worship), as well a fair at which booklets glorifying the Rani of Jhunjhunu were sold and hymns and songs in her praise were played. Once this fact was publicised in the Bengali daily *Aajkaal*, there was a national level hue and cry.

The state government was in two minds about what to do. On the one hand, it was cautious about offending conservative voters; on the other, it wanted to maintain its secular image after all its fundamentalism-bashing. The police force was instructed not to give permission for the fair and the procession. The Congress leader, Deokinandan Poddar, in a statement issued on 14 November, tried to hoodwink the government: 'This sati has no connection with the tradition of sati. It is the worship of shakti. We do not support the burning of women.'

Local women's organisations and civil liberties groups were not fooled by this. Fearing trouble, the Marwari Yuva Mancha persuaded the organisers to cancel the procession. On 14 and 15 November, this news occupied the front page of *ABP*. That the paper gave due importance to women's protests is borne out by the fact that the march against the procession to the Beleghata temple, led by the Communist Party of India's women's unit, along with women's organisations like Nari Nirjatan Pratiradh Mancha, Sachetana, Prgatisheel Mahila Samiti and others, received front page coverage.

Ultimately, only worship was conducted and the function was restricted to the temple premises. A news report on 16 November highlighted the demonstrations by women while granting less importance to the worship itself. But on 22 November the *ABP* reported in great detail the bandh organised by Congress (I) leaders and legislators, protesting against the cancellation of the fair and the procession. The assertion by these politicians that the programme was just an annual shakti worship which had nothing to do with Deorala was considered dubious by most women's organisations.

Their misgivings about *ABP* were confirmed when the paper published the pro-sati statement of the Shankaracharya of Puri: 'If sati is voluntary, it is sublime and is to be worshipped.' This, in their view, was given undue prominence compared to the introduction in Parliament of legislation proposing modification of the Indian Penal Code to prevent sati. Reactions against sati by well-known Calcutta personalities from the media and in the fields of literature, cinema and theatre were not given the kind of coverage accorded to the Shankaracharya's statement. This convinced concerned persons that *ABP's* anti-sati stance was insincere, mindful of its image, and that the basic attitude of the paper revealed some covert sympathy for sati which would keep conservative readers and patrons happy.

Such a position was in direct contrast to the article by senior assistant editor Gouri Chatterjee (after a trip to Deorala during which she met many people, including the parents and in-laws of Roop Kanwar) which was unbiased and tried to judge the incident not in isolation but as part of tradition and culture, and in the context of the political set-up. She pointed out that sati has been glorified in text books and local literature and highlighted the commercial reasons that keep such customs alive, concluding that women's oppression is commercially gainful. She also brought to readers' notice the fact that the issue was a matter of prestige among Rajputs and united them in their resentment against the government. She mentioned the hypocrisy of the Rajasthan government, which customarily declared an annual holiday and arranged special buses for the mela at the Rani Sati temple at Jhunjhunu. She also deplored the silence of political leaders on the tragedy. She gave due weightage to the fact that the issue was essentially about women's oppression.

The first editorial on the subject appeared on 29 September as a comment on the central ordinance for the prevention of sati. It was long on anger but short on logic. While the edit blamed government policies and politicians (including leftists), who secretly glorify sati but adopt anti-sati postures in public for political gain, it did not say much except for calling for the eradication of the feudal, patriarchal culture. It made no mention of the economic deprivation of women or the low status and vulnerability of widows; nor did it specifically condemn the Rajput tradition under which a widowed daughter's dower went back to her father.

An edit page article by Shibdas Bannerjee, on 14 October, openly criticised the support given to sati by the Shankaracharya of Puri. On the same day there was an edit entitled 'Who Will Dispel The Darkness Of The Hindu?' The main thrust of the edit was not against Hindu fundamentalism; instead it was an attack on the convention against communalism and fundamentalism held by the Left parties, which was seen as an attempt to gain political mileage. 'Social change can be brought in only by widespread socio-economic movements for reform and not by politicians,' the edit claimed. This attack fitted in perfectly with *ABP's* declared hostility towards the Left. Politics got the better part of the argument and the monstrosity of Hindu fundamentalism was neutralised with the mention of the Muslim Women Bill and communal riots.

The paper commented editorially on sati on two other occasions. The edit on 2 December was severely critical of the Shankaracharya of Puri whose views on sati were seen as inimical to the right to life recognised by the Constitution. It linked the oppression of women to orthodoxy, citing the Shah Bano case as another example. The edit also praised the role of women's organisations in mobilising public opinion against sati and suggested that similar efforts be made to fight the ill-treatment of widows.

While welcoming the new anti-sati law (18 December), the paper expressed cynicism over the fact that such legislation was still necessary 158 years after the first law banning sati was passed. The editorial suggested that the Bill was essentially an evasion of government responsibility, a poor substitute for a socio-political movement aimed at enlightening people.

The lead article in the magazine section's review page, by Bijon Behari Purakayastha, titled 'The Aim And Progress Of Fundamentalism,' discussed Hindu fundamentalism in very strong terms. He devoted one paragraph to the issue of sati itself, stating: 'The primitive emotional upsurge and fundamentalism over sati has destroyed two centuries of social reform and scientific thinking.' The second article, by Nityo Priyo Ghosh, headlined 'Do We Need The Old Religious Texts?' questioned their relevance in the modern context in the light of the Deorala incident. 'The kind of religious and traditional orientation that is usually given to girls over centuries legitimises sati.'

A political article on the edit page by Amal Mukherjee, on 10 November, dealt mainly with fundamentalism. He criticised the reactions of the non-Congress (I) and non-Left parties who had remained ambivalent towards the sati issue and were critical of the new ordinance. 'Their diplomatic silence is a support for fundamentalism for the sake of political gain.'

The Rajasthan High Court's judgment declaring that sati was not a religious rite under Articles 25 and 26 of the Constitution got front page coverage on 27 November. *ABP's* recognition of the significance of the judgment and its further support to anti-sati views, culminating in the detailed coverage on the front page of the President's assent to the new Bill, ultimately gave it a clean image in the context of the sati controversy.

The preparation of the anti-sati Bill and its presentation in Parliament were given due prominence, as was the news item about a case filed in the special court in Jaipur against eleven prominent people, including politicians like Balram Jakhar, Natwar Singh and Vasantdada Patil, for publicly glorifying sati.

The sati issue received wide coverage because of its political fall-out at the national level. From an example of women's oppression it became a symbol of Hindu fundamentalism. The involvement of political parties diverted media attention from such issues as the basic inhumanity of the practice, the criminal denial of life that it entailed, the low economic and social status of women and the commercialisation of women's oppression. Instead, the press tended to present the entire issue as a matter of political patronage and religious fundamentalism. This angle justified, as it were, the tremendous publicity and space devoted to the issue.

The commercialisation of the sati issue is clear in the prominence given on 24 December to the news of the Censor Board's refusal to grant a censor certificate to the film *Antar Jali Yatra* on the grounds that it glorified sati. The paper promptly organised a debate among prominent film and literary personalities on the censors' decision and published their comments the very next day. Most of them were against the banning of Gautam Ghosh's film. *ABP* gave more publicity to the controversy generated by the film than to the fact that its theme centred on the marriage of a young girl to a dying man who had been brought to the river-side just before his death. Without the Deorala incident and the resultant outcry, this aspect of the film would have gone unnoticed. The review committee passed the film with the stipulation that it should begin with a dedication to the victims of sati.

DESH

The coverage of women's issues in *Desh* was and is meagre in the extreme. In 1978-89—the period of the study—the only women's issues covered by the magazine were those that had political repercussions, like the Shah Bano judgment and the consequent Muslim Women Bill, as well as the Roop Kanwar incident. There was the occasional small editorial concerning bride-burning, but apart from two short articles on amniocentesis and harmful drugs, the only articles it carried on women generally dealt with well-known individuals from the Tagore family. Occasionally, however, the literature slot has carried brief pieces on a woman writer.

Women writers whose fiction is sometimes serialised in the magazine usually follow the traditional girl-meets-boy formula. One of them, describing her experience, said she was expressly told to write sweet stories befitting a woman. Although on one occasion *Desh* did serialise a long story by a woman writer which dealt with lesbianism, at present *Desh* heroines are beautiful, gentle, obliging, conformist and self-sacrificing.

For a brief period *Desh* published a woman's page. But this was a sponsored page containing the usual chit-chat, besides tips on fashion, beauty and interior decoration. The page was discontinued suddenly without explanation.

The reason for the poor coverage of women's issues in *Desh* can be traced to the attitude which presumes that such issues do not interest readers. The average *Desh* reader is intelligent, aware and well-informed and it is likely that serious articles on women would find takers. Strangely, however, the magazine continues to be indifferent to women's issues. It did once bring out a special edition on women to mark the International Women's Day—with articles on the dowry system, the women's movement in India and women working in the unorganised sector—but this was not due to a spontaneous or thoughtful editorial decision. The proposal for such an edition came from a woman activist who was then expected to suggest topics and collect articles, pictures, etc. The issue was well received by the public but also carried an article procured by the magazine's staff which dismissed the women's movement as a craze.

Dowry Deaths

Although it was the leading general interest magazine in Bengali during the period under review, *Desh* published only one editorial condemning the practice of dowry. The edit elaborated upon the latest legal definition of dowry, which included not only hard cash but also ornaments, land and other assets, and hailed the Supreme Court ruling as a positive step towards plugging legal loopholes. But there was no attempt to place the problem in a social or economic context. Considering that the cream of Bengali intelligentsia read *Desh*, the proposed solution—that grooms demanding dowry should be boycotted and that brides should opt for spinsterhood rather than marry such men—was simplistic. The socio-economic position of women was neither discussed nor linked to the question of dowry.

This indifference to a burning social problem smacks of intellectual snobbery on the part of the editorial hierarchy of *Desh*. Its failure to see the problem in perspective can be attributed at least in part to the class background of its editors and readers and their tendency to assume that demands for dowry are alien to their lifestyles and values. It was also obvious that dowry was seen as a mere women's issue and, therefore, not important enough for examination within the hallowed precincts of *Desh*.

Rape

The Mathura rape case, the amendments in the law relating to rape and the agitation and debates around these found no mention at all in *Desh* during the period under review. In contrast, *Ananda Bazaar Patrika*, the daily which belongs to the same publishing house, was far more comprehensive in its coverage of women's issues in general, overcoming the mental block that relegates vital social issues like dowry and rape to the women's page.

Desh, unfortunately, is rigid in this respect and has, by and large, excluded such topics from its pages, refusing to give them any kind of intellectual respectability. Its editorial policies and priorities show little awareness of women's problems. The subtle but definitely sexist bias against women's issues on the part of the editors of *Desh* also reveals a lack of sensitivity about the changes taking place in society vis-a-vis women.

The Shah Bano Controversy

Since the mid-1980s, *Desh* has developed a format which includes a series of articles on one major topic, accompanied by a cover illustration. The edition dated 14 December 1985 had Muslim women and the Shariat law as the special topic of the week. The cover, designed by Wasim Kapur, a leading artist of West Bengal, depicted the face of a burqua-clad woman with only her eyes showing. An eight-page long article, headlined 'Muslim Woman Versus The Shariat Law,' by Hassainur Rahman (Professor of History at Calcutta University and well-known for his secular outlook) was accompanied by eight photographs depicting different aspects of the community—prayers, festivals, customs, education, men and women—as well as a large colour photograph of Shah Bano herself.

The captions to the photographs sometimes contained communal insinuations. For example, the picture of Shah Bano was captioned: 'The Supreme Court has saved a woman from insult, hunger and social deprivation.' Another picture of a young Muslim girl hugging her brother was captioned: 'This innocent Muslim girl will one day be hidden behind a burqua.' A third picture displaying a huge mass of people at *namas* in front of the Jumma Masjid carried the caption: 'Islam claims religion is the unity of God with human beings; today that unity suffers a serious crisis.'

The article went beyond the issue of a Muslim woman's right to maintenance to make the point that religious regulations need to be updated from time to time in order to enable communities to keep pace with the general conditions of the time. In this context, the writer stressed two aspects of the judgment: the declared stand of the Supreme Court, that morality was more than mere religious dogma, and the need to activate Section 44 of the Constitution.

The author argued for the absolute necessity and importance of a Uniform Civil Code in a secular state. He described Muslim women's support for the Supreme Court judgment as an expression of revolt in protest, anger and frustration against the Shariat. The support of women belonging to other communities made the issue more social than religious. The author cited the examples of Turkey and Egypt to prove that so-called Islamic regulations actually vary according to the customs of specific countries to suit changing needs.

He concluded by stressing the importance of Indian Muslims' acceptance of their being members of a secular society and the willingness to evaluate their religious dictums against the needs of the present so as to bring about necessary reforms. He said he hoped that all educated Muslims would view the Shah Bano judgment as really revolutionary and would fight to spread its historical significance: 'Today's Muslims must evaluate Islam by today's thought and morality. In the present world, a basic sense of values is more important than anybody's own distinctive religious codes.' *Desh* used the clever policy of asking a Muslim scholar to evaluate Islam. The same points raised by a Hindu would have read like interference in a minority religion.

The second article on the subject in the magazine (24 May 1986) was a translation by Syed Mustafa Siraj of Madhu Kishwar's article in *Manushi*. By the standards of *Desh*, the issue was well-covered—once at the time of the judgment and then as an ensuing debate.

Female Foeticide

In the period under review, *Desh* had only one editorial on the subject of sex determination tests and female foeticide, and even that did not directly focus on the issue. While praising the scientific achievements in the field of in vitro fertilisation and the benefit of such advances to society, the edit pointed out that given the social conditions in India, scientific knowledge could be misused, citing the case of prenatal sex determination. It mentioned in passing that indiscriminate female foeticide could lead to a perilous imbalance in the sex ratio. Although the edit acknowledged that women were grossly devalued in the male-dominated Indian society, it stopped short of making a telling comment on the dangers of an apparently amoral attitude in scientific research—possibility of a womanless society.

This casual approach can be attributed to the practice of rigidly partitioning views from news. Amniocentesis was not yet a force to contend with in West Bengal. Therefore it did not merit the status of a major issue on the pages of *Desh*. It is likely that the editorial was meant to serve the purpose of merely indicating that the publication had taken note of the issue.

The Roop Kanwar Tragedy

The reaction of *Desh* to the Deorala incident did not befit a magazine that had held sway for fifty years as a friend and guide of serious and cultured persons. *Desh* ignored the political significance of the incident and was quite unaffected by all the publicity given to the issue even by its sister publication *ABP*. All that it had to offer on the subject was an editorial and one article tracing the evolution of the custom and tradition of sati.

The title of the editorial published on 17 October was in itself suggestive: 'Women In The Household And A Burning Pyre'. It began by condemning the glorification of Roop Kanwar's death and went on to make the connection with the general position of women in society. Pointing out that the murder of women took many forms, it concluded with the suggestion that men involved in glorifying the Roop Kanwar incident were of the worst variety (unfit to be called human beings) and ought to be punished. According to the edit, only then would the lot of women in our country improve.

The correlation of the Roop Kanwar tragedy with the general condition of women in a one-page editorial diluted the argument about the heinousness of the custom of sati. The suggestion that a handful of 'bad men' were responsible for such a state of affairs amounted to a denial of the fact and nature of women's oppression in India. The 'handful of bad men' theory made it possible to ignore the role of patriarchy in women's oppression. The entire editorial seemed more akin to a juvenile debate rather than a reflection of the viewpoint of a serious magazine.

The 19 December edition of *Desh* carried an article on sati by Dr. Ranjana Mukherjee. The title, 'Suttee Burning A Stigma On India,' was somewhat misleading because the article contained no condemnation of the practice. Rather, it traced in minute detail the historical evolution of the custom of sati—how far back it could be traced, its different forms, the countries where it prevailed, and so on. The article pointed out that cases of sati were often voluntary although there were also instances of forced immolation. Historical sources of information on the subject were mentioned. The article ended with a reference—which seemed rather out of context—to the barbaric nature of the Roop Kanwar incident; it exhorted the government to take positive measures against the custom of sati because it was a slur on the nation's dignity. This denouncement seemed somewhat cosmetic since it was not accompanied by any analysis and had little bearing on the theme of the article.

Why an article documenting the historical evolution of sati was published at this juncture, when people were exercised over the Deorala incident, is not clear. The writer was reportedly rebuked by many for what they felt was a pro-sati article. Some even accused her of glorifying the practice, albeit indirectly. But she was vehement in her denial of such accusations, maintaining that her intention was just to show how deep-rooted the custom was in our culture and tradition.

But the fact remains that an established, widely circulated magazine like *Desh* did not consider the issue important enough to accord it cover story status even at the height of the controversy. The editorial and the article, which were the magazine's only contributions to the discussion, and were published in different editions, appeared unconnected to each other; thereby reducing their impact even further. A kind of cultural arrogance and snobbery seems to have worked to devalue the issue in the minds of the magazine's editors.

SANANDA AND SUKANYA

A women's fortnightly published by the Ananda Bazaar Patrika group, *Sananda* is one of the two magazines selected for this study in an attempt to cover the entire period. In appearance (glossy cover, clear type, neat layout) it marks a departure from *Sukanya*, the other fortnightly Bengali women's magazine included in the study, which closed down some time ago.

Sananda is contemporary, daring and, in advertising parlance, meant for 'today's women.' Launched in July 1986, it has been able to establish itself as a trendsetter among middle and lower middle class Bengali women. It does not have the stodgy, proper approach of traditional women's magazines. In fact, it has often offended conservative tastes and opinions with its salacious and titillating choice of subjects. These range from adultery and extra-marital bliss for the married woman to fifty questions (often of the soft porn variety) you want answered but are too afraid to ask. The magazine also publishes pictures of women in revealing clothes, including skimpy swimwear (the launch issue, for example, carried one such photograph of actress Moon Moon Sen).

Sananda has regular sections on cooking, beauty care, gardening, fashion, travel, interior decoration and shopping. Occasional editions are devoted to the working woman (dealt with in a very superficial manner). Regular features also include legal advice, fiction, debates and opinions, as well as profiles of people. Subjects for debates range from wall graffiti and sex after menopause to well-dressed women and the proposed move to reserve 30 per cent of jobs for women.

Sananda constitutes a cavalier mix of the frivolous and the serious. It is successfully doing for Bengali housewives and working women what Hindi films do for the proletariat: dream peddling. There is hardly anything on poverty, unemployment, malnutrition or the other problems faced by women from economically weak backgrounds. The household hints, fashion tips and recipes are far beyond the reach of the average Bengali woman. Glamour is the key word. With actress and film-maker Aparna Sen as its editor, the magazine has acquired a certain aura of chic and class lacking in the other Bengali women's magazine still in existence—the monthly *Manorama* (published by Mitra Prakashan of Allahabad). Although the latter does not lag much behind *Sananda* in terms of circulation, it is clearly more like a country cousin, lacking *Sananda's* flair.

In the ultimate analysis, *Sananda*, with its glamorous exterior continues to reinforce media stereotypes of the Indian woman: she has to look attractive for her man, keep a beautiful house, be the ideal mother, the perfect cook and, in the case of a married working woman, fit the superwoman slot. It is essential for her to be cleansed, steamed, creamed, nourished and properly made up, with immaculately plucked eyebrows and elegantly coiffured hair. There is no mention of the joys of single womanhood. Marriage is the ultimate El Dorado and men are the final arbiters in assessing a woman's worth.

How do articles on subjects like wages for housework, rape, bride burning, Shah Bano, etc., fit into this scenario? In its maiden issue, *Sananda* had carried an article on wages for housework, along with a few interviews. The suggestion raised hackles and there were quite a few indignant letters from women criticising the demand, stressing the love aspect supposedly valued by Indian women, unlike their 'mercenary' counterparts in the West, and so on.

But reader response to other serious issues that have appeared in

Sananda was quite lukewarm. A senior editor is of the opinion that the occasional serious features in *Sananda* are more gimmicks than articles of faith. They do not appear consistently or frequently; and they probably have little impact because the readers buy the magazine for entirely different reasons.

Another editor expressed his assessment in interesting terms: he suggested that *Sananda's* attempts at tackling serious issues are akin to selling cosmetics for the woman's mind, not unlike the magazine's offer of advice for the beautification of the body. Naturally, he said, it has the same short-term effect. Since talk of women's emancipation is fashionable, the magazine wants to cash in on that. The occasional serious article is merely an exercise in image-building, with no corresponding sense of commitment.

Thus the media's ideal woman continues to be beautiful, well-groomed, up-to-date, a super cook, a talented interior decorator, the anchor of the family, successfully combining career and home. The advertising campaign that accompanied *Sananda's* launch declared that it was for the kind of woman who shopped for a party, never missed her yoga exercises, was the hostess with the mostest, drove her own car and was a busy executive. *Sananda's* ideas about a woman's sexuality, her needs and desires are quite close to those promoted by the patriarchal value system, all the tips about extra-marital bliss notwithstanding. Its advice to women on sex subtly suggests that they must above all keep their husbands happy and be tactful about their own needs—the stoop to conquer approach.

Sananda's cover feature on Sharmila Tagore and Mansur Ali Khan Pataudi was presented as a dream love story come true. Similarly, reams of paper (spanning several issues) were devoted to Prince Andrew and Sarah Fergusson's wedding—the guest list, the banquet, the ceremony, the haute couture of the hoi polloi, the bridal dress, the jewellery, etc. An article on devadasis skipped unpleasant facts and splashed colourful pictures.

The feminist concept of a woman being the mistress of her own destiny is just not evident in *Sananda*. On issues like abortion, while the magazine did carry one or two supportive views—in terms of mothers' health or as a family planning measure—it highlighted the 'pro-life' stance that abortion is a kind of murder. The moral aspect of the subject was upheld, not the right of the woman to her own reproductive choices.

The elegant *Sananda* woman is clearly happily married, picnicking with her family, holding down a glamorous job and living in style. She is not fighting for issues like the right to decide whether or not to get married, equal sharing of housework or the right to inheritance. For example, an article on inheritance rights for women was accompanied by an interview with a woman judge who advised readers to adjust and accept their fate because that is the Indian tradition; if property rights led to acrimony in the natal home, women should forego their share for the sake of peace. Why women should always be at the sacrificing end is not the kind of question dealt with in *Sananda*.

Sukanya began unambitiously in 1981 but found a following in traditional Bengali homes. Its basic approach was conservative: in essence, it promoted the idea that women should have impeccable moral credentials. Its fiction (serialised novels and stories) endorsed traditional virtues. There were some beauty guides, but proportionally less than in later publications like *Sananda* and *Manorama*. The magazine published profiles of prominent women, as well as occasional interviews with a woman politician or an achiever in some other field. There were also the inevitable recipes and tips galore on how to win over husbands with sumptuous food. In fact, *Sukanya* was the first publication to bring out a cookery special.

Unfortunately, after a while, *Sukanya's* pages also began to deal with films, music and entertainment; as a result, its strong women's focus was diluted. With the Peerless group which owned it facing financial trouble, *Sukanya* and its sister publications, *Paribartan* (a weekly) and *Khelar Asar* (a sports fortnightly), ceased publication in 1985. Its revival in 1988-89 was short-lived as the market had by then been captured by *Sananda* and *Manorama*.

Dowry Deaths, Rape

Certain women's issues, like the Mathura rape case and the Maya Tyagi case (where a pregnant woman was paraded naked after her husband and some other accompanying males had been shot dead) went unreported in this category of magazines because there were no women's magazines in Bengali during 1979 and 1980. *Sukanya* was launched in 1981 and *Sananda* in 1986. The former took almost a year to be regularised and the editions published did not appear during the periods under review; in any case, even those issues which appeared outside the period during 1983-84 had nothing on dowry or rape. The magazines partially catering to women, like *Naba Kallol*, did not care to focus on issues like rape for fear of offending their conservative, down-market, semi-urban readership.

Under the circumstances, even though *Sananda* is basically a commercial magazine guilty of commodifying women, it did highlight issues like rape, albeit in a non-analytical and simplistic manner. However, its endorsement of the view that provocative dressing by women invites rape detracted from its condemnation of the act.

The Shah Bano Controversy

All that the women's fortnightly *Sukanya* could offer on the subject of maintenance for divorced women and Muslim Personal Law was an article by Nilu Taulid from Bangladesh in the edition dated 1-15 November 1985. The title of the three and a half-page article (used without any pictures) was 'Different View On The Monthly Maintenance Of A Talaq-Struck Woman'. It presented the reactions of some well-known women (writers, scholars, activists) of Bangladesh to the Indian Supreme Court's judgment in the Shah Bano case. Most of them welcomed it and felt it was a step towards restoring women's position as equal citizens in society. Those against the judgment observed that monthly maintenance after *iddat* was anti-Islam.

A commendable aspect of the article was that it threw some light on the practice of talaq which it described as an immoral act in Islam, to be resorted to only in the case of severe misconduct on the wife's part. The writer pointed out that discussions in the Koran on talaq made it clear that wives were not meant to be driven out empty-handed. She also enumerated the maintenance periods stipulated in different kinds of talaq. However, she refrained from commenting on the injustice of a situation that does not address the question of how a divorced wife is supposed to continue her life beyond these periods. She acknowledged the need to settle such questions legally since it was difficult for most wives, except those who were educated and employed, to carry on with life after a divorce. Although she advocated the fixing of responsibility on the husband, she was not clear how this could be done, ending instead with a generalised suggestion that institutionalised arrangements should be specified for the life-long maintenance of divorced women.

Throughout the article it was clear that the author was careful not to offend her co-religionists. Instead of stating, as Shehnaaz Sheikh has done, that the Shariat basically discriminates against women, she trotted out the usual claims that Islam actually put an end to inequalities among people 1,400 years ago, ending the insult and torture meted out to women in those days and according a high status to women. The caution was, of course, understandable because of the lack of freedom of expression in Bangladesh.

It was, however, disappointing but somehow not surprising that this issue did not merit any indigenous analysis or debate within the pages of *Sukanya*, the only Bengali women's magazine in existence during this period. Perhaps, according to the perceptions of the publishers, the readership (coming largely from the non-westernised, Hindu lower and middle classes) would not be too concerned about the issue. The overwhelming emphasis on maintaining the traditional feminine character of the magazine precluded intelligent discussions on women's issues.

Female Foeticide

There was no mention, let alone discussion, of sex determination tests and female foeticide in the two women's fortnightlies, *Sananda* and *Sukanya*. This omission is an eloquent testimony to the real aims and character of a magazine like *Sananda* which claims to be a trendsetter aimed at 'today's woman.' Here again, the class of the readership was probably an important factor, making it possible to pretend that such nasty things happen only to others, especially those from the lower classes with big broods of children.

The Roop Kanwar Tragedy

Sananda's handling of the 'sati' controversy did not satisfy women's organisations in Bengal because its condemnation of the practice was accompanied by a substantial, four-page interview with the Shankaracharya of Puri whose statement—'A sati does not feel the burning'—was actually used as the headline for the interview. It was published along with a photograph of the seer and two large photographs of paintings depicting a 'sati' jumping into her husband's pyre and people celebrating the event.

The Shankaracharya insisted that the protests against sati were part of a political cover-up to divert people's attention. The special ordinance was, according to him, an assault on Hinduism and went against the government's declared policy of secularism. The government was accused of showing leniency towards Muslims and criticised for spending money on the Pope's visit to India. He said he did not believe that Hindu widows suffer much; nor did he believe that any law could prevent sati from taking place from time to time for it was 'a natural urge for women devoted to their husbands.' He continued: 'When a soldier dies for the country, isn't that a case of suicide also? Sati is like that. Since you people don't call a soldier's death suicide but death to save the motherland, I'll say that sati is a death to save one's own virtue.'

The prominence given to such views was probably because large numbers of women, who comprise the bulk of *Sananda's* readership, revere gurus like the Shankaracharya. In its effort to widen its readership base, *Sananda* once did a cover story on Santoshi Ma, with a cover picture showing a short-haired, jeans-clad woman bending reverently in front of a cow. The brief edit in this issue, carrying editor Aparna Sen's byline, even condoned such practices as a bulwark against the tensions of everyday life. So *Sananda's* coverage of the Shankaracharya's 'heroics' were quite in character with its apparent goals.

The four other articles on the subject in *Sananda* went into the etymology as well as meaning and significance of the term 'sati,' the history of sati, the practice of jauhar and the inevitability of incidents like the Roop Kanwar tragedy in the existing socio-economic set-up. The last of these articles, written by the eminent writer and crusader for tribal rights, Mahasweta Devi, was the only one that related the custom to women's economic status and the feudal structure of upper caste society; it put the issue in a meaningful context and highlighted its relevance to other problems of women.

Mahasweta Devi drew attention to the commercial potential of the practice of sati for an impoverished, upper caste family, as well as to its linkages with land and property. She also pointed out that sati deaths did not occur among tribals and lower castes, indicating that these 'backward' communities were more liberal towards their widows. Sati, she wrote, was linked to the idea that women were expendable. She strongly opposed a separate ordinance for Rajasthan because it would make incidents like Roop Kanwar's death appear stray and isolated. Sati deaths, she said, should be legally treated as murder and the practice ought to be condemned through popular resistance.

Mahasweta Devi's ideas were in consonance with the demands put forward by women's organisations and supported by human rights ed groups. But the impact of this article was neutralised by the prominence accorded to the Shankaracharya.

The brief discussion on the etymology of sati, by *Sananda's* staff correspondent Bisakha Ghose, did not make any significant point. R.P. Gupta (a well-known writer on period topics), while tracing the history of the practice, pointed out that a particular Vedic *sloka* had been deliberately misinterpreted to support this custom. He trod a familiar path, emphasising that no law can eradicate a social custom. While exposing the process whereby a tradition gets invented, he neglected to explain that a socio-economic reorientation is a must for the success of social legislation.

Hossainur Rahman, Department of History, Calcutta University, dismissed the fall-out of the Roop Kanwar tragedy as a storm in a teacup, sensationalised by the media, and called the uproar stupid and insignificant. It was rather unfortunate that a scholar should thus devalue the public indignation and horror generated by the gruesome death of a young girl on her husband's pyre at the end of the twentieth century.

His scholarly article, differentiating between Hindu and Muslim attitudes to marriage and widowhood—the spiritualistic view of the former and materialistic approach of the latter—and outlining the opposition to the custom of sati down the ages, provided a historical overview. He claimed that Muslim rulers had kept quiet about the practice for fear of a Hindu revolt. He linked the practice of *jauhar* to Hindu-Muslim clashes. The main content of his article—the historical reasons underlying the custom, the rigid structure of upper class Hindu society, the fact of male domination and oppression of widows within this class, the denial of rights to Hindu widows, the implied dishonour and shame of widowhood and the sense of guilt encouraged among widows—were all familiar arguments which contributed little to a better understanding of the phenomenon.

The magazine also carried two insets on sati-related temples. One dealt with the history of the Hangsheswari temple in Bansberia (Hooghly district) which was built by Rani Shankari, widow of the landlord Nirsimha Devraj. (Incidentally, Hooghly district holds the record for the highest number of sati deaths in West Bengal.) The second inset described a temple in Calcutta built to commemorate the sati of a queen in Jhunjhunu (Rajasthan) 700 years earlier.

The cover of *Sananda's* edition focussing on sati was quite sensational, featuring an enlarged photograph of Roop Kanwar's face, surrounded by flames. Other pictures accompanying the articles were historical photographs from the British India period depicting women 'committing sati.' Photographs of women's protests over the Roop Kanwar incident were also included.

Sananda's coverage indicates an awareness of the issue but, barring Mahasweta Devi's article, there was no attempt to point out the incongruity of an educated girl 'committing sati' towards the end of the twentieth century. The fact that even women who were graduates were going on pilgrimage to Roop Kanwar's funeral pyre was never questioned. There was no outright condemnation of the practice.

CONCLUSION

The handling of women's issues by a major daily like the *Ananda Bazaar Patrika*, over the decade under review, underwent a welcome change despite some negative bias. Important women's issues, like the sati incident and the Shah Bano controversy, were given extensive coverage although this was at least partly due to political reasons. Even so, women's issues increasingly figured in the paper during the 1980s and the coverage was more organised than it was in the 1970s. The wide publicity given to the women's decade, the formation of autonomous women's groups and their increased visibility in urban areas have combined to make the media take note of women's issues.

Atrocities against women are also reported somewhat differently now. For example, in May 1976, Surupa Guha, a young woman belonging to a well-known and wealthy family, died an unnatural death. The entire Bengali press treated the incident as a scandal in an aristocratic family, providing sensational coverage in the form of gossip. Almost ten years later when Debjani Banik was murdered by her in-laws, the case was given equally wide coverage but the death was viewed as a crime against women.

This shift can be attributed, in fair measure, to the activism of women's groups which forced the language press to become aware of the status of women and the struggle to change it. The mid-1980s have, therefore, witnessed an important turn in the coverage of women's issues in Bengali papers.

Even the style of reporting has changed. Not only are the unnatural deaths of married women reported but such news is accompanied by information about protests and demonstrations over such incidents.

The term 'wife-murder' has gained wide currency entirely because of media exposure. Of course, there is an urban bias and the mechanical presentation of such news tends to reduce the publication to a mere recording device or a source of statistics. But after a spurt of such incidents, *ABP* often does publish edits condemning domestic violence, dowry, etc., and linking women's oppression to their low economic status.

The paper's approach towards women's issues is not totally in consonance with the aims and ideals of the women's movement. But perhaps that would be expecting too much. At least the problems are recognised. While it is true that protests and demonstrations at the local level are covered only if prominent women are involved or if the organisers have good press connections, it is nevertheless a positive sign that the mainstream language media is increasingly taking cognizance of women's participation in protests.

Interestingly, none of the major issues that have been taken up for review in this survey were featured in *ABP's* weekly women's page 'Stree.' Week after week, this page is devoted to beauty tips, fashion and light-hearted articles. It is difficult to reconcile its content with the same paper's stance on sati or the Shah Bano case—issues which were featured prominently in the general news section, often accompanied by edits and editorial page articles. While the integration of women's issues into the total perspective and scheme of a big newspaper—a welcome development—did take place in the case of these two issues, it was clearly linked to their political repercussions.

Nevertheless, the *Ananda Bazaar* has the best track record vis-a-vis women's issues among Bengali newspapers, and not only because of its coverage of the Shah Bano and sati issues. Its Sunday magazine section, for instance, devotes page two (broadly termed review section) to theoretical articles on topics of current interest. Women's issues are featured quite frequently on this page. Analytical articles on the involvement of women in crime, mothers' rights and the ethical aspects of surrogate motherhood, the question of justice under the rape law, the growth of consumerism among women and sexism in textbooks have been published in this section.

In the news section, reports on crimes against women are usually based on police handouts; but the headlines and style of recent reporting do show an increased awareness of the issue, especially in terms of recording local people's protests against incidents in their area. The edits, some of them quite strong and written by a team of senior persons, suggest some consciousness about the issue despite the preponderance of generalisations.

Although the quantum of coverage given to women's issues has increased, there appears to be an unspoken differentiation between what constitutes purely 'women's issues' and issues concerning women which are of national importance. This was evident in the difference between the coverage of issues like the Shah Bano judgment and the Roop Kanwar incident and those of rape and dowry deaths. The latter were clearly seen as primarily women's concerns and therefore not necessarily part of the main editorial content of a newspaper or general interest magazine.

The neglect of virtually all the topics covered in the survey in *Desh* corroborates this view. The coverage of what are seen as purely women's issues without obvious political or legal overtones is not the same as that of politically exploitable ones like those raised by the experiences of Maya Tyagi, Shah Bano and Roop Kanwar or, more recently, the ghastly assault on three women officials at Bantala or the incident of gang rape at Birati.

Politics remains the dominant concern, while the economic and social aspects of issues invariably take a back seat. This is largely due to the rigid conventions of political reporting, which again is a reflection of the Indian reality. In a situation where even a decision like the setting up of a new steel factory depends not on economic realities but on political exigencies, it is only natural that the print media are also preoccupied with politics. The societal values of the milieu in which the media exist are bound to be reflected in their focus or perceptions.

This is clearly established in the magazines. Both *Desh* and *Sananda* (especially the latter) are representatives of glossy magazine journalism even though *Desh* has created an aura of respectability through its mix of contents. There is some recognition of the relevance of serious issues to the general readership. But the identification of these issues does not reflect current awareness of women's concerns. The handling of uncomfortable social realities, like homosexuality/lesbianism, prostitution, unwed motherhood and abortion, find no place in these magazines. The middle class character of the bulk of its readership makes the perpetuation of conventional morality a dominant concern.

Sananda (a Bengali cousin of the English language magazine, *Savvy*) has a clever content mix which specialises in superficial treatment of serious issues—the hallmark of publications aimed at the middle class. The magazine's handling of the sati issue is a good example. In its special edition on sati, the emphasis was more on packing in as many well-known bylines as possible rather than on studying the topic in depth from various angles. The features seem to have been carefully selected to practically neutralise each other, so that the magazine could get into water without wetting itself. It is difficult to say whether it was, in the ultimate analysis, pro-sati or anti-sati; this ambivalence served the interests not of women but of patriarchy.

The use of exploitative themes and photographs was common to *ABP's* Sunday section as well as *Sananda*. The front page of the newspaper's Sunday section twice featured provocative articles, on Jaqueline Onassis and Merle Oberon respectively, accompanied by salacious quotes in bold, black type and sexy photographs. Yet, on the very next page (the review section) appeared serious articles on various important women's concerns.

The very fact that the *Ananda Bazaar* took cognizance of the emergence of the women's movement and its aspirations, the problems of working women, the importance of careers for women, and so on, should be viewed as a positive step because *ABP* is the unchallenged pace-setter in Bengali journalism. Its tacit recognition of issues beyond marriage, home and motherhood, which are central to the lives of a large number of urban and semi-urban women, has certainly influenced other Bengali publications. However, for *Sananda* such issues have become a convenient peg on which to hang their claim of catering to 'today's women.' The magazine remains fully oriented to the consumerism prevalent today and is more interested in serving the cause of its patrons—the advertisers—and in protecting the interests of the upper-middle class, Bengali *bhadralok*, which forms its readership base, than in promoting women's emancipation.

13

The Gujarati Press

Sonal Shukla

Gujarati journalism has had a strong tradition of social reform. Some of the best known writers and editors of the state, like Karsandas Mulji Narmad and Kabaraji, were social reformers. Kabaraji edited *Rast Goftar*, founded by Dadabhai Naoroji in 1852. Karsandas and Kabaraji were part of a group of reformers who launched *Stree Bedh* in January 1857; this was probably the first journal for women in this country. A few copies of the first edition are still available. *Stree Bedh* continued to be published until 1952.

Although revivalists came out in great force against the reform movement and began to publish their own papers, the next strong influence on Gujarati journalism came from Mahatma Gandhi and nationalism. Gandhi himself wrote extensively in Gujarati and he represented a liberal social reform tendency. Respected Gujarati journalists and publishers still reflect Gandhian liberalism. This began to change, especially in Ahmedabad and Baroda, after the 1985 communal riots; many newspapers now openly flaunt their anti-minority, anti-dalit and anti-poor attitudes.

Most Gujarati newspapers have also distanced themselves from liberal or radical positions in respect of the issues raised by the controversy over the Narmada Dam. With the exception of one long investigative article by Sheela Bhatt in *Abhiyan* and a few tentative writings against big dams in some columns, mainly originating in Bombay, Gujarati newspapers have been totally pro-dam in their approach, thereby choosing not to go against the dominant sentiment in the state.

On women's issues, they are not yet openly hostile. But as the radical stand taken by feminist groups on issues like communalism, health, housing, etc., have become clearer, the earlier support has been withdrawn and feminist baiting has begun in the form of barbed comments in editorials and articles.

Gujarati magazines find it difficult to survive financially. Of the scores of magazines that appeared on the scene in the post-Independence period, apart from *Chitralekha*, only *Abhiyan* and to a much lesser extent *Yuva Darshan* have managed to bring out regular editions. Some of the best and most prestigious magazines—including *Sanskruti*, brought out by Umashankar Joshi, the Gyanpeeth Award-winning poet—have ceased publication over the past ten years.

For this review of women's issues in the Gujarati press, three publications were selected: *Janmabhoomi*, an evening newspaper; *Chitralekha*, a weekly newsmagazine; and *Stree*, a women's journal.

JANMABHOOMI

Janmabhoomi was the second largest selling Gujarati newspaper in Bombay in 1979, next only to *Mumbai Samachar*—the oldest newspaper in Asia. While the latter would have been a better choice for the survey, especially since *Janmabhoomi* is an eveninger, the option was not available. The management does not permit researchers to access their old issues because in the past people have allegedly cut out pages instead of taking notes. Another Gujarati morninger published from Bombay, *Janshakti*, brought out by the Free Press group, was closed down in June 1979, at the very beginning of the survey period.

Pravasi, a morning daily, was launched by the Janmabhoomi group in August 1979, a few months after the period selected for this study; while *Samkaleen*, another morning paper, was started by the Indian Express group only in 1985. As a result neither could be included in the study.

Although *Janmabhoomi* is an evening paper, it is not a tabloid. This broadsheet newspaper was started in 1934 as a nationalist publication. It attained immense popularity under its founder editor, Amritlal Sheth, who became something of a journalistic legend in his lifetime. Zaverchand Meghani, the most popular nationalist poet in Gujarat, was also associated with the paper from its inception. The paper is now run by the Saurashtra Trust and its editor is Harindra Dave, a famous poet. Dave has won several awards for his literary work as well as for journalism. He won the B. D. Goenka Award for Excellence in Journalism in 1991.

Janmabhoomi's readership includes professionals as well as educated, liberal sections of the business class. Gujarati families, particularly in Bombay, often take an English newspaper in the morning and read *Janmabhoomi* in the evening. The paper's circulation was about 45-50,000 in the 1970s but it has dropped to 40,000 over the last ten years. The reasons could be the entry into the market of an evening tabloid, *Madhyantar*, in the mid-1980s and the growing popularity of English tabloids like *Mid-day* and *The Afternoon Despatch and Courier*.

Janmabhoomi is a broadsheet daily comprising at least ten to twelve pages every day. It has an edit page as well as an op-ed page. On Sundays, the group's morning and evening papers are combined into a morninger called *Janmabhoomi Pravasi*. The Sunday edition has always been very popular—it enjoys a circulation of one lakh, almost double that of *Janmabhoomi*. The Sunday magazine section has various columns, including a 'family' column which discusses women's questions in a superficial way, sometimes by fictionalising a conversation between mother and daughter, or mother-in-law and daughter-in-law. This section is called *Sansar Chakra*. Other regular features include a children's page, a serialised novel and literary columns by some major writers. Although the editor, Harindra Dave, is himself a leading writer, most of his creative work is published elsewhere.

In terms of placement, the most important pages, after the front page, are the back page and the op-ed page. The main stories on page one usually continue on page two. Of the five issues studied, the Shah Bano issue received the maximum coverage, with a total of nineteen items, followed by dowry deaths and rape with twelve each. Surprisingly, *Janmabhoomi* carried a total of only fifteen items on the sati issue in the months studied, a low count compared to the coverage of this subject in most English and other regional language newspapers surveyed in this study.

The Shah Bano issue was accorded more importance than the others not just in quantum of coverage; it occasioned three editorials while dowry deaths, female foeticide and sati were commented upon in only one editorial each, and rape was totally ignored in terms of editorials.

Dowry Deaths

Of the twelve items on dowry deaths in *Janmabhoomi*, seven were routine reports. Only one news story was displayed on the front page in a box; this was, oddly enough, an item about the rehearsal of a play against wife murder by a women's group in Ahmedabad (14 March 1984). It is not entirely clear why this item merited page one coverage when news about the passage of anti-dowry legislation was reported routinely on an inside page. Even the unusual story of a bridgroom from Gwalior, who got his prospective father-in-law to give up smoking as a precondition to marriage, was boxed and placed on an inside page under the headline 'Rare Story Of An Unusual Dowry'. The only mention of the public outcry against dowry deaths came as part of a report on parliamentary news (5 July 1979) which mentioned the anti-dowry Bill expected to be soon introduced in Parliament.

Around 1983, the paper introduced a regular column on women's issues on its edit page, written by two well-known women activists and members of the Chhatra Yuva Sangharsh Vahini, Chetna and Alka. In the edition dated 13 August 1983, they wrote on the dowry issue from a clearly feminist perspective, drawing attention to the death in Bombay of a Dr Varsha Venkataraman. Varsha, a Gujarati Lohana girl, who had married outside her caste and community and was resented by her in-laws for not bringing a dowry, was found hanging in her matrimonial home. She had left a suicide note absolving anyone of blame. In another piece (9 March 1984), the columnists touched on the issue of crimes against women and the reasons why they go unpunished, referring to the Sudha Goel and Varsha Venkataraman cases. It was only in this column that dowry deaths were actually discussed and analysed.

Janmabhoomi was clearly not affected by the coverage of dowry deaths in the rest of the media, especially the English and Hindi press, which carried reports on and investigations into the crime. Although Bombay, from where the paper is published, was not the centre of the dowry death phenomenon or the campaign against it, this explanation does not hold throughout the period surveyed because the issue had become widely known all over the country by 1983-84.

Rape

The majority of the twelve items on rape published by *Janmabhoomi* during the survey period were routine reports. There was not a single edit on the subject. Although the paper carried an item announcing (21 February 1980) the public meeting called by the newly-formed Forum Against Rape in Bombay, which was to be followed by a *morcha* on 8 March, there were no reports on the meeting or demonstration.

Only once did rape figure on the front page, in the form of a small news item about a case of dacoity and rape near Nagpur (22 March 1980). Another rape case which caught the paper's attention was the infamous Bandra rape case. This story had first appeared in a Marathi newspaper before it was front-paged by the Bombay edition of the *Indian Express*. The reporter had described how a man and his wife, heading home on the Western Express highway after watching a late-night movie at the drive-in theatre, were held up at knife-point by three men. According to the report, while the man was allowed to go, the wife was allegedly taken away and raped. She returned the next morning, told the tale and then committed suicide.

The sensational story raised a hue and cry in the city in April 1980. Eventually, its veracity was seriously questioned and the paper had to issue a retraction. *Janmabhoomi*, like other Bombay newspapers, responded to public interest in the case by carrying several news items in the course of the first week of April concerning demands by Jan Sangh leaders for the resignation of the then Home Minister, Zail Singh, and the order by the then Prime Minister, Indira Gandhi, for a thorough investigation into the case. However, there was no comment on the case and the fact that it had been proved false. The only such response was from a reader (14 April 1980) who wrote a letter criticising the journalist who had reported the rape case.

Janmabhoomi did not carry reports on discussions—even in Parliament—regarding changes in the rape law. Although the Forum Against Rape was a Bombay-based organisation which had initiated public action on the issue, it received no coverage in the paper over the period surveyed.

The Shah Bano Controversy

Of all the issues studied, the controversy following the Supreme Court judgment in the Shah Bano case on the question of maintenance drew the greatest response from *Janmabhoomi*. Three of the total of nineteen items on the issue were edits while one was an edit page article. The paper's news coverage included an interview with Shah Bano; published as a special report, which included details about the question of *meher* and developments in her home-town Indore in the aftermath of the judgment. The interview appeared on 19 December 1985 when the proposed legislation barring Muslim women from the purview of Section 125 of the Criminal Procedure Code was being hotly debated throughout the country.

The tone of all the three edits, appearing on 18 November and 21 December 1985 and 28 February 1986 respectively, was non-communal. The first, strongly supportive of Muslim women's interests, stated: 'The Muslim community should introspect about the status of women.' It mentioned the reformist group Muslim Satyashodhak Mandal which had been travelling across Maharashtra, encountering opposition from conservatives on occasion. It also advocated the adoption of a uniform civil code.

The other two edits were comments on the personalities involved in the controversy rather than on the issue itself. While one criticised Z. A. Ansari, a minister in Rajiv Gandhi's cabinet, for his comments on the Supreme Court judgment and referred to progressive laws prevailing in some Islamic nations, the other was a strong and forthright critique of the government following the resignation of Arif Mohammed Khan on the question of the Muslim Women (Protection of Rights on Divorce) Bill. It stated: 'Loss of faith in the government's credibility cannot be made up for Rajiv's government has revealed it is immature and superficial.' It lavished high praise on Arif Mohammed Khan, saying that he believed in 'value-based politics in the tradition of Lal Bahadur Shastri, Chagla and Asoka Mehta....'

Apart from the three edits, two more items on the subject appeared on the edit page. One was a box item (5 March 1986) headlined 'Why Should Muslim Women Be Deprived Of This Right?' This criticised the roles played by the then Prime Minister and Muslim fundamentalists in the controversy. A similar article three days later told of reactions across the country against the Muslim Women Bill and condemned Ansari, Rajiv Gandhi and the Congress (I) party.

Neither Arif Mohammed Khan's resignation nor some of Shah Bano's statements made it to the front page of the paper. But a news item on a press conference held by the wife of the Prime Minister of Iran (5 March 1986), in which she reportedly stated that in her country a divorced woman got a share in her husband's income, was placed on the front page under a three-column headline.

Female Foeticide

Janmabhoomi, like its English language counterparts, paid scant attention to the controversy over the misuse of amniocentesis and other such technologies for sex determination. There was a total of just three items on the issue, all appearing in January 1988 after the Maharashtra government had announced its intention to introduce legislation restricting the use of sex determination tests. However, one of the items was an edit which welcomed the law and stated: 'An Act like this should be a model for the country' (2 January 1988).

The Roop Kanwar Tragedy

The death of Roop Kanwar in Deorala and the furore over it elicited a total of only fifteen items in *Janmabhoomi*. However, of these, one was an edit, two were edit page articles and six were special reports. Five of the reports were featured on the front page. Thus, what the paper failed to do in volume, it made up for in content. For instance, as early as 15 September, it carried a report on the indifference of the authorities in Deorala to the task of preventing the preparations for the *chunri mahotsav*. The next day, a front page report once again highlighted the Rajasthan government's failure to prevent the gathering and mentioned the opposition to the ceremony by women's groups who were threatened for their anti-sati stand.

Again, on 17 September, two special reports appeared on the front page, one of them accompanied by a large photograph of Roop Kanwar in the sati image. The two items were headlined 'Was Roop Kanwar Screaming For Her Father On The Funeral Pyre?' and 'How Does Sati Fit With The Prime Minister's Talk About The 21st Century?' The tone of both news items was decidedly pro-women. They gave additional information about police investigations into the incident and about the occurrence of sati cases in Rajasthan over the past decade. On the same day, a half-page article on the edit page by the famous columnist Vijaygupta Maurya traced the history of the custom. The tone of this article, too, was clearly anti-sati.

On 18 September, a front page special report carried the opinions of men and women in Bombay under the headline 'The Husband Should Also Commit Sati'. However, the edit on that day strangely laid the blame for the continuance of customs like sati and child marriage on the women's movement. It posed the question: 'Why did not women activists rush to the sati *sthal*? Why didn't they offer a satyagraha? Gandhiji has shown us this way. Why isn't there a survey on the condition of widows who have not committed sati?' It is interesting that although the paper demanded such a survey, it did not feature a single article over the period studied on the plight of widows. It did, however, carry a front page anchor story which commented on the status of married women in Rajasthan. Despite the rather misleading headline, 'Committing Sati The Best Alternative,' the article criticised police support for the custom.

All the writing on the issue appeared in September 1987. There were no items in October, November or December. Editor Harindra Dave explained that there was no particular reason for this and that the paper carried editorials on the issue in 1988 and 1989. The last one was a particularly strong condemnation of the deification and glamorisation of sati, for which the paper blamed politicians.

Dave explained the difference in the coverage of the Shah Bano issue and that of Roop Kanwar's death, saying that the former stretched out over a much longer period because of events such as the resignation of Arif Mohammed Khan, the ambiguous stand taken by different political parties and the fact that millions of women were affected by the new Muslim Women Bill. In contrast, he said, Roop Kanwar's death, horrible as it was, was more limited in its overall impact.

CHITRALEKHA

Chitralekha began as a film magazine in 1950 but some years later it was converted into a news magazine. Its publishers started a separate film magazine called *Ji* which now also has an English edition.

Both its founding editor, Vaju Kotak, and one of its two present editors, Harkisan Mehta, are well-known novelists whose books are bestsellers. *Chitralekha* is popular because of its serialised novels, humour column and news stories. It does not have a women's section, art column or book reviews. The new trend of investigative journalism was pioneered in Gujarati by *Chitralekha*. Besides at least one long news story on a current political topic, the magazine has special articles on a variety of subjects, ranging from lesser known tribes in Gujarat to the latest medical discoveries in other countries. These specially commissioned articles and stories are in-depth and profusely illustrated but generally non-commentative.

Only the main article focussing on political developments is characterised by analysis and comment. The magazine has no editorial although some news analysis or an article on a current topic appears on the first page where the logo and details of the publication are printed. However, this is written not by either of the editors but by the well-known, progressive writer Vasudev.

Over the past ten years, the circulation of *Chitralekha* has risen from over one lakh to more than three lakhs. This survey of *Chitralekha's* coverage of the five selected issues is incomplete because some editions of the magazine could not be located. According to the publishers, these must have been misplaced when their office moved from south Bombay to an industrial estate in a suburb of the city.

Dowry Deaths

No coverage of the dowry death phenomenon or the campaign against it could be found in *Chitralekha* over the months surveyed. Two editions of the magazine—dated 26 March and 2 April 1984—were missing from the files and there was no way of ascertaining whether they carried any articles on the subject. But given the overall editorial attitude of the magazine to women's issues, it is improbable that they did. It may, therefore, be safe to conclude that *Chitralekha* gave little, if any, coverage to this burning topic of the day.

Rape

Similarly, no articles on the rape issue appeared during the survey period, although it must be noted that the editions dated 3 March, 31 March, 7 April and 12 May were missing from the 1980 file.

The 21 April 1980 edition carried a long article on a journalist's problems after filing a false report on a rape case, wittingly or unwittingly. This was a three-page article by Kanti Bhatt headlined 'Around A Report On A Rape Of A Housewife'. The article discussed the issues that had arisen following the report by *Indian Express* reporter Shirish Kanekar, on the alleged rape of a woman in Bombay, which was subsequently proved false. Bhatt's article was sympathetic towards the journalist but neither commented on the issue of rape nor mentioned the anti-rape movement in Bombay.

The Shah Bano Controversy

The Shah Bano case received better coverage than the earlier two in *Chitralekha*. Although only three items appeared over the period surveyed, one of these was a long article which dealt with various aspects of the issue. Written by Sheela Bhatt, the article headlined 'Both Sides Of The Matter Of Shah Bano's Maintenance' (November 1985), was well-displayed, with a total of seven photographs as well as spot interviews. It provided some idea of the feelings of Muslim women and men in Shah Bano's family and neighbourhood. However, the author failed to meet Shah Bano herself. Nor did the article contain any comment or analysis of the issue.

This piece was followed by a long period of silence on the subject, broken by a small item (12 May 1986), in the miscellaneous column on the last page, which described Shah Bano as 'the world-famous woman of 1985-86' and projected her as an oppressive mother-in-law. The item quoted her daughter-in-law who had spoken to a journalist about her situation. However, neither the name of the journalist nor the publication in which this report originally appeared was mentioned. The item was accompanied by a photograph of Shah Bano with her daughter-in-law, captioned: 'The daughter-in-law brings a house (a family) into disrepute.' This is actually the opening line of a famous Gujarati folk song.

The third and last item on the issue appeared in the edition dated 19 May 1986. This was an angry and forthright analysis and comment by Vasudev in a piece equivalent to an editorial. The headline, 'Bill To Make Beggars Out Of Deserted And Divorced Muslim Women,' was placed alongside a photograph of a Muslim woman. The writer criticised the then Prime Minister, Rajiv Gandhi, accusing him of sacrificing the interests of Muslim women in his attempt to find some middle ground between progressives and fundamentalists. He stated that communalism had been greatly supported in the name of secularism; and that although Rajiv Gandhi tried to project himself as a strong, quick-thinking, decisive and no-nonsense leader, his handling of the Shah Bano case had actually lowered his image in the minds of millions of people.

Female Foeticide

No articles on the controversy over the misuse of sex determination tests leading to female foeticide could be found over the period surveyed. However, this researcher remembers reading an article by Hari Desai and Varsha Pathak in *Chitralekha* which justified the tests in the name of women's right to choose, the need for family planning, and the desirability of preventing the birth of handicapped children. It was not possible to ascertain whether this article appeared in the edition dated 28 July 1986 which was missing from the files.

The Roop Kanwar Tragedy

There was only one article on the sati controversy during the period covered by the survey. This is surprising because this issue had fired the imagination of the media across the country. Roop Kanwar's death and its aftermath had received more extensive coverage than any of the other issues included in the survey in virtually all sections of the press—in English as well as the other three regional languages covered by the study.

Chitralekha's one report from Deorala appeared in the edition dated 16 November 1987. The article, by Varsha Desai, was accompanied by several photographs, including the popular picture postcard made from a wedding photograph of Roop Kanwar which was sold in Deorala during this period. The article was essentially descriptive and reported on the worship of sati by the local people. The writer had also interviewed Gayatri Devi of Jaipur who condemned the anti-sati uproar as an example of the persecution of the Rajput community. The former maharani claimed that if a Jat woman had committed sati, no one would have protested.

Although the report reflected a basically anti-sati stand, it criticised women's organisations 'for not doing grassroots work.' It is interesting that both *Janmabhoomi* and *Chitralekha* used instances of violence against women to lambast the women's movement.

Overall, the coverage of women's issues in *Chitralekha* during the ten years surveyed was extremely patchy. The only exception was the Shah Bano issue which probably drew a response because of its political fall-out. However, measured by the same yardstick, the sati issue should have drawn more coverage than it actually did.

STREE

All the Gujarati women's journals of the nationalist period, including

Stree Bedh which had been in existence since the 19th century, ceased publication soon after Independence. Lalhuben Mehta, daughter of the famous Amritlal Sheth, brought out a journal called *Grih Mandir* for a while. The *Janmabhoomi* group of publications had also launched a journal called *Sudha* under the editorship of the well-known writer Dhiruben Patel (who wrote the dialogue and lyrics for the film/play *Bhavani Bhavai*, among other things). Later the magazine was edited by the popular novelist Varsha Adalja. Dr Neera Desai, a noted sociologist and former head of the Research Unit on Women's Studies of the SNDT University, Bombay, was also a member of its editorial collective. However, *Sudha* did not prosper financially and in 1980, after ten years, publication was discontinued. (Dr Desai, activist and researcher Vibhuti Patel and this writer form the editorial collective of the women's studies quarterly in Gujarati, *Nari Mukti,* which began publication in March 1987.)

In 1979, at the beginning of the survey period, *Sudha* was the only real women's magazine in Gujarati and this ceased to exist in 1980. Both *Gujarat Samachar* and *Sandesh*, dailies published from Ahmedabad, bring out women's magazines in tabloid form. Of these, *Stree*, which belongs to the Sandesh group, is the more popular and regular. Edited by Leelaben Patel, the publisher's wife, the tabloid has an estimated circulation of over 72,000 (1987 figures). In the Indian and Eastern Newspaper Society (IENS) yearbook of 1987, the publication was described as a 'weekly for women folk.'

Ahmedabad is the home of several active and well-known women's organisations. Apart from the world-famous organisation, the Self-Employed Women's Association (SEWA)—whose founder and head Ela Bhat has won national and international recognition and has served in important positions in the country—several other radical women's groups, such as the Ahmedabad Women's Action Group (AWAG) and Chingari, are based in the city. None of their activities are ever covered by *Stree*; nor does the periodical carry any articles by women activists.

Regular columnists who contribute to *Stree* are generally men. The most progressive articles in the magazine were by Ishwar Petalikar who died some years ago. Petalikar was known for his reformist zeal, evidenced in his novels and other literary work. A popular feature of *Stree* is its section containing matrimonial advertisements. The most regular features seen in the magazine are serialised novels, columns on beauty, food and health, astrological predictions, letters to the editor and reports of the activities of Stree Niketan—an association of women readers, with several branches, promoted by the journal. From the reports on its activities, it appears that Stree Niketan is a traditional, middle-class organisation which concentrates on holding competitions, exhibitions, etc.

Stree regularly publishes articles on 'family values,' such as togetherness and harmony in marriage, of the type analysed by Betty Friedan in her landmark book *The Feminine Mystique*. Women's issues generally appear only in editorials which are sometimes surprisingly progressive and forthright, adopting a tone which is at variance with the image of women projected by the rest of the magazine.

Dowry Deaths

Stree carried four items on dowry over the period surveyed—a mention in an advice column, a passing reference in a regular column by a male writer, a special article by the same male columnist and a reference in a work of fiction.

As early as in the edition dated 12 June 1979, the advice column dealt with a query from a young woman who was wondering what to do about the insistence of her boyfriend's parents on settling the dowry before giving the couple permission to get married. The progressive agony aunt suggested: 'Get the man to resist his parents' pressure for dowry or forget him.' She added, in bold letters for emphasis, 'One is shocked that parents can commit the sin of forcing two lovers to part for the sake of dowry.'

Anwar Agewan, a regular columnist, touched upon the dowry issue in two of his contributions. In the 17 July 1979 edition, he made a passing reference to the custom in a column in which he discussed the issue of marriage to an older woman.

A few years later, in the edition dated 10 September 1983, he addressed the issue more frontally. In his article headlined 'Dowry: A Vicious Cycle,' accompanied by a photograph of a bedecked bride, he suggested inter-caste marriage as one of the solutions to the problem. The writer also advocated simple weddings, efforts to raise awareness amongst women, compulsory registration of marriage and a complete list of gifts. Two box items accompanying the article carried quotes on the issue. One said that to consider women as weak was an insult and an injustice while the other explained that cash and other things were given at the time of marriage because Hindu women did not have inheritance rights. Despite this last statement, the column was exceptionally pro-women, besides being in-depth and analytical.

The fourth mention of dowry in *Chitralekha* appeared in a trivial short story in which a woman was quoted as saying, 'Our academic qualification is our dowry.'

Rape

This issue elicited a surprisingly prolific response from *Chitralekha*, with a total of ten articles appearing over the period surveyed (one was in an edition dated just two days before the selected period and was taken into account). Rape was not only covered in a larger number of items than any of the other issues, but it also occasioned four editorials. Of these, three were fairly radical in their approach while one took the conservative line that women should not be out alone at night.

For instance, the editorial in the 30 July 1983 edition was headlined 'Rape Is A Crime Against All Women And Not Just Against One Victim'. Adopting a serious and pro-women tone, it quoted various people on the issue, including the then Prime Minister, Indira Gandhi.

Just two weeks later, on 13 August 1983, the magazine carried another editorial on rape under the headline 'The Crime Of Rape Should Be Uprooted, We Should Create A Climate In Which The Victims Can Speak Out.' The edit stated that rape victims should not be maligned but instead encouraged to lodge complaints. It commended the work of the Delhi-based women's group, Saheli, which had worked with rape victims and helped rouse public opinion against the perpetrators of the crime. Again, a fortnight later (3 September 1983), another editorial, prompted by a rape case in which a couple who had taken a lift in a car was assaulted, commented that rape was a shame on all civilised society.

Compared to the tone of these three editorials, the fourth—which actually appeared earlier, in the edition dated 27 May 1980—was strangely conservative. It suggested to its women readers: 'To reduce crime, we ourselves should be cautious.' There was not a word in the editorial criticising rapists or social attitudes towards rape victims or even the inadequacy of the law in this regard. This may be because this comment appeared during the initial period of the anti-rape movement in India when the editors' writings were probably not informed by an awareness of the new, feminist analysis of the rape phenomenon. In later editorials, the edit writer seems to have incorporated the feminist perspective and dropped the practice of victim-blaming.

An article, which appeared a couple of months before this editorial and conveyed a decidedly different message, illustrates the dissonance that often crops up in publications. The 4 March 1980 edition carried a full page article as well as a smaller one by Neela Shah—regular columnist for *Stree* over a short period and author of some excellent articles on women's issues. The main piece was headlined 'Great Outrage Over Rape Issue, Time Is Ripe For Concrete Steps'. It made the point that eve-teasing was a prelude to rape and criticised the attitude which made victims' families shy away from lodging police complaints. The writer suggested that the solution lay in creating social awareness and supporting rape victims.

The introduction of the anti-rape legislation in Parliament was touched upon briefly in a small news item in the 10 December 1983 edition. It is not clear why the rape issue invited so much more comment and interest in this women's magazine than, say, the dowry question which would have been of direct relevance to many more of its readers.

The Shah Bano Controversy

There were only two items on this issue—an editorial and an article, one of them appearing just outside the period under review. Both concerned the Muslim Women (Protection of Rights on Divorce) Bill. The editorial in the edition dated 8 March 1986 discussed the new legislation, criticised Muslim Personal Law for restricting women's rights and appealed for the supremacy of humanitarian considerations in the issue. Although the editorial was progressive and non-communal and discussed ways to ensure that the law really did protect women, as it claimed to, it did not touch upon the condition of Muslim women today or the question of whether the existing laws provided them with any protection.

The second item, a full page article describing reactions to the Muslim Women Bill (21 June 1986), bemoaned the limitations of the law and was accompanied by a box item which raised the issue of a common civil code. It is interesting that both these items concentrated on the law without going into the question of the status of women or the plight of deserted and divorced Muslim women.

Female Foeticide

This issue received no coverage at all from the magazine over the period surveyed.

The Roop Kanwar Tragedy

Once again, this issue, given extensive coverage by most newspapers and periodicals in the country, was dealt with in only one item in *Stree*. The editorial, published in the 3 October 1987 edition, just short of a month after the death of Roop Kanwar in Deorala, was sensitive and conveyed progressive sentiments. Headlined 'We Can Certainly Not Afford To Go Back To The Dark Ages,' it condemned the Deorala incident, emphatically stating that it was defintely not an act of voluntary sati. It expressed regret that scientific progress and rationalism had not reached all parts of the country.

CONCLUSION

From this scrutiny of three categories of Gujarati publications, it is clear that the selected newspaper gave much better coverage to the five women's issues chosen for this survey than the newsmagazine. *Janmabhoomi* provided wide, if sporadic, coverage to the issues concerned. The broadly liberal editorial line of the paper has, no doubt, contributed to this reality. Besides, a daily does have more scope to follow up stories, and the constant pressure to fill up column inches plays a part in ensuring that items are included. However, this paper's approach to women's issues is clearly different from other mainstream newspapers. This is evident from some of its unusual content—for example, it serialised the first feminist novel in Gujarati, titled *Batris Putlini Vedana* by Ila Arab Mehta, in its Sunday edition. The second such novel, *Saat Pagalan Akashma* by Kundanika Kapadia (which made publishing history because it went into a second edition within two months and a third edition within the year and was particularly well-received by women readers), was also first serialised in the Sunday edition of *Janmabhoomi*.

Another proof of the fairly unique policy adopted by *Janmabhoomi* and its sister publication *Pravasi*, lies in its early decision to invite feminists, among others, to write regular columns. This researcher, for instance, began writing a feminist column in *Pravasi* in 1980—the first of its kind in Gujarati. Later, two other newspapers published from Gujarat introduced columns by Ela Bhat of the Self-Employed Women's Association and Ila Pathak of the Ahmedabad Women's Action Group. Alka and Chetna from the Chhatra Yuva Sangharsh Vahini also wrote a column in *Janmabhoomi* for two years. This researcher's column in *Pravasi* has run throughout the decade surveyed in this study.

The articles by Neela Shah in *Stree* stand out from among the other signed articles appearing during this period. While they were written with feeling, they were also analytical. For example, her article on rape, pointing out that women from socially and economically backward communities were the worst victims of rape, stated: 'It is time responsible people in society gave an assurance to women, who are all feeling insecure.' In her other piece she drew a parallel between eve-teasing and rape, underlining the fact that they are rooted in the same attitude towards women. She also advocated support to rape victims and programmes for social awareness.

While both *Janmabhoomi* and *Stree* commented on some of these women's issues during the period surveyed, publishing six editorials each, *Chitralekha* carried only one equivalent of an editorial—on the Shah Bano controversy. It is noteworthy that while *Janmabhoomi* carried as many as three editorials on the Shah Bano issue, in *Stree* it was the rape issue which prompted four editorials. This could be attributed to the fact that while the Shah Bano issue had legal and political implications, rape was more obviously a 'women's issue' and therefore appealed more to a women's magazine like *Stree*.

The two issues which received the widest coverage in newspapers and magazines were the Shah Bano case and the 'sati' incident. Apart from the controversial nature of these issues and the fact that both had acquired political overtones, there was another possible underlying reason for their preponderance; that it is easier to condemn old traditions and feudal practices and their revival and misuse in modern times, than to take on modern manifestations of patriarchy, as seen in the dowry death or female foeticide phenomena. Also, in the Shah Bano and Roop Kanwar cases, there was a single woman victim through whose struggle or sacrifice an issue could be highlighted. Readers and journalists generally like to highlight individual struggles and sufferings or achievements and acts of heroism. Another aspect is that both were examples of how blatantly anti-women some traditions can be and readily permitted a righteous tone and outraged feelings.

It must be said that all three publications retained a non-communal tone in their comments on the Shah Bano case. Still, the three editorials and wide news coverage around this issue in *Janmabhoomi* and *Chitralekha* suggest that it is relatively easy for the Gujarati press to wholeheartedly condemn Islamic fundamentalism without arousing guilt feelings among the majority of its readers whereas far more soul-searching would be necessary on issues like the misuse of sex-determination tests, dowry and sati.

It is also significant that the issue of female foeticide received scant coverage in these publications although the problem is quite rampant in Gujarat. This could be because the element of discrimination and oppression implicit in the misuse of sex determination tests is not always obvious and the practice can be rationalised in many ways. Only *Janmabhoomi* gave some importance to the issue through an editorial supporting the ban on sex determination tests. *Stree* remained completely silent on the issue, while *Chitralekha* published an article supporting the tests.

III

Television

14

A Critical Focus

Deepa Dhanraj

'There is no available official material which could provide insights regarding Doordarshan's planned strategy and programmatic efforts on behalf of women. No such thought seems to have been given in Doordarshan's generally ad hoc approach to programme content and programme schedules.' [1]

This quotation from the 1985 report of the Working Group on Software for Doordarshan, set up in 1982 and chaired by P.C. Joshi, holds good even today. The report, which has a chapter on women, indicts Doordarshan as a government-controlled and financed medium for failing to fulfil its expected role in furthering the stated national objective of women's equality.

Noting the failure of efforts to raise women's status through development measures and constitutional guarantees and emphasising that despite such interventions the position of women had deteriorated, as brought out by the 1974 report of the Committee on the Status of Women, the Joshi Committee report made the following observations about Doordarshan's approach towards programming for women:

> Middle class ideologies of women's roles as wives and mothers provide the underlying basis for most programmes. In a country where 36 per cent of the agricultural workforce is female, women continue to be projected as predominantly non-producers and as

[1] *Report of the Working Group on Software for Doordarshan: An Indian Personality for Television*, Ministry of Information and Broadcasting, New Delhi, 1985.

playing a limited role outside the home. Women are basically seen as performing a decorative function and as being marginal to national growth and development. Their primary place is seen as being within the home and this value is reflected in the content and setting of most television programmes. The plural nature of Indian culture and the diverse roles that women play is neither acknowledged nor communicated. This results in a reinforcing of the stereotyped images and role specifications of women in a unidimensional projection of their reality.

Urging that Doordarshan should formulate clear-cut guidelines at the earliest regarding the positive portrayal of women, the Joshi Committee report recommended that this portrayal must take note of all facets of their lives as workers and significant contributors to family survival and the national economy, and that it must further endeavour to integrate women in all sectors of national life and the development process on equal terms. These guidelines, it said, must emphasise that the 'women's' dimension forms an integral part of all Doordarshan programmes and not be merely confined to the 'women's programmes.'

The Joshi Committee report exposed two premises: (*a*) that the integration of women into the development process will automatically achieve equality for them and (*b*) that Doordarshan ('post-independent India's gift to society,' as the Joshi Committee Report puts it), since it is a government department, is beholden to execute this national objective. (See Appendix E, Growth of TV in India.)

Another assumption, that seems to be implied rather than stated, is that given Doordarshan's duty to implement the national objective of equal rights to all citizens, including women, as enshrined in the Constitution, it must ensure equitable representation on Doordarshan to all sections.

Women and Development

To understand Doordarshan's approach towards women with respect to programming, it is relevant to examine how and whether the process of integrating women into the development process has worked. Various recent studies have revealed that these attempts have largely been a failure.

One meaning given to the term 'development' is: a planned process of improvement in various aspects of people's lives—economic, welfare, civil, and so on. If development is seen in this broader sense of the process of socio-economic transformation, then the notion that women need to be 'integrated' into development is clearly false.

Demands for the addition of women's components onto projects or women's quotas for jobs are examples of well-intentioned actions which have confused means and ends. They should not be regarded as ends because, by themselves, they do not alter the structures of subordination. They are means which can only become effective if they are combined with an awareness of the process by which real change can be achieved. This is not an easy task. For instance, despite studies on women's work such as those recording the widespread incidence of women in agriculture, the delivery of agricultural resources continues to be directed towards men.

Where power relations are entrenched within institutions, the effort to benefit subordinated groups encounters resistance from those it threatens: women whose security lies in stable patriarchal relations or in the privileges of their class and men whose identity and dominance may be undermined if women's life options are increased. Consequently, all attempts to transform gender relations have a political character and have to be analysed in terms of politically unequal categories. Politics is not simply about elections, political parties or voting. It is about contests for power, mechanisms of control and battles over policy.

A gender sensitive approach to development focuses on interlinkages within a holistic perspective; that is, it looks at the totality of social relations in the economy, the family and society in order to understand how gender operates between and within particular arenas of social life. Women's subordination has to be investigated rather than assumed because its various cultural expressions are dependent on the intersection of class, caste and regional factors. What we can assume on the basis of what we know is that gender relations are structured in dominance; they are not generally relations between equals but are produced as categories of power and hierarchy.

Affirmative Efforts

Current affirmative efforts by Doordarshan on women's issues, during the period examined in this study, through the afternoon transmission, spots on the girl child, family welfare, and so on, stem firmly from the traditional model of 'integrating women into development' referred to above. These token attempts of the 'add women and stir' formula are doomed to be ineffective just as this approach has failed to deliver tangible benefits to women.

Another aspect of affirmative action which tries to address 'women's needs' is based on the assumption that all women share the same needs. This assumption of unproblematic unity among women is based on their common biology. It ignores the class, caste and social structures that separate different groups of women. Which women did Doordarshan seek to affirm? In the serials under review, the category 'women' largely referred to those from middle class, upper caste, Hindu and predominantly urban backgrounds. In the few instances where working class or rural women were included, they were defined and assimilated by a homogenising ideology based on middle class assumptions.

Doordarshan had to respond to pressures to achieve the stated national objective of raising the status of women exerted by other government departments. It also could not ignore the contemporary Indian women's movement which, by the end of the women's decade (1975-85), had established itself as a vocal and visible lobby.

Mobilised in the late 1970s around issues of rape, dowry murders and family violence, women's groups had, in close to ten years, succeeded in changing the frameworks within which these issues were previously articulated and understood. For example, the demand that led to the reopening of the Mathura rape case initiated a debate on the problematic question of 'consent' and thereby led to an examination of the rape law itself. Women began to question the structures and ideological apparatus that produce rape in our cultures. By the end of the decade, these re-articulations had acquired visibility, validity and public space.

Targeting Women

This study attempts to analyse the implications of Doordarshan's efforts towards the affirmation of women's concerns, using the model of positive images (role models, success stories) and, more often than not, the soap opera form. In this context, the questions which need to be addressed include: How were women's concerns and their empowerment constructed at that historical moment by Doordarshan? Why did Doordarshan attempt the exercise at all, given its abysmal track record of women's representation? What impact did the commercialisation of Doordarshan, with the attendant system of sponsorship, have on the production of these images, given that the producer-viewer relationship is mediated by Doordarshan?

The period between 1982 and 1987 saw Doordarshan launch for the first time a massive refurbishment of its traditional image as a 'purveyor of male elite interests' [2] by telecasting a deluge of women-oriented serials. Two or three such serials, on an average, were telecast on prime time every week. Some of these, obviously prompted by the need to integrate women into the development process, focussed, for example, on women's legal rights and career possibilities.

For instance, *Adhikaar* (Rights) dealt with laws relating to women's rights to property, equal pay, *streedhan*, maintenance and breach of promise, among others. *Aur Bhi Hain Raahein* (There Are Other Ways), consisting essentially of vocational guidance, outlined different career options for women, with some information on training opportunities. *Udaan* (Flight) offered the possibility of an unusual career for women—it traced the main character's struggles to become a woman police officer.

Stri (Woman), the only one to be filmed in a docu-drama style, created portraits of women who had negotiated the public world of power successfully. The stories of positive heroines (role models) told by this serial cut across class and regional lines. They focussed on a welder, a press photographer, a theatre director and a tribal activist, among others. *Kashmakash* (Struggle or Conflict), based on short stories written by well-known women authors in various regional languages, examined the lives of women as they coped with oppression both within and outside the home. *Air Hostess* was about the trials and tribulations of single working women in a service industry. *Swayamsiddha* (Self-determination) dealt with the growth into selfhood of a divorcee. Literary classics, like Munshi Premchand's *Nirmala*, which centred around a female protagonist, were also telecast at the same time.

Since that brief and aberrant period, women and their concerns have been relegated either to the women's programme or the programmes telecast during the afternoon transmission where they are projected as part of a troika of underprivileged groups: the elderly, children and women.

While the serials seem to have mechanistically absorbed the more topical or sensational aspects of issues which the women's movement has taken up, they have also deflected their subversive potential of re-articulation onto individual women, by exhorting them to rise above the

---

[2] Krishnan and Dighe, *Affirmation and Denial*.

difficulties and problems they face. There is no understanding in the serials of the systemic nature of women's oppression. The fundamental premise of the women's movement that the personal is political finds no echo here. Issues, attitudes and radical re-articulations thrown up by the movement have been incorporated into the traditional ways of looking at the women's question. This process of assimilation not only tames oppositional ideas but creates the illusion that change has been affected. This concept becomes clearer in the detailed analyses of some of the serials, which follow.

Parallel Images

Before that, however, it is important to note that at the time that these serials were being telecast, the television version of the *Ramayana* was also on air. Without essaying an analysis of Ramanand Sagar's presentation of the epic, it is clear that five minutes of watching Sita iconised as the ideal, chaste wife is enough to undercut even the limited effectiveness of the so-called women-oriented serials. This simultaneous telecast also reveals the lip service paid by Doordarshan towards any sort of redressal of its representation of women's issues. (In keeping with an ad hoc policy of throwing something in to please each segment of society, the progressives got—say *Adhikaar*—while rest of the country got the *Ramayana*, and Doordarshan earned huge profits.)

All the serials were sponsored by national and transnational companies producing consumer goods, leading to the ironic situation of Doordarshan using private capital to finance welfarism. The practice of using a commercially-sponsored soap opera form for unpalatable or development messages started with *Hum Log* (We folks) which dropped its family planning messages after the first eight episodes to settle into an audience-maximising family drama.

As the broadcaster, Doordarshan allots the time of telecast and, through an osmotic chain of command, of which little or no documentation exists, indicates to producers the current issues it wants to promote. In this role of middleman, Doordarshan controls not only the content of the programme but its placement as well.

The code for commercial advertising on Doordarshan has minimal regulations for advertisers. No advertisement is permitted which derides any race, caste, colour, creed or nationality; glorifies violence or obscenity in any way; or is against the Constitution of India.

No advertisement shall be permitted which projects a derogatory image of women. Women must not be portrayed in a manner that emphasizes passive, submissive qualities and encourages them to play a subordinate, secondary role in the family and society. The portrayal of men and women should not encourage mutual disrespect between the sexes. The advertiser shall ensure that the portrayal of the female form is tasteful and aesthetic and is within the well-established norms of good taste and decency.

The text of the commercials which preceded the 'affirmative' women's serials under review often gave out contradictory messages. As Prabha Krishnan and Anita Dighe have observed:

In the current climate of commercialisation, even feminist texts cannot be telecast without sponsorship which effectively denigrates and demeans women. Since these commercials are the norm, and feminist texts are rare, it is likely that the message of the text is processed as aberrant, and that of the commercial validated.[3]

The producers of the serials are all Bombay-based, with previous experience in the production of advertising commercials or commercial cinema. Only Kavita Chaudhari of *Udaan* had no previous film experience.

Selection Criteria

The original intention of this study was to review samples of different categories (soap opera, sit-com, self-help, docu-drama, fiction-based, etc.) of the 'women-oriented' serials telecast by Doordarshan during this unusual period when a plethora of such programmes inundated the audience.

However, such a planned selection proved impossible because Doordarshan does not have the rights to part with their copies of the serials (for which they have only multiple telecast rights), even for research purposes, without the permission of the producers who hold the copyright. The majority of the producers were unresponsive, elusive, disorganised or a combination of these (in one case nobody involved with the serial seemed to have the mastertapes or knowledge of where they might be). Ultimately, at the end of arduous and largely futile

[3] *Ibid.*

attempts to procure the serials originally selected, there was no choice but to take what was given by a few cooperative producers.

THE VISUAL MESSAGE

Arguments for a more radical analysis of women's role and position in society or a more socially extensive representation of women—more working class women, for example—are valid but finally limited in their political scope. This is because these arguments accept filmic reality as life itself and, in comparing it with life, find it lacking. Yet what is taken for 'reality' in films is a carefully constructed world, with its own set of conventions.

The images of women on television or in any other media appear 'natural' to the audiences them watching.[4] This is not just because we have grown accustomed to seeing these images from our earliest days, but also because we are socialised into categorising women according to those images. The predominant social relations outside the media—in the family and at work—give rise to these categories.

In constructing these images, the audio-visual media have their own preferred codes. Fragmentation of women into stereotypes, such as sex object, mother and housewife, is one method. To paraphrase British feminist theorist Sheila Rowbotham, the media has considerable power to throw back to us a version of ourselves which is presented as the norm.[5] If we examine this normative image of ourselves, we find that women are defined only in relation to men.

Media or film practices contribute to the construction of 'woman' using varied techniques—camera angles, shot composition, framing, lighting, editing and music—to create and place a woman in a coherent and complete world. All manner of devices are employed to give spectators the sense that what they are watching is unmediated reality itself.

'Our society,' wrote philosopher Roland Barthes, 'takes the greatest pains to conjure away the coding of the narrative situation—the reluctance to declare its codes characterises bourgeois society and the culture issuing from it: both demand signs which do not look like signs.'[6]

---

[4] Helen Butcher et al., *Images of Women in the Media*, Centre for Contemporary Cultural Studies, University of Birmingham, 1974.

[5] Sheila Rowbotham, *Woman's Consciousness, Man's World*, Penguin Books Ltd., Harmondsworth, 1973.

[6] Roland Barthes, *Introduction to the Structural Analysis of Narratives in Image-Music-Text*, Fontana, London, 1977.

If we want to investigate the codes or signs by which a film conveys meanings other than the most obvious ones (what the film apparently says or means), we have to look at how the 'reality effect' is achieved.

Realist Narrative

Realist narrative films (all the serials under review come under this category) almost always open onto an enigma or a lack which disrupts the existing order or equilibrium or status quo in the central character's life situation. A child is lost, or a woman is abandoned or lovers are separated. The story then proceeds through a series of complications to restore order by making good the lack. The pleasure of the narrative lies in raising our anxieties by the various twists and turns of the plot so that we welcome the resolution: the child is reunited with her parents, the abandoned woman wins her husband back and the lovers are reconciled. We identify both with the narrative events as they unfold and with the central protagonists who are delineated with great attention to character, motivation, psychology and so on.

When we look at how women are constructed in realist narrative and the role they play in furthering the movement of the plot we find certain repetitive patterns. Very often women are the problem that sets the story into motion. Narrative closure then depends on returning the women to their proper place so that order is restored to the world. This may mean that she falls in love or gets married; if not, she may be suitably punished for her transgression from the normal order (marriage) by banishment or even death. It is always a sexually definitive resolution, based on the male/female courtship bond.

Cinematic Codes

The cinematic devices which contribute to the creation of the illusory reality effect and help to keep the narrative going are, primarily, cinematography, editing and music.

Cinematography has its own codes, with different meanings in, say, long shots or close-ups. A close-up of a character may serve to emphasise her emotional state; a close-up of a detail or an object may demand that we see its special significance in the narrative. Music is another device which guides the spectator into appropriate responses towards the characters or events in the story. Editing—particularly continuity editing which relies on unobtrusive cuts to create a seamless fictional world—also emphasises that what we are seeing is reality itself.

All these seemingly invisible devices are designed to get the spectator to believe in the meaning that the narrative has produced. The success of narative realism lies in its ability to conceal its methods of production so well that the spectators are unware of its working and assume that they have come to understand the final resolution independently.

Narrative or dominant control constructs the closure from the very beginning by keeping our noses firmly to the narrative track and demanding that we come to certain conclusions or meanings. It is this process of dominant control that feminists have argued recreates patriarchal culture. The devices employed create such falsifications of women that one critic, Christine Gledhill, asked: 'Though they are women-centred narratives, can there be women in such films?'[7]

By using pyschoanalytic concepts, it is possible to attempt an understanding of how spectators are drawn into the cinematic world and how they construct meanings of what they see.

One school of thought built on the basis given by Sigmund Freud sees the child's understanding of the different cultural meanings of male and female genitals as crucial to the development of personality and, in particular, the unconscious part of the mind. The learning of languages is based on the child having internalised the distinction between subject and object. For this to take place, the infant has to first see his or her body as separate from the world around him or her; in the mirror phase (a term describing a stage of personality development), the infant's reflection in the mirror establishes his own body as separate from that of his or her mother, for example. This is also pleasurable looking, a narcissism based on the enjoyment of one's own reflection.

Identification

Christian Metz has argued that cinema generates pleasurable viewing by offering the spectator two kinds of identification—narcissistic and voyeuristic. In the first, by looking at representations of the human body, or parts of it, the spectator identifies with himself, much like the identification of the mirror phase. In the second, the spectator identifies with the position or look of the camera. However, the cinema screen is not a mirror: the spectator is not actually reflected in it. Voyeuristic

[7] Christine Gledhill, 'Contemporary Film Noir and Feminist Criticism' in E. Ann Kaplan, ed., *Women and Film Noir*, British Film Institute, London, 1978.

looking is pleasurable precisely because the object of the look cannot respond or return the look in any way.[8]

Laura Mulvey, on the other hand, in her pathbreaking essay, 'Visual Pleasure and Narrative Cinema,' argues that women have always been constructed in dominant cinema as objects of the look—'as erotic object for the characters within the screen story and as erotic object for the spectator in the auditorium.'[9] This suggests that dominant cinema constructs itself for pleasurable viewing, both narcissistic and voyeuristic, by male spectators.

Considering that women also watch films, what implications does this have for women viewers? Women are placed in the position of identifying with the masculinisation of the address, with the male protagonist who is in control of events on the one hand; or, masochistically, with the construction of women who are either punished by the narrative or treated as a fetish on the other. If we interrogate the narrative film form, we come to an understanding of how a filmic representation of a woman is constructed. It is clear, therefore, that narrative filmic conventions are not gender neutral. When the form itself creates women as subordinate, how then can we use narrative realism to present positive or alternative representations of women?

While these analytical tools are useful in enabling us to take apart how dominant cinema constructs women, one should not be paralysed by their implications. Meanings that are made at the point of reception of these images rest on the interaction of the viewer with them. We can stand at a distance from these constructions, observe their ideological operations and arrive at our own meanings.

One unifying characteristic that seemed to run through all the serials was the self-conscious construction of a positive image of women: *Stri* featured accomplished role models; *Adhikaar* dealt with successful cases; *Aur Bhi Hain Raahein* showed women attaining economic independence; and in *Udaan* the protagonist succeeded in her goal of becoming a police officer.

'Positive' Images

Theoretically, the concept of 'positive' images raises the question of definition: what are 'positive' characteristics and how are they determined? Obviously each woman's life is shaped by her class, regional and

[8] Christian Metz, *The Imaginary Signifier*, Indiana University Press, Bloomington, 1985.
[9] Laura Mulvey, 'Visual Pleasure and Narrative Cinema,' *Screen*, vol. 16, no. 3, 1975.

language background, age and her understanding of these factors; 'positive' characteristics are not universal absolutes—they have a relationship to a particular social reality.

Diane Waldman, a feminist film critic, raises a crucial point while critiquing a compilation of non-sexist films and audio-visuals for young people:

> The notion of a positive image is predicated upon the assumption of identification of the spectator with a character depicted in a film. It has a historical precedent in the positive hero and positive heroine of socialist realism.
>
> The mechanism of identification goes unchallenged and unchanged and introduces, I think, a complacency associated with merely presenting an image of the positive heroine. If the mechanism of identification goes unchallenged, how are students to distinguish between positive and negative images? And, more importantly, does this concept allow or does it militate against the development of those critical tools so necessary for dealing with the dominant media and society? As teachers we should stress analysis, critical distance and discussion of any material we use rather than rely upon the identification implied by the positive image concept.[10]

PRIME TIME IMAGES

The primary purpose of this detailed analysis of six prime-time television serials in Hindi, telecast in the 1980s, is to assist women viewers to critically examine their texts, particularly of those specifically designed for their consumption.

Adhikaar

Produced by Manju and Navjoth Singh and presented by writer-journalist Mrinal Pande, *Adhikaar* (Rights) dealt with women's legal and constitutional rights in the family, the community and the economy.

Successful case studies were dramatised using actresses and actors. Each episode dealt with a single case. The presenter, Mrinal Pande, introduced the case at the beginning of the episode, ending either with

---

[10] Diane Waldman, 'There's More to Positive Image than Meets the Eye' in Peter Steven, ed., *Jump Cut: Hollywood, Politics and Counter Cinema*, Toronto, 1985.

a summary of the unique points of the case or an extension of the analysis to other situations where the legal arguments were applicable.

Despite the limitations of the serial, *Adhikaar* was found to be a meaningful programme by many women, judging by the flood of letters from viewers. Predominantly written by women, the letters described problems in detail and asked for legal advice or access to sympathetic, free legal aid. The tone of the letters was supplicant in nature, as if written in the certainty that an appropriate answer would be forthcoming.

Doordarshan has never implied that it permits dialogue with its viewers. Why, then, in this instance, was it perceived as an essentially benevolent and paternalistic institution by the people? One hopes that the letters were either a misreading of Doordarshan's role and intentions in the case of this serial or an indication of the desperation of women trapped in intolerable situations who felt that appealing to another 'official' government organ for justice might be of help.

The opening credits of the serial were accompanied with grainy black and white stills of poverty-stricken women, followed by shots of women in a meeting and finally of women marching in a procession on the streets. It telegraphically established, in the traditions of social-realism, the fact of women's oppression and the beginnings of collective political activity. The stills appeared to be news photographs, connoting that what we were about to see was truth, not fiction. Mrinal Pande, a credible presenter (social activist/writer/editor of a progressive women's magazine), introduced the serial with these words:

> In every age, in every society and in every country, victims of oppression and exploitation are those who are ignorant of their legal rights. In our society, women are unaware of their legal rights and, even if they are aware, they are afraid to assert them. Times are changing, society is changing and it is very necessary for women to march shoulder to shoulder with men in every walk of life. The rights that have been provided by law should be fully understood by women and this is the primary motive of our serial. The incidents you will see are all based on true life incidents, about women who fought for their rights using the law and were successful. These women are not figments of the imagination of a poet or writer—they are mothers, daughters and sisters who live in our communities, homes and families.

The makers of the serial were obviously concerned enough to

involve a credible presenter—her association with this serial was an extension of her public political work; and in their efforts to ensure affirmation and identification for women viewers, selected only those cases which were successful.

However, the 'successful' case strategy was a trap—it resulted in the concealment of the patriarchal attitudes of the judiciary in respect of cases that were either not admitted or were lost.

Not one episode addressed issues such as rape, prostitution, domestic violence, restitution of conjugal rights or loss of land. None of the cases focussed on women belonging to minority communities or the personal laws that apply to them. Except for one episode dealing with a working class situation, all the cases were centred on the problems of middle and upper middle class women.

Two cases fell into a general category: one involved a prejudicial confidential report that affected the future promotional prospects of an upper division clerk and the other was a consumer grievance case which seemed totally tangential to the women's rights issue. The woman who had bought a defective fridge in the latter episode was not even a canny consumer; in fact, she was quite the opposite—more like the woman in the refrigerator advertisement on television who calls the mechanic because the fridge is not making a noise!

But the most problematic point about the serial was the basic premise that the judiciary is free of gender prejudice. Instead of initiating a debate on women and the law, the serial suggested that women viewers had to bear the onus of their intolerable situations: if you don't file a case, it is your fault. Yet, for every successful resolution, there are countless failures. The abysmal record of the judiciary in innumerable rape cases (even those involving minors), the few convictions obtained in the cases of 'dowry deaths,' the many loopholes in the laws relating to the property rights of women, so that victory in a court case is purely ephemeral, are all indicative of the patriarchal nature of the legal system and the judiciary. In cases of rape, women lose because their past sexual history and the question of 'consent' are used as evidence to damn them. 'Dowry death' cases are converted into suicides. This aspect of the legal system vis-a-vis women was completely ignored by the serial.

Going beyond evaluating the inadequacies of the text in terms of its omissions of 'representative' cases, it is important to examine how the chosen form (family melodrama) enabled the entire issue to be sidetracked, enabling Doordarshan to, ideologically, have its cake and eat it too. On the one hand, Doordarshan acquired a progressive image by seeming to accommodate and yield to the national debates raised by an increasingly vocal women's lobby; on the other, by using a sleight of hand to transfer the definition of the problem and solution onto individual effort and will, it managed to evade an analysis of the social and patriarchal constructions of power and powerlessness.

The inadequacies of a limited, distorted analysis, combined with a limited form, create an intriguing situation. The viewer is rushed along, narcotised by the details of the drama as it unfolds. As certain forms, using a complex set of codes, generate a certain response, it is crucial to question the unthinking use of forms drawn from dominant cinema because they are counter-productive.

In this case, the issue was emasculated and retrieved self-consciously only in the book-end sequences with the presenter. Mrinal Pande's analytical sections at the beginning and the end were like appendages—at that point the viewer was snapped out of the cinematic hypnosis to register that the serial was about women and law. The maximum amount of time was spent on the details of the crisis, not on encouraging an understanding of the legal issues involved.

The first episode showed a young widow being duped by her in-laws into signing away her rights to the insurance policy of her husband Ramesh. When she questions her father-in-law, he asks her to leave the house accusing her of only having greed for Ramesh's money. A sympathetic sister-in-law advises her to stay put and consult a lawyer who obtains an injunction, and she gets the money. The presenter closes the episode with a warning about the dangers of not leaving a will.

The second episode revolved around a doting mother who signs her property away to her son and is later evicted by him. She ends up in an old people's home where she is advised by the social worker to seek legal help. She obtains maintenance but only after a lot of agonising over whether she should risk the scandal of exposing family feuds to the public. The presenter wraps up with the advice of not giving away wealth to anyone during one's lifetime and information that aged parents are entitled to maintenance under the law.

This serial was telecast at the height of the controversy over the Shah Bano case involving the maintenance of an old, indigent Muslim divorcee by her ex-husband. As feminist activist Sonal Shukla pointed out in an interview with this researcher, other beneficiaries under the law cited in this episode include ex- and present wives. If the producers had given this information, they would have also had to mention that, thanks to the Muslim Women (Protection of Rights on Divorce) Act,

1986, Muslim wives are now excluded from this list of destitutes. This omission is significant because it exposes the limitations of government-controlled Doordarshan's efforts towards affirmation for women.

The third episode was a dowry-murder case where the dying declaration was sympathetic to the killers. The case was filed and the dying declaration challenged. The writer of the serial, Sunil Shanbag, admitted in an interview that since, at the time of writing, no dowry-murder case had resulted in a conviction, they had to stop at the point of admitting the case.

The episode dealing with the well-known case of the first woman secretary to win a case under the Equal Remuneration Act was the most carefully directed—by film-maker Jahnu Barua. Not only was its presentation of the Goan ethos and culture credible (minority cultures are generally caricatured on Doordarshan), but it also managed to convincingly portray the frustrating toll that such a long drawn out legal battle can take (the petitioner won in the Supreme Court after six years of litigation).

The heroic nature of her struggle becomes apparent in the documentation of the various odds against her—marginalisation and betrayal by the union, suspension, intimidation by the company management and the painstaking persistence required to keep the case going through the Labour Court, Sessions Court, High Court and Supreme Court. On the personal level, her sense of low self-esteem when she is suspended—'For a working woman it's like losing your whole world'—indicates a more complex approach to the case than those in the other episodes. Though she is proud to have won the case, she is unhappy that the other women secretaries in the company did not take advantages of the ruling. 'I didn't fight for myself alone,' she states.

The only episode that dealt with working class women was a case involving women fish workers who were incarcerated in a fish processing plant. These rural women, under contract to the factory to work for a nine-month period, worked under exploitative conditions. They were assisted in their efforts to form a union by a trade unionist who was smuggled into the factory by a sympathetic truck driver. The episode explained the provisions of the Factories Act as they apply to women.

This episode suffered the most from the 'successful' case treatment. The bracketing of the dramatis personae into mechanistic social types—the 'indifferent' management, the 'cruel' overseer and the 'exploited' workers—made it difficult to 'suspend disbelief.' The scene in which the women were persuaded to join the union appeared ritualistically brief;

a necessary chore to sustain the narrative before racing to the real plot resolution—slapping of the Factories Act onto the management. The producers revealed their politics by privileging the 'action' sequence of vanquishing the villainous management over the more valuable processes of how rural women arrive at an understanding of their exploitation and of their engagement for the first time with intimidating institutions of the state.

Two episodes were constructed around women opting for *streedhan* and maintenance instead of divorce. In the first case, the husband, who had not consummated the marriage, was threatened with public exposure and agreed to return his wife's jewellery; in the second, the woman herself felt divorce was too extreme a step and was prepared to wait for the man to emerge from under his mother's influence.

The episode on bigamy seemed to be constructed not to illustrate any legal point—except the question of the child's share in the father's ancestral property—but to issue a moralistic warning through the presenter: 'Bigamy is a crime; marriage is not just a *madhur milan* (sweet union/meeting) but a long relationship. Bigamous relationships are illegal and frowned upon by society. The brunt is borne by innocent children who can't lift their heads in society.'

In another episode, a widow who wishes to remarry is threatened by her husband's family that she will lose her rights over her husband's property. She is advised that widows have full rights to property and custody of the child even if they remarry. The right of daughters to a share in the ancestral property was the subject of another episode.

All the family cases' exploitation of cinematic conventions from the traditional 'women's weepies,' to represent masochism and passivity, was so crude that the women's ultimate decisions to act on their own behalf seemed perverse and unconvincing. Excessive time and emotions were invested in scenes dealing with the loss of male protection—the death of a father or a husband. It was seen as the point at which discrimination against women began and they were reminded of the horrors that awaited them if they left their husbands' families or transgressed sexually. The majority of the cases in the serial had sensational and voyeuristic elements—non-consummation of marriage, bigamy, a widow having an affair.

The only case which exposed the patriarchal attitudes of the judiciary was one which dealt with breach of promise. It was a double-edged case because even though the petitioner won, she was publicly humiliated and punished by an aggressive lawyer for admitting that she had had a sexual relationship with a man without being married to him. He used the classical arguments that turn the victim into the accused: she was no better than a whore and by trying to coerce her lover into making the relationship legitimate she was harassing him. Such women, the argument implied, were not fit to get married. What saved the day was certain correspondence that she was able to produce as evidence. Even though this sequence was obviously constructed for male gratification and to sound a moral warning to women through the presenter, it was useful in that it showed what the law doles out to women when they dare to seek its intervention, particularly in cases relating to sexuality or the family.

Mrinal Pande wound up with 'Madhu won, but it's a good warning for all girls who get lost in love and repent later. She wasn't broken, she fought back.' Concluding the entire serial, she continued, 'Lots of things have to be left out but treat the series as the beginning of a new consciousness. The struggle is hard, long and painful but till you fight you're not going to get your rights.'

It is impossible to disagree with this statement but, a qualifying statement should be added: the legal system as represented in the serial is not only lacking in gender prejudice but is shown to be completely fair. This is a deliberate falsification. One must not only fight for one's rights but also force the legal system to examine its sexist preconceptions about women. Since the law has serious implications for women's lives and is a fundamental aspect of the oppressive social structures surrounding them, women should be vigilant and continue to examine and fight the way the law sees and treats them. By not including this perspective, the serial served a limited function.

Kashmakash

Kashmakash (Struggle or Conflict), a serial based on short stories written by well-known women authors in various regional languages, was produced by Asrani and directed by Manju Bansal Asrani.

The producer's 'affirmative' intentions towards women's empowerment were indicated in the use of stories by women authors only. This was a significant redressal of past wrongs by Doordarshan—in all the other short story compilations on television, such as *Katha Sagar*, women writers were conspicuous by their absence.

The chief criterion for the selection of the stories seems to have been that the central characters were women. Some of them endeavoured to struggle against oppressive social practices, such as dowry or segregation of widows; others tried to redefine their familial roles within the home. A unifying theme running through all the episodes was the women's self-discovery and strength. Notwithstanding the diverse regional backgrounds from which the women came, the episodes showed the universal nature of their oppression and marginalisation.

Despite the presence of all the elements necessary for a uniquely 'feminist' representation, why was the serial so disappointing? Without access to original literary texts, it is impossible to assess the adaptations; but the construction of the narratives and the uniform privileging of the scenes of women awakening to and denouncing their oppression suggest that considerable effort went into assembling a progressive, 'feminist' text.

The form followed a rigid agitational–propaganda (agit–prop) style: delineation of oppression, point of awakening, action/denunciation. The political ideals and issues articulated by the women's movement were appropriated and presented in their most caricatured form, ensuring the loss of their subversive potential. Worse, the realistic treatment made the viewer believe that at the end of each episode a change in consciousness had taken place. The following detailed analysis seeks to examine how this process took place.

The opening titles of the serial were superimposed on close-ups of Kangra miniature paintings. Some shots had Radha and Krishna together in a Holi sequence; in others the *nayika* was alone—pensive and longing for her lover (these shots were crudely framed so that the male object of her look was, quite literally, cut off); and one shot showed Chandi slaying Mahisasura. This title sequence bore little relation to what followed. The attempt to draw connections between the representations of femininity in the paintings and the serial, given the totally different historical, social and aesthetic contexts in which the two sets of images had been produced, was ludicrous.

Depending on the region, each episode had appropriate ethnic art direction, locations, and costumes but the same all-purpose Hindustani of Doordarshan, with concessions only to terms of address, like Baba, Boudi or Appa as the case may be. The casting was done from the same pool of popular Bombay-based actresses and actors who looked very unconvincing in the South Indian stories.

The first episode taken up for analysis is *Alta* (original title *Suhag Chinh*) by Mahasweta Devi. A serious writer, she has extended not only the delineations and analyses of feminity but the use of language as well.

Her inclusion in this serial came as no surprise; her prominence in literary circles and her political activity make her compulsory viewing.

Alta is a red dye that married women in Bengal wear on their feet as a sign of marriage. The story plays ironically with this signifier of marital status. A woman and her teenaged daughter are practically imprisoned at home by an old-fashioned, over-protective husband/ father. His intention is to protect them from the goonda raj (rule of criminals) that exists outside. He dies of a heart attack after a marriage proposal for his daughter falls through. The family's dream of seeing their daughter's feet painted with *alta* is unfulfilled and the two women are now destitute.

The widow, who steps out of the house for the first time, returns dispirited and angry. Unused to traffic, she barely escapes being run over by a car, is sexually harassed by a man and finds the simplest transaction of buying food an intimidating task. She confesses her terror of the future to her daughter and blames her husband for keeping them so ignorant. A local lecherous landlord, who has designs on the widow, sends an offer of help and is told off. He discovers that a young man visits their house every night and takes a gang of young men to the house to expose her 'immoral' activities which, he claims, are corrupting the locality. However, it turns out that the gentleman in question is an agent for an *alta* company and that the women are working at sticking labels on the bottles. The widow accuses the landlord of daring to insult them only because they lack male protection. He retreats in confusion.

The serial was generically constructed around the turning points of oppression, recognition and self-assertion. The changes in the widow's consciousness were depicted in the most telegraphic, connotative way. When her husband is alive, she is shown—in appearance (colourful Bengal sarees, sindur, etc.) and demeanour—with all the signifiers of a good wife. After her husband dies, she is stripped of colour, her body posture loses its erectness, she is uncertain. In her final form, denunciating the lecherous landlord, she is portrayed as Kali, the devouring goddess. Photographed from a low angle, the vengeful icon advances menacingly; the music—conches and drums from Durga puja—adding to the effect. The landlord's retreat, it was implied, was more from fear of the goddess than enlightenment through a powerless female mortal.

The episode evades the central question of who controls the women's sexuality and deals with it only in rhetorical dialogue. 'If a good wife doesn't die with her husband, she has to dance to the tune of a new The protector. My daughter and I will live with self-respect and dignity.' The statement seems to be directed in equal part to the viewers.

The second episode, *Suhag ka Chinh* (original title *Nalla Pusalu*), was based on a Telugu story written by Raj Lakshmi. A young woman who lives with her widower father wears a mangalsutra to college to avoid being harassed by male students. The totemic power of the marriage chain, signifying possession by one man, is supposed to be a guarantee against sexual harassment by other men because they respect a fellow male's property. Many misunderstandings later, she marries a man she loves. While tying the mangalsutra around her neck during the marriage ceremony, her husband mocks her saying, 'Let me tie the real one around your neck—you tied the false one yourself.' Having acquired a legitimate protector, she smiles.

While *Alta* at least qualifies as a 'progressive' text, this story opens up a Pandora's box of contradictions. Sexual harassment of women—on the roads, in public transport, in educational institutions—is an ugly fact of life in the ambivalent relationship between the sexes in India. It is always the first issue that women students take up when they start to organise politically. Male hostility and violence towards women are on the increase within and outside the home.

Compartmentalising violence towards women and suggesting that it takes place only outside the home is a travesty of the tortures that many women face in marriage—both psychological as well as physical (starvation, battering and even murder). A woman's mangalsutra is no protection against the sexual abuse she might have to tolerate from her own husband. In the early days of the women's movement, many married women decided to publicly throw away their mangalsutras as they considered them shameful social symbols of sexual possession. In Maharashtra particularly, public debate in the press and women's magazines was fierce.

To return to the episode, the troublesome question is again: who controls the woman's body? The narrative refused to address this. While violence against women was taken as a given, it was not analysed. The suggested solution was to maintain purity and virginity by whatever means possible so that it could be handed over to the husband after the woman had successfully essayed a brief, perilous period of being in charge of her own virtue. Her husband's remark during the wedding ceremony properly addressed her own attempts to protect herself as a foolish, feminine ruse, charmingly childish and naive.

This brings one back to the problematic nature of 'progressive' texts.

The question is, 'progressive' on whose terms? The objective underlying the construction of these 'feminist' texts seems to be either to delineate women's powerlessness and passivity with ethnographic fidelity or to indicate a resistance to existing conditions in the most mechanical way possible.

Having created a 'feminist' formula, the producer expects audience reaction to be instant feminist consciousness. This naive understanding of the interaction between a film text and audience needs to be recognised.

Both these episodes of *Kashmakash* drew women viewers into a recognition of situations of female powerlessness without male protection. Though the plots delineated the two different strategies of negotiating out of powerlessness, the emphasis was on a straightforward narrative which moved towards a resolution of their ambiguous status. In both the episodes, the portrayal of the women's bodies (the problematic central issue) was so conventionally glamorous that the fact that their bodies became sites of dispute came as no surprise.

The strident manner in which the central protagonist denounced the landlord in the contrived last sequence in *Alta* was unconvincing. Anxieties raised about the future of the mother and daughter were only temporarily allayed; they had won the first round but they were still vulnerable.

No clues were given as to how they were going to re-establish themselves with 'self-respect and dignity.' One reading could suggest that the real *Alta* was not a visible indicator of the protection of marriage but economic independence. As their transition from destitution to wage labour, sticking labels for exploitative wages, was never shown, the Kali incarnation came as a surprise. The emphasis on plot movement precluded even minimal character exposition. Their destitution was built up in such great detail that instead of the final rhetorical statement, the mother's abject capitulation would have been just as easily acceptable as a possible resolution.

Films are complexly coded texts which offer more than one meaning. Both episodes set into play more elements than could be resolved by the narrative closure.

Aur Bhi Hain Raahein

Aur Bhi Hain Raahein (There Are Other Ways) was aired on the national network on Sunday mornings (prime time). Written by Karan Razdan and directed by Mazahir Rahim, it was targeted at women viewers, encouraging them to be economically independent by choosing their own careers. Each episode delineated a possible career choice with concrete information about where training could be acquired. It was presented by film actress Tanuja who moved the plot along and was central to all the episodes. She played herself as an actress and columnist for *Women's India*, a fictional women's magazine.

Of the thirteen episodes, three dealt with working class women: a domestic worker from an urban slum, a widowed rural woman migrant in an urban slum and a group of fisherwomen in a coastal village in Kerala. One episode featured an upper middle class woman. The others were all structured around middle class women who were introduced in the serial to careers in various fields—para-medical work (pathology, physiotherapy, occupational therapy, etc.), catering, beauty care, special education for the handicapped, computer programming, product design, management, the services (the police, the Indian Administrative Service) and career guidance itself (administering aptitude tests, etc.), in addition to activities such as setting up creches. The alternatives presented to working class women were the special vocational training programmes for poor women run by the Bombay-based Women's India Trust and the setting up of fishworkers' cooperatives.

This can be read as an impressive list of options to the permanent post of housewife. But the serial always places these options in the context of marriage. Implicit in the title is another notion; that which is left unsaid—'There are other ways' of living, perhaps? Such as being single, choosing not to marry, not being defined only by marriage. An understanding of the intentions of the film-makers who have articulated the problem and come up with solutions will be attempted here through an analysis of all the episodes.

Before launching into a critique, it is important to acknowledge the positive achievements of the serial. It acknowledges and analyses, even if partially, the double-edged quality of the *char diwari* (four walls) concept (connoting shelter and safety as well as confinement and insecurity). Further, it does not limit itself to the violence that women can experience within the home (from husbands, fathers or in-laws) but examines the subjugation of women as they participate in their own oppression. It also deals with the sense of low self-esteem and the terror of coping that women experience when thrust into the public world for the first time after a lifetime spent inside the home (four walls). By including this analysis, the concept of women's work in the 'public' sphere takes on new meaning. The analysis then incorporates the question of why so many women are 'technically unfit,' lacking the educational qualifications to enter job markets.

However, the serial does not go beyond presenting various professional alternatives. Tanuja repeatedly asserts, 'My job is only to suggest vocational training,' with less and less conviction each time. At one point in the serial, confused about what advice to give, she does concede that women's work seems to be inextricably linked to their personal lives.

This said, a review of the occupations suggested reveals that, except for the management and services jobs, to which privileged women have always had access, they all reflect a distinct gender affiliation. The service industry—to which catering, para-medical work, beauty care and running a creche belong—has traditionaly been 'reserved' for women. (The rationale for this could be that since many of the women featured in the serial had never worked before, it was only appropriate that they be offered career choices that are more accommodative, requiring fewer skills or shorter training periods.) There is no critique in the serial of this reality; it is accepted as a given.

The serial also fails to suggest that women have always performed productive tasks, in addition to those associated with human reproduction, which contribute to the welfare of their families and the community. So it is necessary to ask why this aspect of women's labour has not been given the significance it deserves.

Looking at the language in which a great deal of women's work is described, it is clear why this is so. The description of women's labour as 'unpaid family labour' is a good illustration of the fact that 'family labour' is seen as an extension of their natural mothering roles rather than real work—biological in origin rather than the result of conscious effort. Thus women look after children, the sick and the elderly because it is in their nature. This umbrella term, 'family labour,' also gets stretched to other aspects of work that are assigned to women. This is the ideological justification given for the sexual division of labour—a set of social relations by which men and women are assigned separate sets of activities based on their 'natures' or 'aptitudes'.

These social relations are not, however, constructed in a neutral way. Rather, they are relations of power that assign women to a position of subordination by devaluating their labour and denying them control over political, material and human resources. They also legitimise ideologies which perpetuate this condition.

If production is conceptualised only in terms of a market economy, then commodity production, as opposed to subsistence production, is seen by planners and local communities themselves as an indicator of socio-economic transformation. What this perspective hides is the fact that this form of production relies on a form of labour not bought or sold on the marketplace—primarily the subsistence labour performed by women. Therefore, the emphasis on efficiency, which views all individuals as free economic agents, ignores women's greater embeddedness in familial or domestic responsibilities and relationships. If production has to be reconceptualised, it becomes glaringly obvious that giving women equal opportunities will not work if no account is taken of the unequal conditions from which they begin. The contents of the serial have to be viewed against this conception of women's work.

The first episode introduces the presenter, Tanuja or Tanuji, relaxed and at ease in her elegant, upper class home, complete with leather furniture, low marble table, antiques and art objects. Throughout the serial she plays herself: Tanuji, the star (people react to her consciously as a star) and Tanuji, the women's rights activist. It is an interesting construction, since one part is truth (she is an actress in semi-retirement) and the other is fiction (she has never been active in social movements, unlike Nargis Dutt, Shabana Azmi or Smita Patil).

This also raises a point about the form of the serial—featuring a celebrity to not only tackle unpalatable issues, but also sell the serial to sponsors and viewers. Tanuja is consistently in character as an upper class women (it is difficult to imagine her sitting on a pavement during a dharna)—confident, imperious, surrounded by liveried male servants and without a visible family.

In the serial, Tanuji takes up the offer to do an 'agony aunt' column in *Women's India* with one stipulation: she will choose and respond to one letter at a time, go into the problem, find the solution and then write about the process in her column. This device enables her to enter various situations in a credible manner. She is accompanied in her crusade by a deferential male employee of *Women's India*. He is the editor but, in an ironic role reversal, he functions like a meek male secretary.

The first episode deals with a young girl who is frustrated at her inability to obtain a medical seat despite her high marks. Her parents can afford to put only one child through medical college and inevitably choose the son; marriage is suggested to her as a career option. Tanuji's suggestion that she pursue a para-medical career is gratefully accepted, thereby setting the tone of the serial—accommodation and compromise without tackling the fundamental issue of gender discrimination.

When friction arises between partners in the case of married or engaged couples because of the woman's work, Tanuja is quick to bridge the gap with requests addressed to the men for 'understanding' and a 'change of heart.' The language used by Tanuja sounds like familiar feminist rhetoric: women's work is a 'double burden' (*dohra bhoj*), she works outside the home and within it, child care responsibilities and other domestic tasks need to be shared, especially when her workload gets too much, and so on.

The emotional investment of the serial seems to lie in these scenes. Punished for having articulated these ideas, women now need Tanuji to grant their problems legitimacy. The phrases, 'new modern women' or 'times have changed,' offer another clue. Tanuji, the agony aunt, in conspiracy with the women, has to guide the men by the hand into the modern age and introduce them afresh to their wives.

With the number of middle class women entering the workforce on the increase, tensions generated by the traditional familial role expectations and the impossibility of juggling responsibilities at home with those at the workplace have assumed primacy. The disproportionately large amount of time allotted to this section of the serial and its overwhelming intensity, while paying only lip service to the priorities of working class women, is revealing. It illustrates how Doordarshan gives the impression of addressing a problem while actually deflecting and disarming it.

Such an approach leaves unaddressed the more radical questions of the right to work, equal pay and equal participation in the workforce, as well as precludes analyses of the kinds of jobs that patriarchal capitalism has permitted women to enter and the demands that the system makes on them. Instead, the debate takes place within their homes with a plea for 'understanding' and 'sympathy' on the part of men and other authoritarian figures in the family.

Where the sisterhood breaks down is in the episodes dealing with working class women. The construction of 'women' as the subject of address is based on a predominantly middle class, upper caste Hindu model. Thus, while the film-maker and Tanuji construct a 'we'—women like us—with the middle class subjects, when they come to working class women, it is 'you'—women obviously not like them.

An episode involving a young girl working as a domestic help reveals this all too clearly. The girl is rescued by Tanuji's male side-kick (the editor) from a vicious female employer who starves and beats her. She is brought to Tanuji's house and there ensues a graphic, if stereotypical, account of how the poor live—a drunken, incestuous stepfather, five siblings, an exhausted mother whose meagre earnings as a domestic worker do not stretch enough to feed the family. Tanuji is practically in tears by the end of it, but the voyeuristic delight in observing that an alien world lives so predictably, according to her expectations, is obvious.

While the search for suitable training/employment is on, the girl is visited by a boy who offers to liberate her from her family as well as the rich. At this point, Tanuji bursts into the room and abuses the boy, threatening him with the police. Then, still seething, she attacks the girl: 'Here I'm trying to do something for you and you are carrying on with this good-for-nothing character.' When the girl protests that he is ready to marry her, her would-be benefactor shrieks, 'And then what? You want to end up like your mother?' And that is the point: the lower classes lead amoral lives and need to be bullied, threatened and manipulated into submitting to the middle class mode—for their own good, of course.

Contrast this bullying, self-righteous, moral tone with the one adopted in the episode involving a product designer whose fiance wants her to give up working after they are married. Tanuji asks her to rethink his demand and consider the implications of stopping work for her creativity and self-esteem (clearly middle class women's work equals self-expression, self-esteem and economic independence, in that order, while working class women's work equals economic sustenance). The young woman breaks off the engagement; Tanuji is stricken with guilt and remorse, agonising over her responsibility for the estrangement. She wonders whether she should not intervene to bring about a 'change of heart' on both sides. When women from the same class as herself are involved, it is clear that the primacy of the couple and the family as a social unit, with their own private space, is a given deserving respect.

In the episode with the fisherwomen, it was apparent that the entire crew was floundering, totally at sea. The fisherwomen graduate from 'false' to 'true' political consciousness and set up a union in twenty-two and a half minutes, aided only by some literature from the Self-Employed Women's Association (SEWA) which Tanuji has to abandon in a hurry because the 'goondas' (middlemen in the fish marketing chain) are after her. All the filmic conventions of social realism are employed, including a torch-light procession at night, a rousing song and some eyeball to eyeball confrontation with the management goons (dressed in the stereotypical goonda costume: lungi, vest and scarf knotted at the throat, appropriate for smugglers, rapists, etc.). Tanuji in the role of a political activist or catalyst strains one's credulity, leading one to suspect that the whole episode must have been structured as low comedy.

It is a pity the episode was handled so shoddily as it was the only one in which women workers examined their situation, collectively, at the workplace. The site of the struggle was not the home which would have been an ideal context for discussing the dependence of exploitative markets on women's cheap labour. The cliched treatment of the path to political understanding and empowerment was unforgiveable.

The undifferentiated 'we'/'women like us' articulated by Tanuji should have been clarified to mean middle class, literate, urban and upper caste Hindu. It is their concerns and experiences that were being structured and articulated—through women privileged by class and ethnicity. The problem is that Doordarshan iconises these images as the only or dominant representations permissible.

Stri

The last line of a Brooke Bond Tea commercial jingle for its 'Special' brand puns on the word 'special.' It reads in translation, 'My life and my dear wife are both very special.' The line fades on an image of a beautiful young woman smiling tenderly at her tired husband, off-camera, whom she has just revived with samosas served in a silver dish and 'Special' tea. Her immaculately made-up face in close-up is tilted to one side, her elbows rest on an elaborately arranged dining table and steam rises from the teapot. It is her face or, should one say, the construction of the image which is so familiar: the soft, diffuse lighting, the expression of pleasurable anticipation which, while it is directed explicitly at the male viewer, is also fairly masochistically noted by women viewers—the only possible stance women are allowed to adopt in such compositions.

The scene changes to a big close-up of a woman's eye. The transition from advertisement to serial is fairly imperceptible. The music also changes and the close-up of the woman's eye is intercut with 'negative' photography images—of various women who seem to be at work. The same set of shots is then repeated, but this time the sequence uses positives.

It appears that the elaborately made up single eye shots belong to a model and are photographed in the commercial genre (somehow reminiscent of a 'slasher' or suspense movie where the eye could belong to a nubile victim who witnesses a crime or is about to become the target of one). On the other hand, the 'positive'/'negative' photography images seem to be of a police officer, an old Rajasthani woman, a woman welder and sundry other women—among them the celebrities Vijaya Mehta (theatre director) and Kiran Bedi (police officer). The women are photographed in straight, news reportage style in different work situations.

The commentary starts during the sequence with 'positive' photography images. Translated from the Hindi original, it reads: 'Every week we will be introducing you to an Indian woman, a woman who has not only wrested her individuality by her own efforts but has reached a position which was previously considered out of bounds for women.' Black and white titles come on: *Stri* (Woman), produced, written, directed and edited by Shridhar Kshirsagar.

Stri, a prime time serial, was advertised as a 'real-life' journey through the lives of successful women. It used the docu-drama format to draw portraits of a group of 'extraordinary' women drawn from all regions and all classes. Though the form of the serial will be discussed at length later, here docu-drama signifies live interviews with the women, intercut with dramatised portions enacted by professional actresses and actors.

When Shridhar Kshirsagar was asked about his motivations for making this serial, he replied:

> I was tired of reading about all the negative things that happened to women—bride-burning, dowry deaths, torture. It struck me that it cannot be that this is common, in the sense that it happens to everybody. I know of women who are perfectly happy, perfectly adjusted, coming from different strata of society, who seem to be leading relatively full lives. Why not do something which talks about such successful women?

This raises the problematic question of 'positive images'. The title sequence is an indicator of the director's intent. The first query arises in relation to the close-up of the eye: who is watching whom? The eye is obviously not Kshirsagar's nor is it representative of the female audience—we mercifully watch with both our eyes and, in any case, that eye is observing us. Could it be that Kshirsagar would like the eye to be his, that he is using the shot to create a bond between male/creator and woman/audience? Except for the close-up of the eye, which is in a 'positive' photographic image, shots of the women whose lives are about to unfold before the viewer are in 'negative' photographic images until he chooses to breathe life into them, during the sequence using positives, with a commentary in a female voice.

However, built into the concept of 'positive images' is, presumably, an analysis of the status of women in Indian society. Apart from dismissing stories of bride-burning, dowry murders and torture, Kshirsagar's analysis is lacking. Depicting individual predicaments as personal struggles, rather than relating them to the larger social oppression faced by all women as a group, is particularly objectionable.

The valorisation of 'successful' women in order to create 'positive' role models is a dangerous strategy. Implicit in its dialectic is a judgmental exclusion of 'negative' images and a simplistic, corrective notion of redressing the balance. In his own words:

The women I chose are no different from anybody else. They have not had chances or opportunities thrown into their laps. What they have done, they have done quietly, without any major drama, and they have managed to achieve for themselves a sense of individual identity. I believe very firmly that these kinds of women are in the majority. *Now, if there are millions of women who watch this and feel that they have not been able to do it, then the purpose of this serial is really to ask these women, why not?* (Emphasis added.)

One must put on record at the outset that, given the scarcity of non-fiction programmes centred around women, practically any images are to be celebrated. There is a genuine hunger on the part of women viewers for material which makes women visible, names their experiences and validates their struggles. However, while it is commendable that the serial got made and aired, it is also important to look at how it was made.

Asked about his criteria and methodology for selecting women to be portrayed in his serial, Kshirsagar said he had used a 'most simplistic rationale'—the women must come from different regions and from across classes. He had written letters to voluntary agencies and activist groups working in the rural areas asking for potential candidates. In certain instances, the references had been given by friends. Of interest to him were also 'women who typified a certain kind of individual, women who had made changes for themselves.' Unusual (male) job skills seem to have been another qualification: welder, news photographer, doctor specialising in aviation medicine, police woman, collector, theatre and film director. Most of the women were shown as having personally struggled to attain these skills and persist in their current occupations.

A cursory glance at the selection of women for *Stri* indicates that it does fulfil these criteria. Much like the television graphic of the map of India that comes on before the national network programmes (Kathakali mask in Kerala, etc.), the serial featured women from Kerala, Karnataka, Tamil Nadu, Delhi, Aligarh, Rajasthan, Bengal and Mizoram.

The serial used a linear narrative structure. The women were introduced to the viewer using a female voice-over which identified the name of the actress who would play the part in a particular episode. Asked about the construction of this format, Kshirsagar said:

> The easiest way to do it would have been a straight documentary—a day in the life of or a portrait but audience sensibilities would have been turned off. I felt the issue was important; I needed the audience. I dramatised incidents critical in her personal evolution to make it more interesting.

The assumptions being made here by the director are that audiences prefer the narrative form and that the documentary style cannot elicit the same sort of identification nor generate sufficient dramatic tension to sustain interest. The choice of 'dramatisation' as the only possible mode for handling emotions and feelings is indicative of Kshirsagar's brand of politics—he locates women's strengths and responses in the individual, instead of critiquing the systemic roots of their oppression. This form—searching for the psychological sources of their unique strengths to construct their characters—was imposed uniformly on all the episodes.

The form did not work. Strait-jacketing the women's stories into the 'family drama' genre only served to diminish the women. The dramatic scenes played by Bombay-based, Hindi-speaking actors and actresses resulted in some grotesque parodies, such as Farida Jalal playing Sunderambal, the welder, who lives in Madras. The dramatic scenes were privileged over the documentary scenes.

The documentary scenes were stilted and brief, constructed more to present the women as visual evidence. Every cut from the real situation to the dramatic parts came as a shock because even the locations—the interiors of, say, Shipra Das' actual home and her 'theatrical' home—did not match.

Every episode starts with the woman in her youth, at the first turning point, when she is made aware of her gender identity as either valuable or inferior, or identifies with a tribal heritage (Toda and Mizo), or articulates a desire to become a doctor or news photographer. Obstacles are placed in her path by male family members or material constraints. Some of the women fall in love and marry, usually mid-point in the narrative. This section was always dramatised with great fidelity to the romantic conventions laid down by popular cinema: softly-lit close-ups of the couple staring at each other, a combination shot of the woman reading a love letter and her lover—in a cut-out in the upper right-hand corner of the frame—speaking passionately to the camera. These scenes, set to appropriate music, were the most carefully crafted, occupying top place in the hierarchy of dramatic sequences. The rest of the narrative is an exposition of the woman's current status. It ends with a freeze-frame of the woman whose name is announced by the accompanying commentary—for example, 'Kiran Bedi, an Indian woman of today.'

The episode on Vijaya Mehta, the theatre and film director, was the only one, done in a straight, biographical documentary style, with no dramatised bits. She speaks in Hindi, is extremely articulate and describes her attitudes to her work and family with sensitivity and insight. Moreover, she was accorded a very reverential space—the episode on her ended the series. The relationship of the film maker to all his other subjects—who were spoken for by actresses and spoken about in the third person by the commentator's voice—was an uneasy one.

The women's struggles to achieve their goals were translated into a valorisation of male values like ambition, the courage to take on the public world of work and power and the ability to succeed despite all odds. The constrictive perspective imposed by the producer's concerns could not, however, contain the women completely; one often suspected that they had different stories to tell.

The pan-Indian strait-jacket imposed on them—note the concluding 'an Indian woman of today'—did not permit attention to the differential experiences of the women. For example, in the episode on Parthe of

Mizoram, only one line indicated that the status of women in that area was radically different from that in other parts of India. Nor was much attention paid to the fact that she was Laldenga's daughter and had lived through a very violent and repressive period of her state's history. Apart from showing a tame encounter with an Indian government official who had arrested Laldenga, there were no references to the specificity of that experience. Scene after scene delineated her sense of discrimination by and alienation from Indians, experienced first as a student in college and then later as an adult. The discriminatory attitude of Indians towards Mizos was presented as an 'ignorant' and provincial form of social ostracism. Without an exposition of the long struggle for Mizo self-determination, the exhortations of Parthe's mother and grandmother to be proud of her Mizo heritage lacked meaning.

Similarly, with Evam Pilgin's story, the audience was left with no sense of the process by which she decided to work for Toda rights and the preservation of the tribe. It was hard to picture tribal gender relations even though the commentary mentioned, again telegraphically, that they are more equitous than those in the rest of India. Her elevated status in Toda society as a spokeswoman for 'her' people was revealed but not her working methods except in the most cliched social worker style—supervising embroidery groups and translating an interview where people spoke of the devastation of the environment. The imposition of this kind of framework led inevitably to the enactment of a classic Films Division tribute or darshan (divine audience) scene, with the young Pilgin placing a Toda shawl over Jawaharlal Nehru's shoulders.

Kshirsagar does this to all his subjects—claiming to speak on behalf of all women, he obscures the specificities of their experiences and muffles their individual voices. His attempts at conveying a superficial and duplicitous 'speaking from the inside' understanding of and intimacy with regional, class and linguistic diversity are exposed in every story. Kshirsagar does not trust his subjects and has, instead, caricatured them by uniformly casting them in the synthetic '*Bharatiya stri*' mould of Doordarshan.

Air Hostess

Air Hostess, a thirteen-episode serial on the trials and tribulations of air hostesses working on Global Indian, an international airline, was written, produced and directed by Vinod Pande. He also played the male lead, a divorced business magnate who is emotionally estranged from his son. Kausalya (Kittu) Gidwani, a successful model who performed the main role, was also used in the publicity to 'sell' the serial.

Her character of Ritu linked the episodes. Jilted by her fiance, who allows his calculating mother to bulldoze him into an arranged marriage, she goes through the serial doing good work. These include rescuing other hostesses and some passengers from incredibly messy personal and professional crises.

The serial chalked up a first on Indian television in its varied representations of heterosexual possibilities outside of marriage. Except for Ritu's loving parents, who are transferred midway through the serial to another town and reappear only briefly, all the other characters were daringly deviant or, at least, non-normative—legally single but sexually active.

The divorced industrialist is emotionally reconciled with his son and falls in love with Ritu, but she wants to bring him and his ex-wife together. One hostess is pregnant when her fiance dies in a Global Indian aircrash weeks before their marriage; she decides to go ahead with the pregnancy, even if it means losing her job. Another star-struck hostess is seduced by a conman pretending to be a film producer. She is used as a drug courier by her lover and only realises what she had been carrying when she is arrested.

A third hostess, who is supporting her layabout brother, has been the mistress of a married colleague for three years. She resolves to give him up after Ritu convinces her that the man will never leave his wife and children.

Air Hostess can serve as an allegory for all single working women. The serial constructs their economic independence only to undercut it with sexual transgression—either pre-marital sex, an obvious taboo, or adultery. The self-consciously casual treatment of these relationships is unusual; the air-hostess who wants to go ahead with her baby is warned of repercussions from 'society' by Ritu and her male boss but their attitudes are sympathetic and without censure.

Despite the self-conscious foregrounding of the 'modern' single working woman—who uses English in love-making as well as abuse, lives alone outside the paternal family and is sexually active—as normal or, at least, nothing out of the ordinary, the dominant male discourse of the serial is voyeuristic and punitive.

A patriarchal construction is apparent in the enactment of a dichotomy between legitimate desire within marriage and its transgressional nature outside the marital framework. The air hostesses are placed firmly on the outside, looking in. The prime narrative motivator is the desire for integration into society through marriage and family. The reverential space that family and marriage occupy is a given. The women, then, are constructed as sites of male desire.

This leads to objectification, so that they were photographed in a fetishised 'advertising commercial' style, with soft lighting and careful compositions, to be consumed by the male protagonists within the serial as well as male viewers watching it.

Ritu's rejection by her lover opens the serial. His mother, in listing the attributes of the rich, finishing school polished bride she has arranged for him, stresses the virtues of good family and decent girl (read virgin).

Other hostesses in later episodes speak of similar experiences but they never articulate to each other the public perception of their roles, as the major obstacle in the cycle of unsatisfactory relationships. When it is articulated, the words are given to a man.

Ritu accepts a dinner invitation from a male passenger who has defended her against the abuse of another male passenger. Discussing the latter's hostility, Ritu says it has to be seen in the light of prevailing male attitudes towards air hostesses, which presuppose that they are fair game: 'They all think we are whores, lacking character or morals.' Her date flares his nostrils and, appropriating her outrage, declaims: 'All men are afraid of working women, their economic independence, their freedom, their possible rise to men's status. This is a deep, irrational fear, in the blood.'

Vinod Pande's analysis (the statement has a distinctly sonorous, authorial tone, though spoken by another male character) and his attempt to align himself with the air hostesses are not convincing. As in the scene detailed above, he first creates the problem by structuring the serial with a view to male gratification—it reaffirms every titillating myth about women in the service industry—and then offers a feeble defence in the best liberal-humanist tradition: 'They are also human beings, they have their joys and sorrows, too.'

Except for one episode where the serial moves into the 'action' genre, with an improbable plot involving a bomb and a crash landing, the serial voyeuristically builds crises and resolutions around the air-hostesses' personal lives, firmly in the genre of 'melodrama.'

This is combined with a meticulous portrayal of the exotic, elite, luxurious nature of air travel itself. To enable the viewers to vicariously experience the thrill of flying, all the usual procedures are shown. The sequence on the take-off has a shot of the Captain against a mock-up of the cockpit (inexpert carpentry in full evidence); as the plane lifts, we hear the opening bars of Beethoven's Fifth Symphony. Appropriate passenger behaviour is also shown. Unlike the gregarious gabble and clack characteristic of those travelling by Indian trains, the passengers maintain a studiously quiet poise (most staring directly ahead). However, the air hostesses are treated no better than domestic help or abused contemptuously. They appeared to grin and bear it in the best traditions of courteous service. A lot of time was spent, again in a suspiciously apologetic fashion, on constructing the job as a 'profession' and debunking the traditional perception of female cabin crew as sexually available ayahs in the sky.

In the construction of the fantasy world peopled among others by the industrialist, inordinate time was devoted to observing the ethnographic rituals of the wealthy. His estate is enormous—the camera tracks along the manicured green lawns, the landscaped gardens, the stables (although he looks extremely uncomfortable on a horse), the cars; as it lingers on the dining table, we observe the elaborate arrangements and the innumerable dishes of food and the way the affluent eat, their leisure activities, as well as the industrialist's imperious behaviour in his office.

Positioned centrally in this artificial but seemingly coherent world are the beautiful airhostesses. This is in keeping with the aim of selling the viewer the entire package—consume the lifestyle, consume the woman.

Ritu, the main character, in deflecting her desire, by effecting a reconciliation between the industrialist and his ex-wife, aligns herself with the ex-wife. This comes late enough in the serial for viewers to have speculated pleasurably on the resolution of her marriage to the industrialist.

She manages to navigate the perilous shoals of temptation as a single working woman deprived of the protection (moral and financial) of her family. When her father is transferred, Ritu offers to look after her younger sister till she completes her education. They can only find cheap accommodation in a boarding house in a seedy neighbourhood. One of the occupants, obviously a prostitute, comes over to their room for a neighbourly chat and retreats in confusion at the two sisters who are so obviously 'respectable'. Ritu refuses to solve her housing problem by accepting the industrialist's offer of his flat or agreeing to her fiance's suggestion that he set her up in an apartment as his mistress.

Here the ambivalence and covert politics of the serial become all too apparent. Despite the valorisation of Ritu's choice to be her own woman, the implicit message of aligning her with the prostitute, with the corollary of the inevitable exposure to male advances, is clearly to caution all single working women: leave the shelter of paternalistic protection and look at what awaits you! It also follows then that the solution is not to be financially independent but, instead, to move from father to husband in one fluid step.

The other air hostesses' entrapment in and enactment of transgressional sexuality highlighted Ritu's self-control and strength, but Ritu was only permitted autonomy by the narrative because she acknowledges her sexual attraction towards the industrialist and sublimates it by attempting a reconciliation between him and his family.

Her powerful and disturbing screen presence was effectively neutralised by her belief in monogamy sanctioned by marriage. Her pep talks to the industrialist, his ex-wife and their son constantly upheld the stable nuclear family as the only viable social unit. Her own idealised family was no doubt the model. It was subtly implied that the other hostesses would not have gone astray if their families (read fathers) had not let them down.

The mother-to-be did not have a father, only an ineffectual mother; the drug courier had parents who were provincial, meek and easily intimidated by authority/the police; the mistress had no parents but an exploitative brother.

In the episodes dealing with their crises—each one was an emotional roller-coaster ride lasting exactly twenty-two and a half minutes—the serial revealed its violence and misogyny. Male fantasies were first projected onto the air hostesses and then, as male fears rose, the women had to be punished.

The star-struck air hostess who becomes a drug courier and ends up in prison does so because she is seduced by a conman who impersonates a film producer. The pregnant air hostess who loses her fiance in the air crash wants to keep her baby as a 'sign' of their love and thereby loses her job. The unscrupulous brother who exploits his air hostess sister can only do so because she is vulnerable and depressed in a dead-end relationship with her married colleague.

While the representation of the transgression of sexual codes could be enjoyed voyeuristically, a reappropriation of the text by the male protagonists and the male spectators was necessary. The threat that the woman's desires posed had to be contained and dealt with for all the narrative ends to be tied up.

Udaan

Kalyani is eight years old when her younger brother is born. His birth as the first grandson in a zamindari family is celebrated with due ceremony. When her grandfather, a feudal patriarch, objects to Kalyani attending school and arranges a marriage for her, Kalyani's father decides to defy his diktat. He leaves the parental home to set up an independent base on a small piece of land gifted to him by his late mother. After a couple of years of hard work, the land becomes fertile and is ready to yield profits when the family is brutally evicted in an illegal land-grab operation by a smuggler/criminal.

Kalyani's father is determined to take the battle for the restitution of his property to the courts. Undeterred by the frustratingly long and unsuccessful legal battles in the lower courts, he appeals to the High Court. Even when physically assaulted by the smuggler's goons in the court grounds, in an attempt to terrorise him into withdrawing the case, he remains basically noble.

Kalyani, by now a young woman, decides to carry on her father's struggle for the return of their land. Confronted with humiliation and an increasing awareness of powerlessness in every encounter with the police or bureaucracy, she resolves to achieve power as a police officer, faces and rises above discrimination in a male-dominated force, and finally brings the smuggler to book.

Udaan (Flight), which was aired from 28 April to 21 July 1988, was written, produced, directed and enacted by Kavita Chaudhari, a graduate of the National School of Drama, as her first film-making effort. According to the Indian Market Research Bureau (IMRB), during its run, *Udaan* was rated as the second most popular serial in the prime time 9 pm slot in the metros and the most popular one in the small towns. Critics and viewers were vociferous in their condemnation of Doordarshan when, in keeping with its new policy, it initially refused to grant the popular serial an extension beyond thirteen episodes. (It reversed its decision in 1991).

Critics were unanimous in their praise for *Udaan*. Jyoti Punwani stated:

> It's not just an aesthetically satisfying serial when you thought that kind were dead; it's a thought-provoking serial in a sea of juvenile and cliched muck; and, more important, it's a woman-oriented serial that says things about women you want to listen to, at a time when

women-oriented serials are bad news.... But is being on 'the other side' (a police officer), Kalyani's '*Udaan*', a worthwhile ambition?[11]

Amita Malik wrote:

Where Doordarshan revealed its 'broadmindedness' was with the serial, *Udaan*, scripted, directed and acted (of all people) by Lalitaji of the Surf ad fame. *Udaan* was an example of how women-oriented serials can be hard-hitting without being loud and how one does not have to indulge in polemics to prove a point.[12]

Chaya Datar, a feminist activist and writer, was quoted in Jyoti Punwani's article as saying, '*Udaan* is simplistic—it is true what they say, such serials make women happy. They are fantasies which provide relief for women and a catharsis. But better an *Udaan* fantasy than a *Shah-en-shah* fantasy.'

Despite Chaudhari's claims to the contrary—'The woman's story is just one of the themes of *Udaan*, not the only one' (in an interview to this writer)—she has produced what can be described as the first Indian women's soap opera for TV.

Vladimir Propp, analysing the fairy tale as a narrative form, has indicated that the agent to motivate action is a 'villainy' or a 'lack' which disturbs the existing equilibrium—for example, the hero has to regain a lost object, or evil personified by a witch or dragon has to be slain. The world of the narrative has to return to its original order by the act of vanquishing the 'villain' or liquidating the 'lack.' The villain is either killed or suitably chastened and the princess won.[13]

In a significant reversal, Kalyani not only assumes the role of the hero but also takes on the patriarchal world of crime, law enforcement and the judiciary. We identify with her humble origins, suffer and empathise with her humiliations and rejoice in seeing her deal with the villains as a feared police officer.

Filmed and presented in the classic realist tradition, the world of *Udaan* was easily accessible. Actual locations, photographed as far as possible in natural light, and continuity editing made for a transparent narrative that moved inexorably towards its foregone conclusion, leaving Kalyani successful and triumphant, a 'winner.'

[11] Jyoti Punwani, *The Indain Post*, 14 July 1988.
[12] Amita Malik, *Sunday*, 19-25 March 1989.
[13] Vladimir Propp, *Morphology of the Folktale*, University of Texas Press, Austin, 1968.

It is difficult to knock a fairy tale which works so well but it must be admitted that one's unabashed enjoyment was tinged with guilt. As a feminist, it is difficult to valorise the Indian police force with their notorious reputation for custodial rape, 'encounter' murders, their propensity for torture leading to infamous lock-up deaths and their magnetic attraction to supporting and enabling the most exploitative elements (landlords and factory managements, for example) of Indian society. Even if they did not have such a reputation, it still goes against the grain to understand and empathise with a woman's burning ambition to qualify for, and succeed in, joining the police force, with its quasi-military character.

The most significant aspect of *Udaan* lay in the construction of Kalyani who gradually acquires the status of a 'hero.' Donning the male police uniform, to do battle to reinstate her father's land and honour, she perforce surrenders and represses her 'femininity.' However, this negation of her female sexual and social self does not mean that she escapes being projected in male fantasy. Iqbal Masud, a prominent film and television critic, in an interview to this writer, admitted that 'Kavita Chaudhary looked quite sexy in a police uniform.'

If Kalyani enacted 'masculinity,' her father had to be emasculated in the 'feminine' sphere of powerlessness, passivity and narrative inertia. Kalyani's mother and other female characters in the serial were not only positioned marginally but also shown as derogatory examples of how the sexual/social enactment of familial roles can paralyse and confine them in the claustrophobic private space of domesticity. The main players were definitely father and daughter; and in returning to a detailed analysis of the text one will attempt to examine the construction of the masculine/feminine positions in the serial.

The serial opens with the *naamkaran* (naming ceremony) of Kalyani's baby brother. Kalyani is not part of the festivities—a crane shot establishes her watching from a distance: alone, diminished, an exile. An encounter with a widowed grand-aunt, who serves throughout the serial as a representation of women's extreme dependence on male charity, makes her aware for the first time of not only her gender identity but also its inferiority in the culture into which she has been born. This damage to her self-esteem manifests itself in nightmares; refusing to be comforted, she sobs, 'You won't love me anymore now that you have a son.'

Kalyani, the child, is not the only one who is shocked into an understanding of inferior gender status. In declaring his intention to make Kalyani self-reliant, her father is reminded crudely of his own financial dependence on the joint family. Earlier, his emasculation has been hinted at—he is accused of being soft on tenants, unreliable and so on—and this absence of traits usually associated with the male gender causes him to be treated as a step-son, not a true heir to the old patriarch. His decision to leave the joint family coincides with an appraisal of his previous 'feminine' status and his effort to move into the 'masculine' sphere of self-determination; with his attempt as the patriarch to take control of and responsibility for his nuclear family.

Kalyani, the girl child, and the conflicting plans for her future, act as the first narrative problem. Its enactment enables the plot to move forward. As Kalyani grows up, the relationship between father and daughter is mutually obsessive and pleasurable. His trying nobility is immaculate; his views on caste, social relations and the dignity of labour (he always works with his hands—in the field, as a weaver; the artisan/labourer construction attains a purity later on when counterposed by his enemies, the smuggler/middleman/criminal) are all firmly in the liberal, humanistic tradition.

Kalyani's mother is shown as a side-player. Presenting a role model Kalyani should perhaps never emulate, she is timid, worried about keeping up social appearances, afraid of the consequences of taking on the smuggler but loyal to her unusual, eccentric husband. This repression of her influence on Kalyani's development in the text is a significant omission; an indicator of where the unconscious of the narrative was really being played out—between father and daughter.

For example, the father, stripped to a dhoti, tucked *langoti*-style, is shown clearing rocks from his fields. He is alone; Kalyani is watching him. He tries to lift a huge rock which comes up to his chest. His attempts to move it are presented melodramatically, with low angle shots of him straining with the huge rock (reminiscent of an exaggerated phallic symbol) inter-cut with Kalyani's face growing increasingly anxious and frightened. The music rises to a crescendo as he succeeds, his expression resembles a sexual climax. Later on in the serial, Kalyani describes her father as the man who does not know the meaning of the word 'impossible,' whom no obstacle can stop.

The old patriarch sells his own, if estranged, son's land illegally to a smuggler. The armed goons of the criminal brutally evict Kalyani, her mother and brother on a night they happen to be alone in their house. The family moves to an urban slum. Kalyani's father loses the case for restitution of his land in the lower courts, ignores a warning from his lawyer to abandon the case and decides to appeal in the High Court. He is physically attacked by the armed goons of the smuggler in the court compound and is hospitalised—prone and immobilised. He is now firmly in the 'feminine' sphere of narrative paralysis.

Kalyani decides to step into the narrative vacuum. Her efforts to seek justice from a hostile state apparatus that favours the 'powerful' or well-connected are futile. Her humiliation as a powerless citizen is compounded by her gender status. Four incidents are made the primary determinants of her propulsion towards the desire for *'udaan'* to 'the other side of the desk.'

A senior police officer forbids her to return to his office: 'They send a girl to get more sympathy; the officer will get impressed and they may get more out-of-court compensation.' A minister, after dismissing the case as a family feud, asks her, 'Who are you with?' She is the only woman there; she replies, 'I am alone.' Defeated, she emerges into the corridor and sees a young woman not much older than herself walking confidently into her office with three or four clerks flapping files in her wake, trying to keep up. People stand at attention as she passes. This apparition, Kalyani discovers, is an officer in the Indian Administrative Service (IAS). The final straw comes when she is sexually harassed (or 'eve-teased') on her way home.

In an impassioned speech on her return home, she speaks of her ambition to obtain power and a special status for herself and her father. By including her father in the definition of ordinary and powerless, she circumscribes him in a feminine space, to be enacted upon. In the serial, the state appropriates the right to demand submission from those of its subjects, regardless of gender, who lack all access to economic and political power and upward mobility.

At this point it may be useful to delineate the Arundhati myth with special reference to the castration fantasy of turning all men into eunuchs. According to the story, Brahma (the creator) displays desire for his daughter, Sandhya (twilight) as soon as she is born and she reciprocates. As a result of this, Brahma curses Kama (Eros), who had caused the trouble, to be burnt by Siva. When everyone has departed, Sandhya resolves to purify herself and to establish for all time a moral law: that new-born creatures will be free of desire. For this she is prepared to offer herself as an oblation in the fire.

Knowing her intention, Brahma sends the sage Vasistha to instruct her in the proper manner of performing *tapas* (penance). Vasistha disguises himself as a *brahmachari* (a celibate seeker of the truth) with matted locks and teaches Sandhya how to meditate to invoke Siva. Siva then appears to her and offers her a boon. Sandhya asks:

> Let all new-born creatures be free of desire, and let me be reborn as the wife of a man to whom I can just be a close friend. And if anyone but my husband gazes upon me with desire, let his virility be destroyed and let him become an impotent eunuch.

Siva says, 'Your sin has been burnt to ashes, purified by your *tapas*. I grant what you ask; henceforth, creatures will only become subject to desire when they reach youth and any man but your husband who looks upon you with desire will become impotent.' Then Sandhya, meditating on the chaste Brahmin for her husband, enters the sacrificial fire. Her body becomes the oblation, and she rises from the fire as an infant girl, named Arundhati. She grows up in a sage's hermitage and marries Vasistha.[14]

As psychologist Sudhir Kakkar suggests, even though the Arundhati myth is a patriarchal projection, it uncovers two significant features. One, the young girl's fantasised erotic feelings towards her father and her subsequent repudiation of these wishes by transforming them into their opposite—no feelings, a freezing over, an absence, leading automatically to chastity.

Second, the castration fantasy of turning all men into eunuchs is an illustration of the ambivalence that governs the relations between the sexes. Women's feelings of worthlessness and inferiority, in societies which have traditionally devalued women in cultural terms and so blatantly prefer men, can easily be transformed into envy and hostility. It also serves as a warning against seeing women as the sites of desire.[15]

During her training and subsequent rise as a successful police officer, Kalyani so completely denies her female sexual/social self that one of her bosses calls her 'our best man.' Enacting an active/masculine sexual/social self, she rejects all her feminine 'baggage,' demanding and obtaining dangerous assignments. She disdains soft jobs, such as traffic control and crimes against women (there are none in her police station), and wants to be where the action is, as one of the boys. But it is precisely at these moments that she is perceived as a pornographic staple or

---

[14] Wendy O'Flaherty, *Asceticism and Eroticism in the Mythology of Shiva*, Oxford University Press, London, 1973.
[15] Sudhir Kakkar, *The Inner World*, Oxford University Press, New Delhi, 1978.

cliche—a fetishised image of the woman masquerading in an authoritarian garb. The force of her desire and passion were focussed on empowerment (achieving status and respect in her profession) and seeking revenge.

A thaw seems possible when she meets an attractive IAS officer while trying to extricate a bullock cart wheel out of the mud because it is blocking the road. 'Lara's Theme' from the film *Doctor Zhivago* soars on the sound-track but it amounts to nothing—he is only a red herring; her hero/sexual partner is her father.

The collective anxiety of critics and viewers on this question is interesting. Most critics felt a romantic diversion would only retard the action and delay the gratification of watching the smuggler get his due. But words like 'jarring' indicated another area of unease. If Kalyani was to get side-tracked into confronting her sexuality and affirming it (through marriage, in her case; the way the character was set up, there could be no other option), she would be instantly mired in the messy world of emotions, desire and subjugation, and every woman knows where that leads: disempowerment and abrupt loss of momentum.

Kalyani is shaken but not deterred. She pursues the smuggler relentlessly, destroys his underworld empire and brings him grovelling to her for a ceasefire. But when she tries to lay this trophy at her father's feet, reclaiming in a sense his honour and manhood, she is met with a lukewarm reaction and her triumph turns to ashes. Now order, which by definition is patriarchal, has to be restored. It is given to Kalyani's father to guide her back to her 'essential' femininity both in character and in the narrative.

Kalyani's rejection and implicit criticism of her mother's and, by extension, all women's spheres of passivity, weakness, subjugation and service in marriage, has to be revealed as a mistake. She is returned to the female world of emotions, anxiety and despair. For the first time since she embarked on an active path of personal empowerment and persecution of the smuggler, she is unsure. She asks her father, 'Was my flight meaningless?'

The narrative of dominant cinema or fairy tale has no space for strong single women who are not contained and defined by marriage and family. She has to be either married or banished beyond the pale of such a possibility through the mechanisms of rape, celibacy, suicide or even death. The containment has to be a sexually definitive one.[16]

Kalyani, like Arundhati, is asked to metaphorically burn up all her desires, in this case 'masculine' ones like selfishness, violence, anger and vindictiveness, to emerge cleansed and pure, reconciled to her female sexual/social self.

In Wendy O'Flaherty's reading of the Arundhati myth, she suggests that Arundhati's *tapas* (penance) is an angry reaction against her relationship with her father, Brahma, and that it is he who sends Vasistha to sexually distract her from her *tapas*. The fact that Vasistha is in disguise and that Arundhati does not recognise or desire him does not alter the fact that as the man who diverts her penance he earns the right to possess her. This shows that the myth uses the seduction device, though its overt purpose is the opposite—to extol the power of chastity. By manoeuvring such that Kalyani is forced to terminate her *tapas*, her father can restore the patriarchal order, having resolved all his erotic ambivalence towards her.[17]

What implications does *Udaan* have for women? On the one hand, Kalyani succeedes in a male world, supported by a sympathetic, idealised family who believe in the economic independence of women. On the other hand, the analysis does not extend to the construction of power within patriarchal institutions such as the law enforcement machinery and the judiciary. These systems are perceived as 'male-dominated' only because women have not attempted to storm them. Any analysis of how power is deployed in these patriarchal institutions will reveal the naivete and limitations of this approach.

The representations of the socialisation of Kalyani in the feudal joint family and the critique thereafter of appropriate female behaviour—interest in romantic pulp fiction, gossip about prospective grooms, embroidery, values of subjugation and passivity—are insightful. This perspective, which sees family as the site for the socialisation, discrimination and violence against women in the family, has been represented continuously by activists in the women's movement in street theatre, songs, posters and slide-tape programmes. Kavita Chaudhari's familiarity with these efforts (she used to attend meetings of the Women and Media Group in Bombay) enabled her to attempt a similar exercise but in a mainstream, government-owned broadcasting service.

Kavita Chaudhari believes in the need for consciousness-raising on women's issues; she also feels television is an ideal medium for reaching out to women. Yet, in an interview to Jyoti Punwani, she has said:

[16]Mary Beth Haralovich, 'Women's Proper Place: Defining Gender Roles in Film and History,' unpublished paper, University of Wisconsin, Madison, 1979.

[17]O'Flaherty, *Asceticism and Eroticism*.

To isolate the women's issue and to become too aggressive about it is not as effective. I was frightened of making yet another women's serial—before you know it, every issue has become a caricature. Creatively one can say very little about dowry now, it's been so overdone already.... The Indian audience is very attached to tradition, so you have to go about showing these things very carefully.[18]

She has thus, in her own words, articulated the limitations of *Udaan*. The defensive definition of the subject matter and the anxiety about not alienating a 'traditional' audience may indicate an ambivalence about political affiliation. To maintain a position in mainstream media, political affiliations are a handicap.

And finally there is the irreconcilability of the two discourses—the apparent, dominant narrative comprising the success story of a small town girl's rise to power with the unconscious discourse of the containment of her sexuality within patriarchal ideology.

CONCLUSION

It is evident even from this limited study of select women-centred serials that the dominant image of woman being constructed as the norm for representation on Doordarshan is urban, middle class, literate and upper caste. All women are defined according to this norm, making for the distortion and falsification of those coming from an entirely different socio-cultural milieu. And, the power of this image, this misrecognition, is a dangerous one.

Homogeneity of construction—that is, middle class women— and homogeneity of address, to middle class or other women who aspire to those values, suits advertisers who envisage an India united by the same products in every home. In other words we will achieve national integration by eating Fryums and drinking Frooty simultaneously in front of our Solidaire/Uptron TVs while the rest of the country pledges to do the same as soon as they are able. Thus, the values of materialism are constructed as a uniting factor. Advertisers prefer middle class address because the members of this class have the purchasing power.

The dominant image also does not seem to have a specific regional identity. Even if there is a Hindi voice-over, the limited choice of

---

[18] Punwani, *The Indian Post*.

actresses imposes a homogeneity. This construction of homogeneity could be due to the need to create a pan-Indian culture, even if it is artificial and self-conscious, to combat rising caste, religious and ethnic conflict.

One explanation for the evident bias in Doordarshan's programming is that politically it is important that vocal urban electorates be kept pacified with the kind and quantum (as a percentage of the total telecast) of entertainment they want to watch. Consequently, the allocation of resources for imported programmes, for instance, which cater to a very small elite seems out of proportion.

As a result, despite their individual and different motivations, the interests of programmers, bureaucrats, advertisers and audiences have coincided and converged to make the middle class bias inevitable. Even if this has not occurred due to deliberate design, the convergence of interests is more than evident.

Finally, Doordarshan's affirmative efforts for women have been a failure because women's concerns were emptied of 'subversive potential' in both content and form. This either reflects adhocism or a deliberate policy of toning everything down because beaming feminist messages to a politically heterogeneous audience is problematic.

In this instance, Doordarshan acted benevolently to do its bit for promoting welfarism for women. This projection of a pro-women image is not just good public relations but ideologically shrewd—by such acts the government is seen to be progressive, thereby building up its political credibility. However, these exercises deflect the attention of viewers from the continuing and gross neglect of women in other spheres.

Postscript

In the five years since 1988, when we conceptualised and began working on this study, a number of significant changes have taken place—both in the media and in the women's movement—which have a bearing on media coverage of women's issues.

In the press, for example, there have been noticeable changes in the presentation of news and views, dictated partly by the growth of the electronic media and partly by the increasingly consumer-oriented nature of the Indian economy. However, one characteristic of the press that has not significantly altered in the intervening years is its continuing event-orientation. Nor has the press deviated much from its traditional definitions of news and its customary hierarchy of news values.

A second noteworthy development has been the remarkable increase in the number of media women who have been able to make a mark in the 'hard' news areas of politics and economics which until recently were all-male bastions. Interestingly, however, while many women journalists, especially within the English language press, were openly supportive of the issues raised by the women's movement during the period covered in our study, female journalists today are by and large wary of being labelled as feminists, of being associated with the women's cause and even of being categorised as 'women journalists'.

Meanwhile, the women's movement has also changed pace, with many more groups concentrating on grassroots activism or empirical research rather than on the highly visible propaganda campaigns of the past.

All these factors have had an impact on press coverage of women's issues over the past few years. For instance, as our study has amply demonstrated, women's issues are usually given significant coverage when they fit the dominant norms of what constitutes news. Since the media continue to emphasise events rather than processes, the shift in the women's movement, from high decible, single issue, public campaigns centred around atrocities against women to more consistent but low-key work that acknowledges the complex nature of women's oppression, has meant some diminution in the media's coverage of women's issues.

Changed Emphasis

Women's groups which campaigned in the late 1970s and early 1980s against dowry deaths, rape and domestic violence are in the 1990s also expressing concern about issues that are not exclusively gender-based but certainly have an impact on women's lives. Thus they are forming coalitions with groups fighting against environmental degradation and for sustainable development. They are also joining forces with those opposed to fundamentalists and communalists who capitalise on women's faith even while placing oppressive restrictions on their lives and using them as cannon fodder for their causes.

At a workshop on Women and the Media held in Delhi in September 1992, a feminist and activist, who works with the Action India Women's Programme in the capital, spoke about media coverage of women's issues from the perspective of women's groups. Describing the current thinking in the contemporary Indian women's movement and the new directions in which it is moving, she explained:

> What perhaps has not been conveyed to the press is that the women's movement is not at the peak of the early 1980s. Women's own perceptions are changing. Many groups in the autonomous women's movement have widened their field, getting involved in anti-communalism and environmental issues. Women are talking of human rights and state repression. Women are beginning to intervene in mainstream politics, to get a foothold in decision-making bodies. Women are getting organised, taking the initiative and assuming leadership roles at the community level. The women's movement has come of age and shows a wider perspective.

This is probably one of the reasons why there has not been a single, coordinated national campaign on a women's issue by women's groups since the Roop Kanwar tragedy in 1987 which galvanised many groups in the capital and in Rajasthan to launch a campaign for changes in the law relating to 'sati' and other crimes against women ostensibly sanctioned by religion.

A Commercial Break

As the women's movement has been evolving, the press, too, has been adapting to a number of external factors. This is especially true of the English language press where the very nature of news coverage has been affected.

One of the major change agents has been the growth of television and its emergence as the prime medium for advertisements. The displacement of the press from its position as the most important vehicle for commercial messages has had severe financial consequences for the print media. Newspaper economics has to be rethought. The larger newspaper chains have been compelled to diversify. Many have invested in television companies to make programmes for Doordarshan and thus cash in on television's advertising boom.

At the same time, in order to corner as much of the available print advertising as possible, each newspaper has had to seek new ways of making itself commercially attractive. As the editor of a new Sunday newspaper in Bombay recalls, just fifteen years ago, staff of the advertising department would not even be seen in the editorial section of a newspaper like *The Times of India*. Today, editors and advertising executives in many newspapers, including the forementioned one, meet and plan joint strategies to attract more advertising revenue for the paper. Every section of the paper is up for sale, including the daily weather report! So far the editorial page has remained sacrosanct but judging by the way the wind is blowing, it may not be long before it too is modified so that it can be sponsored by some private company.

While the economic compulsions which have led to such decisions are understandable, the current overriding emphasis on commercial viability has undeniably affected the quality of journalism. With the growth of the video and consumer culture, it is now taken for granted that the attention span of the average reader will not last beyond 600-800 words. All issues must, therefore, be reduced to small, easily digestible nuggets. Some newspapers even frown upon two or three part investigative stories. According to the typical 'new-look' editor, if an issue cannot be covered in one part, it is not worth covering. As a result, newspaper readers are given a heavy dose of generalisations on all manner of issues—from health and education to pollution and popular culture.

The motto of the new model editor, 'No flag-waving,' is music to the ears of the new-style managements of newspapers. Gone are the days when journalists could investigate social evils such as bonded labour or police atrocities, write a series of reports, follow them up with a strong opinion piece and even pursue justice for the victims in court through public interest litigation. Today such a 'committed' approach would be deemed unacceptably unprofessional.

This new world-view of the media directly affects those in the profession who remain convinced that the concerns of the silent and deprived sections of society must be reflected in media coverage. They are given little encouragement today. Those who undertake such assignments on their own initiative are rarely given the space to present all their findings in full. And, certainly, they are unlikely to reach the higher echelons of the editorial hierarchy.

Of course, not all social issues are ignored. Even today sections of the press do carry the occasional front-page report on atrocities or exploitation. And the press has not forgotten that women exist. They continue to leap out of the grey columns of newsprint as rape or dowry death victims, or as participants in beauty contests or as women achievers in some other field or as subjects of a scandal.

However, the regular columns on women's issues that were a significant feature of more than one mainstream newspaper some years ago have all but disappeared. Also, unlike in the late 1970s and the early 1980s, when many editors not only encouraged staff to work on such stories but often actually took the initiative to assign them, in the 1990s journalists concerned about social issues have to take the initiative and work on their own. Further, they sometimes have to 'sell' their stories to the editorial higher-ups, bargain for space and serve up their findings in a 'palatable' form, which invariably means short and superficial.

The 'yuppiefication' of newspapers is most noticeable in the Sunday magazine sections of major newspapers. During the period of our study, each of these had a distinct personality and often carried well-researched and argued articles on a variety of serious current topics. Today, the majority appear to have no focus and provide readers neither light-hearted entertainment nor serious information and analysis. In fact, many of them seem to be little more than advertising supplements.

Gentlewomen of the Press

'You've come a long way, Baby!', the copy of a cigarette advertisement in the U.S. which received much flak from American feminists in the

1970s for misrepresenting women's liberation, sums up the current position of Indian journalists who happen to be women, especially those working in the English language press. While in the 1970s, women reporting on politics and economics were rarities, in the 1980s a few women began to make inroads into 'hard' news areas. In the 1990s it is widely acknowledged that women journalists have given some of the best coverage of issues ranging from Kashmir and Punjab to Sri Lanka. Furthermore, the story of the biggest financial scandal in India's post-Independence history was broken by a woman journalist in 1992.

However, many well-known women journalists are allergic to being categorised as such. Their attitude is: 'I am neither a feminist, nor a "woman journalist". I am a professional.' The implication is, clearly, that anyone who identifies herself as a feminist or accepts the appellation 'woman journalist' is somehow less than 'professional' (whatever that means).

Ironically, many of these women admit that their approach to an issue has often been different from that of their male colleagues. For instance, at the Women and Media workshop mentioned earlier, a female journalist who had covered the conflict in Sri Lanka said she focussed on the human tragedy unfolding in that country while also dealing with the obvious geopolitical aspects of the ethnic strife. By contrast, the latter was the sole preoccupation of most of the male journalists covering the conflict. Her reporting from the island nation was clearly outstanding and, not surprisingly, she was snapped up by a leading international publication to serve as their India correspondent. However, she does not accept that her perception of the conflict, which made her stories exceptional amongst the plethora of reports coming out of Sri Lanka at the time, had anything to do with her gender.

Another prominent journalist, recently referred to as 'the first lady of Indian journalism,' took umbrage at the notion advanced by a colleague at the workshop that the media's preoccupation with politics leads to its neglect of vital social issues. Identifying herself as a political journalist, she pointed out that all issues are essentially political. Indeed she herself uses her popular political column to write with conviction, passion and sensitivity about the violation of human rights, corruption in high places, the continuing neglect of the impoverished countryside, the cynicism of communalists, as well as about rape and other crimes against women. But, ignoring the fact that her kind of political writing is the exception rather than the rule, she insists that she is 'just a professional journalist.' She also spoke disparagingly about what she called 'the Mother Teresas of the press' who she believes do disservice to their cause by ignoring the political aspects of issues and writing what she described as long, boring, naive, bleeding heart type articles which nobody would read.

The high visibility and intensely competitive nature of the media profession today, the opportunities now open to women in the press, combined with the persistent assumption that coverage of national politics (as defined by the major political parties and personalities) comprises the acme of journalistic practice have led many women journalists, earlier noted for their writing on women's and other social issues, to move over to the fast track of political reporting. Although some of them have retained a personal interest in the issues they once covered, they believe that in the interest of career advancement they need to serve time on the political beat. Unfortunately, they find it difficult to balance the two impulses.

This is particularly so because writing on women's issues today involves more than reportage on atrocities or campaigns. It means keeping track of a broad spectrum of government policies in order to analyse their impact on women's lives and status. It entails staying abreast of the wealth of empirical and analytical material produced by the growing number of institutes and departments of women's studies. Thus writing on women's issues today is as complex and specialised as writing on politics, economics or the environment. However, few journalists can afford to specialise in women's issues because there is still no legitimate 'women's beat' and, in any case, such a low priority specialisation will not push them up the ladder of professional success. As a result, coverage of women's issues continues to be ad hoc—dependent to a large extent on the personal commitment of a few writers who are willing to risk professional ghettoisation in order to call public attention to issues of special concern to women.

Meanwhile, several women have made their way to senior positions within the major newspapers, in particular the *Indian Express* and *The Times of India*. Even *The Hindu*, the last national, English language daily to admit women into its journalistic ranks, now has female correspondents in several centres apart from two women (members of the proprietorial family) in important editorial positions. Yet these positive developments have neither significantly changed the traditional definitions of news or the hierarchy of news values nor enhanced the amount of space devoted to subjects other than politics or economics.

An issue left largely unaddressed in this study is the status of women working at various levels in the press. Discussions on the experiences and working conditions of women journalists—both during the Delhi workshop on Women and the Media and earlier—have revealed that those employed in the English language press are considerably better off than those working within the Indian language press. While this theme clearly requires further investigation, the few superficial surveys that have been conducted suggest that the latter often face many direct forms of discrimination and harassment from which the former are generally shielded.

Vanishing Liberal Consensus

Women's groups complain that the press has lost interest in the condition of the deprived sections of the population amongst whom many of them work. This, in a sense, is the crux of the issue. The liberal consensus that underlay the investigative stories and other types of press coverage in the post-Emergency period up to the late 1980s had largely vanished by the early 1990s. Today, the press is once again fixated on politics (in the narrow sense of the term), scandals (involving powerful personalities) and the lifestyles of the rich and famous.

Despite the yuppie nature of current journalism, the open sexism of the 1970s appears to have been finally buried. No longer do the third edits routinely attempt humour at the expense of women. By the early 1990s, few writers in the national press could be found deliberately using derogatory terms with reference to women. While 'Eves' still make an appearance in newspaper headlines, less common now are terms like the 'fairer' or 'weaker' sex. Blatantly sexist terminology is definitely out as far as the national press is concerned though non-sexist language has yet to be incorporated into Indian journalese.

In a departure from the trend towards the light and superficial, one newspaper now devotes an entire weekly page to 'Gender' while another features a page on 'Development' every week. Both these spaces allow serious discussion on women's issues and other related subjects. There is considerable debate on whether such special pages are good news or bad. Some people believe that they lead to ghettoisation and represent a step backward to the days when women's issues were invariably relegated to women's pages in magazine sections. Others argue that such regular slots provide an opportunity for journalists concerned about such issues to consistently focus public attention on them. They believe that in view of the changes in the very nature of newspapers, such subjects would otherwise be completely ignored.

Invasion from the Sky

Another significant factor affecting the media scene today is the growth in the reach of the electronic media. In the 1990s, satellite and cable television have begun to pose a serious threat to Doordarshan which had hitherto enjoyed a virtual monopoly. The government, which kept national television on a tight leash for years, now finds it has no control over the programmes and advertisements—both Indian and foreign—being beamed into Indian homes through these new communications technologies.

The original purpose of Doordarshan—to promote education and social progress—and the recommendations of the P.C. Joshi Committee on Software for Doordarshan (1982) have been steadily eroded ever since the television network began to accept advertisements and sponsored programmes. Of late, even the earlier pretence at a higher purpose has been thrown to the winds as Doordarshan braces up to meet the challenge posed by this virtual invasion from the skies.

The portrayal of women on television will, therefore, require fresh assessment in the light of this onslaught and its consequences for Indian television. Compared to the new images of women being projected on say MTV (Star TV's twenty-four-hour music video channel), the efforts made by Doordarshan in the early 1980s to highlight women's problems appear positively noble. Besides, Doordarshan's code on advertisements kept some check on the images it telecast. Now, however, satellite television channels are bombarding lakhs of Indian viewers with stereotypical images of women, some of which are not even rooted in Indian reality.

Among the many ads projecting women as doll-like creatures, who hang helplessly on the arms of their all-male protectors, are some which actually mock women's progress. For example, one Indian ad for a men's fabric shows a woman supervisor—provocatively dressed in red—overseeing female workers in a steel plant. Her pretensions at being the boss woman collapse when a tall, handsome, male worker picks her up in his arms and strides off as if he has won a trophy.

The power of the advertising image, a major subject by itself, has not been touched upon in this study. But there is clearly a pressing need for the study and analysis of advertising messages, especially those transmitted through the television medium, in the present media context. The combined effect of the growing consumer culture in India and the images projected through advertisements is bound to affect the way women are eventually perceived by large numbers of people, including themselves.

The growing power of the media—both electronic and print—and their increasingly commercial nature, which obviates all pretence at a higher purpose, suggests that the commodification of women, so evident in the West during the 1960s, is likely to become far more virulent in India in the near future. Media watchers and those concerned about the status of women need to be ever more vigilant in the days to come.

Kalpana Sharma and **Ammu Joseph**

Notes on Contributors

Ammu Joseph, a professional journalist since 1977, has worked with several publications in Bombay, ranging from *Eve's Weekly* to *The Indian Post* (where she edited the daily's Sunday magazine). She has been a close associate of the contemporary Indian women's movement, actively seeking to incorporate women's voices into the publications with which she has worked. She is currently a freelance writer, media researcher and communications consultant based in Bangalore.

Kalpana Sharma has worked as a full-time journalist since 1972 in the alternative and mainstream press. She began her career with a small alternative weekly, *Himmat*, of which she became the editor during the Emergency. She has also worked with the *Indian Express*, where she edited the Sunday magazine section, and *The Times of India*. At present she is a Special Correspondent with *The Hindu* in Bombay writing on development and environmental issues.

Shubhra Gupta is a Delhi-based media critic with a regular weekly column on television in *Sunday*. She also writes on films for newspapers. She has worked with *The Hindustan Times* and *Sunday Mail*.

Prasanna Ramaswamy, a Madras-based freelance journalist, writes on women's issues, the traditional arts and contemporary theatre. She has worked for a women's magazine and a daily newspaper. For some time she edited a page for women in *Dina Mani*, a Tamil daily. At present she is working with the Goethe Institute in Madras.

Vasantha Surya is a Madras-based journalist, poet and translator. She writes investigative articles on development, culture and social change for major English-language publications. She has published two collections of poems in English—*The Stalk of Times* (Cre-A, 1985) and *The*

Ballad of Budhni (Writers Workshop, 1992). The latter is a translation from Bundeli Hindi. She also translates from and into Tamil, her mother tongue.

Maitreyi Chatterjee, a Calcutta-based freelance journalist, has written extensively in English and Bengali. She has been involved with the women's movement and at present belongs to the Nari Nirjatan Pratirodh Manch which is engaged mainly in organising campaigns on issues that affect women and human rights. She also runs a women's library-cum-documentation centre.

Sonal Shukla has been actively involved in the women's movement from 1980 and was one of the founder members of Forum Against Oppression of Women (formerly Forum Against Rape), Bombay. Since 1980, she has written a weekly feminist column in *Pravasi*, a Bombay-based Gujarati paper. She is a member of the editorial collective of *Nari Mukti*, a women's studies journal in Gujarati.

Deepa Dhanraj is a Bangalore-based documentary film-maker. She has made a number of documentaries on women, including *Molkarin* (1981), *Tambakoo Chakila Oob Ali* (1982), *Sudesha* (1983), *Modern Brides* (1984), *Many Ways to God* (1985) and *Kya Hua Iss Sheher Ko?* (1986). Her latest film, *Something Like A War* (1991), on India's family planning programme and its effect on women, has won critical acclaim.

Appendix A

Quantitative Analysis

ISSUE-WISE DATA

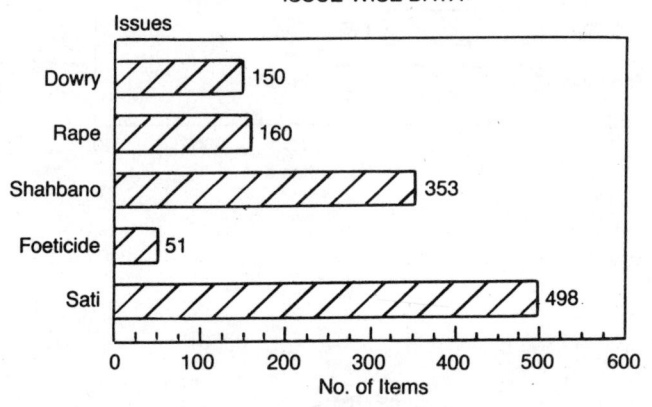

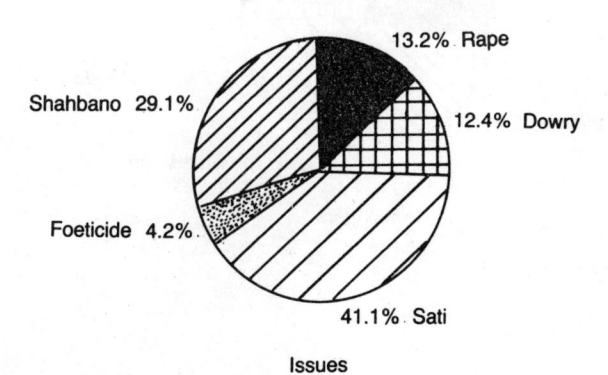

Issues	No. of Items
Dowry	150
Rape	160
Shahbano	353
Foeticide	51
Sati	498

Issues

- Shahbano 29.1%
- 13.2% Rape
- 12.4% Dowry
- Foeticide 4.2%
- 41.1% Sati

NEWSPAPER-WISE DATA

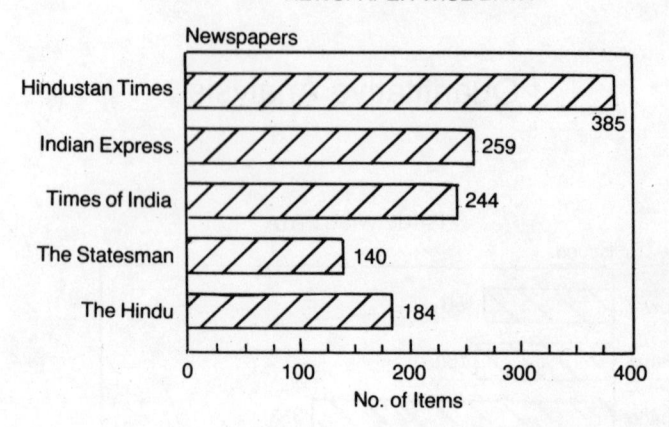

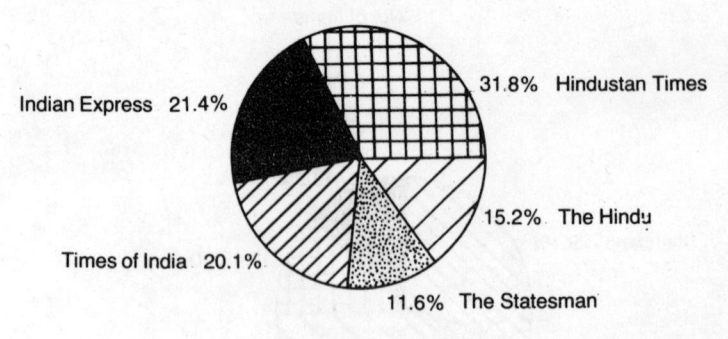

Newspapers / No. of Items:
- Hindustan Times: 385
- Indian Express: 259
- Times of India: 244
- The Statesman: 140
- The Hindu: 184

Newspapers (pie chart):
- Hindustan Times 31.8%
- Indian Express 21.4%
- Times of India 20.1%
- The Hindu 15.2%
- The Statesman 11.6%

COVERAGE OF DOWRY DEATHS

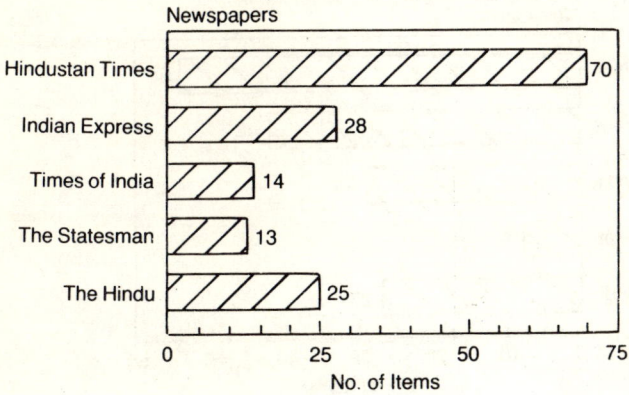

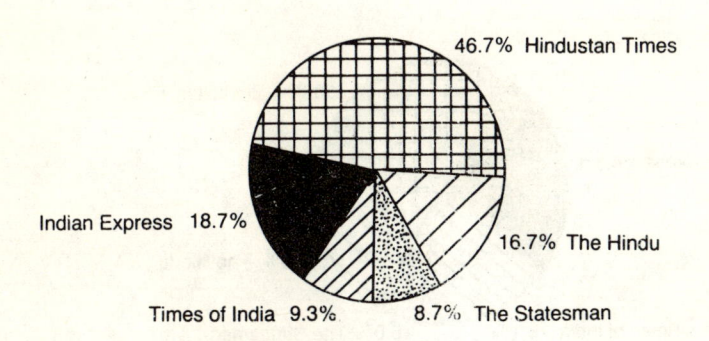

Newspapers:
- Hindustan Times: 70
- Indian Express: 28
- Times of India: 14
- The Statesman: 13
- The Hindu: 25

No. of Items

- 46.7% Hindustan Times
- 18.7% Indian Express
- 9.3% Times of India
- 8.7% The Statesman
- 16.7% The Hindu

Newspapers

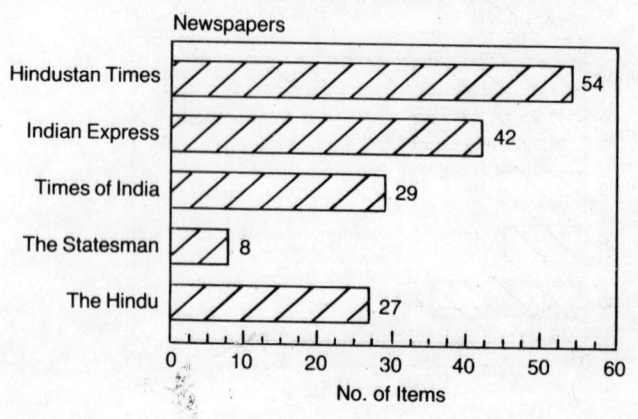

306 Whose News?

COVERAGE OF RAPE

Newspapers

- Hindustan Times: 54
- Indian Express: 42
- Times of India: 29
- The Statesman: 8
- The Hindu: 27

No. of Items

Newspapers

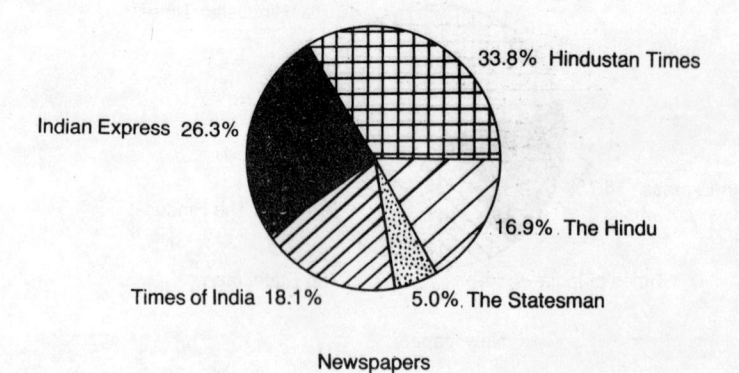

- 33.8% Hindustan Times
- Indian Express 26.3%
- Times of India 18.1%
- 5.0% The Statesman
- 16.9% The Hindu

Appendix A 307

COVERAGE OF THE SHAHBANO CONTROVERSY

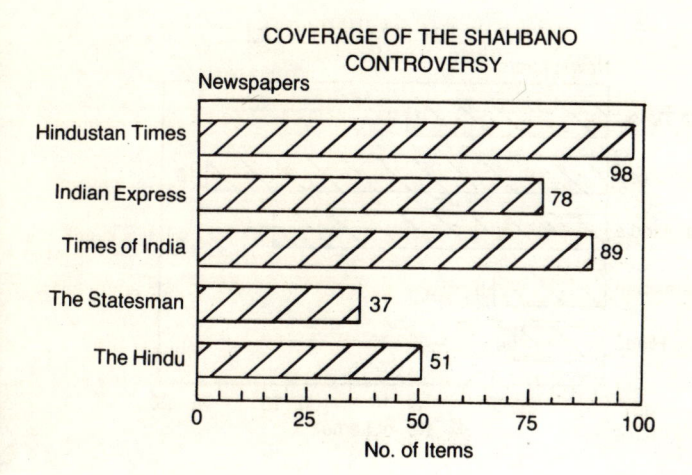

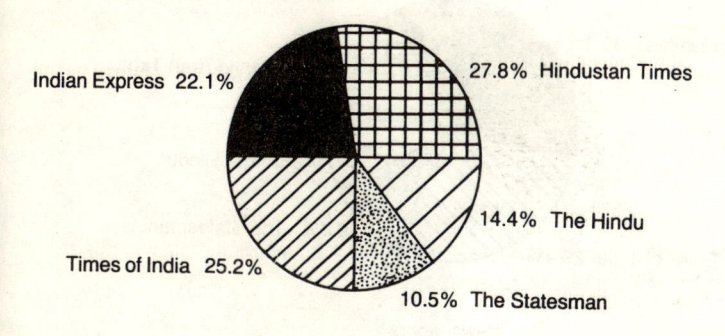

Newspapers

- Hindustan Times: 98
- Indian Express: 78
- Times of India: 89
- The Statesman: 37
- The Hindu: 51

No. of Items

Indian Express 22.1%
27.8% Hindustan Times
14.4% The Hindu
10.5% The Statesman
Times of India 25.2%

Newspapers

COVERAGE OF FEMALE FOETICIDE

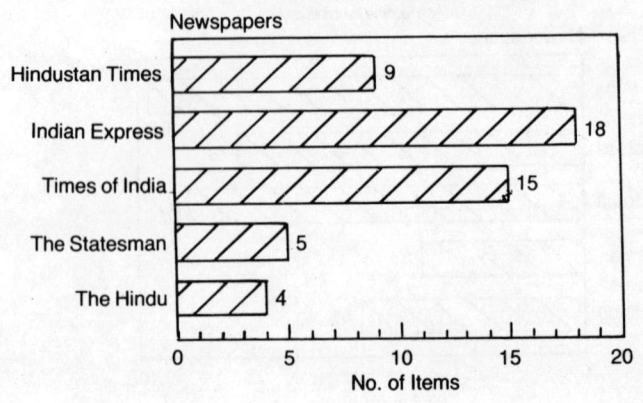

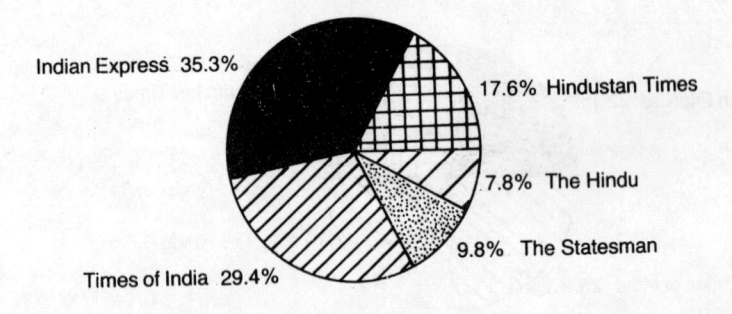

Newspaper	No. of Items
Hindustan Times	9
Indian Express	18
Times of India	15
The Statesman	5
The Hindu	4

Newspapers:
- Indian Express 35.3%
- Times of India 29.4%
- Hindustan Times 17.6%
- The Statesman 9.8%
- The Hindu 7.8%

COVERAGE OF THE ROOP KANWAR TRAGEDY

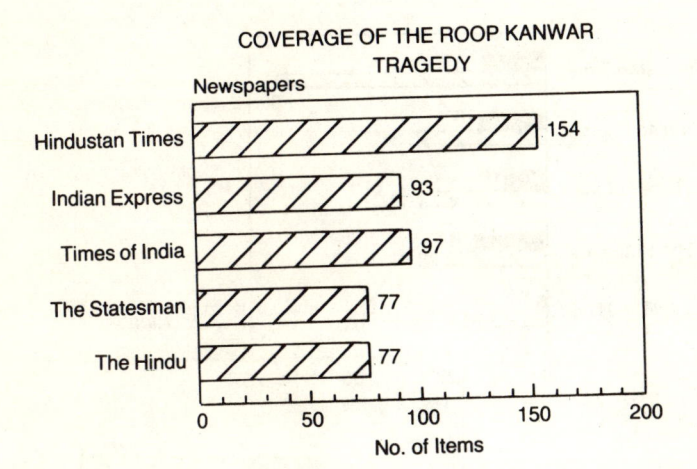

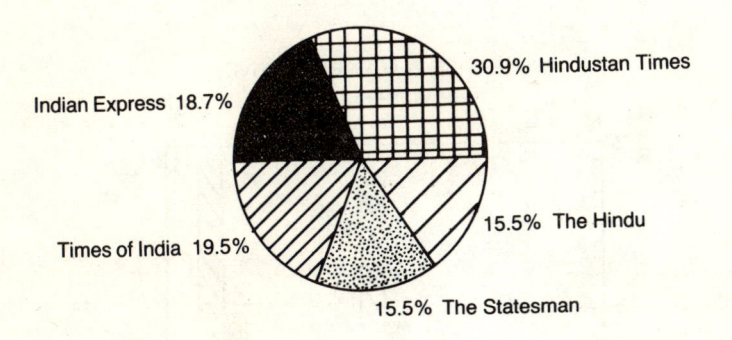

Newspapers:
- Hindustan Times: 154
- Indian Express: 93
- Times of India: 97
- The Statesman: 77
- The Hindu: 77

(No. of Items)

Newspapers:
- 30.9% Hindustan Times
- 18.7% Indian Express
- 19.5% Times of India
- 15.5% The Statesman
- 15.5% The Hindu

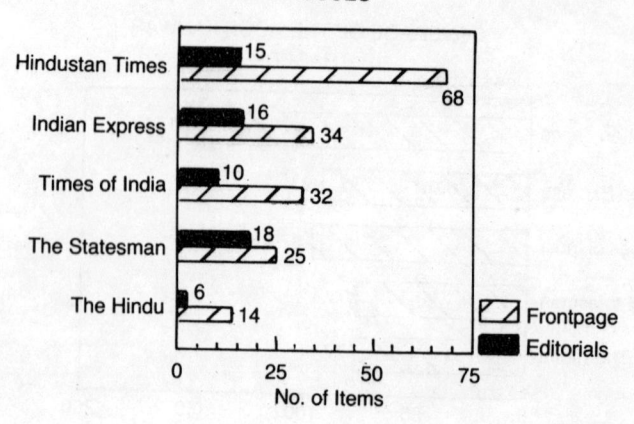

NEWSPAPER-WISE PLACEMENT OF ISSUES

Newspaper	Editorials	Frontpage
Hindustan Times	15	68
Indian Express	16	34
Times of India	10	32
The Statesman	18	25
The Hindu	6	14

No. of Items

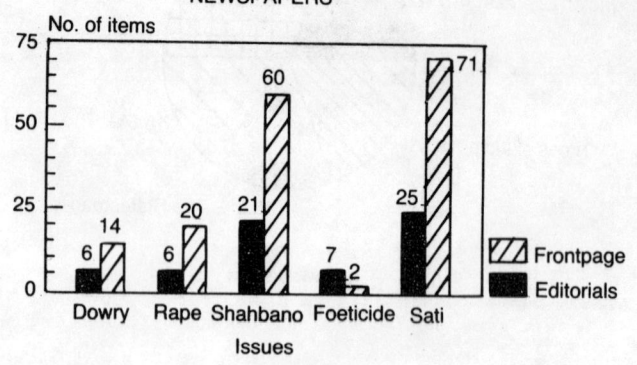

ISSUE-WISE PLACEMENT IN FIVE NEWSPAPERS

Issue	Editorials	Frontpage
Dowry	6	14
Rape	6	20
Shahbano	21	60
Foeticide	7	2
Sati	25	71

Appendix B

Letters to the Editor

Of all the papers surveyed, *The Statesman* had the least number of letters to the editor on any of the issues covered. Whether this is reflective of reader disinterest in these issues or indicates the paper's neglect of reader response is not clear. Interestingly, *The Hindu* registered high reader interest even in issues which were minimally covered by the paper itself. By contrast, although *The Hindustan Times* gave wide coverage to all the issues, its readers seemed relatively unresponsive. Again, whether this is due to the characteristics of the paper's readership or to the limited space provided for letters is a matter of conjecture.

Letters to the editor often give an indication of the seriousness with which readers respond to issues covered in newspapers. However, readers' responses cannot always be correlated to the quantum of coverage. Thus, despite limited editorial coverage of the dowry death phenomenon in *The Hindu*, it published as many as thirteen letters from readers. *The Hindustan Times*, on the other hand, had only nine letters on the subject, which is surprising given the local nature of the phenomenon. None of the other three newspapers carried any noteworthy readers' comments.

The Statesman and *The Times of India* carried no letters to the editor regarding rape. *The Hindustan Times* published ten while the *Indian Express* had eight. *The Hindu* also featured eight before correspondence on the issue was inexplicably closed by the editor on 12 April 1980.

The theme of most of the readers' letters published in the *Express* was provocation by women—in other words, blaming the victim. Responding to Githa Hariharan's article, one reader wanted the Indian Penal Code to be altered so that women are made liable for soliciting. Another, arguing that it was not contempt for women but 'sex stimuli' that led to rape, stated, 'Half-naked breasts, for example, are more provocative than fully naked or fully covered ones...' Other quotable quotes from letters to the *Indian Express* editor on rape:

Girls have every right to wear attractive dresses. Let them don any dress; but let them do it in the privacy of their homes—not in public places to provide a feast to the eyes of potential rapists.

In present-day society, women have conveniently allowed themselves to be exploited for provocative advertisements without batting an eyelid. Society girls wear more and more revealing, see-through dresses, inviting provocation.

The root cause of rape in society, whether urban or rural, is mainly the loose morals of the woman who attracts leering looks due to her provocative behaviour inviting special attention.

Women's organisations must attack the root cause of rape by asking women to behave themselves and conduct themselves with dignity and grace to command respect.

Of the eight letters which appeared in *The Hindu* before correspondence on the issue was closed, two were critical of the Supreme Court judgment in the Mathura case. Another criticised Justice Unwalia for his statement disapproving of the pressure brought to bear on the Court by women's groups. While the majority were broadly supportive of the anti-rape campaign, two were highly critical of the public outcry in this case and the use of 'direct action' against the judiciary.

All the ten readers whose letters were published by *The Hindustan Times* seem to have been supportive of the anti-rape campaign—some offered clarifications on points of law; others pointed out the culpability of the policemen involved in the Mathura case in being drunk and indulging in sexual activity while on duty in a police station. One letter-writer suggested that poverty and poverty-induced sexual starvation were the root causes of rape. Another, endorsing Justice Tulzapurkar's reported views, approved of flogging as a punishment for rapists but believed that provocative dressing by women was usually responsible for rape. The latter also disagreed with politician and activist Pramila Dandavate's comparison of prostitutes with shopkeepers, suggesting that a more appropriate parallel would be black-marketeers.

On the Shah Bano controversy, readers' interest in the issue was evident in the 'Letters' column of all the newspapers. The *Indian Express* carried twenty-seven letters while *The Hindu*, which had not given the issue as much coverage as the other papers, had as many as seventeen letters on the subject. *The Times of India* and *The Hindustan Times* carried twelve and ten letters respectively while *The Statesman* had only four.

Much of the discussion in the 'Letters' column in both the *Indian Express* and *The Times of India* centred around Muslim Personal Law and later the resignation of Arif Mohammed Khan. *Indian Express* readers seemed to respond to the general editorial line which strongly advocated the adoption of a uniform civil code.

The Times of India carried several letters attacking the Muslim Women Bill; in fact, one letter by journalist Rashid Talib (9 December 1985) was given the entire column running down the length of the page. Significantly, this letter appeared before the first editorial comment by the paper on the issue. The writer was against the reversal of the Shah Bano judgment and suggested that the Prime Minister should consult Muslims, including 'educated Muslim women whose interests would suffer most from any hasty reversal of the Shah Bano decision.'

Readers' comments in *The Hindu* also focussed largely on the Muslim Women Bill, with the majority stating their opposition to it. In fact, one reader questioned the claim made by an MP that 99.7 per cent of Muslims in India were against the Supreme Court verdict. He wrote, 'I fail to understand how Islam suffers from any infirmity if unfortunate persons like Shah Bano and others are rescued by the Supreme Court's action.'

Another letter by a woman reader suggested that the Muslim community should look into the conditions of poor Muslim women 'instead of fighting for the removal of a section which for all its faults happens to be the last recourse for many hapless women in the throes of penury.'

The Hindustan Times also carried letters which criticised the Muslim Women Bill, expressed admiration for Arif Mohammed Khan and discussed whether Muslim or Hindu women were worse off. One letter claimed that the avalanche of articles on the issue would create disharmony in homes, break up marriages, confuse young minds: 'Playing up imaginary fears of housewives and working women will only bring further frustration in the homes, thereby destabilising the peaceful atmosphere elsewhere.'

The Statesman was an exception in some ways as all the letters on the issue favoured the Muslim Women Bill and strongly attacked the editorial position of the paper.

The most heated debate on the issue of female foeticide in the 'Letters' column appeared in *The Times of India* in response to Achin Vanaik's edit page article. The controversy was sparked off by a letter (26 June 1986) which stated: 'It is ironical that he (Vanaik) and Dr Ravindran (who was spearheading the campaign) had to expose this social scourge, while so-called women's libbers and MCP-denouncing groups do not find time or inclination to plead for those hapless, unfortunate yet-to-be-born female lives.'

Dr Ravindran responded on 8 July by stating:

Women's liberation groups are in the forefront in this struggle.... It is time we realise the misuse of technology for sex determination and sex preselection will affect us all, men and women. It is not only a women's issue. It should also be a concern for activists in the field of health, human rights and science and technology.

Another letter (17 July), by Maithreyi Krishna Raj of the the women's studies department of the SNDT University in Bombay, stated: 'It is a strange notion that there is a category called "women libbers" whose duty alone it is to take up issues on behalf of women, as though these are not concerns for all of us.'

In the *Indian Express*, all the letters but one argued for a ban on sex determination techniques. The exception, published on 15 January 1988, asserted that the law was curtailing individual freedom:

> So the government decides the composition of my family! And if I have a daughter already, I cannot go in for the test privately. What a totalitarian way of increasing the female population! True, there is a tendency amongst most of us to prefer boys to girls. So what? Let the males outnumber females in the near future. The fear that the feminine gender will become extinct is a hoax.

Among other letters was one which linked the female foeticide problem to 'the dangerous custom of dowry.' The reader asserted that 'unless the punishment for bride burning is death (as in the case of sati), it is immaterial if the girl is killed before being born or after marriage, which causes pain to parents also.' Another letter writer expressed concern for doctors when he wrote: 'The new law will hurt doctors who have invested heavily in ultrasonography machines and create difficulties for couples who have too many daughters and desire a son.'

The readers of *The Hindustan Times* and *The Statesman* responded to the 'sati' controversy with twenty-seven letters to the editor each—an unusually large number, particularly for the latter (it carried no readers' letters on any of the other issues surveyed except for the Shah Bano case which elicited one response). *The Hindu* published ten letters to the editor on this issue, the *Indian Express* seven and *The Times of India* (Bangalore edition) three.

Historian K. R. Malkani, editor of *The Organiser* and associated with the Bharatiya Janata Party and the Rashtriya Swayamsevak Sangh (RSS), wrote in both *The Hindustan Times* and *The Statesman* on this issue. In the former, he distinguished between voluntary and forced sati. He described the burning of unwilling widows as scandalous—it was murder rather than self-immolation. However, in his view, the Deorala incident belonged to 'a very different genre' and invoked 'awe—and not anger.' He wished widowers would also be similarly moved.

In his letter to *The Statesman*, which responded to the two-part article by editor Sunanda Datta-Ray on Hindu revivalism in the context of the 'sati' controversy, Malkani dwelt on the role of the RSS in nurturing an internal movement committed to reform within Hinduism, as opposed to reform sought to be imposed by official fiat. This was an obvious reference to calls for legislation and state intervention for preventing sati and its glorification.

In *The Statesman*, the article which provoked the largest number of responses was the edit page piece by the American scholar, Patrick D. Harrigan. While six of the seven were critical of his support of the practice, one was in favour of his stand. They were grouped together under the headline 'Can Custom Excuse Homicide?'

In *The Hindu*, eight readers condemned *sati* while one questioned the furore over the incident in the context of all the other and more common atrocities; (one described the proposal for special courts to try cases of sati as using a sledge-hammer to kill an occasional fly). It is worth noting that virtually all the readers who responded to Swami Harshananda's article on the 'Open Page' seem to have read it as a positive and progressive contribution to the debate. One of these, a strong letter headlined 'Stop Calling It Sati,' called attention to the fact that the burning of widows was not sati but *stri-dahana* (burning of women).

Ashis Nandy's article in the *Indian Express* brought in several letters, three in support of his stand. One, for example, which called his piece 'refreshingly different,' said:

> Everybody including your leader writer is trying to prove himself more modern and forward-looking than the other man by blindly condemning the incident without going into the deeper psychology and sociology at work.... Also why do leader writers and correspondents of the media consider only themselves to be right and condemn the collective psyche of lakhs of men and women who consider this to be a laudable event? Or do these self-appointed guardians of public morals subscribe to the Hitlerian view of a majority consisting of fools?.... The event was best ignored but the hardening of attitudes due to media breast-beating is there for all to see.

However, there were readers who deplored the practice in the *Indian Express*. One queried, 'Why don't widowers burn themselves? Why only widows?' Another, linking sati to other forms of oppression, stated: 'It is a shame that women in Indian society are fast becoming an expendable commodity right from the foetus to old age, in these enlightened times.'

Ammu Joseph and **Kalpana Sharma**

Appendix C

Newspaper Humour: What's so Funny?

The Times of India and *The Statesman* generally reserve their third edits for humour. Often this humour is at the expense of women. Thus, in September 1979, when the dowry-death syndrome was at its height and women's groups agitated about this issue had begun demanding changes in the law, *The Times of India* carried a third edit, headlined 'H'm, Housewife Power,' which began:

> So the Lib virus, the one with an apron on, has infected Germany. Well, well. We had hoped with a fervour that should have been reserved for a nobler cause, that the strain had run its course, but as is so often the case where the unpredictable sex is concerned, we seem to be off course.

The provocation for the edit was a trade union for housewives established in Hamburg to 'give housewives a new sense of purpose.' Stated the edit:

> And what is the new sense of purpose they are seeking? To blacken the toast or burn the roast?.... If it is a plain case of overwork there surely are better ways of registering their grievances. No self-respecting husband would really mind a short period of ease when there is no button-sewing or sock-mending or bed-making; even a bit of detergent in the soup, a dash of pepper in the coffee, would be tolerated. But certainly not an organised trade union movement. If German men are half the men we think they are they should retaliate by sacking the housewives and hiring computer-run robots. That will teach 'em a thing or two.

Over the period when the issue of sex determination featured in the press, *The Statesman*, which accorded the subject three editorials, ran third editorials which struck a very different note. For example, the one on 12 January 1988, titled 'Love Bytes,' referred to a Saudi Arabian man who used a computer to divide time equally between his wives. The edit concluded thus: '...In the place where he comes from, few males would take such pains to be in the right place: most would opt for the simple expedient of keeping women in their place.'

The Statesman's third edits were generally less offensive than most, but during the period monitored for coverage of the *'sati'* controversy, the headline of one such edit made light of the issue by using the word completely out of context. The edit, on the search for extra-terrestrial intelligence, was headlined 'SETI Not Sati.'

While *The Times of India* and *The Statesman* had their third edits to poke fun at women generally and so-called 'women libbers' in particular, *The Hindustan Times* had the services of their columnist Rajinder Puri. In his column 'My Word,' Puri took a special delight in writing anti-women pieces. For instance, on 5 March 1986, in a piece headlined 'One Woman,' he wrote:

There is a woman who has given a headache to many people .... Only the woman herself did not get a headache.... She continued to exercise a woman's prerogative of changing her mind with painful regularity. And by creating havoc in the minds of many, and in the careers of a few, she spectacularly demonstrated the power of women. Just one woman. Shah Bano.

Shah Bano was once again selected for comment by Puri, on 25 March 1986, in a piece headlined 'Bill For Maintenance Of Women.' He clarified that this was his third reference to the Bill, the second advocating a Bill for the rights of politicians divorced from the party.

This piece was based on a supposed conversation with a friend who claimed, 'Women expect maintenance for all sorts of frills and luxuries which can drive the poor male insane .... (they are) only interested in buying sarees, perfumes and lipstick.' Announcing that he himself was not divorced, he went on, 'I have this problem of maintaining my lawful, happily married wife! The government must make a Bill for the maintenance of wives all over the country.'

The sub-editors of *The Hindustan Times* also could not resist headlines like 'Last Virgin Loses Out' for an article in 1979 on the Silent Valley! And in 1984, between reports of women dying of burns, the paper saw fit to reproduce an article from *The Daily Telegraph* of London headlined 'Women's Lib: Making Both Men And Women Miserable'; and on the continuation page 'Women's Lib Doing Good To Nobody.' If 'Women's Lib' survived this onslaught, it was entirely fortuitous!

The weekly accounts by newspaper correspondents of what transpired in Parliament often tended to trivialise serious women's issues in a number of ways. Sometimes they repeated tasteless jokes made by Members of Parliament in the course of the debate without commenting on the inappropriate jocularity even though, as personalised pieces, parliamentary reviews were often commentative.

In other cases, as in *The Statesman* in the context of sati, the correspondent's comments on the woman minister who piloted the anti-sati Bill in Parliament took away from the seriousness of the discussions. Although the parliamentary review, on 21 December 1987, devoted only two paragraphs to the Bill, it was headlined 'Alva Charms Members.' In a patronising and rather meaningless comment, the correspondent wrote: 'Perhaps because the charming Mrs Margaret Alva was piloting the Anti-sati Bill, the House, particularly the Opposition, was quite literally cooking over it.' Although he highlighted the 'femininity' of the minister (using words like charming, tactful, patient and courteous for her but not for any of the male politicians mentioned), he did not bother to check the veracity of one senior member's suggestion that Alva was the first woman to pilot a Bill in Parliament (which, if true, would have been a historically significant fact worthy of being recorded).

Ammu Joseph and Kalpana Sharma

Appendix D

Lessons from Ahmedabad

(Excerpts from an article based on a report, on the impact on women of the caste and communal disturbances in Ahmedabad in 1985, by the Women and Media Group, Bombay.)

For over five months in 1985, Ahmedabad city witnessed a series of violent disturbances which originated with the caste-based anti-reservation movement but soon developed into communal riots. An unusual feature of the Ahmedabad disturbances was the active involvement of women in the anti-reservation agitation and allegations of police misconduct—including sexual harassment—with women participants. This aspect of the troubles was reported quite widely—often salaciously—and occasioned some comment in the media but the coverage failed to shed much light on the uncommon phenomenon.

The Women and Media Group, Bombay, decided to send a four-member team to Ahmedabad to look specifically at the role of women in and the impact on women of the caste and communal clashes in the city in the first half of 1985. The objectives of the WMG team were to identify the special problems faced by women during the violent period, to understand how women viewed the disturbances and how they responded in the situation, to assess how the communal and caste violence had affected a secular women's organisation like the Ahmedabad-based Self-Employed Women's Association (SEWA), and to piece together differing versions of incidents in which women were involved.

While seeking to fulfil its objectives, the WMG team also gained some useful insights into the sins of omission and commission committed by the media covering the disturbances. Since many of these are applicable to media coverage of similar situations in other parts of the country at other times (there is, sadly, no dearth of such situations), it may be worthwhile to draw some lessons from the Ahmedabad experience.

During the process of inquiry it became clear that major gaps in information and understanding resulted from the normal media practice of reporting crisis situations largely on the basis of what 'the authorities' and leaders of various groups have to say, paying hardly any attention to the experiences and views of ordinary citizens, especially women....

As far as coverage of women's participation in the events was concerned, a perusal of news clippings from Bombay-based English papers, including some with Ahmedabad editions, revealed a striking absence of reports on some of the major incidents in which women, especially Muslim women, had been involved during this period.

For instance, thousands of Muslim women sat on the road in the Dariapur area of the walled city on June 2 to protest against the killings in their locality in the wake of the Rath Yatra that day as well as against the imposition of curfew, which had brought considerable hardship to them. This unusual demonstration was unreported except for the odd passing mention. Similarly, a dharna held in front of the town hall on April 22 by women belonging to 29 organisations to protest against police atrocities was not reported at all.

In contrast, an inordinate amount of attention was given to two incidents involving upper caste Hindu women—the beating up of some women in the Asarva area and the harassment of women in the Gomtipur area in the form of a parade by abusive and allegedly naked policemen. Such selective coverage revealed media biases based on caste and creed, as well as the preoccupation of the media with violence and prurience.

Little attention was paid by the media to the economic hardship suffered by common citizens of Ahmedabad as a result of the disturbances. Particularly hard-hit were those who work in the informal sector, a large percentage of who are poor women, both Muslim and Hindu. Most of them were unable to work during the five months of trouble in the city. Curfew meant that home-based workers could not go out to get raw materials or deliver finished products and that vendors could not operate in most parts of the city.

The polarisation of communities had a direct impact on such workers because employers and employees often belonged to different communities and lived in areas dominated by their communities; the mutual distrust arising from the communal tension and violence was exacerbated by the fact that it was dangerous to venture into each other's areas.

The media's customary devaluation of the experiences and opinions of women, particularly poor women, prevented public awareness of the severe economic impact of the disturbances on large numbers of people in the city. An estimated 29 to 33 per cent of the women organised by SEWA are the sole supporters of their families; a substantial percentage of the rest earn more than male members of their families; and it is widely known that women's earnings go directly towards the basic needs of their families while men's wages are often spent on drinking, smoking and/or gambling. So women's loss of income during the five months of trouble proved disastrous for a large number of people but the media ignored this side-effect of the disturbances.

The media's neglect of this aspect of the disturbances had a serious negative fall-out in practical terms. Apparently ignorant about the importance of women's economic activity, the government, in its relief efforts, did not take into account the loss of livelihood suffered by thousands of women working in the informal sector.

One of the most significant discoveries of the WMG team was the debilitating impact of curfew on the lives of ordinary citizens, particularly the poor, who cannot afford to stock up on provisions. In Ahmedabad, curfew was imposed round the clock, often for as along as seven to ten days at a stretch, at times even touching the maximum permissible limit of 500 hours. Curfew not only meant a total stoppage of work, since nobody was allowed out of their homes, but it forced large families to survive for days on the meagre provisions they happened to have at home when curfew was announced—often in the dead of night. On women fell the task of managing the difficult situation of feeding hungry families with nothing but onions and gram or wheat flour, of pacifying wailing children with black tea....

Even when the army decided that it was safe to relax curfew for an hour at a time just for women, to enable them to buy essential commodities, Muslim women suffered the most. Hindu women, who had shops in their neighbourhoods, were able to get back home before the hour was up, but Muslim women, who had further to go, were often caught between shops and homes when curfew was reimposed and found themselves subjected to various punishments.

If the media had bothered to record and highlight the everyday hardships encountered by innocent citizens as a result of the disturbances, particularly the resultant curfew, perhaps the authorities could have been persuaded to devise practical ways of alleviating their sufferings. But media reports usually deal with the imposition or relaxation of curfew in a single sentence, based on information from the authorities themselves. The WMG team uncovered this aspect of the problem mainly because its primary sources of information were the women of poor, violence-torn localities, for whom, in the words of Ela Bhat of SEWA, 'Curfew is a kind of violence.'

If the lack of coverage given to the problems of poor women was unsurprising, the absence of reportage on the internationally renowned and nationally acclaimed organisation, SEWA, was quite amazing. The media's failure to cover the impact on and perspectives of this influential organisation can be partly traced to its general disinterest in labourers, unless they belong to unions led by people with nuisance value. The fact that SEWA organises women workers probably made it doubly irrelevant in the eyes of the average reporter who probably believed that female workers were of no real consequence and that women could contribute little to reports on such male activities as rioting and violent confrontations.

But this represented a serious lacuna in media coverage because, apart from the yeoman work done by SEWA in organising women workers of the informal sector, it was the only non-governmental organisation which continued sustained relief and rehabilitation work throughout the entire period of the disturbances. In addition, SEWA was actively involved in peace and reconciliation efforts even at the height of the violence. The media missed these significant points because they traditionally do not consider women important sources of information at the best of times, least of all in crisis situations.

Apart from the sins of omission elaborated upon above, the media was guilty of at least one sin of commission with respect to its handling of women's involvement in the Ahmedabad disturbances. For instance, in addition to paying a lot of attention to incidents with sexual connotations, such as the Gomtipur controversy, many papers unquestioningly picked up and repeated accusations typically used to discredit women and justify brutality against them. For example, women involved in the Asarwa incident were dismissed as 'ladies of easy virtue,' while anti-reservationist women in Khadia and Raipur were described as 'traditionally aggressive, abusive and rebellious.'

Further, its coverage of the unconfirmed allegations of sexual harassment of caste Hindu women in Gomtipur by policemen (through the infamous naked parade) contrasted starkly with its total silence on the claims by Muslim women that men taking part in the Rath Yatra procession through their localities harassed them with sexual taunts and gestures. In its coverage of the former incident, the media was clearly promoting its partisan interests in the context of the anti-reservation agitation rather than worrying about the significance of sexual harassment as a weapon.

Similarly, the media paid little serious attention to the strategy adopted by the anti-reservationists in using women (and sometimes children) as a vanguard in confrontations with the authorities and making political capital out of police brutality against them. The WMG team, on the other hand, found this to be one of the most disturbing factors of the Ahmedabad disturbances....

In its coverage of the Ahmedabad disturbances, the media laid bare some of its inherent biases and interests, often based on typical ownership and staff composition patterns. Only an acceptance of the existence of these natural and obvious biases can lead to an effort to consciously counter them by actively seeking to redefine news as well as sources of information and to thereby include the experiences and perspectives of those customarily marginalised by the media, including women.

Ammu Joseph

Appendix E

Growth of TV in India

Television was introduced in India in 1959 with the purchase of a 500-watt transmitter at a nominal price from Phillips, a multinational company, and a grant from UNESCO. A pilot project was set up to study the use of television as a 'medium of education, rural uplift and community development.' Programmes of an hour's duration were broadcast twice a week to viewers who assembled at teleclubs' or community viewing centres in Delhi. Two years later, a specially designed programme was telecast weekly to ninth grade students of higher secondary schools. This was done in cooperation with the Directorate of Education, Delhi, with financial aid from the Ford Foundation.

Up until the mid-1960s, all television hardware, transmitters, studio equipment and television sets had to be imported from abroad. Anticipating the possibility of regular programming soon, wealthy residents of Delhi, who had imported television sets, began to demand entertainment. However, the content of educational programming did not alter till 1965 when regular daily transmission started in Delhi.

Dr. Vikram Sarabhai was the first to raise the possibility of using television as a method of spreading education—'leap-frogging from the state of economic backwardness and social disabilities in decades rather than centuries.' However, at that time, the existing terrestrial transmitters were hopelessly inadequate to implement programmes of rural education unless the country thought in terms of satellite delivery systems. Advocating satellite technology for the direct broadcast of educational television programmes to the rural areas, Sarabhai argued:

> It represents the use of an advanced technology which for the first time does not impose a penalty on account of the dispersal of the receiving units away from the urban centres. The Indian economy in the next two or three decades must lean heavily on the development of rural areas.

He also perceived that stability and national integration were necessary because 'following the division of the country into linguistic administrative units, there is a need to bring together different units through a common mass medium of communication.' He opted for television over radio as it was an audio-visual medium which would have a profound impact given its particular persuasiveness and rare credibility.

The resulting Satellite Instructional Television Experiment (SITE) was launched in August 1975. It was designed to reach rural audiences in community viewing situations in six states (Bihar, Madhya Pradesh, Orissa, Rajasthan, Andhra Pradesh and Karnataka). The programmes were education-oriented, dealing with agricultural practices, health care and literacy. While some evaluators deemed SITE a success, the Planning Commission, after conducting its own evaluation, did not think the programme deserved to be continued. This was a decisive blow to the development of rural television. At the same time the Government was keen on opening TV centres in all the state capitals.

As Minister for Information and Broadcasting, Indira Gandhi was directly responsible for the expansion in hardware and a shift in content to include entertainment. The Indo-Pakistan conflict of 1965 had just taken place and she was in favour of elevating television from its 'experimental' status, limited only to Delhi, into a tool that could be used appropriately for the promotion of education, development and national unity. In fact, she can be described as the architect of the massive and rapid expansion of television in India—unparalleled anywhere in the 'Third World'. In many ways, the expansion of television in the country was directly linked to the ups and downs of her political career. Every time she was threatened politically (during the 1975 Emergency and at the prospect of elections in 1984), capital outlay for television registered a dramatic spurt.

The year 1975 saw the imposition of the Internal Emergency, during which the media were censored, fundamental rights were suspended and practically the entire Opposition was in jail. All India Radio (Akashvani) and Doordarshan were used blatantly as mouthpieces of the ruling party. Satellite technology's potential for conveying propaganda to the electorate was noted, and the green signal to go ahead with an indigenous satellite delivery system was issued by the Cabinet.

The next phase of expansion was undertaken in 1982, just before the Ninth Asian Games scheduled to be held in Delhi. It was decided to switch to colour transmission because coverage of the Asiad in black and white would embarrass India in the international community. The Minister for Information and Broadcasting at the time, V.P. Sathe, defended the conversion to colour in an abrasive attack on critics, claiming that India's 'traditions were audio-visual' and needed to be recorded in colour. The import of colour television sets was placed under the Open General Licence and the licence requirement of already imported sets was waived. This was to enable viewers with purchasing power to enjoy the sports extravaganza.

In July 1983, the Cabinet approved the special plan for the expansion of the television network—126 transmitters were added and networked by the Indian National Satellite (INSAT) system to achieve coverage of 70 per cent of the population within eighteen months. This figure of 70 per cent is used constantly without clarification about the spread of this population, but there is reason to believe that the figure refers only to urban coverage, especially since no provision was made for community T.V. sets in rural areas.

The powerful uses that a government-controlled broadcasting medium could be put to were picked up even by the Opposition parties; expansion plans, though initiated by the previous Congress government, were passed unaltered by the Janata Government after it came to power for a short period in 1977. However, after this period of expansion, the aspects of education and development in programming began to get slowly marginalised. As media analyst Bella Mody says, 'This pattern of television introduction, early public service rhetoric, educational implementation and then implementation on a large scale for elite pacification would repeat itself in India.'[1]

It is important to understand the implications of hardware expansion in the context of the choice of particular technologies. Kalyan Raman, of the Indian Space Research Organisation (ISRO), discussing developments after the advent of satellite broadcasting, argues:

> The satellite freed the television authorities from the constraint of having to put up a programme production facility every time they installed a transmitter. Any transmitter can receive programmes uplinked from Delhi via satellite with the help of a T.V. Receive Only terminal and rebroadcast them over its area of coverage. This meant that there could be a satellite-led expansion in transmission facilities without a concomitant expansion in programme production facilities. So important was it considered to extend coverage that the Delhi programmes, both local and national, were considered fit to be transmitted throughout the country. This policy decision led to an advertising-oriented 'laissez-faire' expansion of T.V. in India by the end of June 1985—147 out of a total of 173 transmitters were dependent on Delhi for programme feed.[2]

This policy, while it enables advertisers and viewers to be locked into a mutually satisfying consumerist embrace, was not designed for the advertiser alone. Dependence on Delhi for programming served a crucial political need. While the ostensible objective was the oft-stated desire to encourage national

---

[1] Bella Mody, 'The commercialisation of TV in India: A Research Agenda for Cross-country Comparisons,' paper submitted to ICA's Inter-cultural and Development Communication Division, 1988.

[2] N. Kalyan Raman, *Communication and Mass Media Development: The Case of Television*, Development and Educational Communication Unit, Indian Space Research Organisation, Ahmedabad, 1988.

integration or a construction of the modern Indian citizen schooled in the appropriate responsibilities and tasks of nation-building, the special expansion plan in 1983 was clearly initiated with an eye on the general elections which were to be held in 1984.

Doordarshan began accepting commercial advertisements in 1976. Initially revenues were low as there were only seven city-centred television stations and few receivers in each city. The period between 1982 and 1987 saw a phenomenal increase in revenues (Rs. 77 lakhs in 1976 to Rs. 185 crores in 1987).[3]

There were four reasons for this spurt. The conversion to colour, thanks to the Asian Games; the start of the national programme in August 1982; the increase in urban transmitters; and the networking of the growing numbers of transmitters (42 in 1983 to 186 in 1987)[4] by satellite, providing a single massive audience and affording advertisers a captive market of an unprecedented size. Today, approximately 30 per cent of the total estimated expenditure on advertising in the country is spent on television in the form of spot advertisements and sponsored programmes.[5]

In looking at the growth of television in India it is important to note how a technology (a hybrid terrestrial-cum-satellite system), designed and intended as a tool for the development of the rural poor, has been distorted and appropriated to provide entertainment and convey political messages to the vocal urban consumer.

Deepa Dhanraj

---

[3]Krishnan and Dighe, *Affirmation and Denial*.
[4]Raman, *Communication and Mass Media*.
[5]Krishnan and Dighe, *Affirmation and Denial*.

Index

Aajkal, 190, 191, 203
abortion, of female foetus, 64, 68, 214
Adalja, Varsha, 235
Addington, Carol, 21
Adhikar, 249, 250, 255, 256–62
Advani, L.K., 60
advertisements, on television, 325; codes for, in Doordarshan, 250, 299
advertisers' influence, on magazine editors, 115, 116
Agewan, Anwar, 236
Aggarwal, Justice S.M., 35, 38, 119
Agnivesh, Swami, 153
Ahmedabad, caste and communal riots' impact on women, 319–22
Ahmedabad Women's Action Group, 235
Air Hostess, 249, 277–81
Akbar, M.J., 110, 196
Akhileshwar, 142
Alka, 227, 239
All-India Women's Conference, 119
Alva, Margaret, 154, 318
amendments to the Dowry Prohibition Act of 1961, 35
amniocentesis, 64, 68, 102, 146, 162, 201, 207, 210; campaign against, 65; in *Femina*, 118
Ananda Bazaar Patrika, 190, 192–207, 212, 220, 221, 223; reports on, dowry deaths, 193–94; female foeticide, 201–2; rape, 195–96; Roop Kanwar tragedy, 202–7; Shah Bano controversy, 196–201
Ananda Vikatan, 168, 169

Ansari, Z.A., 174, 229
Antar Jali Yatra, 207
Anthony, M.J., 49
anti-dowry campaign, 36, 37, 90, 194
anti-dowry law, 39
anti-rape campaign, 44, 45–46, 115
Arora, Kiran, 150
Asrani, Manju Bansal, 262
atrocity-related women's issues, 19
Atyachar Virodhi Samiti, 123
Aur Bhi Hain Raahein, 249, 255, 266–71
Awaz, 164
Azmi, Shabana, 125

Bakshi, Rajni, 103, 104
Bala, Kanchan Sashi, dowry death of, 34, 36
Balasubrahmanyan, Vimal, 92
Bali, Suryakant, 146
Banik, Debjani, murder of, 220
Bannerjee, Shibdas, 205
Bansal, Uttamprakash, 160
Bartaman, 190, 191
Barthes, Roland, 252
Barua, Jahnu, 260
Bedi, Kiran, 273, 276
Bengali press, 190ff
Bhat, Ela, 235, 239
Bhatt, Kanti, 232
Bhatt, Sheela, 224
Bhatty, Zarina, 59
Bidwai, Praful, 80
Bordes, Pamella, 30
Bose, Ajoy, 100

bride burning syndrome, 34-36; *see also*, dowry deaths
British press, women's group and, 21
broadcasting medium, government controlled, 324
Brownmiller, Susan, 123
Butalia, Subhadra, 122

caste groups, politics and, 17
censorship of press, during Internal Emergency, 16
Chabra, Rami, 48
Chandrachud, Chief Justice Y.V., 95, 100, 174
Chatterjee, Gouri, 202, 204
Chatterjee, Maitreyi, 190
Chatterjee, Suman, 196
Chaudhari, Kavita, 251, 282, 283, 289
Chetna, 227, 239
Chhachhi, Amrita, 48
Chidambaram, P., 154, 203
child, marriages, 186, 197
Child in Need Institute, 201
Chingari, 235
Chitralekha, 225, 231-34, 240, 241; reports on, dowry deaths, 232; female foeticide, 233-34; rape, 232; Roop Kanwar tragedy, 234; Shah Bano controversy, 233
Chopra, Kanchan, dowry case of, 91
Choudhury, Saifuddin, 174
cinematography, codes, 253-54
commercials, on Doordarshan, 249-51; in women's magazine's 114; *see also*, advertisements
Commission of Sati (Prevention) Act, 1987, 78
Commission of Sati (Prevention) Bill, 129
consumer culture, women and, 34, 116
Criminal Law (Amendment) Bill, 47
critical focus, 245ff

Dahej Virodhi Chetna Manch, 181
dalit women, atrocities on, 123
Dalmia, Vishnu Hari, 177
Dalwai, Meherunissa, 55
Dandavate, Pramila, 312

Dandiya, Milapchand, 156
Das, Shipra, 276
Das, Veena, 108, 109
Datar, Chaya, 283
Datta-Ray, Sunanda, 80, 314
Dave, Harindra, 226, 231
D'Cunha, Jean, 129
Delhi, dowry deaths in, 34, 35
Desai, Hari, 234
Desai, Neera, 235
Desai, Varsha, 234
Desh, 191, 192, 207-12, 222; reports on, dowry deaths, 208; female foeticide, 210-11; rape, 208-9; Roop Kanwar tragedy, 211-12; Shah Bano controversy, 209-10
Dhagamwar, Vasudha, 59
Dhanraj, Deepa, 244
Dharma Raksha Samiti, 104
Dharmyug, 140, 152
Dighe, Anita, 251
Dina Mani, 168, 169-78; reports on, dowry deaths, 171-72; female foeticide, 175; rape, 172-73; Roop Kanwar tragedy, 175-78; Shah Bano controversy, 173-75
Dina Thanthi, 168, 169
divorce issues, 163
Dogra, Bharat, 142
Doordarshan, programmes on behalf of women, 245ff, 290-91 dowry, deaths, 19, 22, 25, 33, 313; concept of, 120; demonstrations against, 115; institution of, 33; legislation bill, 193
dowry deaths, coverage in papers and periodicals, 90-93, 119-21, 140-41, 160, 171-72, 179-81, 185-86, 193-94, 208, 227, 232, 236
Dowry Prohibition Act 1984, 40
Duggal, Ravi, 67

editorials, 22-23, 27, 29-31, 42, 46-47, 171; on female foeticide, 65; on dowry, 194; policy, 131; on rape, 47-49; on Roop Kanwar tragedy, 79-82, 146; on Shah Bano controversy, 175

education, 183, 184; through television, 323
electronic media, 299–300
Emergency, press censorship during, 16, 70, 71, 324
English language press, 16–17, 22–26, 135, 296
Equal Remuneration Act, 260
Eve's Weekly, 116–31; reports on, dowry deaths, 119; female foeticide, 126–28; marriage customs, 118; rape, 121–24; Roop Kanwar tragedy, 128–30; Shah Bano controversy, 124–26
Ewing, Gulshan, 117
exploitation, of women, 166

'family labour', 268
Farouk, H.M., 174
feature articles, 24
female foeticide issues, 19, 64ff, 101–3, 126–28, 146–47, 162, 175, 183, 188, 201–2, 210–11, 233–34, 313
female infanticide, 201
Femina, 116–31; reports on, consumer complaints, 117; dowry deaths, 119–21; female foeticide, 126–28; rape, 121–24; Roop Kanwar tragedy, 128–30; Shah Bano controversy, 124–26
Forum Against Rape, 45, 123, 228
Forum Against Sex Determination, 64, 65, 68, 102, 128
Frontline 88

Gajraula, rape cases in, 93
Ganasakti, 190
Gandhi, Indira, 194, 228, 324
Gandhi, Mahatma, 15, 224; stand on sati, 80
Gandhi, Rajiv, 145, 146, 153, 176, 182, 183, 203, 229, 233
Gaya, Javed, 98, 100
Gayatri Devi, on sati, 234
gender, perspective, 21, 22, 61–62; relations, 246; status, 284
Ghose, Bisakha, 219
Ghosh, Ashish, 196

Ghosh, Gautam, 207
Ghosh, Nityo Priyo, 206
Ghosh, Sunit, 196
Gidwani, Kausalya, 278
Gledhill, Christine, 254
Goel, Sudha, dowry death of, 35, 38, 119, 227
Grihshobha, 140, 156–63, reports on, dowry deaths, 160; female foeticide, 162; rape, 161–62; Roop Kanwar tragedy, 162–63
Guha, Surupa, death of, 220
Gujarat Samachar, 235
Gujarati press, 224ff
Gupta, R.P., 219
Gupta, Ruchira, 105
Gupta, Shubhra, 139
Gupte, Manisha, 67
Gurcharan, 142

Haksar, Nandita, 123
'hard' news, 24, 27
Hariani, Milika, 123
Hariharan, Githa, 49
Harijan, 15
Harrigan, Patrick, 81, 82, 109, 315
Harshanand, Swami, 85, 315
Hasan, Zoya, 187, 199
Hind Swaraj, 15
'Hindi belt', 17
Hindi press, 136, 139ff
Hindi writers, 166–67
The Hindu, 22; reports on, campaign against dowry, 37; editorials on amendments to rape law, 47; letters to editor, 311–13, 315; rape and role of women, 29, 30; Shah Bano controversy, 62
Hindu Code Bill, 200
Hindu revivalism, sati and, 72
The Hindustan Times, 22; reports on, dowry deaths, 35, 36; humour, 316; letters to editor, 311–13; Muslim Women's Bill, 58–60; rape and law on, 46–48; Roop Kanwar tragedy, 74; sex determination tests, 66; style of presentation of women's issues, 30

Hum Log, 250
human rights violation, 17
humour, in newspapers, 316–17

The Illustrated Weekly, 88, 89; reports on, female foeticide, 101, 102; Gajraula nun rape case, 93; rape victims, 93, 94; Roop Kanwar tragedy, 103–4, 108–9; Shah Bano controversy, 90, 95–96
India Today, 88, 89, 140, 151; reports on, dowry deaths, 90–91; female foeticide, 101; rape law and anti-rape campaign, 93; Roop Kanwar tragedy and sati, 103, 107–8, 110; Shah Bano case, 96; women's issues, 111
Indian Express, 22, 232; reports on, dowry deaths, 35, 36; letters to editor, 311–13, 315; magazine section on women's issues, 84; Rajasthani women, 83–84; rape, 46, 48; Roop Kanwar tragedy, 82; pro-sati views, 75, 81; sex determination tests, 67; Shah Bano case, communalisation of, 54, 57, 60–61; women's issues, 29
Indian National Satellite (INSAT), 325
Indian Penal Code, 110, 197, 311
inheritance rights, 120
International Women's Day, 44, 48, 121, 208
investigative journalism, 16, 71
Iranian wives, financial entitlements to divorced, 199–200
Iyer, G. Subramania, 184
Iyer, Justice V.R.Krishna, 62, 109

Jain, Minu, 105
Jain, Sandhya, 74
Jain, Vineet, 117
Jalal, Farida, 275
Janmabhoomi, 225–31, 239, 240, 241; reports on, dowry deaths, 227; female foeticide, 230; rape, 227–28; Roop Kanwar tragedy, 230–31; Shah Bano case, 226
Janmabhoomi/Pravasi, 137

Jansatta, 106, 136, 164; reports on Roop Kanwar tragedy, 147
jauhar practice, 219
Jethmalani, Ram, 46
Joseph, Ammu, 15, 33, 64, 70, 113, 135, 300, 301
Joshi, Harideo, 79
Joshi, P.C., Committee, 245, 246, 299
Joshi, Sharad, 150, 167
Joshi, Umashankar, 225
J.P. Naik Memorial lecture, 33
Jugantar, 190

Kabaraji, 224
Kader, Justice S.A., 55
Kalia, Mamta, 152, 165
Kalki, 169, 179–83; reports on, dowry deaths, 179–81; rape, 181; Shah Bano controversy, 182–83
Kalvi, Kalyan Singh, 79, 203
Kanekar, Shirish, 232
Kapoor, Ila, 119
Kapur, Wasim, 209
Karandikar, Lata, 149
Karat, Brinda, 80
Karat, Praveen, 188
Kashmakash, 249, 262–66
Katha Sagar, 262
Kaul, Iqbal, 84
Kaur, Tarvinder, dowry death of, 34, 36, 90
Kesari, 15
Khan, Arif Mohammed, resignation of, on Shah Bano controversy, 25, 56, 58, 99, 100, 145, 174, 182, 199, 200, 229, 231, 312
Khan, Hamid, 197
Khan, Mohammed, 197
Khan, Reshma Arif, 187
Khan, Sona, 55
Khare, Vishnu, 148, 149
Kishwar, Madhu, 200, 210
Kotak, Vaju, 231
Krishna Raj, Maithreyi, 314
Krishnan, Prabha, 251
Krishnamurthi, R., 179
Kshirsagar, Shridhar, 273, 274, 275
Kumar, Krishna, 150

Index

Kumar, Kuldeep, 106
Kumar, Radha, 74, 79, 107
Kumar, Rajesh, 179
Kumudam, 168
Kusum, 49, 74

Lajmi, Jyoti, 125
Lateef, Shahida, 62
Latifi, Danial, 59
Law, on rape, 44; on sati, 78-79
Law Commission, 121, 124, 143
legal rights, of women, *Adhikar* on, 256
letters to editor, 24, 311ff

Madar Manoranjani, 184
magazines, 88ff
Mahadevan, Iravadham, 171
Mahajan, Krishan, 49
Maharashtra, ban on sex determination, 65, 66, 69, 127, 146
Mahasweta Devi, 218, 220, 263
Mahila Dakshata Samiti, 119
Mainstream, 163
Maintenance, for divorced Muslim women, 55, 63, 118
Malik, Amita, 283
Malkani, K.R., 314
Mangaiyar Malar, 183-89; reports on, dowry deaths, 185-86; female foeticide, 188; Roop Kanwar tragedy, 188-89; Shah Bano case, 185-86
Mangalwadi, Vishal, 177
Manimala, 148-49, 150
Manorama, 140, 156, 157, 165, 192, 215
Manushi, 42, 210
Marwari Youth Forum, 203
Marwari Yuva Manch, 203
Mathur, Anjali, 61
Mathur, Rajendra, 140
Mathura rape case, 93, 95, 122, 173, 195, 208, 248, 312
Maya, 140, 151-53, 163, 165; reports on; Roop Kanwar tragedy in, 153; Shah Bano case, 153

Maya Tyagi rape case, 154-55
Mazumdar, Anand, 188
Mediastorm's documentary, on Roop Kanwar tragedy, 71
Medical Termination of Pregnancy Act, 66
Meghani, Zaverchand, 225
Mehta, Lalhuben, 235
Mehta, Vijaya, 273, 276
Meri Saheli, 140
Metz, Christian, 253
Mitra, Nirmal, 106
Mitra, Sumit, 92, 99
Mody, Bella, 325
Mohan, Brij, 162
Molotch, Harvey N., 18, 20
MTV, women's projection on, 298
Mudgal, Sarla, 91
Mukherjee, Amal, 206
Mukherjee, Kanak, 193
Mukherjee, Ranjana, 211
Mulvey, Laura, 255
Muslim Personal Law, 20, 31, 59, 96-98, 100, 101, 125, 126, 144, 153, 183, 197, 198, 238, 311
Muslim Personal Law Board, 199
Muslim Satyashodak Mandal, 199, 229
Muslim women, divorced, 54, 97, 99; views on Shah Bano case, 54-55
Muslim Women (Protection of Rights on Divorce) Bill, 25, 31, 56-60, 62, 63, 95, 99, 100, 125-26, 144-46, 173, 174, 182, 198, 199, 205, 229, 238, 312
Mussavir, Hussain, 199

Nandy, Ashis, 81, 82, 83, 109, 314
Naoroji, Dadabhai, 224
Naqvi, Saeed, 54, 55
Narainpur atrocity, 28
Narayan, Gita, 93, 94
Nari Nirjatan Pratiradh Mancha, 204
Nari Raksha Samiti, 119
Narmad, Karsandas Mulji, 224
Narmada Dam controversy, 224
Natarajan, Dr K., 175
Natarajan, Saroj, 129
Nathanael, M.P., 48

National Convention Against Communalism and Separatism, 78
national movement, role of press during, 15
Navbharat Times, 137, 139, 140-51, 163; reports on, dowry deaths, 141-42; female foeticide, 146-47; rape, 142-44; Roop Kanwar tragedy, 147-50; Shah Bano case, 144-46
Nayar, Kuldip, 196
Nehru, Jawaharlal, 110
news, definition of, 18; features, 23
newspapers, reports on, dowry deaths, 33ff; female foeticide, 64ff; rape, 43ff; Roop Kanwar tragedy, 70ff; Shah Bano case, 51ff
Nigam, H.B.L., 59
Ninan, Sevanti, 35
Niranjana, Nirupama, 177
Nirmala, 248
Noorani, A.G., 60

O'Flaherty, Wendy, 289
Ojha, Ashok, 143
Omvedt, Gail, 94
Onassis, Jaqueline, 223
oppression, of women, 17, 293
Organiser, 314

Pahwa, Neerja, 125
Pande, Mrinal, 136, 146, 152, 163, 165, 166, 256, 259, 262
Pande, Vinod, 277, 279
Paribartan, 215
Patel, Dhiruben, 235
Patel, Leelaben, 235
Patel, Vibhuti, 123, 235
Pathak, Ila, 239
Pathak, Varsha, 234
Patil, Vimla, 117, 119, 120
patriarchal system, and values of, 31, 214
periodicals, 88ff; reports on, dowry cases, 90-93; female foeticide, 101-3; rape, 93-95; Roop Kanwar tragedy, 103-10; Shah Bano controversy, 95-101
Petalikar, Ishwar, 235

Philipose, Pamela, 128
photographs, in magazines, 89
Piramal, Gita, 121
Poddar, Deokinandan, 203
Police handouts, against crimes on women, 221
political parties/politicians, role of, in sati and Roop Kanwar tragedy, 71, 72, 79; in Shah Bano case, 56-58, 100; in women's issues, 21, 31, 63
polygamy, sanction by the Koran, 97
Pragatisheel Mahila Samiti, 204
Pratikshan, 191
Pravasi, 225
prime time images, 256-60
print media, importance of, 15; and the State, 16; *see also*, newspapers
Propp, Vladimir, 282
Pro-sati reports, 71, 74
prostitution, 94
proximity, and coverage in newspapers, 26, 41
Punjab Kesari, 139
Punwani, Jyoti, 96, 102, 282, 289
Purakayastha Bijon Behari, 206
Puri, Rajinder, 60, 110, 317
Purie, Mandira, 91

quantitative coverage, of women's issues, 26

Rahim, Mazahir, 267
Rahman, Hassainur, 209, 219
Rahnabad, Ahra, 199
Raj Lakshmi, 265
Rajagopalachari, C., 179
Rajasthan government, 204
Rajasthan Patrika, 164
Rajasthan Sati (Prevention) Ordinance, 77, 78, 106, 107, 176, 189
Rajputs, response to Deorala incident, 82; sati practice among, 72
Ramalakshmi, G., 189
Raman, Kalyan, 324
Ramaswamy, Prasanna, 168
Ramayana, on Doordarshan, 250
Ramesh, Manjula, 184, 185

Index

Rangan, Kasturi, L.S., 169, 170
Rangarajan, L.S., 80, 177
Rao, Amiya, 91
Rau, M. Chalapathi, 15
rape, issues, 19, 22, 25; campaign against, 43ff; of minor girls, 43, 44, 195; newspapers and periodicals covering, 93-95, 121-24, 130, 142-44, 161-62, 172-73, 195-96, 208-9, 227-28, 232, 237-38
Rape Bill, 195, 196
Rashtradoot, 106
Rast Goftar, 224
Ravindran, Dr., 313
Ravivar, 140, 151, 154-56, 165
Razdan, Karan, 266
regional language press, 135-36; problems faced by, 137; readership, 16
religion, role of, 80
Reshma, Syeeda, 99
R.G.K., 41
Roop Kanwar tragedy, 22, 26, 70ff; coverage in newspapers and periodicals, 128-30, 147-50, 153, 162-63, 175-78, 183, 188-89, 202-7, 211-12, 217-20, 230-32, 239
Rowbotham, Sheila, 252
Roy, Raja Ram Mohan, crusade against sati, 177
RSS, 314

Sachetana, 204
Sadashivam, Bharati, 102
Saheli, 93, 237
Sahgal, Nayantara, 48
Saksena, N.S., 49
Samadhaan, 127
Samkaleen, 225
Sananda, 212-20, 222, 223; reports on Roop Kanwar tragedy, 217-20
Sangari, Kumkum, 83
Sankarasubramanian, Khiyambur, 189
Saptahik Hindustan, 136, 140, 152
Sarabhai, Vikram, 323
Saran, Satya, 129

Sarin, Ritu, 96
Sarkar, Lotika, 74, 79
Satellite Instructional Television Experiment (SITE), 324
Sathe, V.P., 324
sati issue, in newspapers, 19, 22, 25, 27, 70, 111, 128, 129, 147, 150, 177, 189, 197, 204, 205, 217-18, 293, 314, 315; anti-, Bill, 206; and Hindu revivalism, 106; justification of, in *Indian Express*, 81-82; voluntary versus forced, 83-84, 103, 109
Saxena, Alka, 154, 155
Self Employed Women's Association (SEWA), 235, 239, 319, 320
Sen, Aparna, 213
Seshu, Geeta, 82
Sethi, Sunil, 91, 92, 93
sex determination tests, 19, 22, 64, 101, 111
sex problems, reports in *Grihshobha*, 157-58
Shah Bano controversy, 19, 22, 25, 27, 31, 111, 205, 312-13, 317; reports in newspapers and periodicals, 51-63, 95-101, 124-26, 144-46, 153, 173-75, 182-83, 186-88, 196-201, 209-10, 216-17, 226, 228, 233, 238
Shah, Neela, 238, 240
Shanbag, Sunil, 260
Shankaracharya, of Kanchi, statement against sati by, 80-81, 178; of Puri, pro-sati views of, 75, 80-81, 87, 176-78, 204, 205, 217
Sharan, V.P., 74
Shariat law, 100, 174, 197, 210, 218
Sharma, Kalpana, 15, 33, 64, 70, 84, 88, 135, 300, 301
Sharma, Udayan, 154, 155, 165
Sheikh, Shehnaaz, 31, 100, 126, 144, 198, 216
Shaikh, W.M., 59
Sheth, Amritlal, 225
Shourie, Arun, 62, 100; interpretation of Koran by, 96, 97-98
Shukla, Sonal, 224, 259

Sidhwa, Shiraz, 104, 106
Singh, Brajendra, 156
Singh, Kushwant, 92
Singh, Manju, 256
Singh, Nalini, 83
Singh, Navjoth, 256
Singh, Payal, 94
Singh, S.P., 140, 165
Singh, Tavleen, 96
Singh, V.P., 110
Singh, Zail, 228
Siraj, Syed Mustafa, 196, 200, 210
soap operas, on Doordarshan, 250
social reform, 178, 184, 197
'soft' news, 24, 27
Somani, J.K., 117
Srinivas, M.N., 33
Srinivasan, Sandhya, 127,128
state, press and, 16
Statesman, reports on, dowry deaths, 35; humour in, 316-18; letters to editors, 310-15; Maharashtra's ban on sex determination tests, 66; rape, and campaign against, 46; Roop Kanwar tragedy, 74; sati, 76-77; sati and its justification, 81-82; Shah Bano case, 57; women's issues, style of presentation, 30
status, of women, 34, 64, 67, 80, 109, 129; in Rajasthan, 73, 83-84
Stree, 225, 234-39, 240; reports on, dowry deaths, 236; rape, 237-38; Roop Kanwar tragedy, 239; Shah Bano case, 238
Stree Bedh, 224
Stri, 249, 255, 272-77
Subramania Bharati, 184
Subramaniam, Chitra, 93
Succession Act, 120
Sudha Goel dowry death case, 186
Sukanya, 192, 212-17, reports on, Shah Bano case, 216
Suman Rani rape case, 44
Sunday, 88, 89, 111; reports on, dowry deaths, 90, 91; female foeticide, 101, 102; Roop Kanwar tragedy, 106, 108, 110; Shah Bano case, 96

Sunday magazine sections, women's issues in, 24, 49, 61, 85-87
Sunday Observer, 88, 89; reports on, female foeticide, 101, 102; Muslim Personal Law, 98; Roop Kanwar tragedy, 103-7; Shah Bano case, 95, 96
Supreme Court, Judgement on, Mathura rape case, 312; Shah Bano case, 62, 98-100, 143, 144, 174, 182, 186, 198, 210, 216; Suman Rani rape case, 43, 44
Suri, Sanjay, 35
Surya, Vasantha, 168
Swaminadhan, Srilatha, 84
Swayamsiddha, 249

Talak Mukti Morcha, 55
Talib, Rashid, 313
Tamil press, 168ff
Tanuja, 267, 269, 270
Taulid, Nilu, 216
Telegraph, 200
television, colour, 324, 326; growth of, in India, 323-26; UNESCO grant for, 323
Tellis, Olga, 101
Tilak, Lokmanya, 15
The Times of India, 22; anti-women articles, 40; reports on, dowry deaths, 36; humour in, 316-17; letters to editor, 311, 314; Muslim Women's Bill, 58, 59; rape cases, 49; Roop Kanwar tragedy, 80; sati, 83; sex determination tests, 65, 67; Shah Bano case, 54, 57, 62; style of presenting women's issues, 30; unnatural widow-deaths, 74-75
Tiwari, Ghanshyam, 104
Tuchman, Gaye, 18
Tulzapurkar, Justice, 312

Udaan, 249, 255, 282-90
Unwalia, Justice, 312
urban educated women, commercial women's magazine for, 131

Vama, 140, 152

Vanaik, Achin, 49, 65, 313
Vasan, S.S., 169
Vasanthi, 186, 187
Vasudev, 232, 233
Venkatraman, M.S., 175
Vishnu Dharma Sutras, on sati, 85
Vishwa Hindu Parishad, on sati, 29, 61, 63, 75, 87
Vora, Motilal, 152

Wakf Board, 153
Waldman, Diane, 256
The Week, 88
widows, 186, 218, 219; rules imposed on, 85; status of, 205
wife-beating, 163
'wife-murder', 221
women('s) and development, 71, 246-47; groups, access to, 20-21, 27; journalists, 28-29, 292, 296-298; journalists, participating in women's movement, 115; libbers', 40-42; magazines, 113ff; movements, 115, 124, 131, 137; movement, and impact on media, 20, 22, 41-42; and news, 20-21; organisations, on legal reforms in rape cases, 44; out of focus in newspapers, 46-49; question, 76-78; serials based on, in Doordarshan, 251
Women and Media Committee of Bombay Union of Journalists, report on Roop Kanwar tragedy, 71, 82
Women and Media Group, report on Ahmedabad caste and communal riots' impact on women, 319-22
Women and Media workshop, 293, 296, 298
Women's Development Programme, 84
Working Group on Software for Doordarshan, report of, 245

Young India, 15

Zakaria, Rafiq, 97, 98